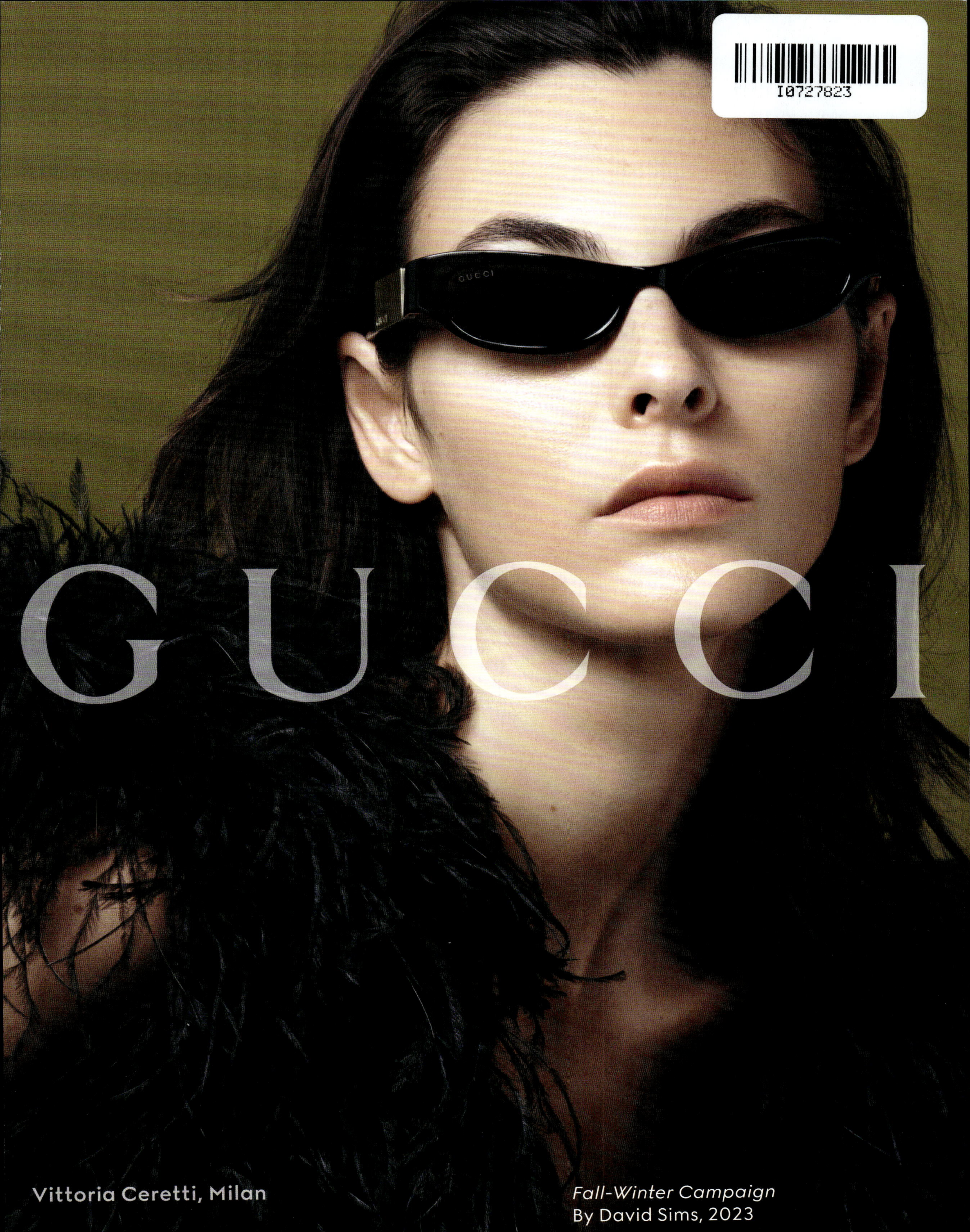

Vittoria Ceretti, Milan

Fall-Winter Campaign
By David Sims, 2023

Winter 2023
Desire

Front

Back

Words & Pictures

Front cover:
Ishiuchi Miyako, *Yokohama
Days #12,* 2011
© the artist and courtesy
the Third Gallery Aya, Osaka
(See page 122)

Subscribe to *Aperture* **and
visit archive.aperture.org
for every issue since 1952.**

LOEWE

Fall Winter 2023
Photographed by David Sims
79 Greene street, New York
loewe.com

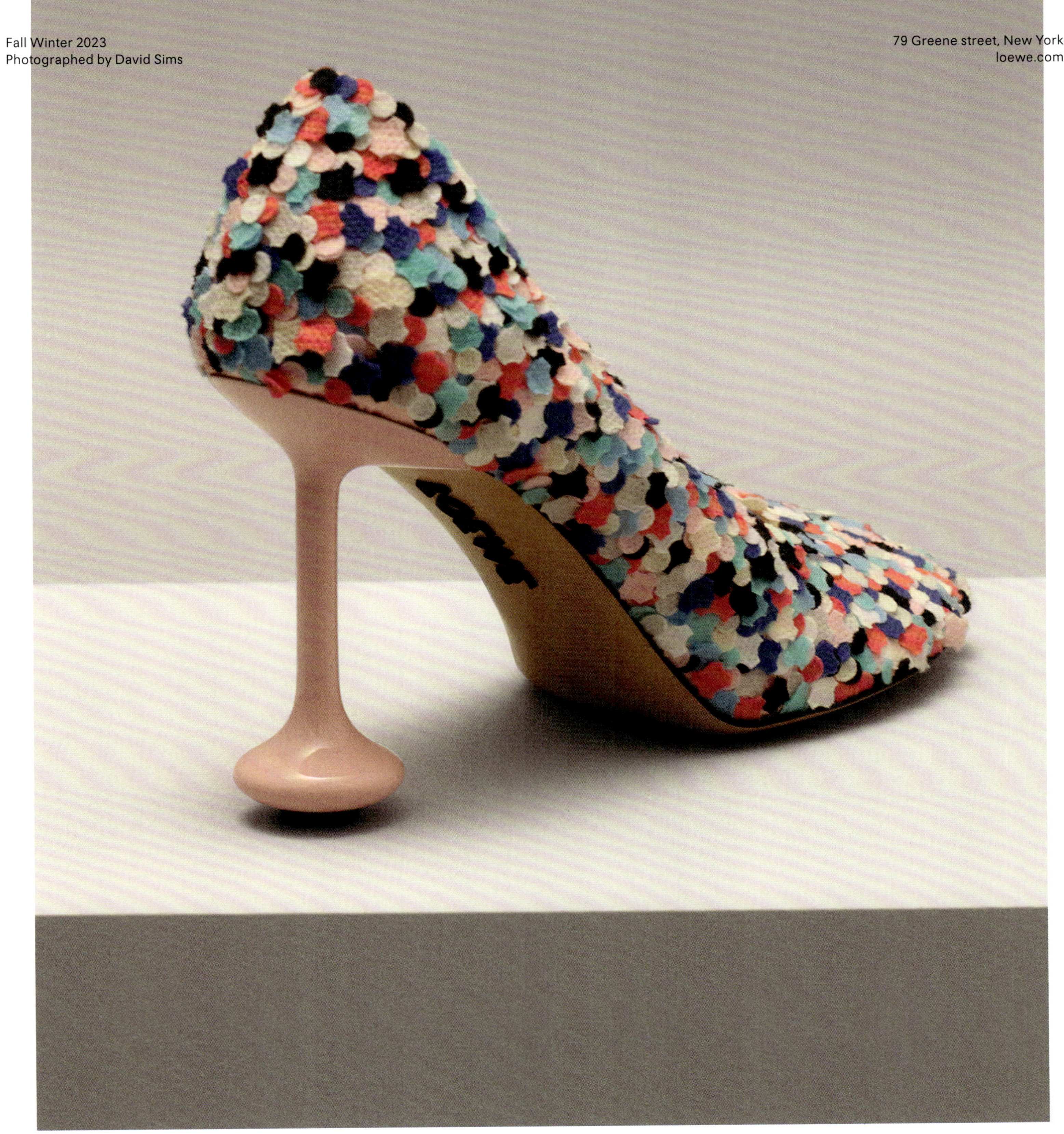

Aperture is a nonprofit publisher dedicated to creating insight, community, and understanding through photography. Established in 1952 to advance "creative thinking, significantly expressed in words and photographs," Aperture champions photography's vital role in nurturing curiosity and encouraging a more just, tolerant society.

Aperture (ISSN 0003-6420) is published quarterly, in spring, summer, fall, and winter, at 548 West 28th Street, 4th Floor, New York, N.Y. 10001. In the United States, a one-year subscription (four issues) is $75; a two-year subscription (eight issues) is $124. In Canada, a one-year subscription is $95. All other international subscriptions are $110 per year. Visit aperture.org to subscribe. Single copies may be purchased at $24.95 for most issues. Subscribe to the *Aperture Digital Archive* at aperture.org/archive. Periodicals postage paid at New York and additional offices. Postmaster: Send address changes to *Aperture*, P.O. Box 3000, Denville, N.J. 07834. Address queries regarding subscriptions, renewals, or gifts to: *Aperture* Subscription Service, 866-457-4603 (U.S. and Canada), or email custsvc_aperture@fulcoinc.com.

Newsstand distribution in the US is handled by CMG. For international distribution, contact Central Books, centralbooks.com. Other inquiries, email orders@aperture.org or call 212-505-5555.

Become a Member of Aperture to take your interest in and knowledge of photography further. With an annual tax-deductible gift of $250, membership includes a complimentary subscription to *Aperture* magazine, discounts on Aperture's award-winning publications, a special limited-edition gift, and more. To join, visit aperture.org/join, or contact membership@aperture.org.

Credits for "Timeline," pp. 18–19: Keïta studio portrait: Courtesy the High Museum of Art, Atlanta; Thomas: Courtesy Yancey Richardson Gallery, New York

Credits for "Curriculum," pp. 24–25: Douglas: © the artist and courtesy Victoria Miro and David Zwirner, New York; Hammons: Courtesy Iolanda Pensa; Queen's Face: Courtesy the Metropolitan Museum of Art, New York

Library of Congress Catalog Card No: 58-30845.

ISBN 978-1-59711-550-6

Printed in Turkey by Ofset Yapimevi

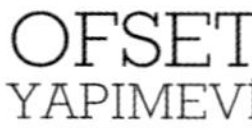

Support has been provided by members of Aperture's Magazine Council: Jon Stryker and Slobodan Randjelović, Susan and Thomas Dunn, Kate Cordsen and Denis O'Leary, and Michael W. Sonnenfeldt, MUUS Collection.

aperture

The Magazine of Photography and Ideas

Editor in Chief
Michael Famighetti
Senior Editor
Brendan Embser
Associate Managing Editor
Varun Nayar
**Contributing Editors,
The PhotoBook Review**
Noa Lin, Lesley A. Martin
Copy Editors
Hilary Becker, Donna Ghelerter, Chris Peterson
Production Director
Minjee Cho
Production Manager
Andrea Chlad
Work Scholar
Cassandra Awad
Press Supervisor
Ali Taptık

Art Direction, Design & Typefaces
A2/SW/HK, London

Publisher
Dana Triwush
magazine@aperture.org

Director of Brand Partnerships
Isabelle Friedrich McTwigan
212-946-7118
imctwigan@aperture.org

Advertising
Elizabeth Morina
917-691-2608
emorina@aperture.org

Executive Director, Aperture
Sarah Hermanson Meister

Minor White, Editor (1952–1974)

Michael E. Hoffman, Publisher and Executive Director (1964–2001)

aperture.org

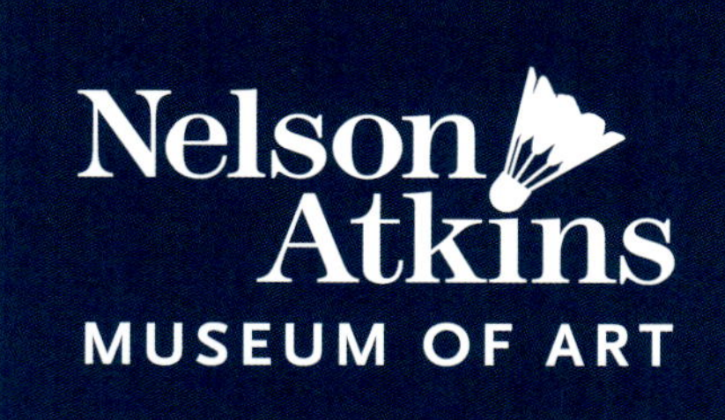

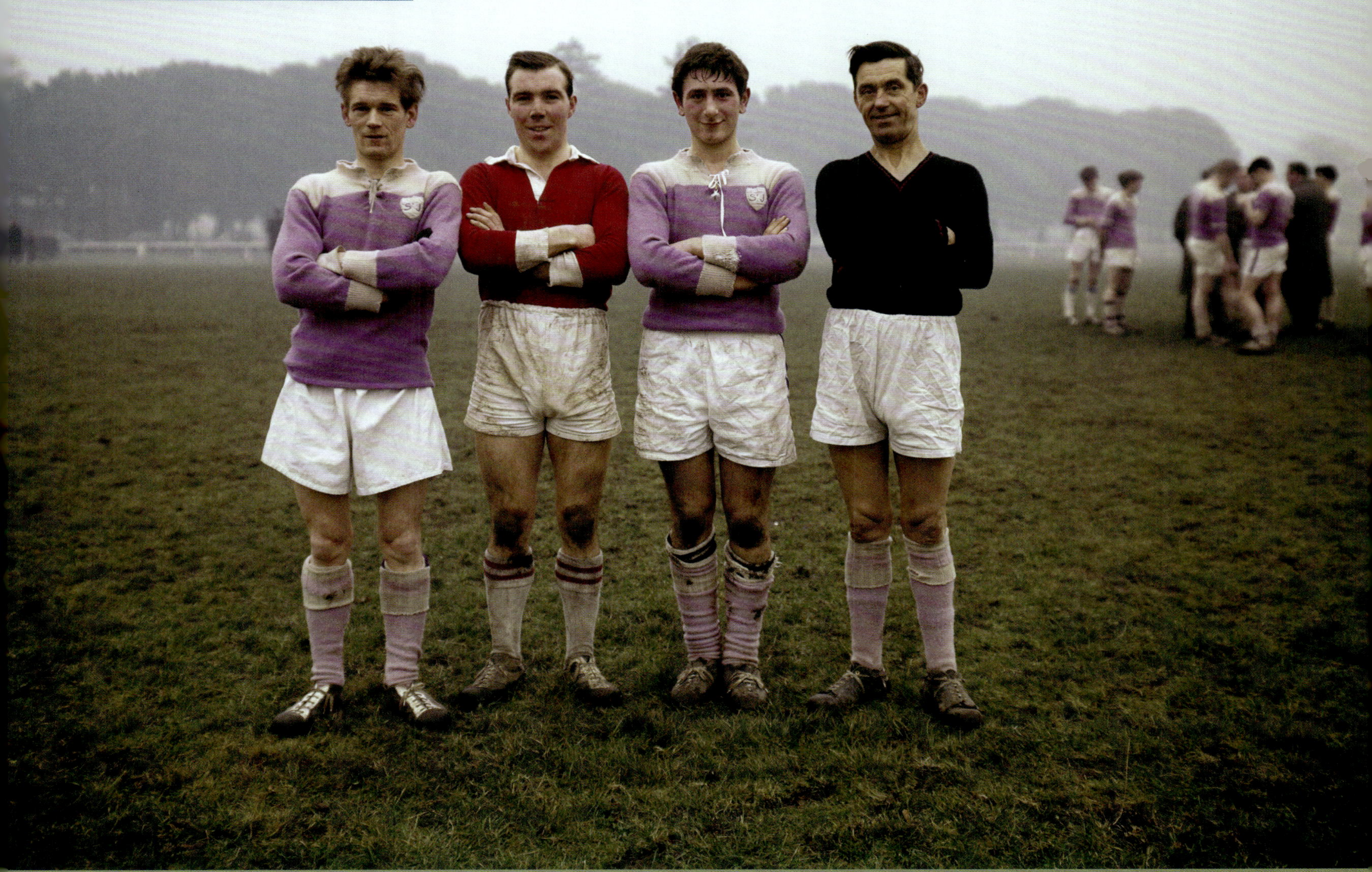

EVELYN HOFER

EYES ON THE CITY

Sept. 16, 2023–Mar. 24, 2024

Evelyn Hofer's insightful and sensitive portraits of European and U.S. cities convey the vibrancy and complexity of urban life in the late 1950s and 1960s.

Co-organized by The Nelson-Atkins Museum of Art and the High Museum of Art. In Kansas City, generous support provided by the Hall Family Foundation.

Evelyn Hofer, American, born Germany(1922–2009). *Phoenix Park on a Sunday, Dublin*, 1966. Dye transfer print,13 5/16 × 16 7/16 inches. The Nelson-Atkins Museum of Art, Gift of the Hall Family Foundation,2019.39.14.©Estate of Evelyn Hofer

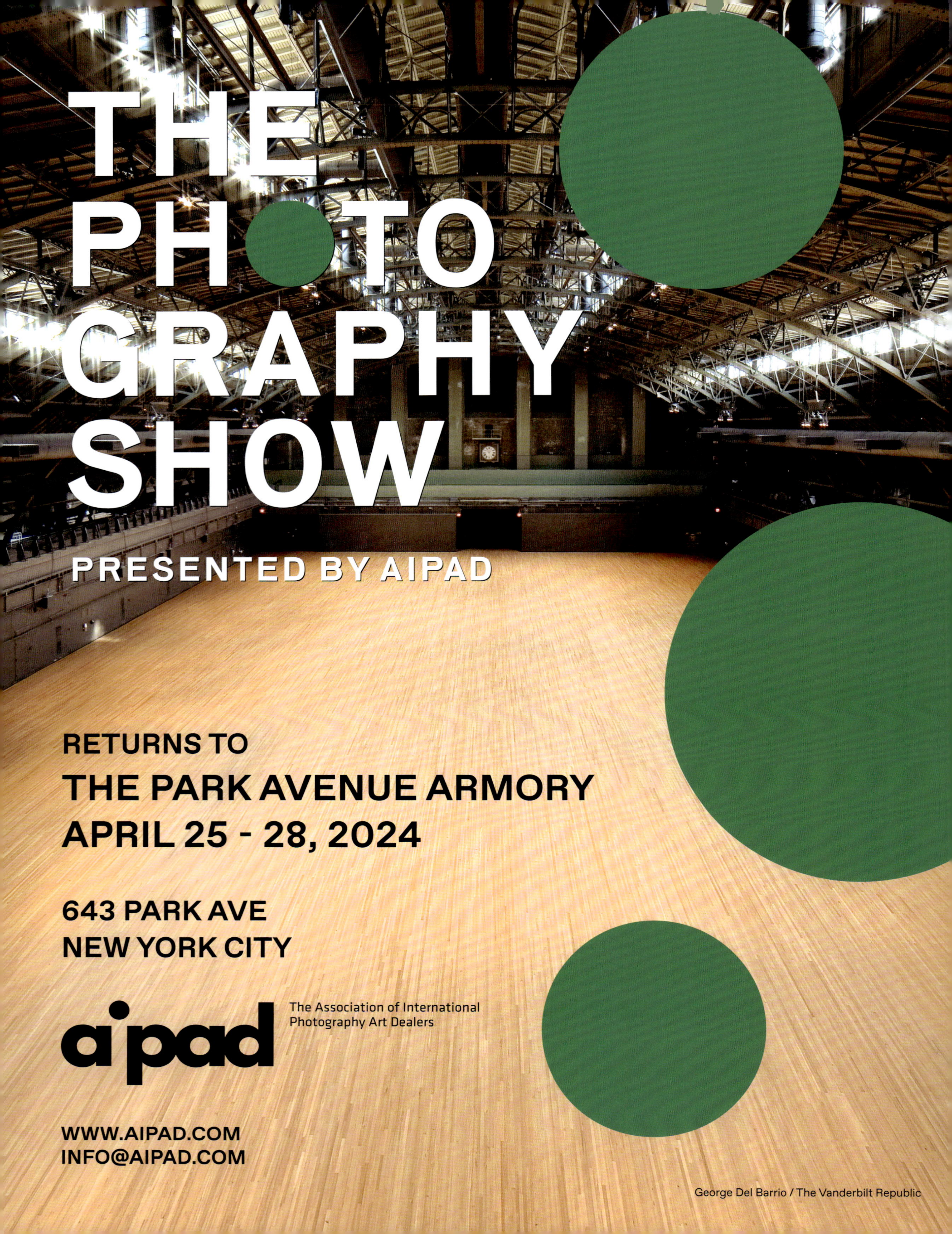

THE PHOTO GRAPHY SHOW

PRESENTED BY AIPAD

RETURNS TO
THE PARK AVENUE ARMORY
APRIL 25 - 28, 2024

643 PARK AVE
NEW YORK CITY

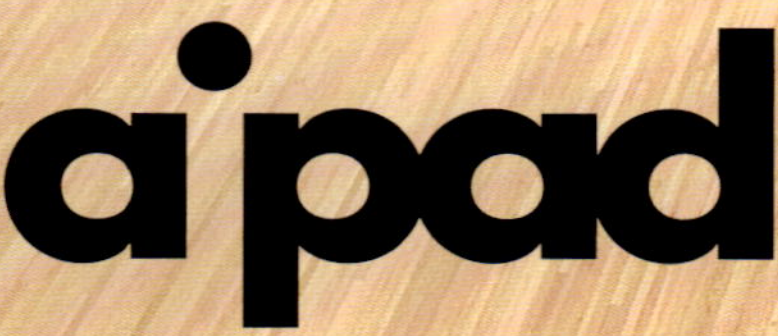

The Association of International
Photography Art Dealers

WWW.AIPAD.COM
INFO@AIPAD.COM

George Del Barrio / The Vanderbilt Republic

Agenda
Exhibitions to See

In Our Hands

When Jaida Grey Eagle studied art at the Institute of American Indian Arts in Santa Fe, New Mexico, she struggled to find a book or exhibition that covered the comprehensive history of Native photographers in North America. Returning to Minneapolis, where she was raised, she joined the curatorial team of an ambitious project to redress that history. *In Our Hands: Native Photography, 1890 to Now* is an exhibition at the Minneapolis Institute of Art organized in collaboration with a fourteen-member council of Native advisors, artists, curators, and scholars. Featured works include portraits by early twentieth-century photographers Richard Throssel and Louis Situwuka Shotridge and photographs by contemporary lens-based artists such as Brian Adams and Wendy Red Star. Grey Eagle, who is also a photojournalist, notes that *In Our Hands* affirms the agency of Native people in their own image making. "It's a really rich and diverse show," she says, "and a real reflection of Native people, because we are a rich and diverse people."

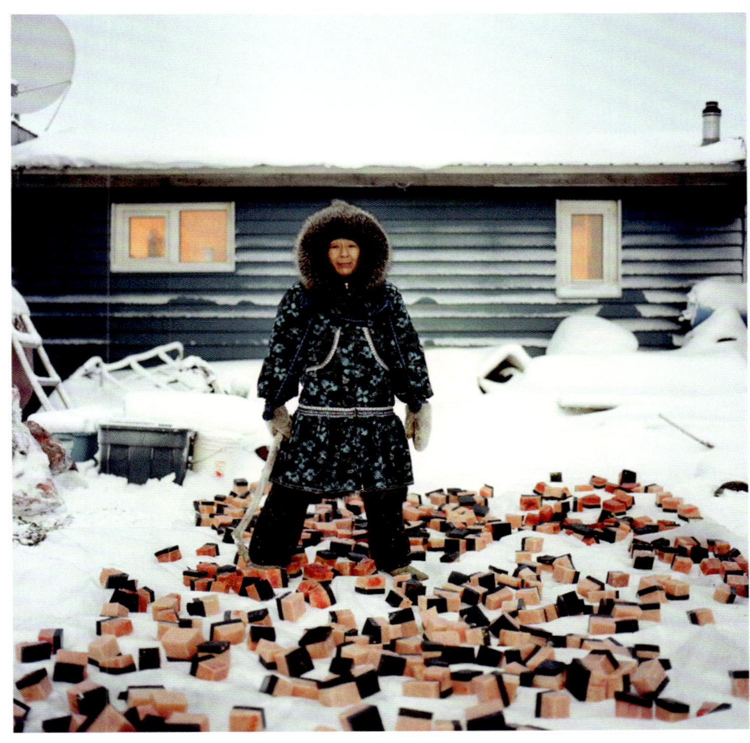

Brian Adams, *Marie Rexford of Kaktovik, Alaska, preparing maktak for the village's Thanksgiving Day feast*, 2015, from the series *I am Inuit*
© the artist and courtesy the Minneapolis Institute of Art

In Our Hands: Native Photography, 1890 to Now at the **Minneapolis Institute of Art, October 22, 2023–January 14, 2024**

Viviane Sassen

Over the past thirty years, the Dutch artist Viviane Sassen's output has spanned conceptual photography and mixed-media work as well as commercial and editorial imagery. Her photographs—often featuring stark color contrasts, severe geometric shapes, and abstracted bodies—have a distinct visual language, equally present in the context of her museum exhibitions and magazine spreads. In 2013, her fashion imagery was the subject of a retrospective at Huis Marseille in her home city of Amsterdam, covering over seventeen years of work. A decade later, the scope of a Sassen retrospective has greatly expanded. Bringing together two hundred photographs across several of the artist's most well-known series, *Viviane Sassen—Art & Fashion* at the Maison Européenne de la Photographie is the first comprehensive exhibition of the artist's work in France. Its two floors incorporate signature work and unseen archives to bring audiences closer to Sassen's commitment to visual innovation. As the curator Clothilde Morette explains, the exhibition oscillates between "exuberant formal experiments and more contemplative iconography, highlighting the ambiguity inherent in Sassen's representation of reality."

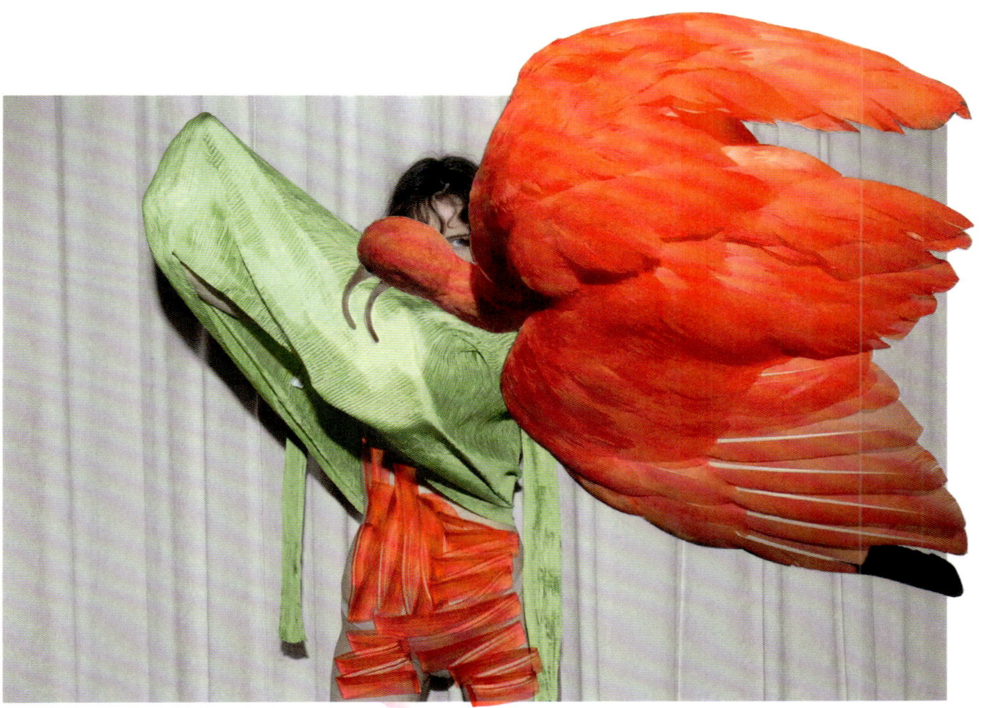

Viviane Sassen, *Eudocimus Ruber*, 2017, from the series *Of Mud and Lotus*
© the artist and courtesy Stevenson, Johannesburg, Cape Town, and Amsterdam

Viviane Sassen—Art & Fashion at the **Maison Européenne de la Photographie, Paris, October 18, 2023–February 11, 2024**

Dorothea Lange

In her biography of Dorothea Lange, Linda Gordon describes a pivotal realization when, in the spring of 1932, the pioneering American photographer "looked down from her second-floor studio window and saw the Depression." Lange was familiar with the effects of the country's economic crisis, but seeing its human tragedy play out in the streets—across breadlines and strikes—had a lasting impact. She went on to have a remarkable career as a documentary photographer, making portraits of migrant workers facing economic ruin, Japanese Americans who had been forcefully interned shortly after the start of World War II, and people she met in her travels to South America, the Middle East, and Asia. *Dorothea Lange: Seeing People*, at the National Gallery of Art, Washington, DC, highlights the effect of her early training as a studio photographer on her later documentary work. "This powerful merging of portraiture and documentary photography expanded the boundaries of both traditions," writes the curator Philip Brookman. Further illustrating this link, a catalog copublished by Yale University Press accompanies the exhibition, with new research on Lange's early career and political thinking.

Dorothea Lange: Seeing People **at the National Gallery of Art, Washington, DC, November 5, 2023–March 31, 2024**

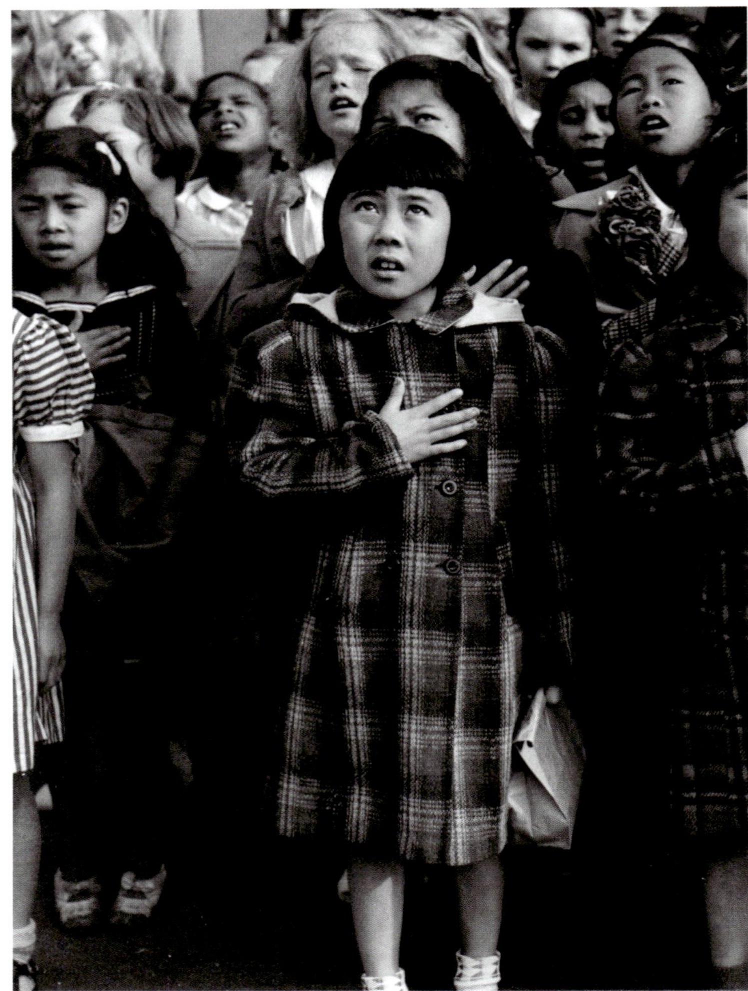

Dorothea Lange, *Children of the Weill Public School Shown in a Flag Pledge Ceremony, San Francisco, California*, April, 1942
Courtesy the National Gallery of Art, Washington, DC

An-My Lê

There are the facts of Vietnam and then there's the Vietnam of the mind—what the photographer An-My Lê calls the world between "experience and chaos versus memory and storytelling." Lê was born in Saigon in 1960 and evacuated with her family to the United States in 1975. For years it was too traumatic to watch films about the war, but then Lê became obsessed by classics of the genre, such as *Apocalypse Now*. In 1999, she traveled to Virginia to take part in Vietnam War reenactments, playing a Vietcong guerilla or North Vietnamese soldier. There she made her trenchant project *Small Wars* (1999–2002), one of several series about conflict and performance featured in *Between Two Rivers*, Lê's retrospective at the Museum of Modern Art, New York. "My concern is to make photographs that are provocative in response to the reality of war while challenging its context," Lê has said. Her career-long fascination with the foggy nuances of history speaks to the enduring debates about the sacrifices of war and the elusive nature of truth.

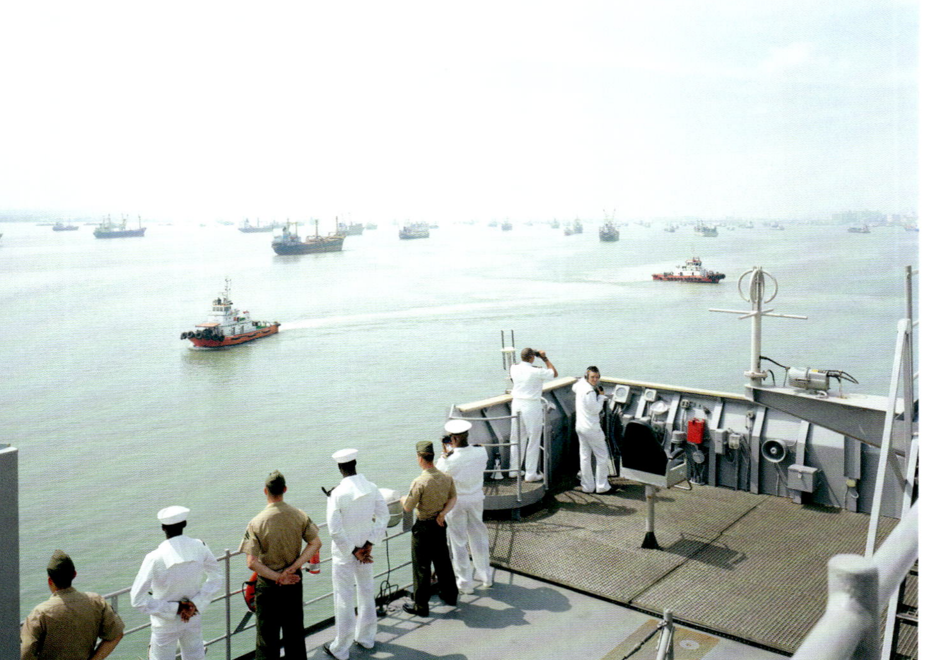

An-My Lê, *New Orleans*, 2011, from the series *Delta*
© the artist and courtesy Marian Goodman Gallery

An-My Lê: Between Two Rivers **at the Museum of Modern Art, New York, November 5, 2023–March 16, 2024**

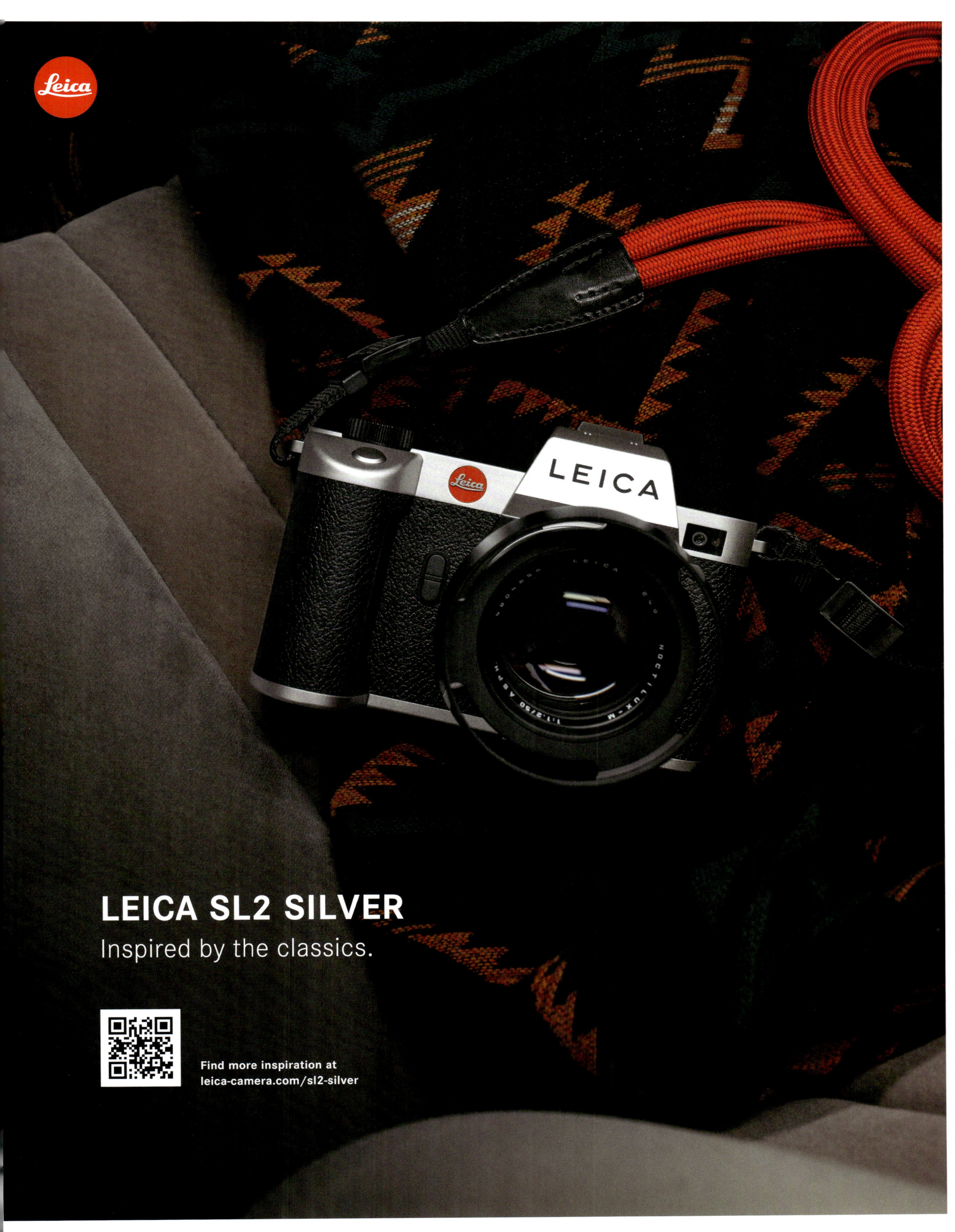

LEICA
LEICA SL2 SILVER
Inspired by the classics.
Find more inspiration at
leica-camera.com/sl2-silver

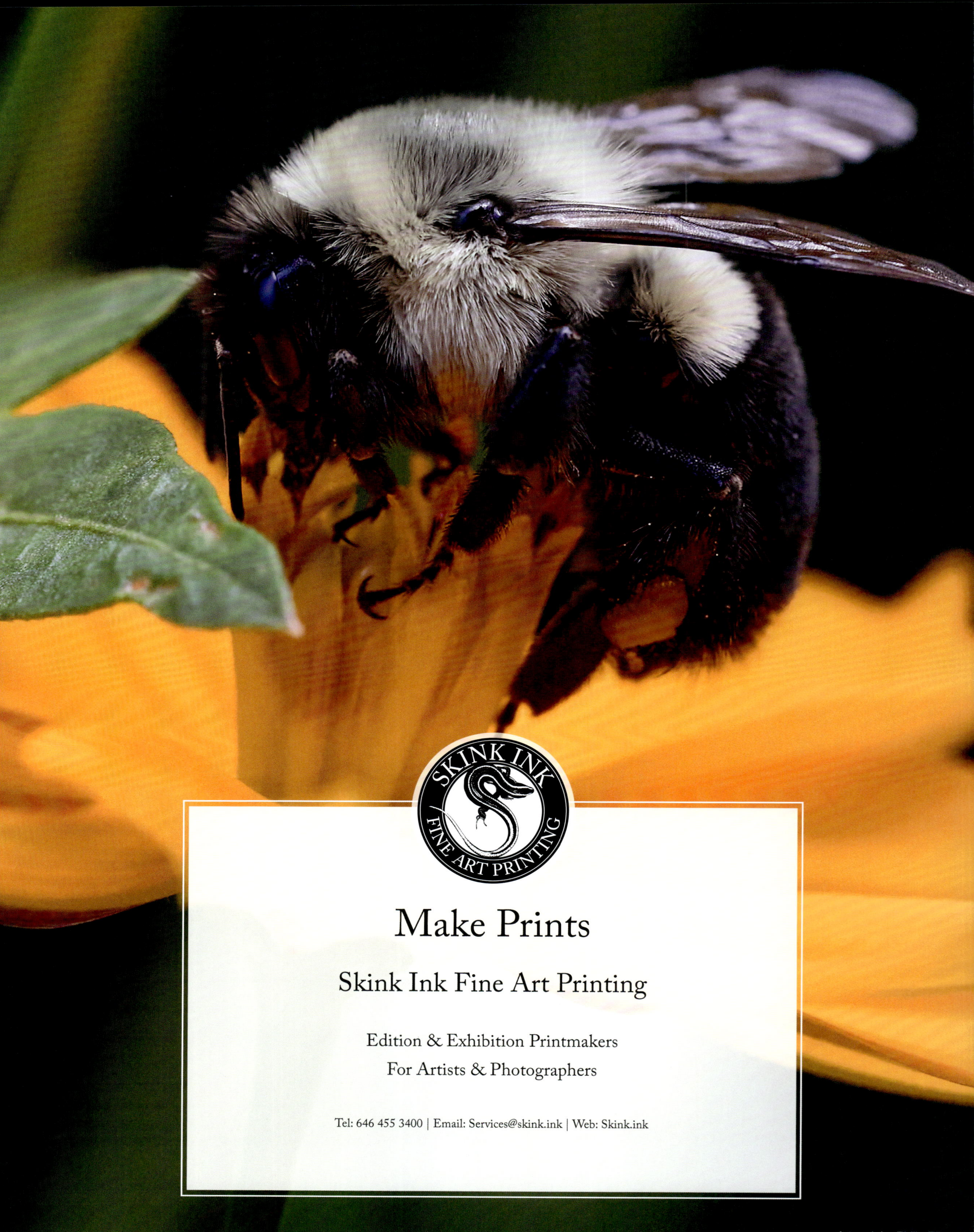
SKINK INK
FINE ART PRINTING

Make Prints

Skink Ink Fine Art Printing

Edition & Exhibition Printmakers
For Artists & Photographers

Tel: 646 455 3400 | Email: Services@skink.ink | Web: Skink.ink

Artwork by Philip Riley

Dispatches

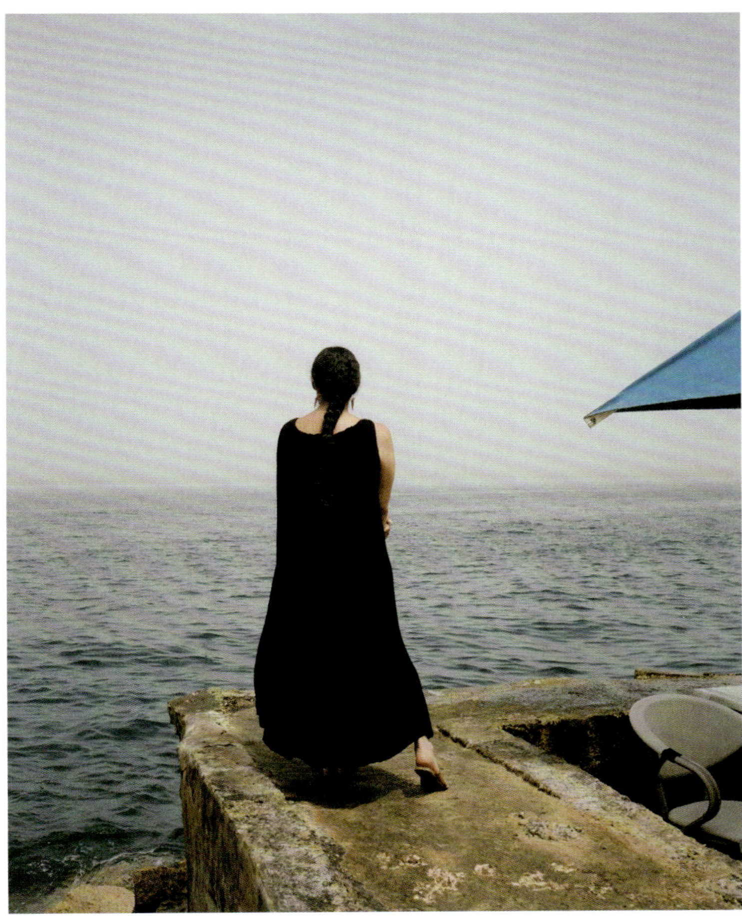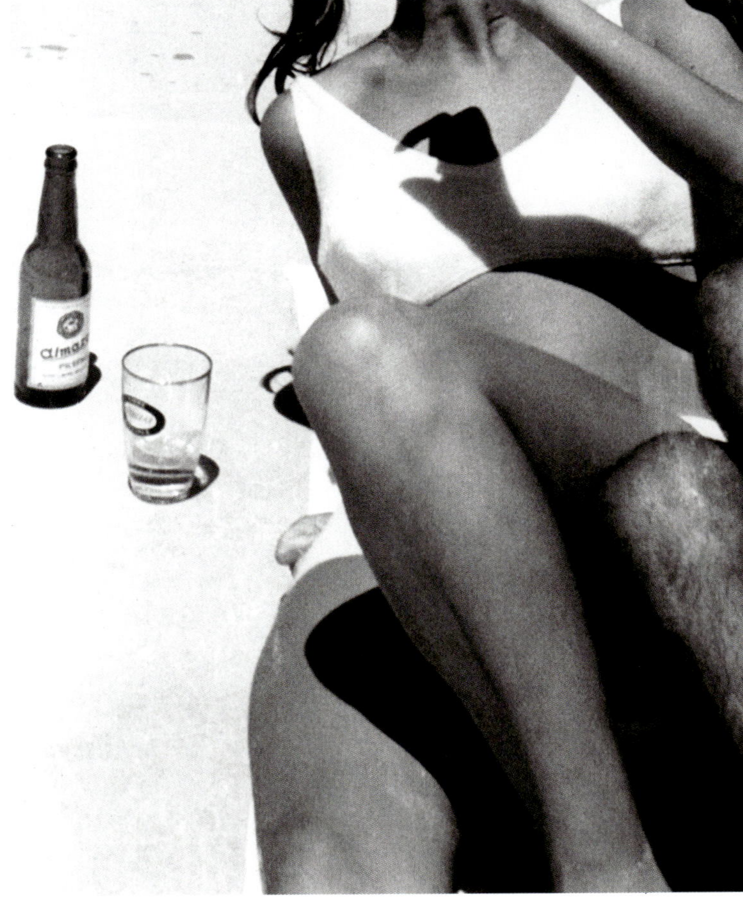

How has Tanya Traboulsi emerged as one of Beirut's most thoughtful and affectionate chroniclers?

Kaelen Wilson-Goldie

Tanya Traboulsi is an ardent observer of the Lebanese coastline. Her photographs probe the ways in which clay tennis courts and fake grass playing fields are tucked into the hills sliding down to the sea in Ras Beirut, on the western side of the city's promontory. She is also a dedicated student of vernacular architecture. She details vestibules, awnings, bougainvillea peeking through tactical breeze-blocks, and the elegant arches of a derelict Ottoman mansion. She returns again and again to the playfulness with which shopkeepers in the Lebanese capital use language to advertise the Renaissance Sporting Club, New Fashion, or Dalida, a tiny chocolatier downgraded under financial duress to an all-purpose *dekaneh*, or grocery store, named for a pop music sensation.

Traboulsi's series *Beirut, Recurring Dream* (2021–ongoing) pairs photographs she has taken in the last two years with images from her personal archive: six large boxes of material, including family albums and pictures she took during her childhood and adolescence. Traboulsi's diptychs are fluid and unfixed. They appear in different configurations, depending on their context. They are also matched by intuition. By placing a photograph of a couple lounging on a beach in the 1960s next to an image of a woman standing alone, her back to the viewer, on the corner of a low wall jutting into the sea, as she gazes toward a blurry horizon and ambivalent skies, Traboulsi isn't suggesting narrative so much as time travel or a flash of inherited memory.

Traboulsi was seven years old when she left Beirut with her family on a boat crossing the Mediterranean Sea. It was 1983. Lebanon's civil war was lurching through its first decade. The center of the capital had been destroyed in the first round of fighting, starting in 1975. Beirut was split in half and the armed forces had fractured. The government was about to collapse. Massacres had occurred all over the country, and there was shelling in densely residential neighborhoods. Syria had intervened, and in 1982, Israel had invaded and besieged the country, which, among other things, closed the airport for months at a time. Fleeing residents had to risk dangerous mountain roads or the ferry lines connecting Beirut to Cyprus.

Traboulsi's parents met before the civil war began. Her mother had moved to Lebanon from Vienna to work as a ski instructor, and Traboulsi's father cut the line to sit with her on the lift. An enduring romance ensued. Traboulsi was born in Austria but spent her early years in Beirut, taking pictures of the city using an Instamatic camera and 110 film. Her family left and stayed away for more than a decade, in part because the civil war lasted so long and in part because it ended with such uncertainty. A general amnesty was announced in 1991, although some argue the conflict continued by other means.

"The moment I left, I wanted to go back," Traboulsi told me this past summer. "The image of how Beirut looked from the sea stuck with me for thirteen years." She was separated from her two best friends in Lebanon and saw them constantly in her dreams. She didn't return until 1996. From that point, she shuttled back and forth between Austria and Lebanon until she finished university. She settled in Beirut in 2003.

As a city, Beirut has been photographed with a prodigiousness disproportionate to its size, even its history. The so-called photographic mission of 1991 invited six leading photographers—Gabriele Basilico, Raymond Depardon, Fouad Elkoury, René Burri, Josef Koudelka, and Robert Frank—to document the tremendous violence done to the heart of Beirut's city center by fifteen years of civil war. In the late 1990s and early 2000s, artists and filmmakers such as Walid Raad, Jalal Toufic, and Akram Zaatari responded to the conditions of postwar and reconstruction-era Beirut with their own trenchant questions. In their wake, Traboulsi has emerged as one of the city's most thoughtful and affectionate chroniclers.

Traboulsi and I are nearly the same age and came to live in Beirut at the same time. In many ways, her photographs

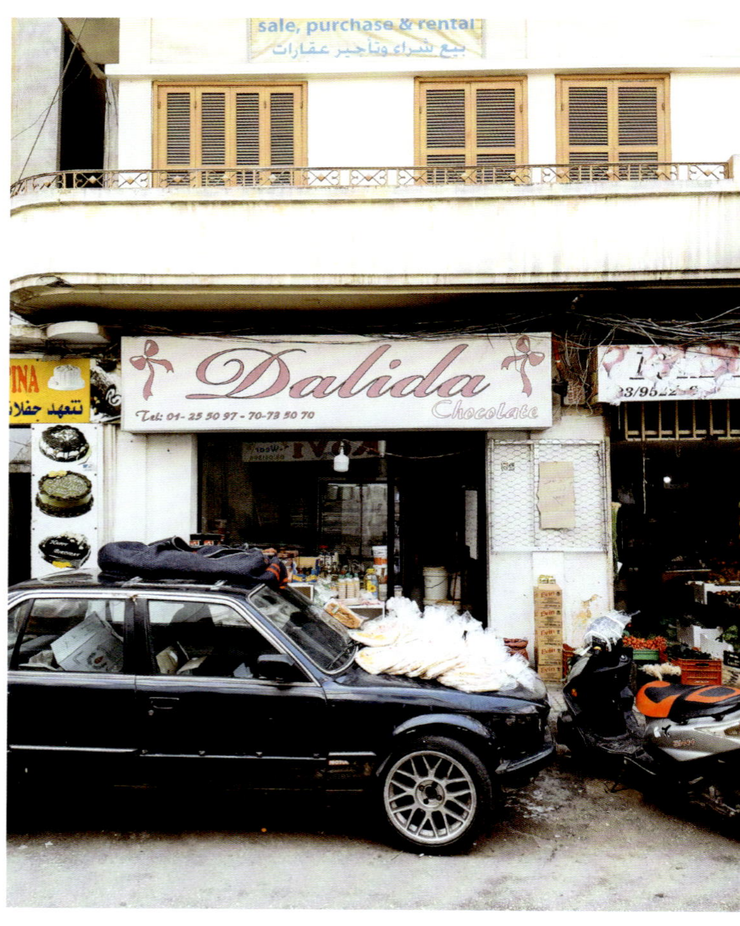

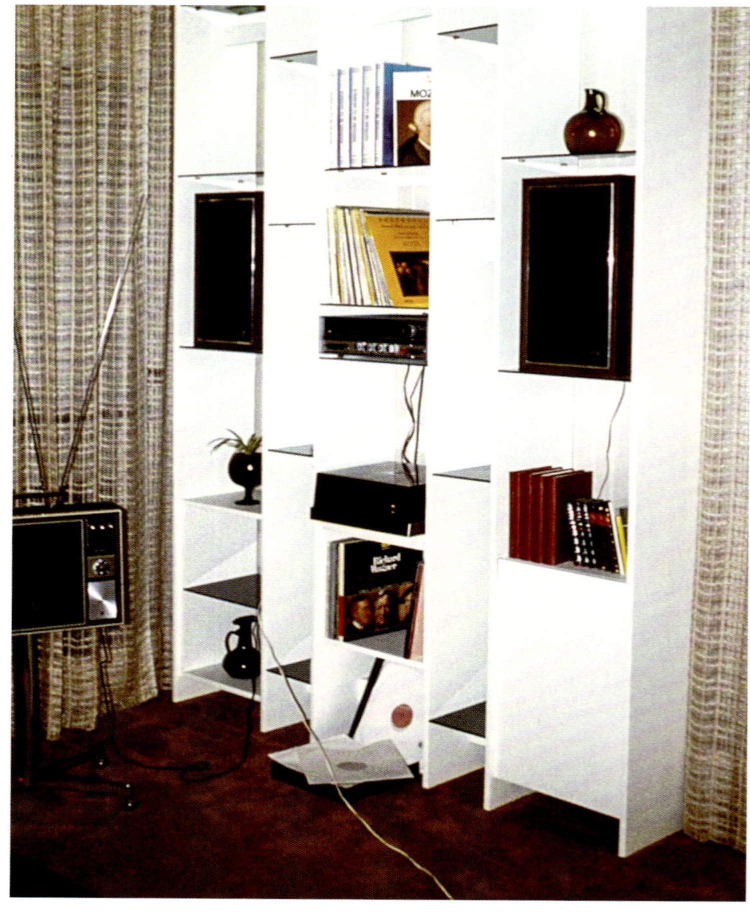

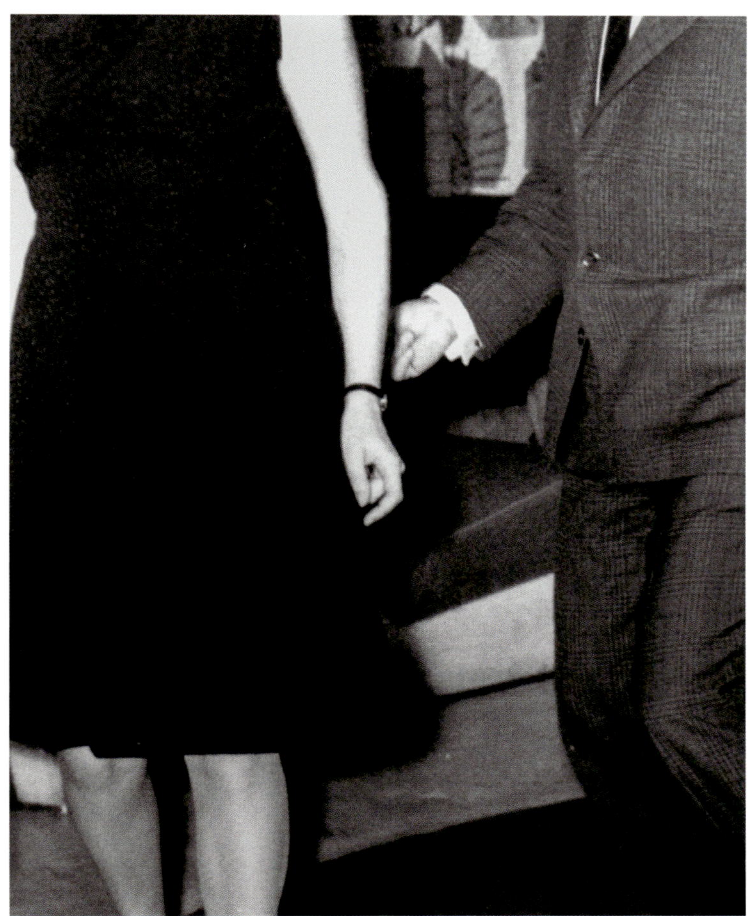 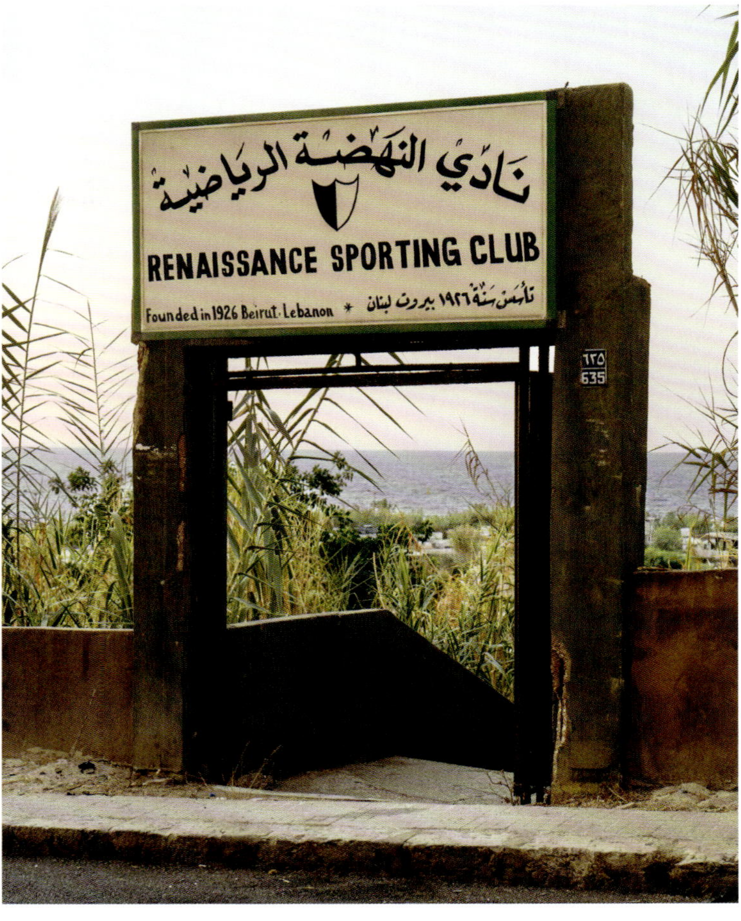

As a city, Beirut has been photographed with a prodigiousness disproportionate to its size, even its history.

narrate my own relationship to the city. She has photographed buildings I have lived in, corners I have loved, places I have walked by and wondered about daily. I vividly remember my first encounter with her work, in a group show called *Be-Sides: How Young Lebanese Photographers See Present-Day Lebanon*, organized by the Goethe-Institut in 2007.

Beirut's photographic history can make the city feel trapped in the past, forever in the rubble of the civil war. But Traboulsi has stayed with the story and followed the city through more recent upheavals. With great subtlety and sensitivity, in *Beirut, Recurring Dream* she gathers traces of the revolution that erupted in 2019, followed by the economic collapse that devalued the local currency by 90 percent and plunged more than half the country into poverty. She captures the afterlives of the catastrophic explosion that ripped through the port of Beirut on August 4, 2020, killing hundreds, injuring thousands, and displacing three hundred thousand people from their damaged homes.

"The explosion changed everything," Traboulsi told me. "It changed me, my friendships, my relationships, my view of love, what I accept and what I can give to other people." Seeing the city so damaged compelled her to admit that Beirut was and always had been her subject.

The Lebanese poet Etel Adnan described a mountain in California as her best friend. She painted it every day, in all kinds of light and weather, for more than a year. This was in the mid-1980s, after Adnan, the ultimate chronicler of Beirut, had made her own exit from the city and Lebanon's civil war. In 2021, Traboulsi made a film with the writer Ibrahim Nehme, unrelated to *Beirut, Recurring Dream*, called *Son of the Sun*. Nehme's voiceover offers a visceral response to the port explosion (he was seriously injured in the blast), but Traboulsi's images are long, steady shots of the sun rising and falling on the coastline, waves lapping the shore. Adnan had her mountain, Traboulsi has her city on the sea.

Kaelen Wilson-Goldie is a critic who lives in Geneva and Beirut.

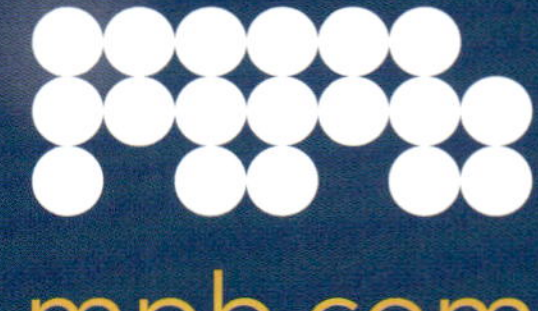
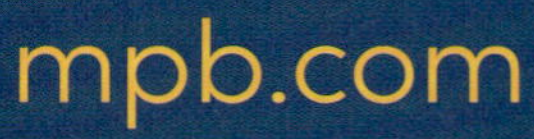

mpb.com
Trustpilot
MPB has thousands of items to choose from.
Shop the full range
mpb.com
Change camera gear for less. Every item is MPB approved with a free warranty.
Buy•Sell•Trade
Create

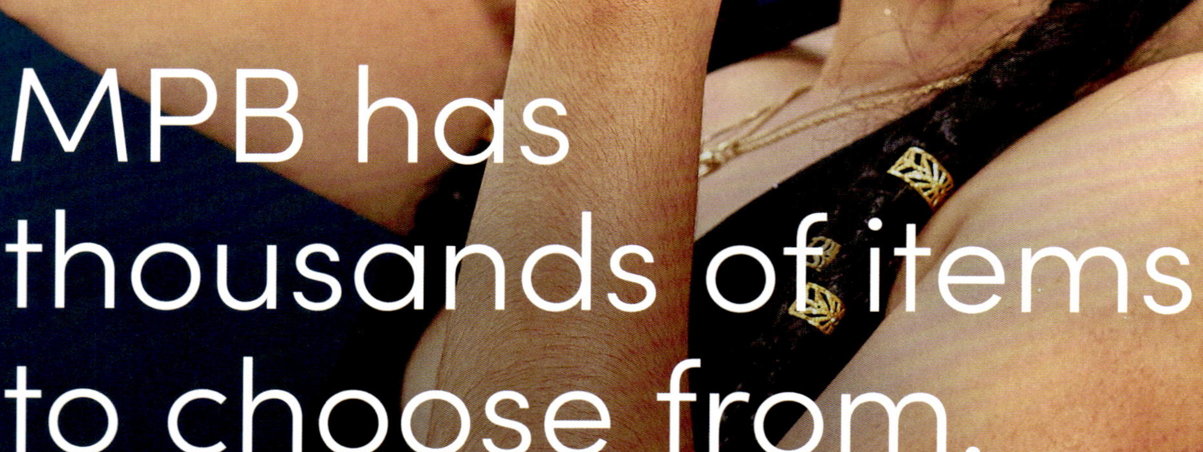
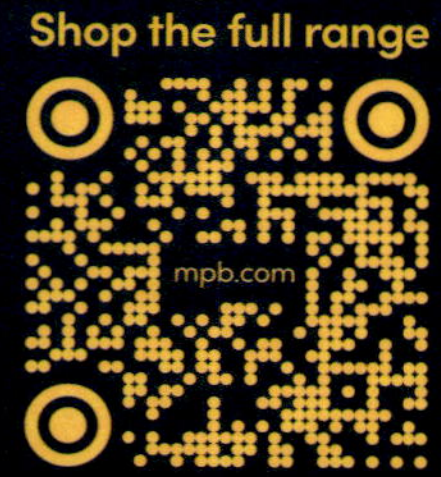

Studio Visit

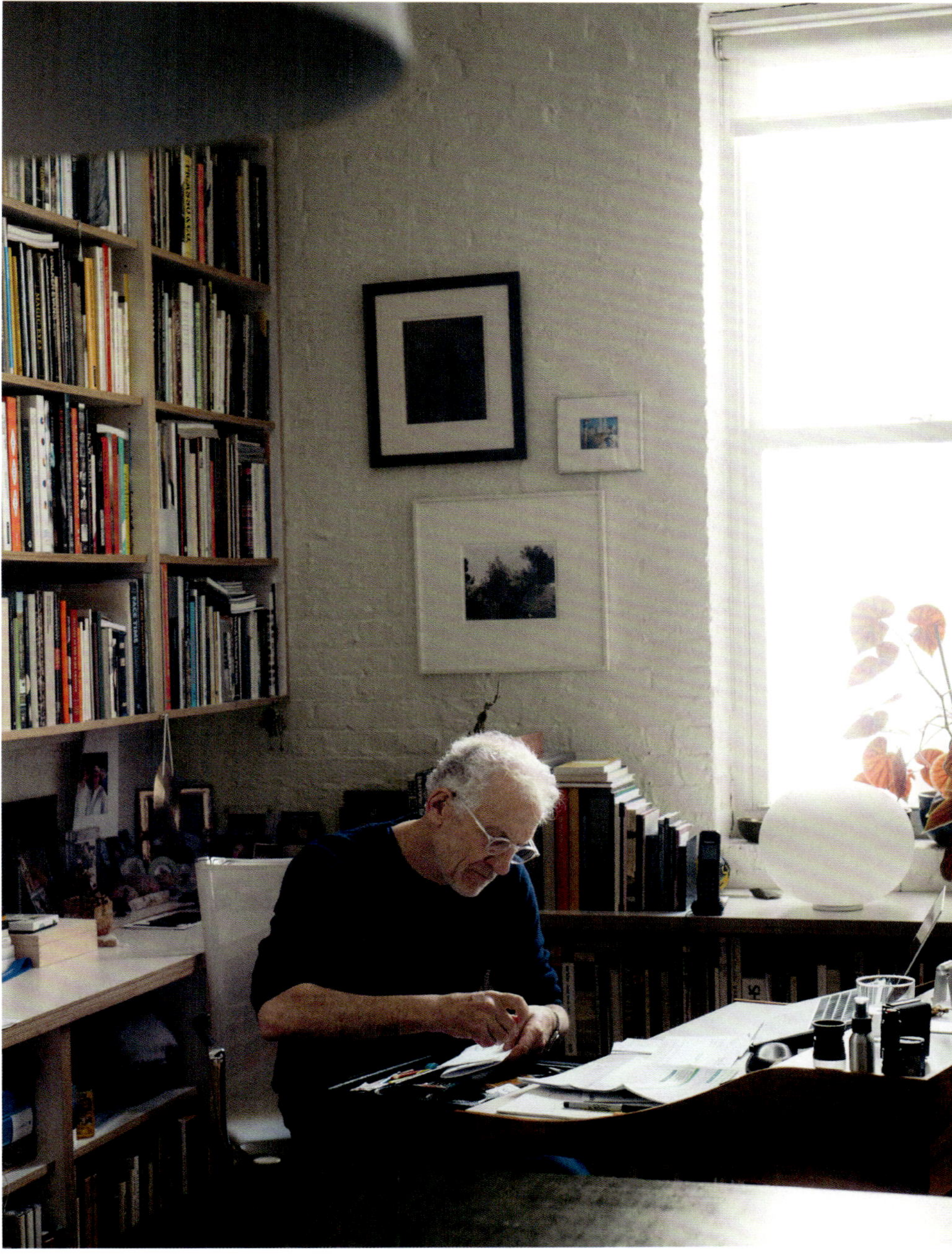

In the 1980s, Mitch Epstein found a loft on the Lower East Side at a time when New York's downtown was the center of the art world.
Brendan Embser

Mitch Epstein and his
studio, New York, May 2023
Photographs by Daniel Terna
for *Aperture*

One Sunday in April 1972, the *New York Times* ran a notice under the column News of the Camera World announcing openings for transfer students to the Cooper Union in New York who "demonstrate a serious and mature commitment to photography." *The Pioneer*, Cooper's student newspaper, highlighted the school's darkrooms and silk-screen facilities, along with the prominent faculty, including Roy DeCarava, Inge Morath, Joel Meyerowitz, and Tod Papageorge. A portfolio of "exceptional merit" would be required for application.

Mitch Epstein happened to see that *Times* piece. "And I seized the opportunity," he told me earlier this year, at his light-filled home and studio on Rivington Street on the Lower East Side of Manhattan. "I came down, submitted a portfolio, did an interview, got in, and it was golden—because there's no tuition at Cooper. It got me here into the city."

At the time, Epstein, who is known for his vivid street photography, long-form documentary essays on India and Vietnam, and *American Power* (2009), a monumental series about energy infrastructure in the United States, was a student at the Rhode Island School of Design (RISD). Artistic experimentation reigned, but his attempts, he once recalled, were "charming and mildly ridiculous." RISD was "fine," Epstein says, but he was just "treading water." He was twenty years old.

His first residence in New York was at 190 Bowery, the seventy-two-room Germania Bank Building—and holy altar for graffiti artists—that the photographer Jay Maisel purchased in 1966 for $102,000. In the summer of 1972, Maisel rented Epstein a former bank office as an

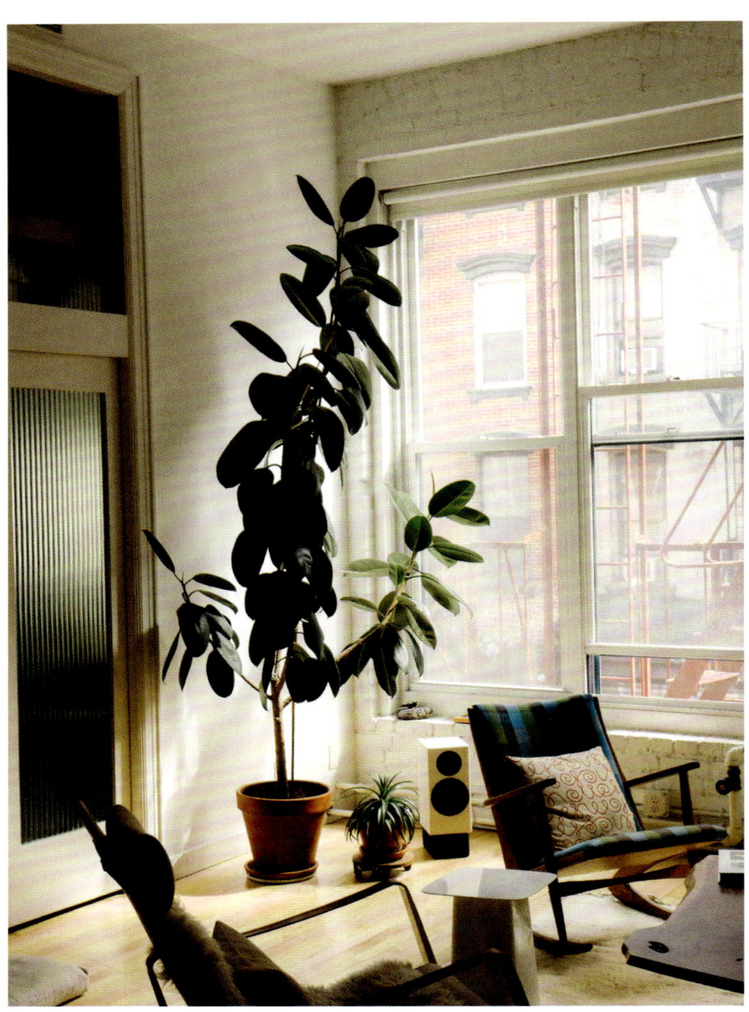

apartment. "The larger downtown area wasn't monetized in the way that it is now," Epstein tells me. Artists were living in cold-water SoHo flats and FOOD, Gordon Matta-Clark's artist-run enterprise, was one of the postindustrial neighborhood's few restaurants.

The Bowery "had a kind of wildness," Epstein says. "You were reminded every day of social hierarchies of the city." Freeman Alley—possibly named for its proximity to an African American burial ground nearby—was littered with needles and condoms. In 2015, Maisel sold 190 Bowery for $55 million and the street-wear brand Supreme now occupies the retail level. Rivington Street today is like an unruly palimpsest: the metal gates to a lumber yard are covered with a fantastical space-scene mural; the galleries once occupied by Eleven Rivington and Sue Scott are now run by Tibor de Nagy and Candice Madey. One night in 2018, a reckless driver slammed into several of the street's decades-old trees, which were later replaced with spindly saplings.

A first apartment is often the opening salvo of any New York story, and so it was for Epstein, who was living on the Upper West Side in the years after studying at Cooper but looking for something permanent. "Downtown beckoned," he explains.

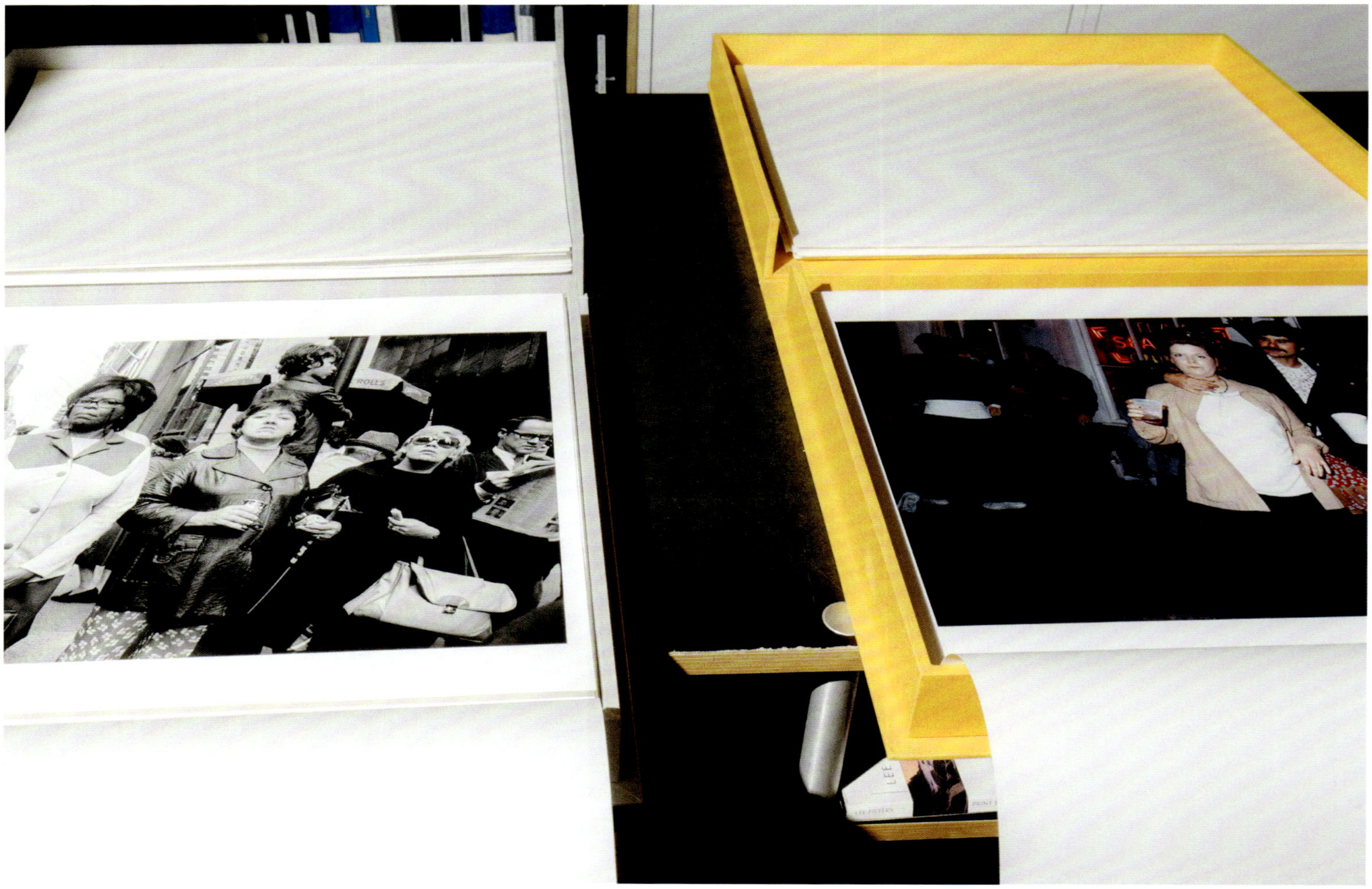

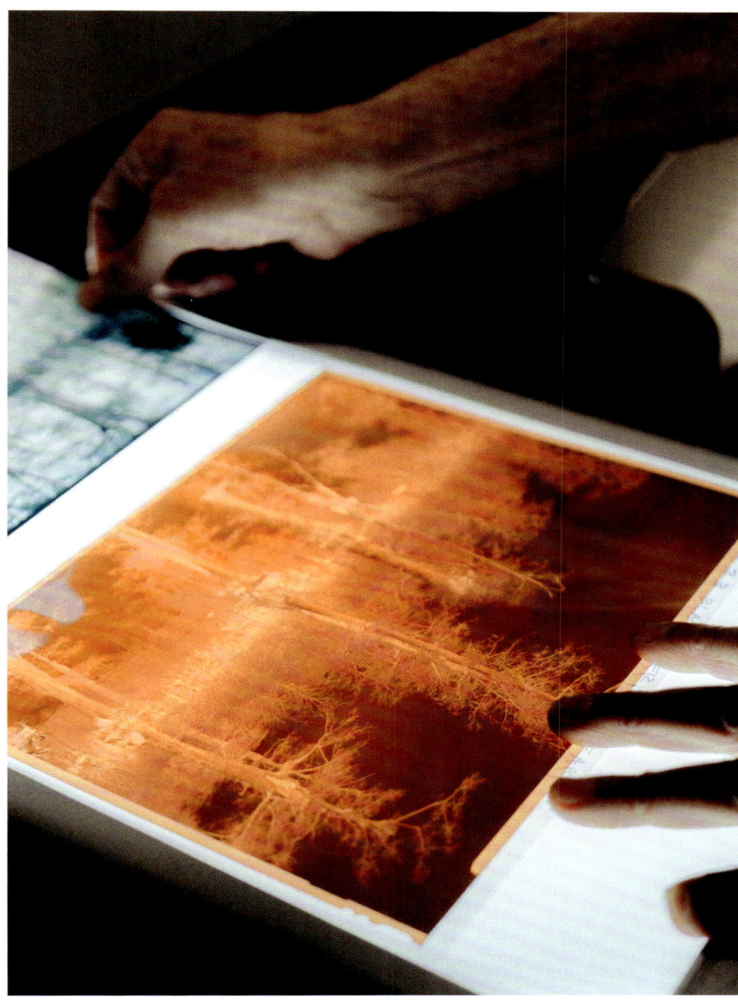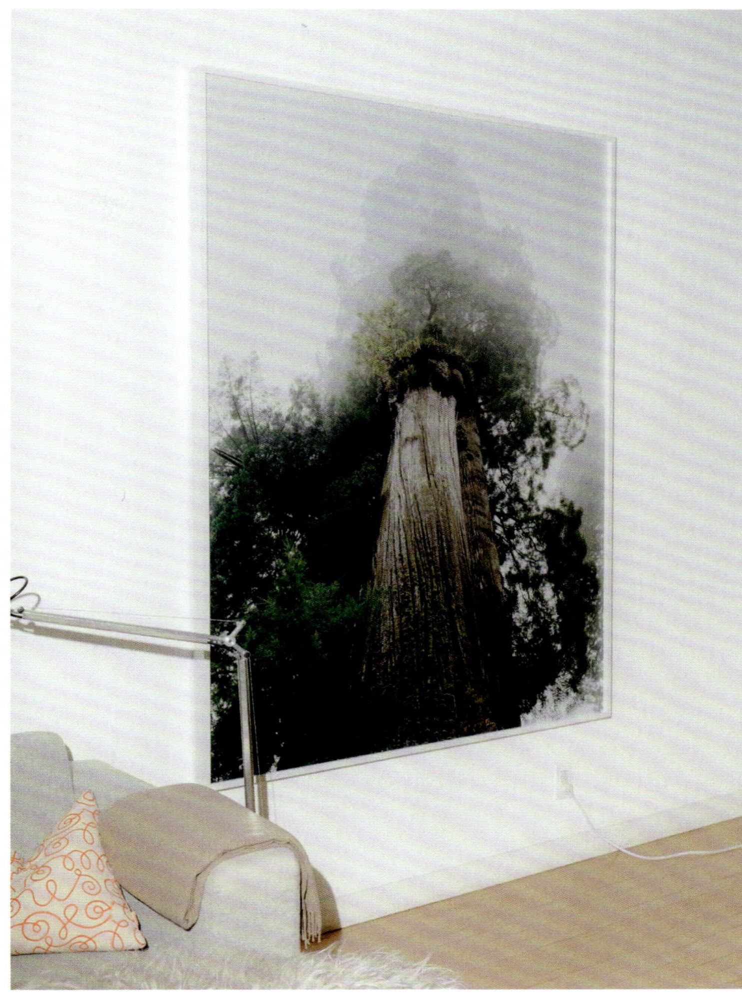

Certain buildings were designated for artists in residence. In 1986, Epstein and his wife at the time, the filmmaker Mira Nair, found a space on Rivington Street and waited out the legal process until, finally, they were able to purchase a floor-through loft, which they promptly gutted. Epstein built a darkroom and studio in the back. The front became the living space.

"I never thought I would be here this long," Epstein says. "But it's enabled me to live a very fertile, very creative life." He and his second wife, the editor Susan Bell, raised their daughter, Lucia, in the loft. In the open-plan kitchen, there's a statement midcentury pendant lamp by the designer Poul Henningsen, and in the living room, a paper lantern made by Tomi Shinagawa, the mother of Mikio Shinagawa, who operated the legendary SoHo restaurant Omen. On a rack of Vitsœ shelving are LPs by Fela Kuti and Pharoah Sanders. In a corner, near the oversize windows, a rubber plant soars toward the ceiling.

In 2008, Epstein dismantled his darkroom. He worked with a contractor and a feng shui advisor to redesign the studio, which, despite facing a back alley, takes in a generous amount of light reflected off white brick walls. The custom-made layered-plywood bookshelves were inspired by Donald Judd and hold a formidable collection of art books. Like Epstein's photographs, the studio has a strong sense of order and clarity, but it's not fussy: his dog, Ginger, has her own bed on the floor. Ryan Spencer, Epstein's longtime studio manager, sits at a desk adjacent to an enormous Epson printer and opposite a refrigerator stocked with film (and sometimes bread). Epstein's own desk is set on a diagonal opposite a magnetic steel wall, powder-coated white by an auto-body shop, on which he examines his test prints. At the center of the room is a black German-made table he's had since the 1980s. Everything happens on this table: from planning an exhibition to sequencing a book.

During his first year at Cooper, Epstein studied with Garry Winogrand, who became a mentor. "He took me upside down and shook out a lot of the gobbledygook that I had in my head," he says. Epstein's work from the early 1970s, collected in *Silver + Chrome* (2022), shows Winogrand's influence—the exuberant street scenes, the beguiling compositions that meld chance and precision. Winogrand suggested Epstein try color film, which would become his medium for decades, from *Family Business* (2003), a book about his parents in Holyoke, Massachusetts, scheduled to be reissued by Steidl next year, to his current project, *Old Growth*, a large-format study of some of the oldest forests and trees in the American landscape.

Epstein has never had another studio—or another home. "I'd like to have a bigger studio. I'd like to have a place in the country," he says. "But do I want those things in lieu of having to give up my freedom to make my work? No. My priorities are very clear." Art is life, and life is downtown.

Brendan Embser is the senior editor of *Aperture*.

Timeline

The Malian photographer Seydou Keïta's portraits are known and celebrated throughout the world. Born around 1921 in Bamako, Keïta ran a successful portrait studio during the late 1940s and '50s. Images of his clients assisted in the construction of middle-class identity in French colonial West Africa. From postcard-size photographs to large modern exhibition prints, the history of their changing formats and circulation tells a story of vernacular photography and African art in global markets.
—**Drew Sawyer**

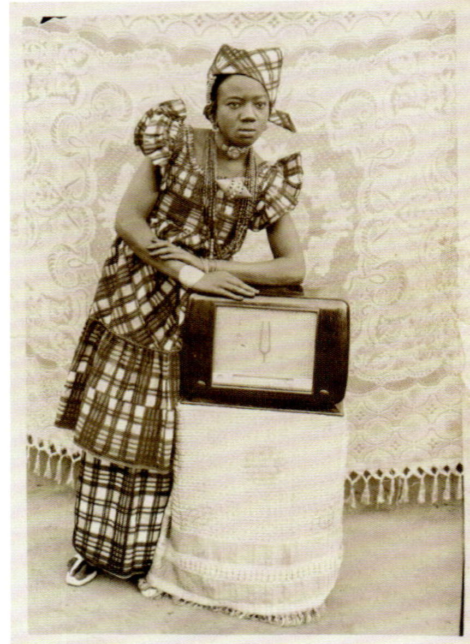

After apprenticing with the photographer Mountaga Dembélé, Keïta opened his own portrait studio, in 1948, in Bamako. Like many professional photographers, Keïta used textile backdrops and provided his clients with props, from jewelry and clothing to vehicles and radios. These visual cues conveyed his clients' social position and aspirations as cosmopolitan and modern individuals. Keïta mostly made contact prints for his clients, retaining the negatives so they could order additional copies.

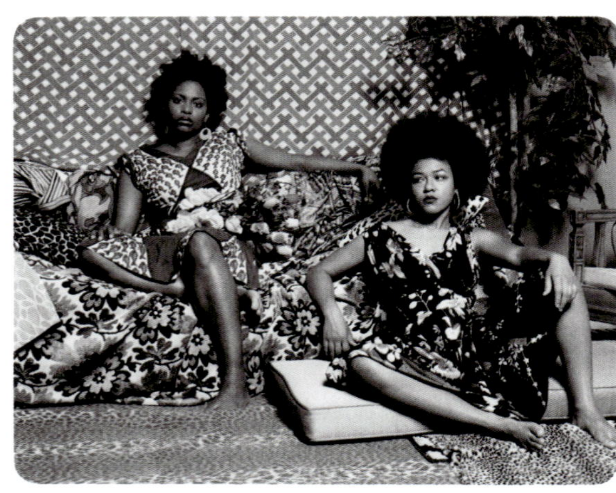

Keïta died in Paris in 2001, prompting a drawn-out legal battle over the ownership of his negatives. Over the last twenty years, and coinciding with a broader interest in vernacular photography, postcolonialism, and Blackness, the circulation of Keïta's photographs has continued to bring Malian aesthetics to contemporary art. Artists such as Mickalene Thomas have openly celebrated some of the visual tropes associated with Keïta's photographs, including patterned textiles and careful yet casual compositions, as in *A Moment's Pleasure* (2006).

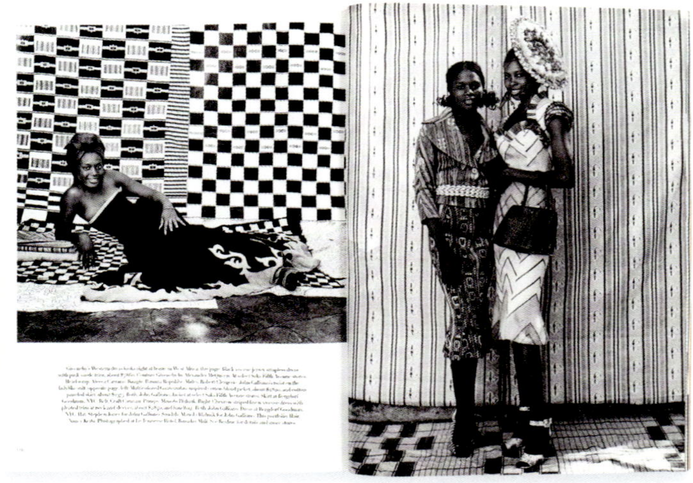

By the late 1990s, Keïta's photographs began circulating in the art and fashion worlds, bringing him new work and financial success. In 1997, Gagosian mounted a solo exhibition. The next year the British fashion journalist Sarajane Hoare commissioned Keïta to produce an editorial for *Harper's Bazaar*. As recounted in Allison Moore's book *Embodying Relation*, Hoare chose clothing by mostly European and American designers, cast the models in Bamako, and bought local textiles for the backdrops to mimic Keïta's portraits from the 1950s.

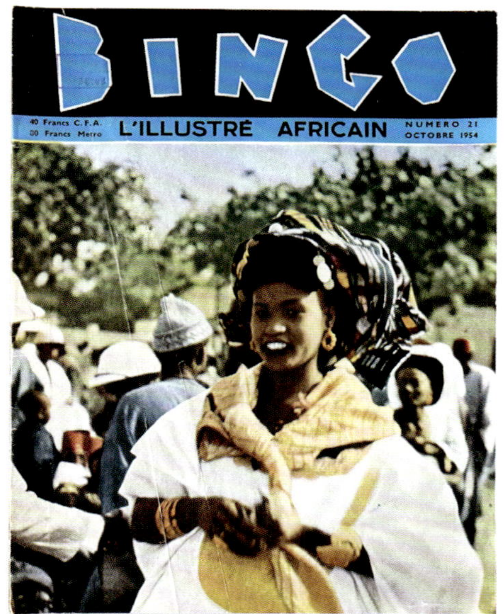

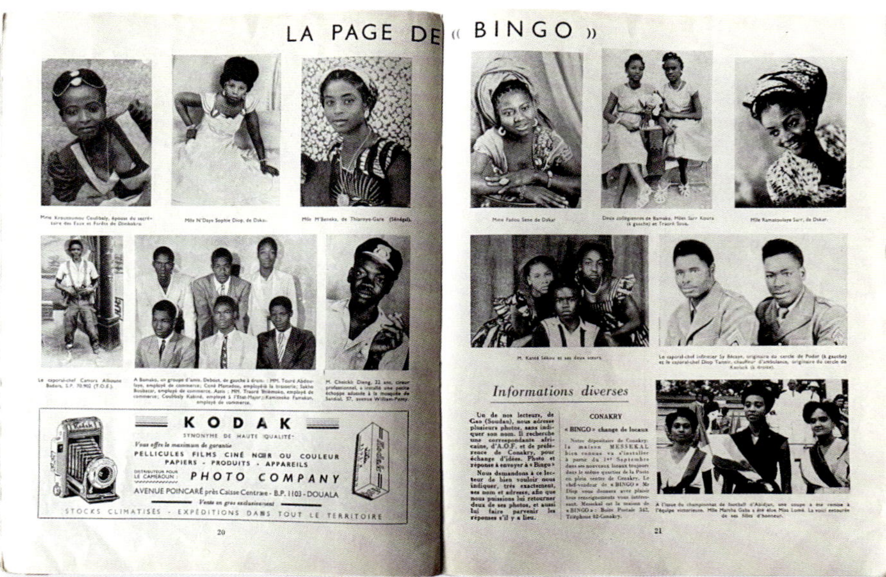

During the 1950s, Keïta's photographs appeared in newly emerging magazines, such as *Bingo*, published in Dakar and considered the first glossy picture magazine intended for Francophone African readers. His images were included in a recurring feature presenting reader-submitted photographs, most often studio portraits with captions that typically identified sitters by name—such as this spread with two schoolgirls, Sarr Koura and Traoré Soua. Scholars such as Jennifer Bajorek have shown how photographs in *Bingo* helped create a "decolonial political imagination" in French West Africa.

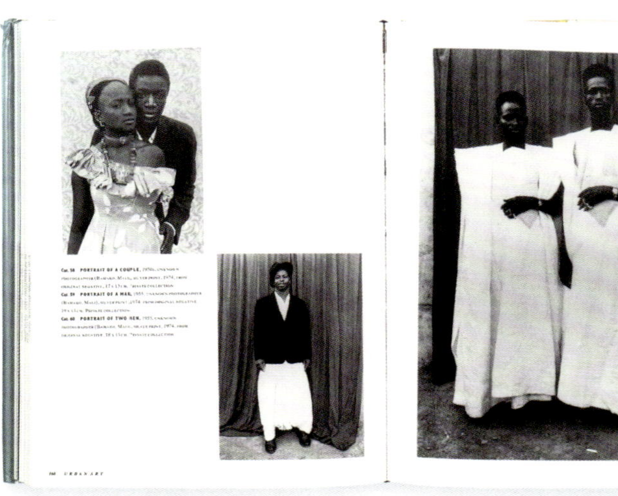

Two decades later, in the 1970s, the art historian Susan Vogel collected negatives by Keïta. She included prints of them in *Africa Explores: 20th Century African Art*, shown in 1991 at New York's Center for African Art and the New Museum, with the credit: "Unknown photographer (Bamako, Mali)." This led to two French photographers and the curator Andre Magnin traveling to Bamako in 1992 in search of Keïta's work. Magnin brought nearly one thousand negatives back to Paris.

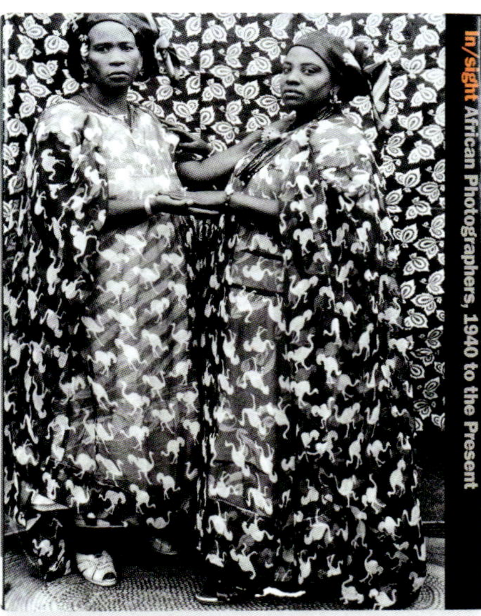

Keïta's credited photographs were presented at the Rencontres Internationales de la Photographie in Arles, France, in 1993. The following year, a traveling solo exhibition opened at the Fondation Cartier in Paris, and his photographs played a central role in the inaugural Rencontres de Bamako. The curator Okwui Enwezor included several works by Keïta, now valued for their aesthetic and historical qualities, in his landmark 1996 exhibition *In/sight: African Photographers, 1940 to the Present* at the Solomon R. Guggenheim Museum in New York.

Drew Sawyer is the Sondra Gilman Curator of Photography at the Whitney Museum of American Art.

PARIS PHOTO

7-10 NOV 2024
GRAND PALAIS

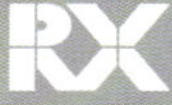

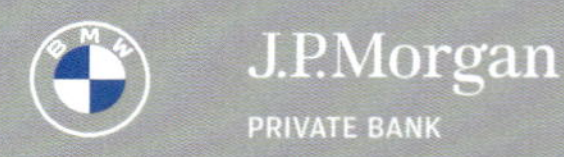

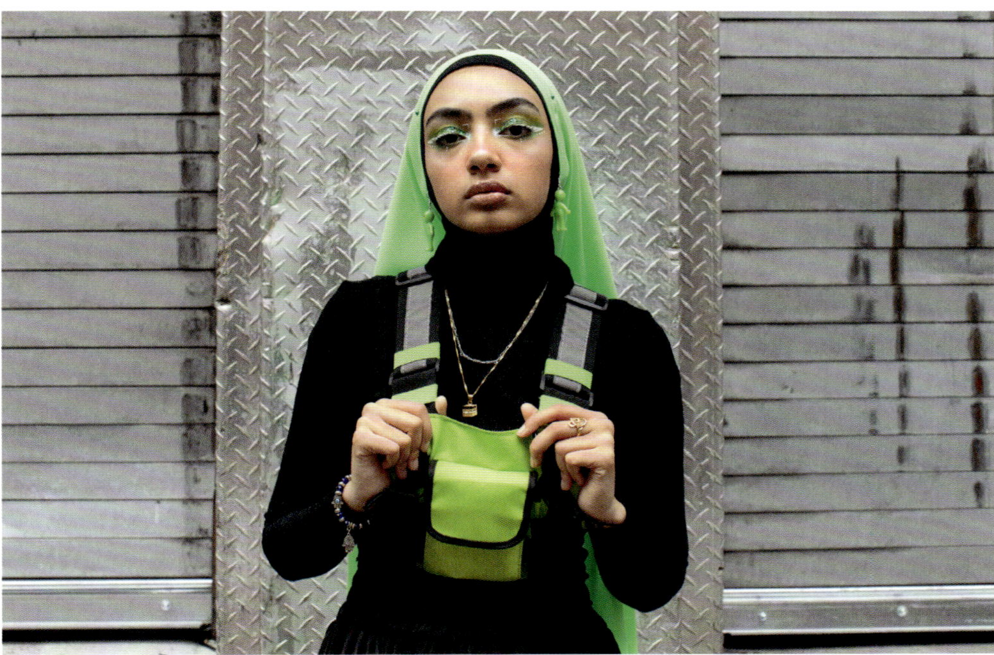

Mahtab Hussain finds warmth and belonging in Muslim communities across the United States.

Suleman Sheikh Anaya

Linda Ahmed, New York,
2022

The first night he arrived at his new apartment in Baltimore, earlier this year, Mahtab Hussain—in town for a residency at the Maryland Institute College of Art—noticed the sound of the *azan*, the traditional Muslim call to prayer. "I stood on the desk and opened the window to hear where it was coming from. That was the only time I heard it from my apartment," he told me recently. "It felt like a sign."

Hussain, a portrait photographer who has been documenting how Islam is lived in his native Britain for the last fifteen years, didn't expect to be confronted with a Muslim presence in his temporary hometown so soon. "It cemented the idea that I had to make work in Baltimore," he says. Immediately, Hussain started to map out the local mosques. Five were a bike ride away, among them Masjid Ul Haqq, first established in 1946 under Elijah Muhammad, at the time the leader of the Nation of Islam. (Its congregation has since shifted to a Sunni practice of Islam.) Hussain visited Ul Haqq the next day.

A prayer call had incidentally set in motion the latest installment of Hussain's ongoing project to bring visibility to a community that is habitually underrepresented in the arts and misrepresented in the public imagination. "I want to visually articulate what the American Muslim experience is," he says, "and make people look at Muslims in a different way." His series *Muslims in America* (2021–ongoing) has already generated segments in Los Angeles, Toronto, and New York, distinct portfolios reflective of the diversity of what it can mean to be an American Muslim today. Muslims in the United States aren't monolithic, the series proclaims; they resonate, instead, with idiosyncrasies from one town to another, like the living communities they are. If the images' subjects in New York are strikingly queer and Toronto's are predominantly Middle Eastern, Hussain "quickly realized Baltimore was going to be a Black experience."

Even though African Americans account for more than a fifth of the US Muslim population (a number that is growing), the validity of their faith and the role it plays in strengthening the social fabric of vulnerable neighborhoods across major cities is rarely acknowledged. For Hussain, Baltimore's Black Muslim minority—routinely ignored by the city's other Muslim communities, not to mention by society and culture in general—stood out as an ideal subject.

Hussain found the vitality of his Baltimore sitters' religious practice and their networks compellingly at odds with the grim reality of where they lived: marginalized neighborhoods with names such as Cherry Hill and Upton/Druid Heights. "The poverty and the violence is right there for you to see," Hussain observed, adding that while in the United Kingdom the aggressive stance of the male youths he portrayed tended to be performative, "in Baltimore, you actually feel your life is on the line." At the same time, Hussain was struck by the warmth, sense of belonging, and empowerment he encountered in Maryland: "Islam really connects with these young men and women, giving them a grounding and peace they badly need." The religion-derived hope Hussain found among individuals who regularly lose friends to drug abuse and gang violence affected him personally.

While Baltimore's Muslim fellowship embraced the forty-two-year-old photographer from Birmingham, England, he, in turn, fell in love with its fluid, accepting, inquisitive version of a religion he thought he was familiar with. "The conversations taking place in these communities are about home, love for those around us, meaning, and, above all, about finding brotherhood and sisterhood," he explains. Hussain, the son of Pakistani immigrants, grew up in a practicing Muslim household but always questioned if he was devout enough. He says that the *Muslims in America* project has made him reassess his faith: "I had no idea that making new friends through my work in mosques in American cities would bring me closer to my faith. These beautiful people are teaching me to see Islam in another way. It always felt to me like either you were in or you were out. But the Muslims I am meeting approach their faith as a journey, less focused on right or wrong."

The fact that most of the men and women in Hussain's portraits appear strikingly attractive isn't by accident; the photographer uses formal compositions strategically and seductively. "I want people to walk out of a museum or gallery space having seen these faces thinking, Wow, they are gorgeous! That's enough for me, because it means they are questioning their preconceived ideas of what a Muslim looks like," he

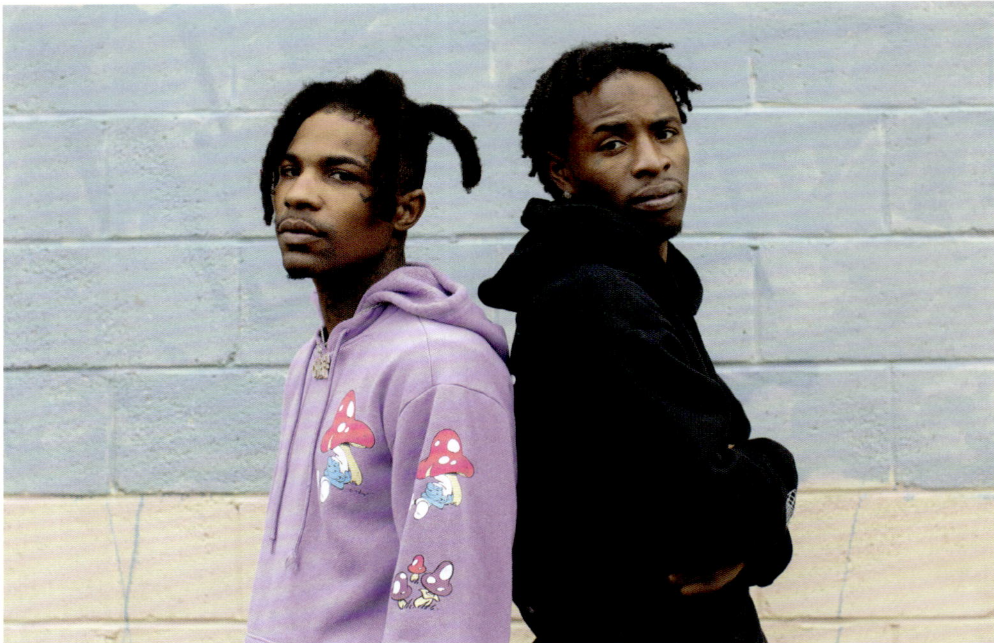

Top:
Creekboyz, Baltimore, 2023; bottom: *Tahira Queen*, Baltimore, 2023
All photographs courtesy the artist

It's no wonder that a sense of pride emanates naturally from the people in Hussain's photographs.

tells me. To this end, Hussain cannily deploys aesthetic devices used in classical portraiture. Whether male or female, young or old, his subjects pose with a preternaturally noble dignity and self-possession that belie the turmoil of their daily lives.

It's no wonder that a sense of pride emanates naturally from the people in Hussain's photographs, who are, for once, being seen rather than vilified. Hussain emphasizes the importance of this approach. "These are men and women who appreciate being celebrated rather than patronized or labeled as threatening. My intention is to let them own their identity and experience. If I show them as the vibrant individuals they are, and people walk away in awe, I've done my job, because a space for a different conversation is now open."

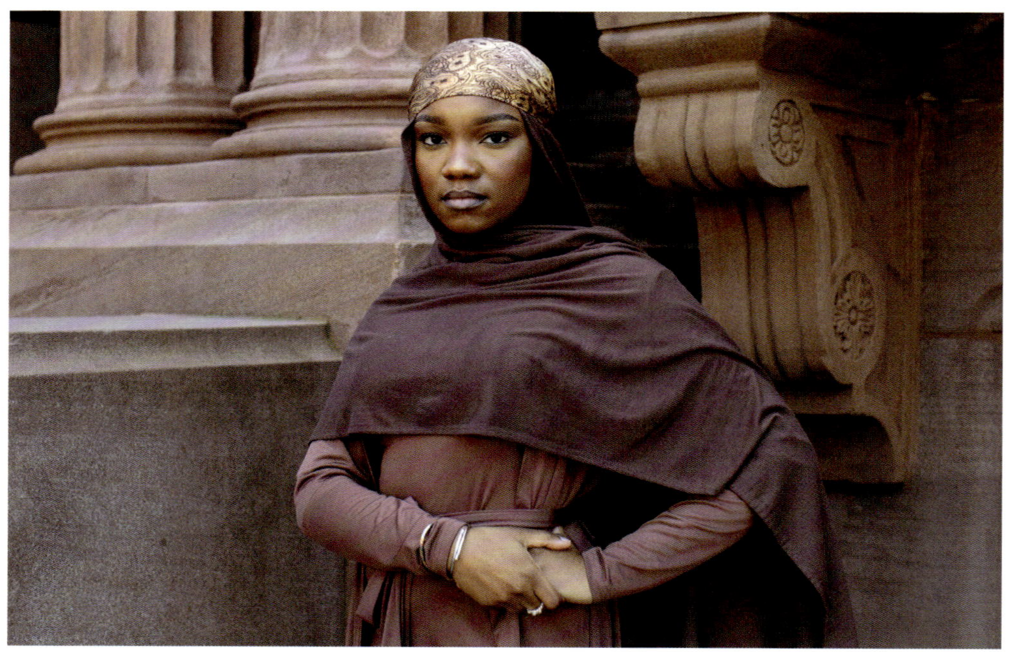

Suleman Sheikh Anaya is a regular contributor to *T: The New York Times Style Magazine* and *PIN–UP*. He lives in New York and Mexico City.

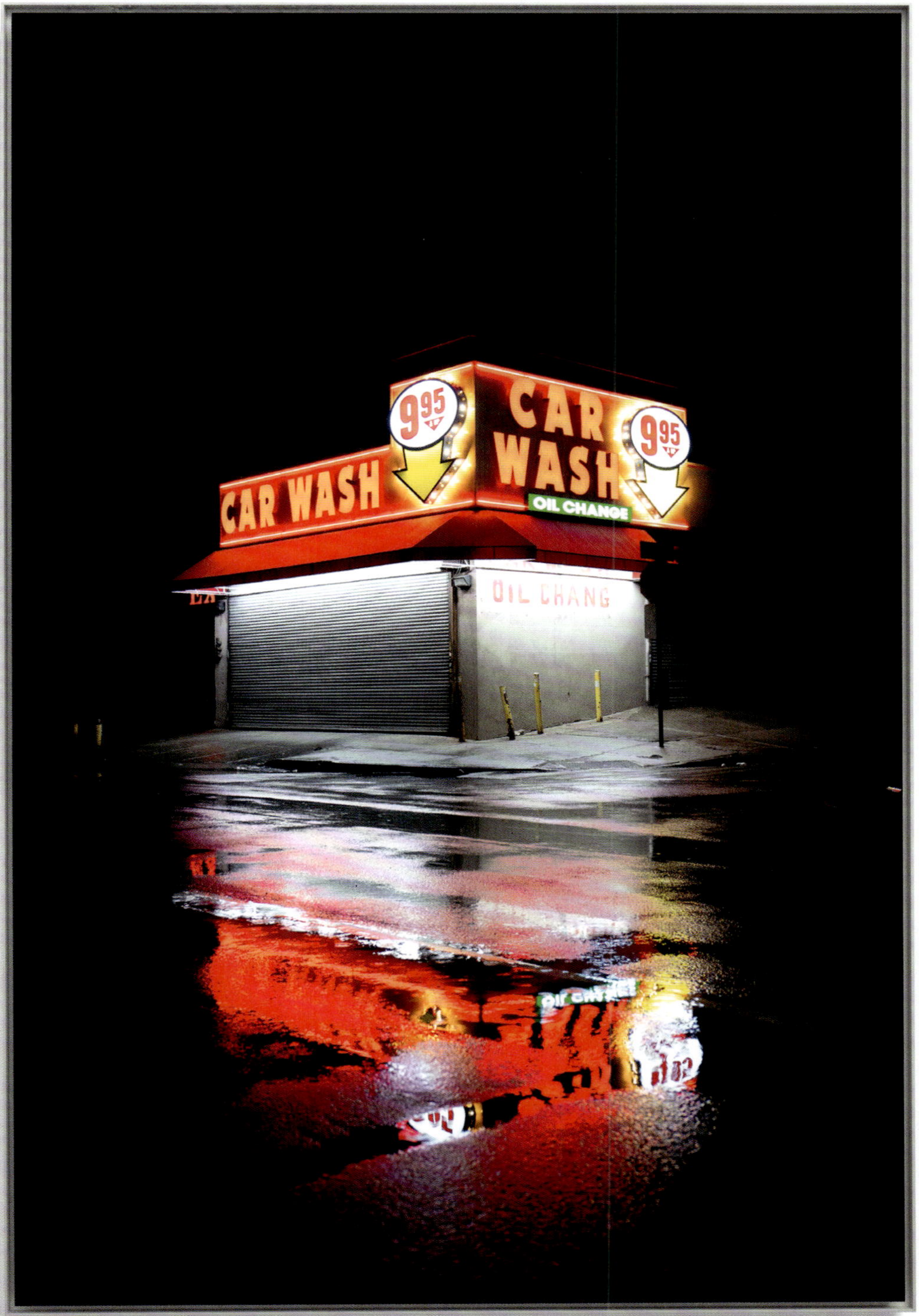

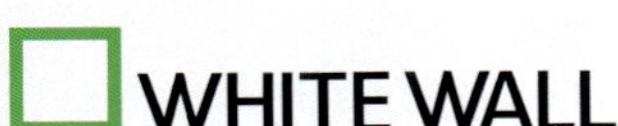

Phil Penman
WhiteWall Ambassador

Photo Print on Fuji Crystal DPII sealed under Acrylic
Aluminium ArtBox, silver | 20 x 30 " | printed and framed by WhiteWall.com

The WhiteWall Ambassadors are among the most respected, talented and influential Professional photographers in the world. Professional photographers worldwide, who rely on the gallery quality of WhiteWall for their WhiteWall gallery quality. Discover individual photo products Made in Germany, such as the original photo print under acrylic glass in a Aluminium ArtBox from our in-house manufacture.

WHITE WALL

Curriculum
Awol Erizku

While some artists are content to create discrete works, Awol Erizku builds an endlessly expanding universe of seductive symbols and visual cues. Born in Gondar, Ethiopia, raised in the Bronx, and now residing in Los Angeles, Erizku fluidly mixes and moves across media. In his indelible portraits, an expectant Beyoncé appears regally perched atop a red Porsche, and the poet Amanda Gorman is a beaming galactic vision. Clever nods to African and African American culture permeate his work—recently published in the Aperture book *Mystic Parallax* (2023)—alongside knowing references to surrealism, spirituality, or whatever salient cultural touchpoint has lately captured his attention.

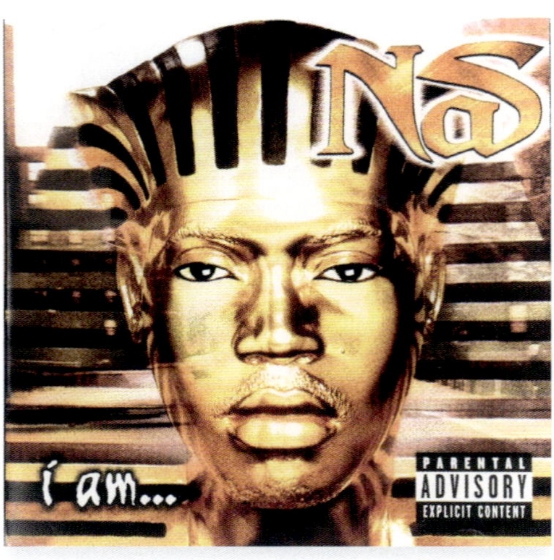

Nas, *I Am...*
With its iconic cover, rich lyrical content, and groundbreaking visuals for the track "Hate Me Now," this 1999 album has given me a metaphorical yardstick to measure how effectively my own art can communicate to the world.

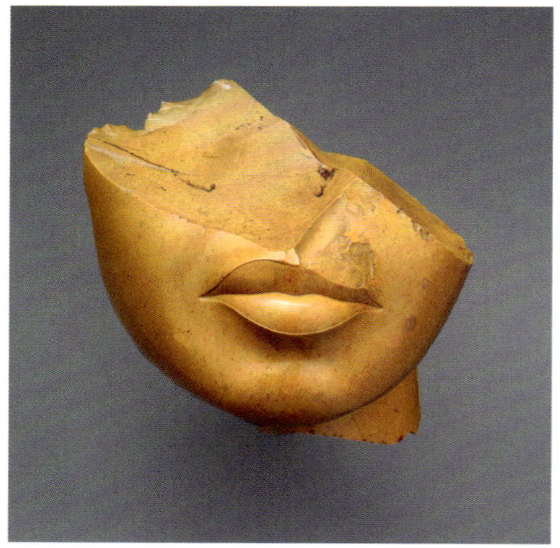

Fragment of a Queen's Face
I probably started going to the Metropolitan Museum of Art as a kid on school field trips. I've never forgotten this sculpture fragment in the Egyptian Wing. Over the years, during my visits to the museum, I would spend most of my time mesmerized by her elegance, beauty, and simplicity. I've probably sketched and made more photographs of this figure than I can count. It's almost always my first or last stop at the Met.

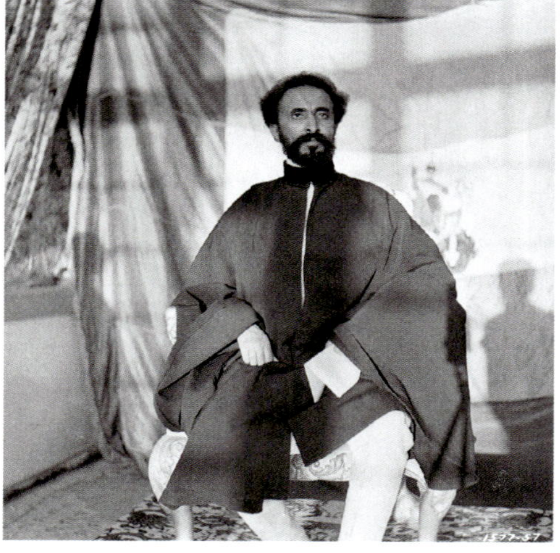

Haile Selassie
A charismatic and enigmatic figure, Haile Selassie, Ethiopia's longtime ruler, died in 1975 but remains influential today. With his famous speech addressing the United Nations in 1963, his sense of fashion (a kind of regal chic), and his recent resurgence in popular culture, he still creeps in and out of my consciousness. Men today often refer to themselves as H.I.M. (His Imperial Majesty), but most are unaware of the term's association with Selassie.

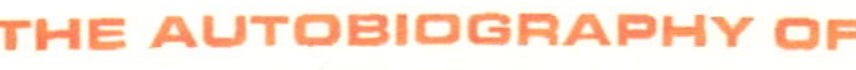

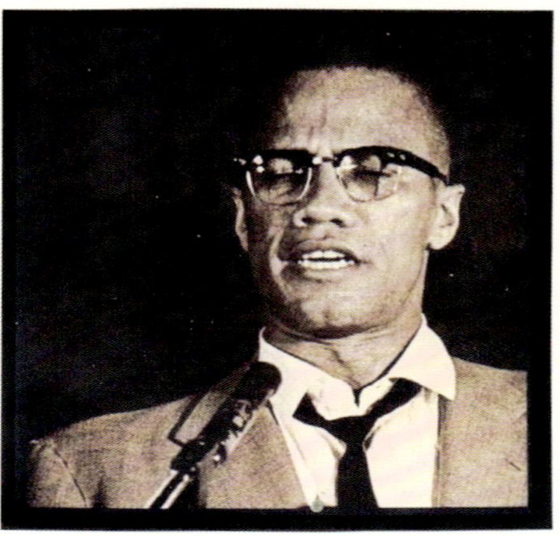

The Autobiography of Malcolm X
My discovery of this 1965 autobiography in my formative years had an impact on me like no other. I was particularly drawn to Malcolm X's evolution—the shift in perspective in how he imagined the world after making the hajj. There's a line in the book where he states: "You will never catch me with a free fifteen minutes in which I'm not studying something." This hit me like a ton of bricks when I was younger and shaped me into a voracious reader.

This spread, clockwise from top left: Album cover of Nas, *I Am...*, 1999; Stan Douglas, Still from *Luanda-Kinshasa*, 2013; David Hammons, *Dak'Art 2004 Sheep Raffle*, photograph by Iolanda Pensa; Moustapha Akkad, Still from *The Message*, 1976; cover of *The Autobiography of Malcolm X*, 1965; Otto Bettmann, *Ethiopian Emperor Haile Selassie Posing in Royal Dress*, 1953; photograph of *Fragment of a Queen's Face*, ca. 1390–1336 BC

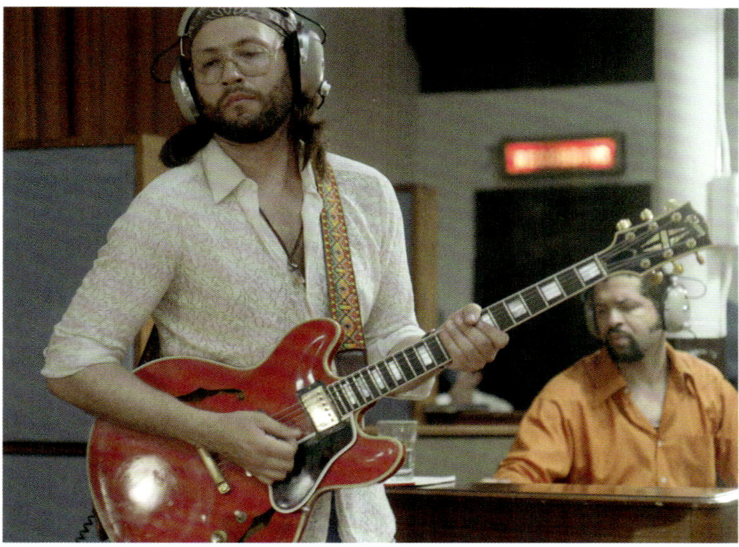

Stan Douglas

Stan Douglas's practice is filled with complexities and idiosyncrasies. When I stumbled on his early work from the 1980s, it made me realize how an artist can incorporate his identity without being heavy-handed, but still be potent. His use of music is only one of the ways Douglas reframes history.

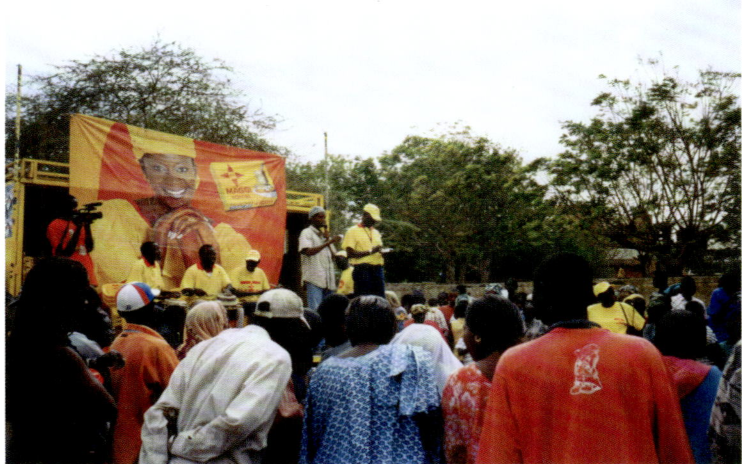

David Hammons at Dak'Art 2004

David Hammons's *Sheep Raffle* at the 2004 art biennale in Dakar, Senegal, resonates because it connected a deep understanding of a rich African Islamic tradition (the slaughtering of animals on the occasion of the Eid celebration) with certain Western tenets (capitalism in particular). Encountering the performance, I observed that Hammons had also made a sculptural, conceptual, and cultural bridge between African and African American values and traditions.

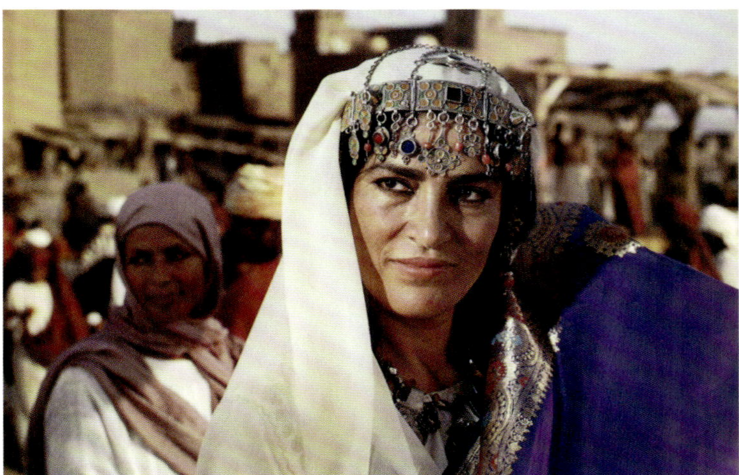

The Message

I spent my early years with my grandmother, and one of my fondest memories as a child is of her playing this 1976 film by Moustapha Akkad during the month of Ramadan. There's a scene in which the Prophet Muhammad (PBUH) returns to Mecca to destroy the idols that people had worshipped. That scene has always come back to me. If nothing else, I learned from a very young age that idol worship isn't permissible. This belief would later inform my relationship with African masks.

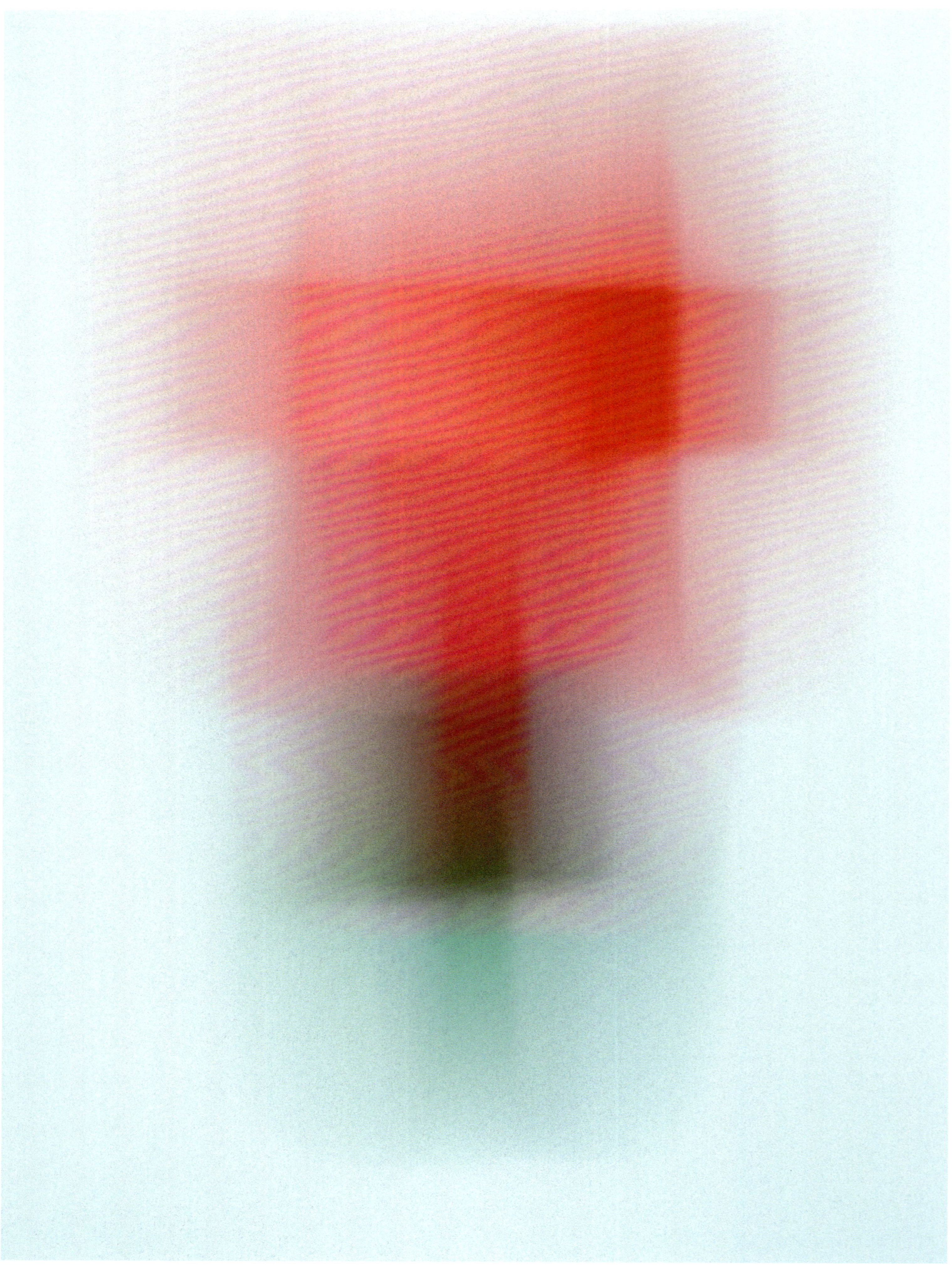

Desire

"Photographs can abet desire in the most direct, utilitarian way," Susan Sontag observed. Hers was a reference to more prurient activities, but she also allowed that desire could be abstract, something more slippery. The compulsion to want—or, in today's parlance, to *manifest*—emerges throughout these pages directly and indirectly, as both an impulse and a state of mind. The manufacture of desire might be fashion's and advertising's most consistent product and its very lifeblood. Ubiquitous and irreverent, Juergen Teller's photographs upend our vocabulary of glamour and aspiration, trading conventional beauty for the more peculiar. Whether it is a luxe handbag, a beaming, wide-eyed baby, or a lithe model making her way to a casting, his binding agent is a hard flash and an arresting directness. He is at the center of a system of material want—but doesn't always make it look very desirable.

Photographers are natural voyeurs. Across this issue, they ask us to look with them to consider what it means to put one's own body on display, to break from long-standing customs, to be seduced by raw beauty found in nature or in uncanny artifice. Histories are conjured through evocative personal objects in the work of Ishiuchi Miyako, who for decades has created beguiling images that in two dimensions are at once surreal and surprisingly physical. Ordinary things are never what they seem: A twisted onion isn't simply an onion but a talisman? Something fetishistic? Elsewhere, the sea appears like a sweetened version of itself, and photography is seen as approaching magic: a medium that renders reality as unearthly, fulfilling a desire to cross a threshold, to take the viewer somewhere else altogether. **—The Editors**

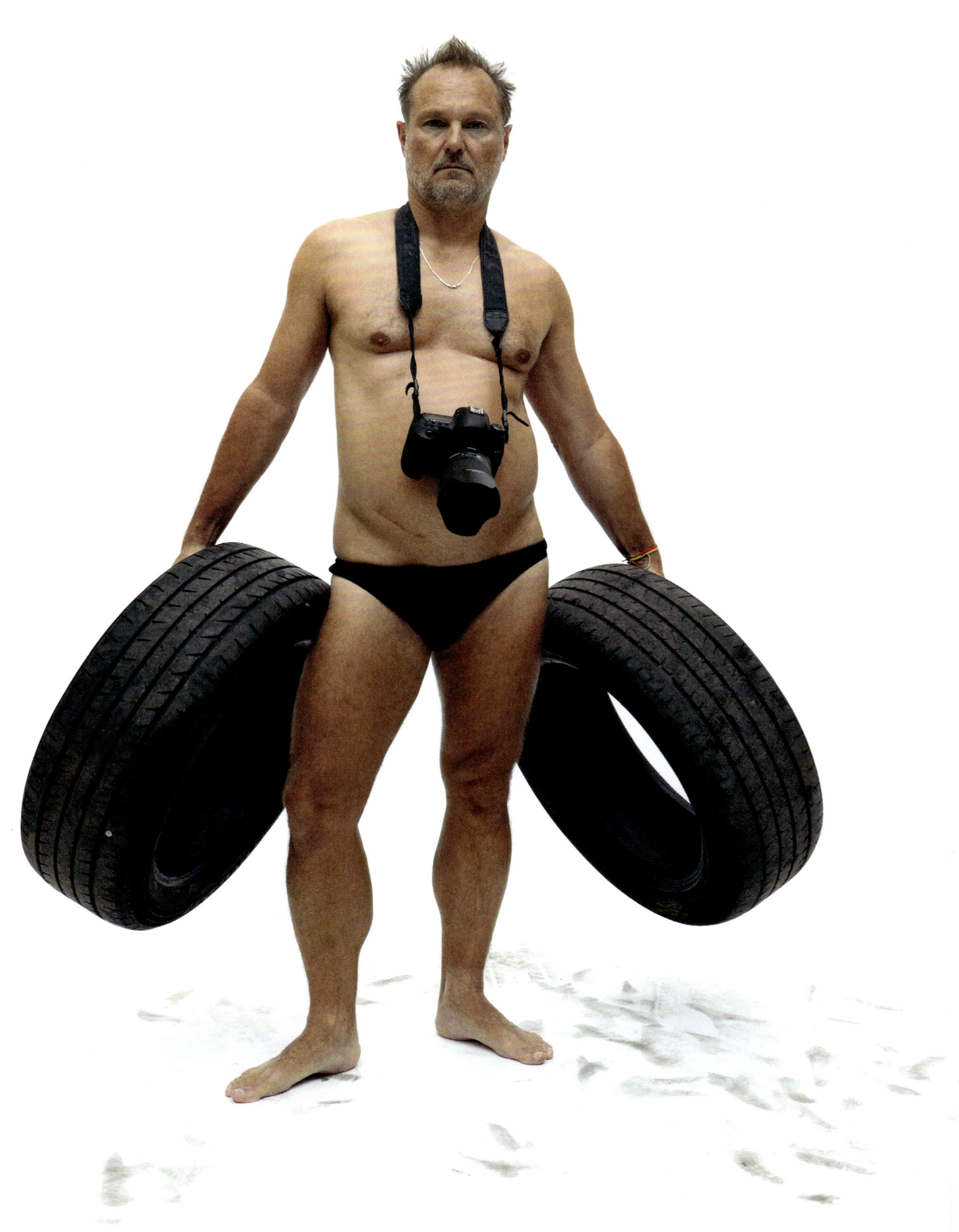

Juergen Teller
The Force of Life

A Conversation with Alistair O'Neill

Over the last thirty years, Juergen Teller has been at the vanguard of fashion photography. His work resists the idea of fashion as the projection of a polished ideal, favoring objective clarity to shine a light through the smoke and mirrors of promotion and commerce. He has shaped the advertising campaigns of visionary designers such as Helmut Lang, Phoebe Philo (for Celine), JW Anderson (including his work for Loewe), and Vivienne Westwood, as well as his memorable editorials for fashion magazines. Running parallel is Teller's ongoing commitment to producing photobooks, in a range of sizes and on a range of subjects, which often irreverently refer back to Teller himself, his personal life, and his own body.

This season, Teller's work is the subject of a major exhibition at the Grand Palais Éphémère, Paris, the cavernous temporary space in the shadow of the Eiffel Tower that replaces the historic Grand Palais, currently under renovation. The exhibition, curated by Thomas Weski, will then travel to the Milan Triennale. By placing Teller's fashion images into dialogue with his personal projects and published works, the show expresses the full vitality of Teller's life and artistic world. Some of his best photographs call into question the exact boundaries between the commercial and the private, examining the crossroads of what takes place on set and what happens off to the side. Alistair O'Neill recently met the photographer at his London studio—an award-winning space designed by the British architects 6a—where they spoke among the many maquettes and display tests for the show.

Alistair O'Neill: **Your exhibition at the Grand Palais Éphémère is large, and the scale of the space is a challenge in itself. There's also a catalog and four additional publications, right?**

Juergen Teller: Four other artist books, yeah.

AON: **Fantastic.**

JT: I've made work specifically for the exhibition, and I would say it's my universe of what I want to show. The title is *i need to live*. We came to the title because of the way that I planned the exhibition in my head. It starts with a photograph taken by my father of me as a baby. And this is followed by my father's suicide, represented by a newspaper article with a photograph of the car crash. And then there's my mother, and then there's me. It's not really chronological, but there is a thread from the beginning, and it guides you through it.

But very early on, there will be some pictures of Dovile [Drizyte, Teller's partner in life and business], which brings in the now within the center of the show. It's very

Page 28:
Self-portrait with tires, London, 2021

This page:
Self-portrait, London, 2023, for *Aperture*; opposite: JW Anderson calendar, Spring/Summer 2022 campaign, London, 2021

I've made work specifically for the exhibition, and I would say it's my universe of what I want to show.

personal and ends with a series we did called *The Myth* (2022). For me, this project is very, very special and very beautiful and very romantic. It's something meaningful, something you can't photograph.

AON: **You said there's a thread that runs through the exhibition. Is it this idea of a life force in the air?**

JT: Yes. There's this religious celebration we did in Sicily just now for our first child together. It's basically this new ball of life. And it means I need to live, I need to be there, I want to be there. And it is the opposite of what my father did. That's the idea about the whole thing. And then, surrounding this central core, there are different projects that I did and different photographs of people who mean a lot to me, who I have collaborated with. There will be commercial work in it as well as videos. I mean, the Grand Palais exhibition is huge. It's huge.

We developed it with 6a architects who did my building here. I really like Tom [Emerson] and Steph [Stephanie Macdonald] a lot. We're friends, and we talk about

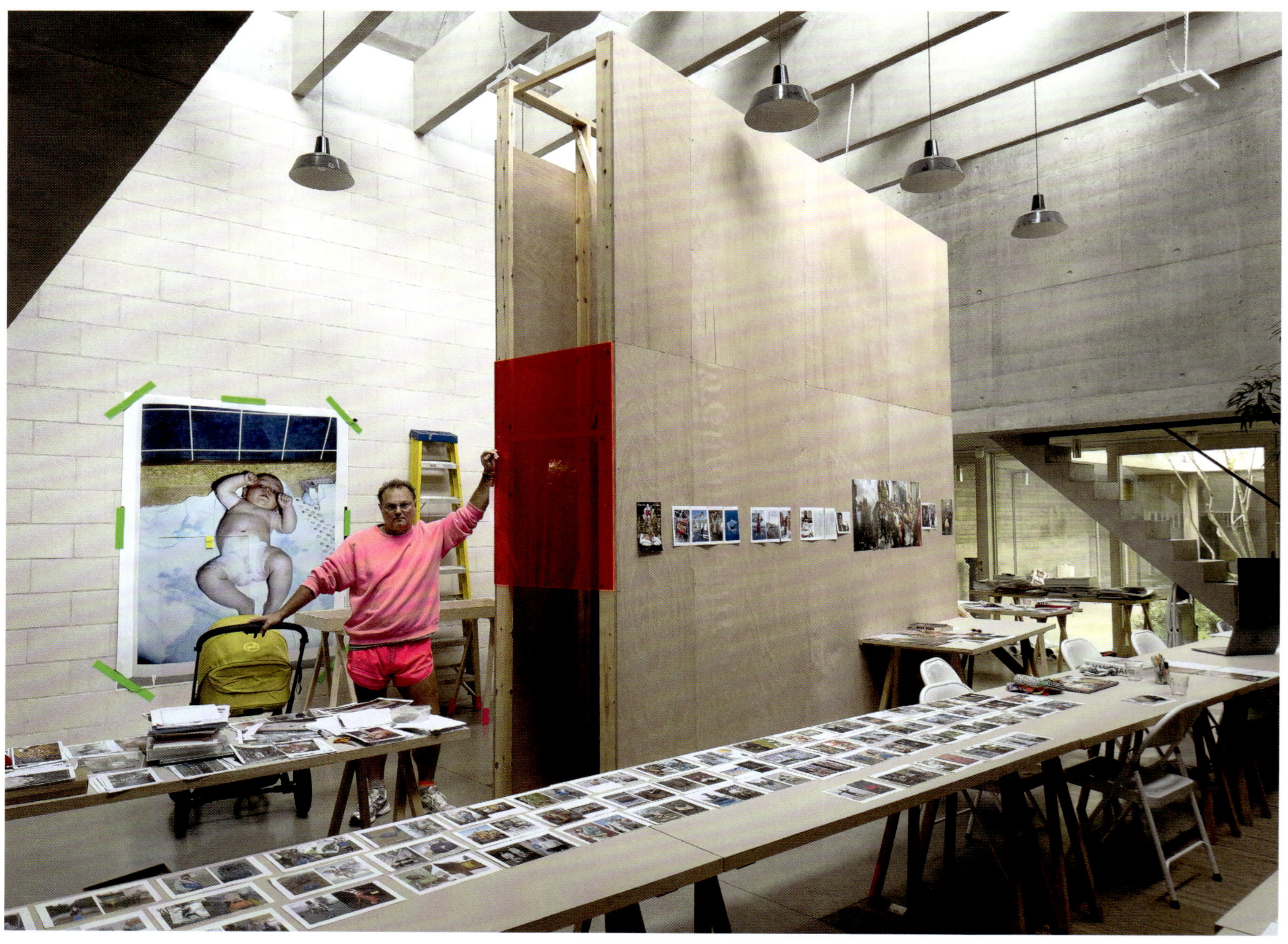

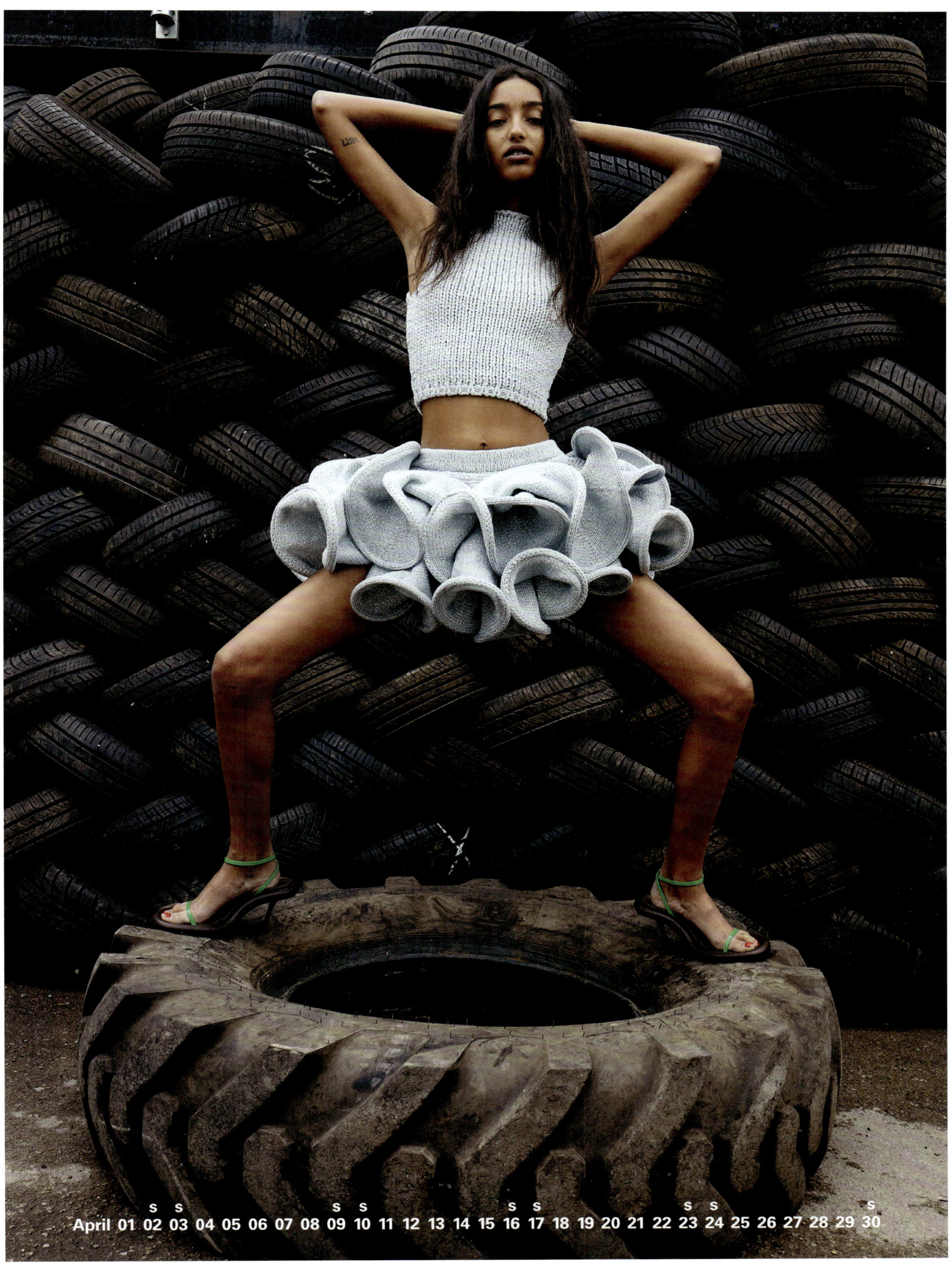

s   s   s s   s s   s s   s
April 01 02 03 04 05 06 07 08 09 10 11 12 13 14 15 16 17 18 19 20 21 22 23 24 25 26 27 28 29 30

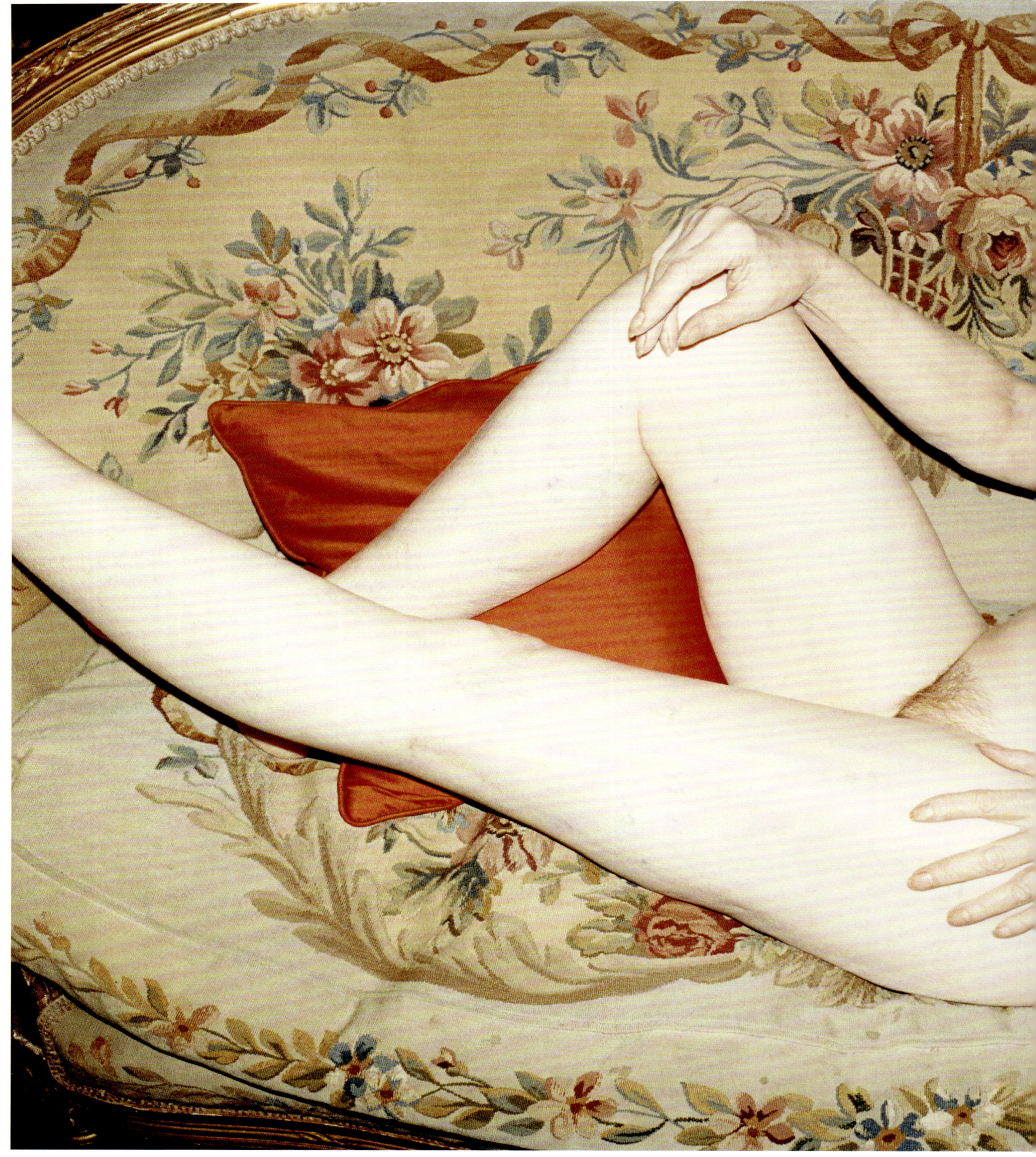

Vivienne Westwood No. 1,
London, 2009

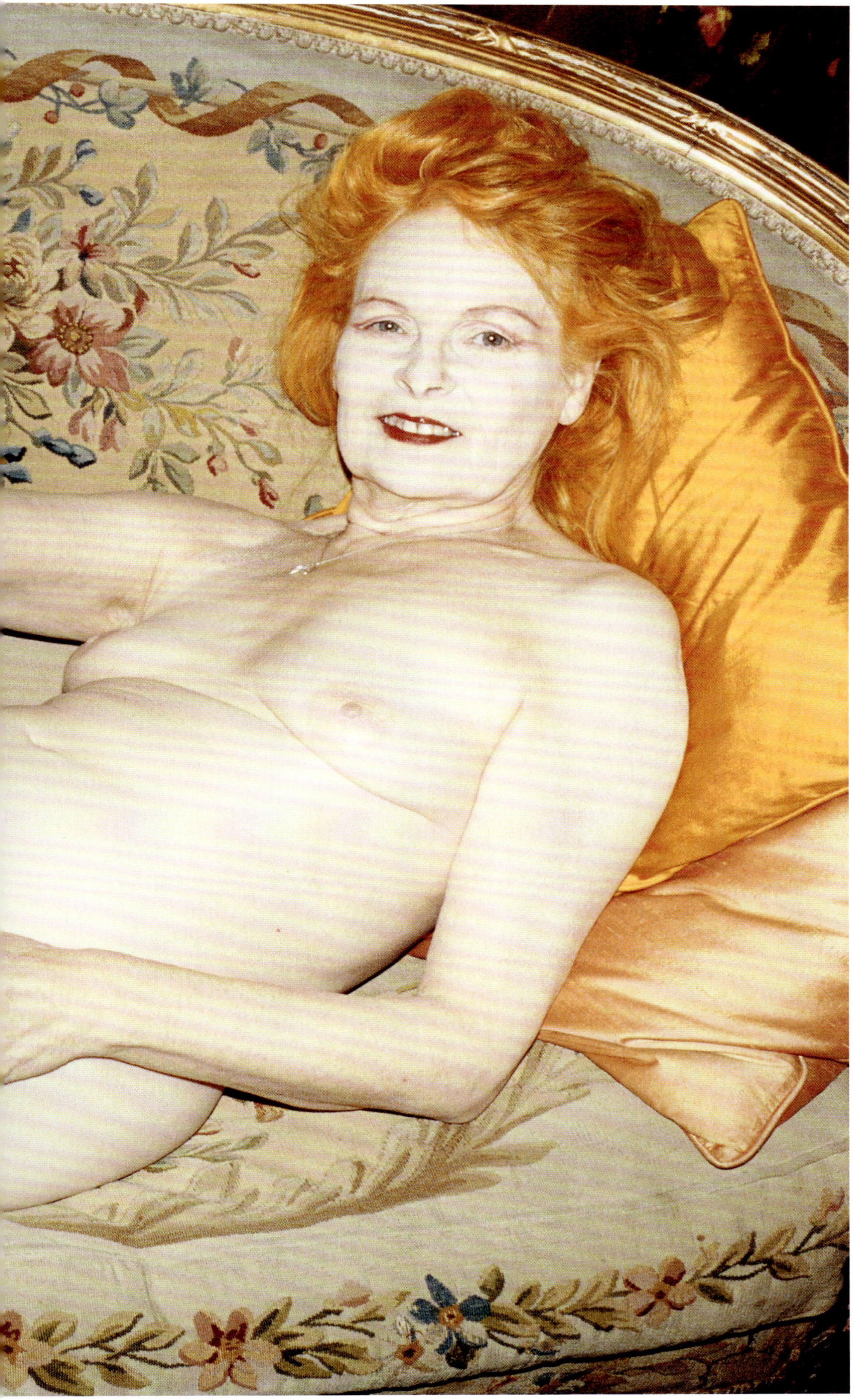

things, and it was very clear to me that I wanted to ask them to help me with it because the space is like an empty shell without rooms. We came up with something that I'm really proud of.

AON: **They're really good exhibition designers. *The Disobedient Bodies* show they did with JW Anderson in 2017 at the Hepworth was fantastic. They designed these fabulous curtain walls, and they used dead-stock fabric from JW Anderson, and they made rooms within rooms because of the very large spaces. It was really clever. Your studio is a great example of their style. I'm happy to hear that you're working with them again.**

JT: Yeah, and that's the wall [*Teller points toward a large, plywood, self-supporting wall section*]. It's four meters, eighty high and four hundred meters long altogether and will feature a lot of new work. It will be very personal. I will also have fifty vitrines and there will be different facets of my work that I'll curate in them. New configurations.

AON: **Is this about lending weight to printed matter because that's something you consider important to how your work is communicated?**

JT: Yes, very, very much so. Sometimes it's just an example of the Marc Jacobs advertising and how it looks. And sometimes, within the vitrine, I will put objects in it.

AON: **So, there will be tear sheets, double-page spreads, and magazines as well as the many photobooks, exhibition catalogs, and monographs you published over the years, but also personal possessions and mementos. They're object-orientated narratives in a way?**

JT: Yes, that's right.

AON: **Is it your intention to let each vitrine display visually breathe so as not to look congested?**

JT: Yes, though some of the vitrines are fuller.

AON: **It seems that, at times, the space and borders around your images, as in your Marc Jacobs advertising campaign, are quite important. The white space that surrounds what is a relatively small printed image in relation to the size of the page magnifies its visual impact and intensifies the color. And you can also**

JT: Yes, and I am also doing a new version of the handbag book [*Juergen Teller: Handbags*]. Since I published that book, in 2019, when I had the museum exhibition in Naples, I've photographed lots more handbags. There will be a new book [*Juergen Teller: More handbags*], but both old and new images will be displayed together on a huge wall.

AON: Great, because I really like what you say in that book about moving on from amassing pictures of models, as in your 1999 book, *Go-Sees*, to amassing photographs of handbags.

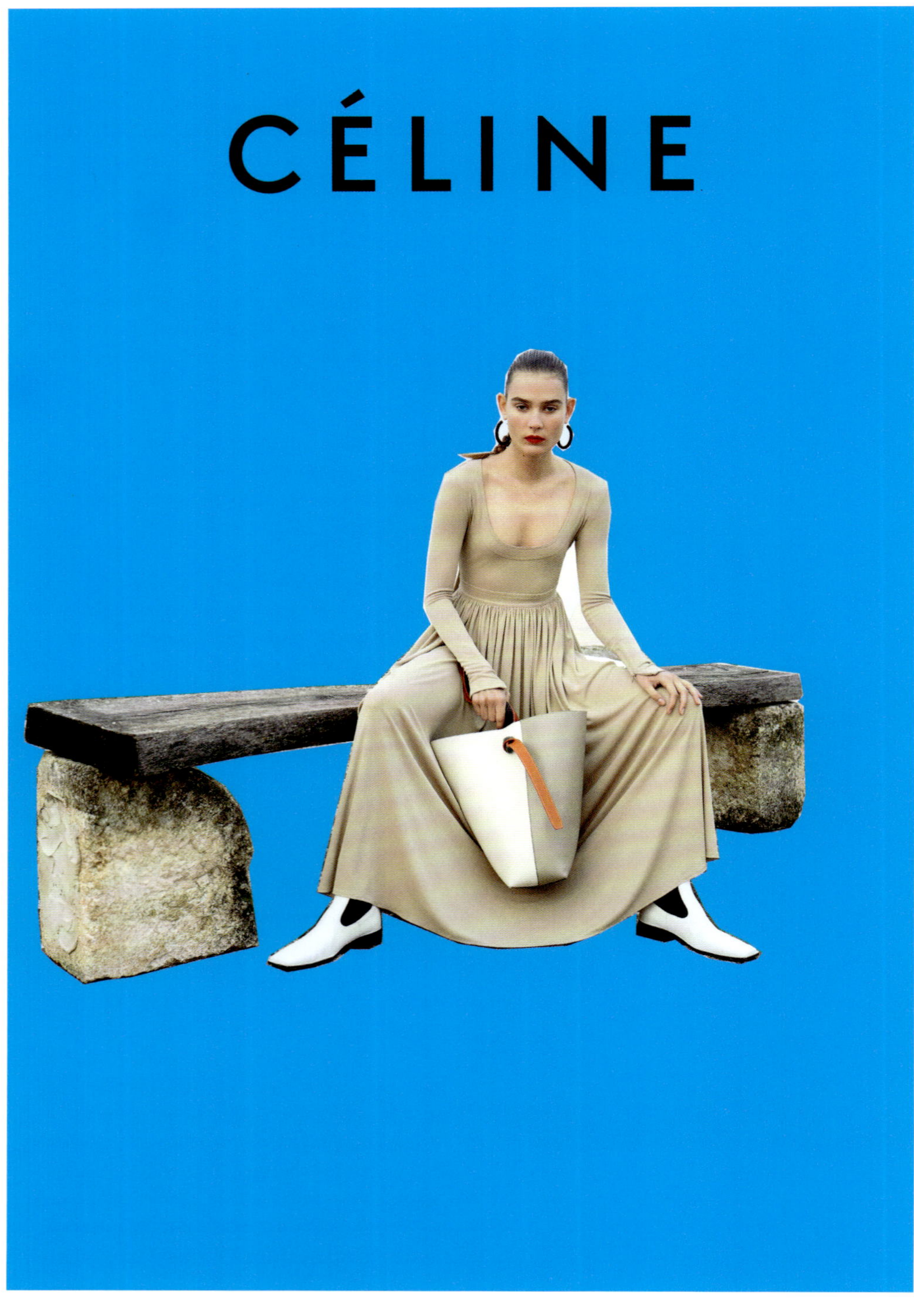

Céline, Spring/Summer 2016 campaign, Tuscany, 2015

JT: When I started in fashion photography, I worked with stylists and fashion designers who all thought that the last thing they wanted in the picture was a handbag. It was all about the clothes, the person, and the mood, to portray a certain coolness or whatever. And nowadays, in every fashion ad, there's a handbag. Everywhere is a handbag. And this is basically what sells and drives the industry alone.

AON: That's really to do with the luxury conglomerates and where they see their profit margin. But it has upended the industry. If you look at Maria Grazia Chiuri and Pierpaolo Piccioli, two of the biggest designers in contemporary fashion, they were accessories designers to start with, and that's really important to the work they now produce. So, apart from the wall of handbags, will the exhibition also deal with your fashion work in full?

JT: Yes, yes, yes, yes.

AON: Good, I'm glad.

JT: And quite proudly so.

AON: Yes, I think it should be unashamed. I really do. Because your work has always expressed itself on a broader canvas. Your fashion photographs never appear as contained exercises in style, as you are often keen to inject a sense of absurdity into them, to expose the unreality of the conditions in which they are made. And while your personal projects reflect the wider sense of your life as it is lived, you remain open about how your commercial work drives it all. You continue to be incredibly prolific as a fashion photographer. Does this work still inspire you?

JT: Simply speaking, yes. Of course, at certain times you get frustrated, and you get bored of it. But it is just, frankly, exciting to work with somebody like JW Anderson, or Anthony Vaccarello, or whoever the good designer is at that moment.

AON: It seems that the creative conversation is an important driving force for your photography. You choose to work with certain designers you respect or want to speak with.

JT: I think I only choose people when I have an instinct or feeling that they understand me. Also, I want to have a relationship that is ongoing, not just a one-off. The excitement of working this one time together, and then, this brings you another idea, and it goes further. That's what I find interesting.

AON: **You've also been quite loyal to the magazines that you've published in. There was a period where you were only publishing in *The Face* and *i-D*, and in more recent years, you've published consistently in *System*. Is this a similar kind of relationship?**

JT: Yes. But in the beginning, when I'm approached, I'm thinking, Not really . . . do I really . . . really? And then, they explain an idea to me, and I'll think, maybe they're right . . . maybe that's an adventure. It's good to be doubtful and think that it could be jumping into the cold water and things could go wrong. Sometimes things don't show their advantage immediately.

AON: **One thing that characterizes the work you've done in *System* is the extended editorial. This is a format that you've done before in *Arena Homme +* or *Pop*, but in *System*, it has a different feel.**

JT: In *System*, it's restricted to the system of fashion. In the other magazines, it's entirely my own universe. And, I think, that's the difference. I like these certain restrictions of having to deal with something commercial, which normally I wouldn't necessarily work with. But there's something interesting about that, and I'm happy to explore.

AON: **Your photographs of Miuccia Prada in her office are a perfect example. It's such a great meeting of your world and her world, in terms of what you picked up on when you were photographing. I really love the detail of that Miu Miu shoe that she's wearing and the close-ups of her feet. That image got me asking, well, what does desire in a Teller photograph look like? And I thought, that is a good example. Another one is your portrait of Roy Anthony Brown in Hydra.**

JT: It's quite interesting because when you start at the beginning of each photograph I take, it's already there, the desire to take that photograph.

AON: **Your desire or their desire?**

JT: My desire.

AON: **Well, what is interesting about those two images is that the desire is so closed off, it's almost their desire only. It's not yours, or that of the person looking at it.**

JT: Right.

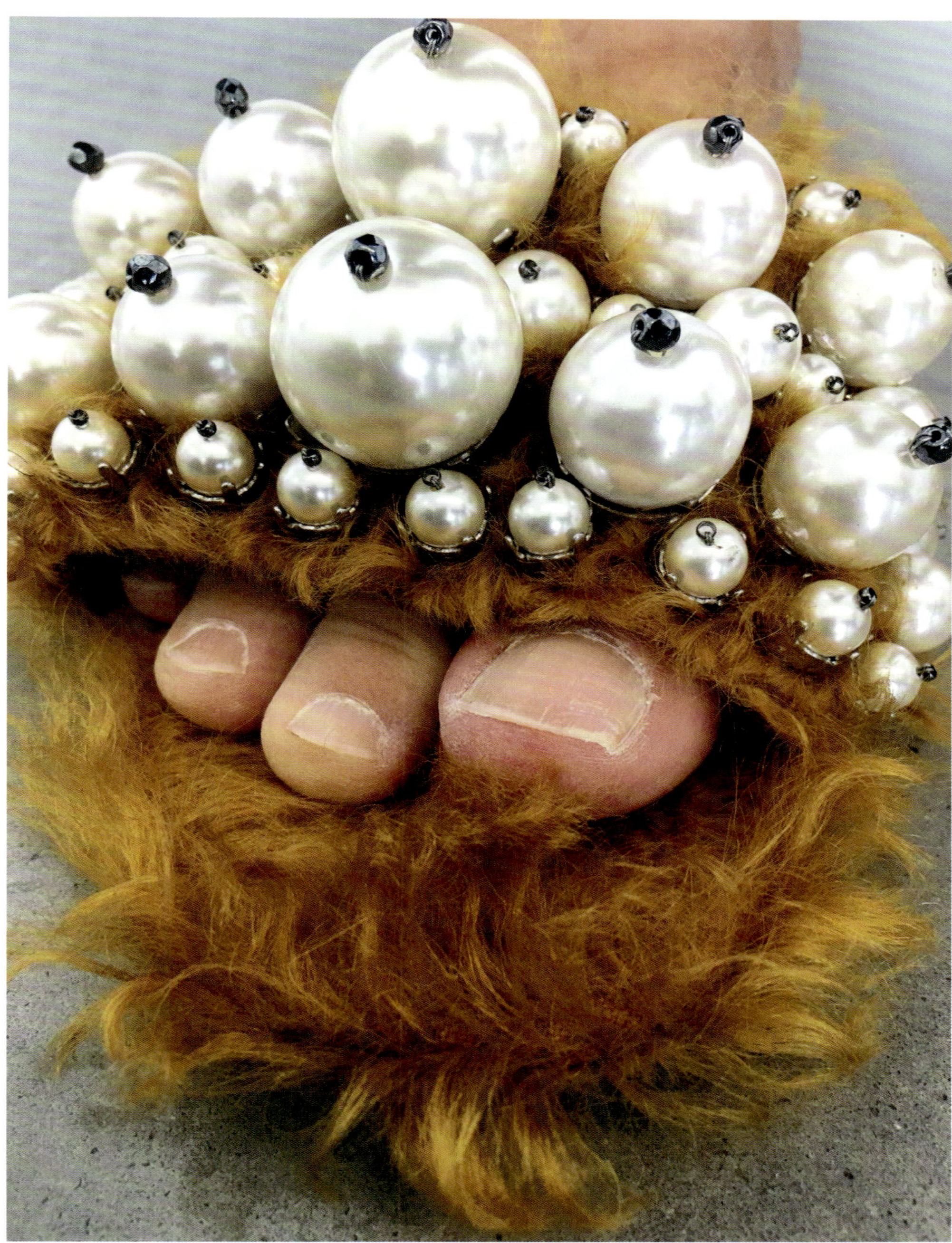

Miuccia Prada, Prada Foundation HQ No. 18, Milan, 2016

I only choose people when I have an instinct or feeling that they understand me.

AON: **But you recognize it in that moment?**

JT: Yes.

AON: **That's a rare skill. Not everyone picks up on those kinds of things.**

JT: You're right about that.

AON: **I also notice that in a lot of your work you conjure desire in an image by turning the scale, or the volume, up. To call this graphic, in terms of quality of line or kinds of shapes, is a bit reductive. Even though this approach might look brash, it's actually quite sophisticated in terms of what it's trying to call attention to, or how it amplifies how people look at things.**

JT: It's very direct, I guess.

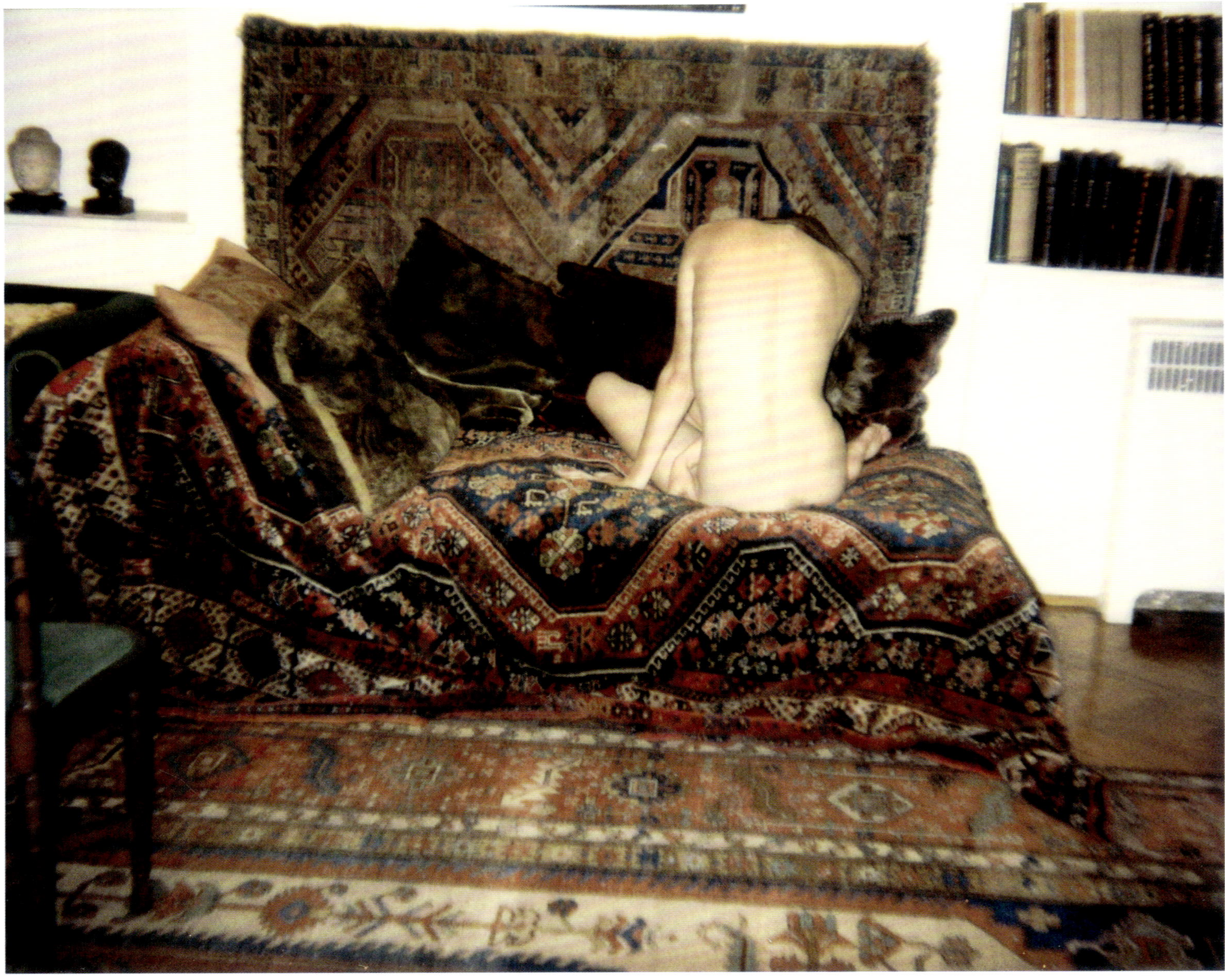

AON: **Visual directness is something you've spoken about before in terms of your German identity and other German image makers you admire, such as the filmmaker Rainer Werner Fassbinder or the photographer August Sander. But when you bring directness in relation to desire, it becomes quite unexpected. It makes me think of those monumental prints of Vivienne Westwood in your 2013 exhibition *Woo!* at the Institute of Contemporary Arts, London. Are they going to be at the Grand Palais?**

JT: The same size.

AON: **Fantastic.**

JT: Yeah.

AON: **Such impact.**

JT: Vivienne came to see the show, and then, either somebody from her family, or Andreas [Kronthaler], her husband, or somebody else, I can't quite recall, said something like, "Do you mind that they're so big?" And she said, "They could be bigger." The way she said it, it was just genius.

AON: **Because they're bigger than life-size, aren't they?**

JT: Yes, yes. They're very, very big.

AON: **You continue to live in London. What is it about the city that resonates with you?**

JT: I feel like people leave you alone to be how you want to be. There are so many good people here and good opportunities to do things. And it's very international. And you are in the heart of Europe. But I have to say, since Brexit, it's been a bit different. The whole political climate, and how expensive things are here, that's just been horrific, really.

AON: **I think it's becoming much harder for London to make a claim to being a creative city because creatives can't afford to be here anymore.**

JT: Yeah.

AON: **But you will continue to stay here?**

JT: I find Monaco visually really exciting, but I would probably get bored there.

Alistair O'Neill is professor of fashion history and theory at Central Saint Martins, London.

This page:
Roy, Hydra, 2010

Opposite:
Sigmund Freud's Couch
No. 10, London, 2006
All photographs © the artist

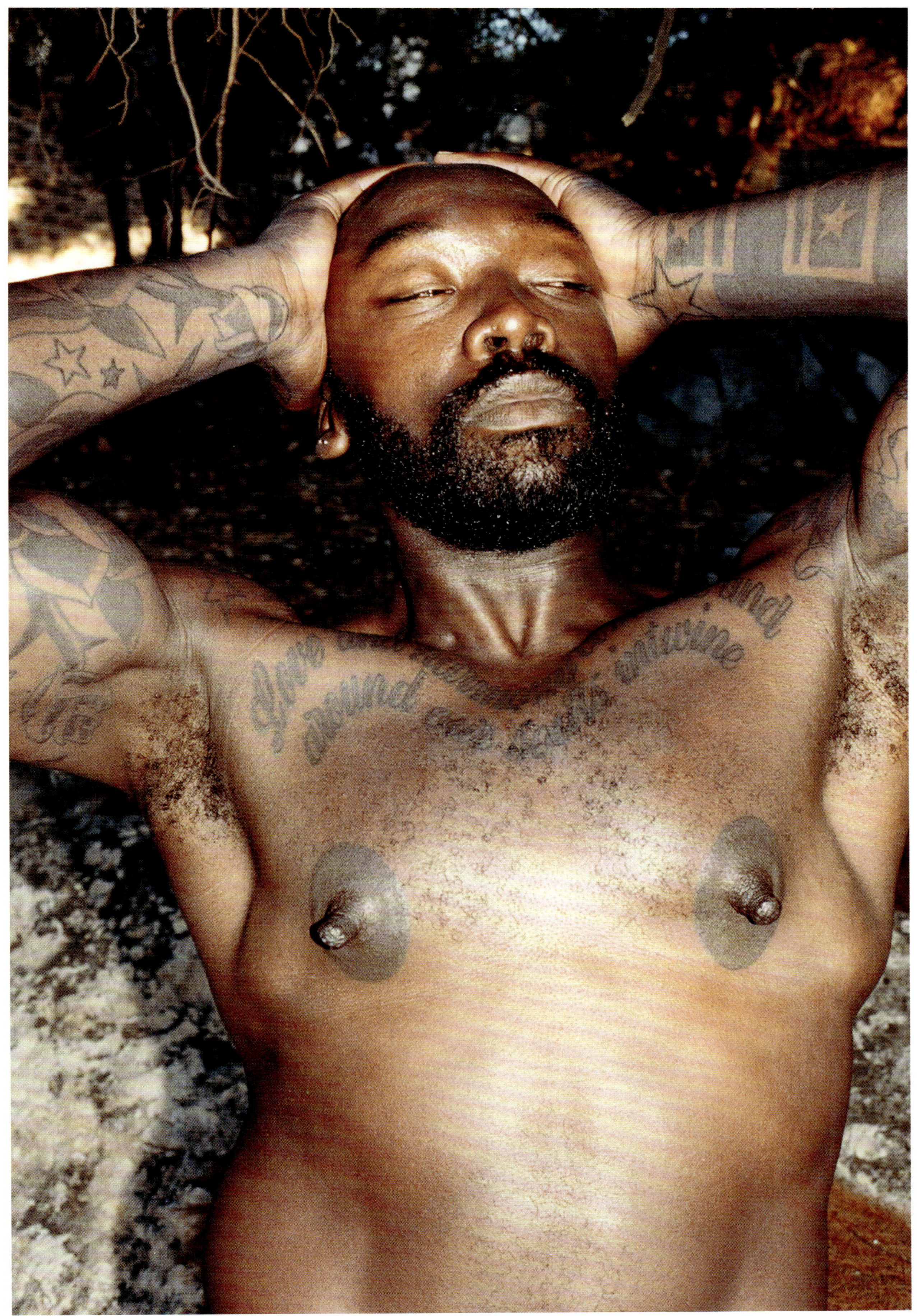

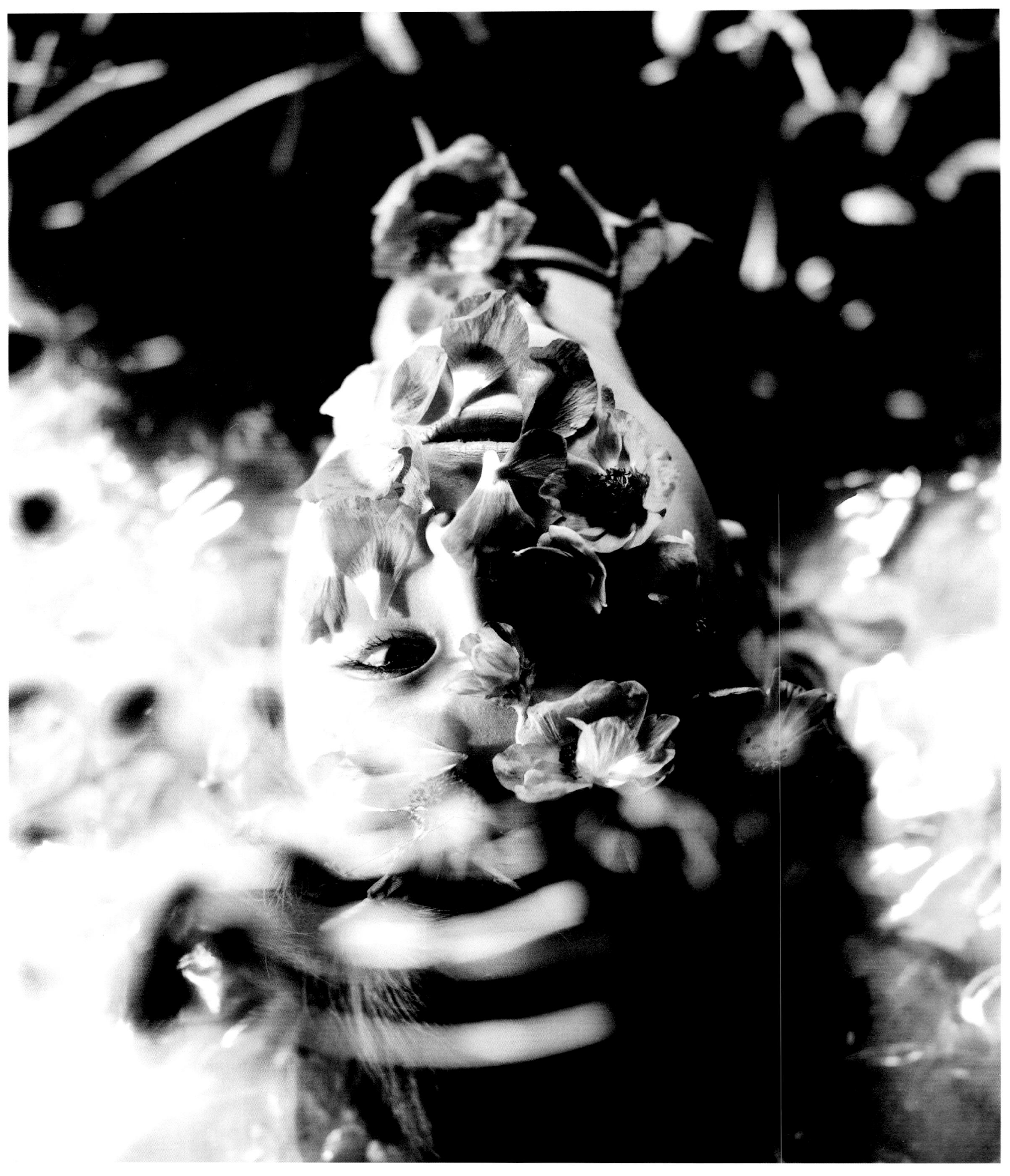

Hisae Imai *Daydreams*

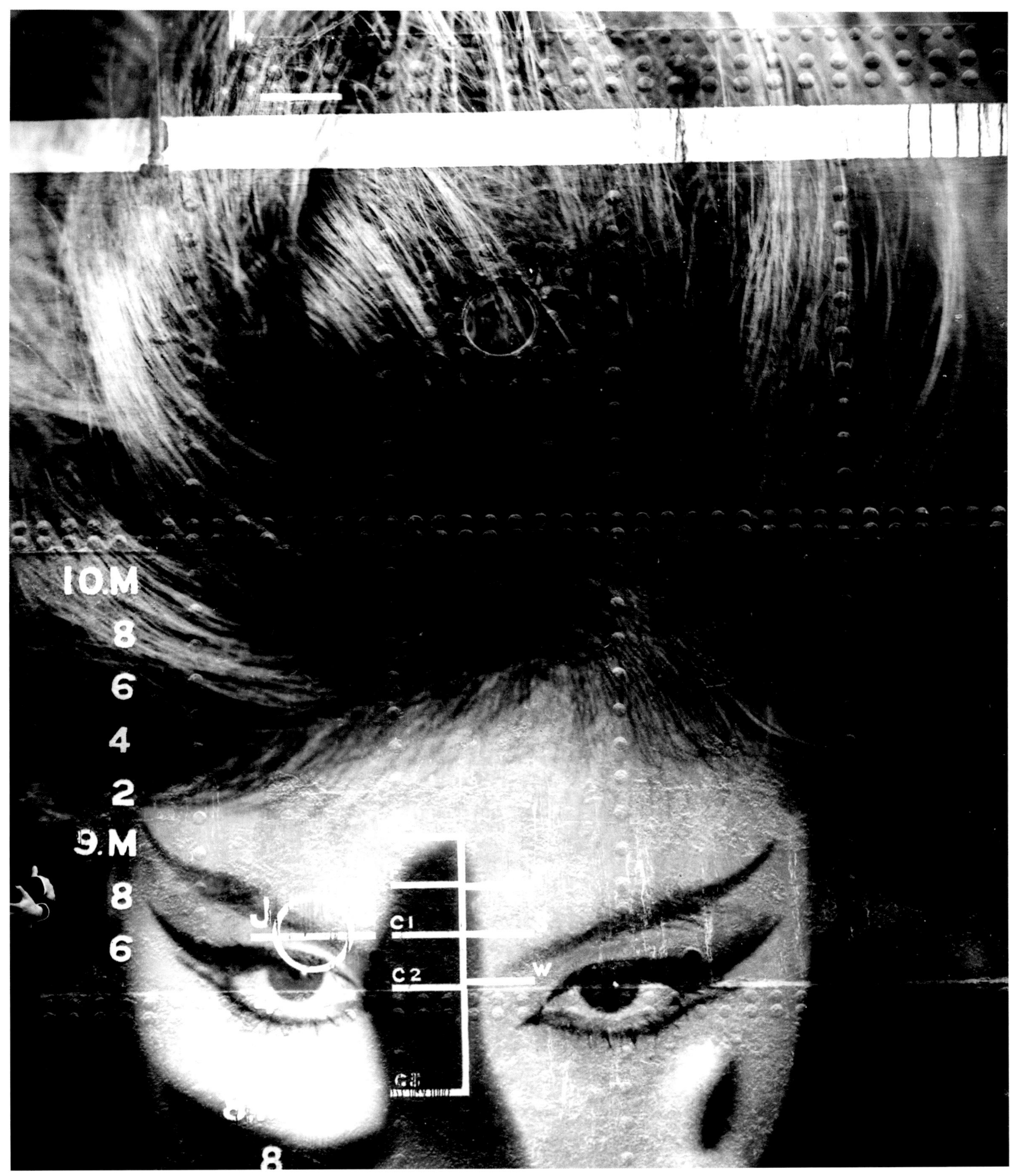

An ascendant figure in Tokyo's art and fashion scenes of the 1960s,
Imai took an unpredictable turn after a terrible car accident.
Moeko Fujii

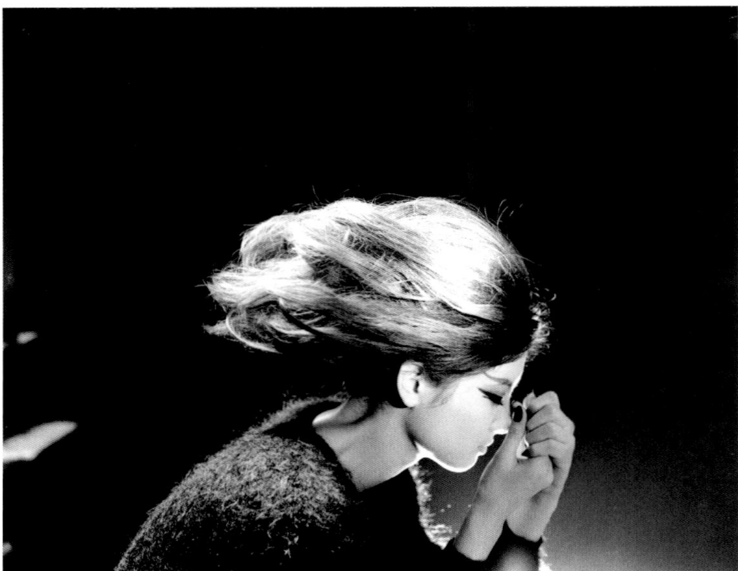

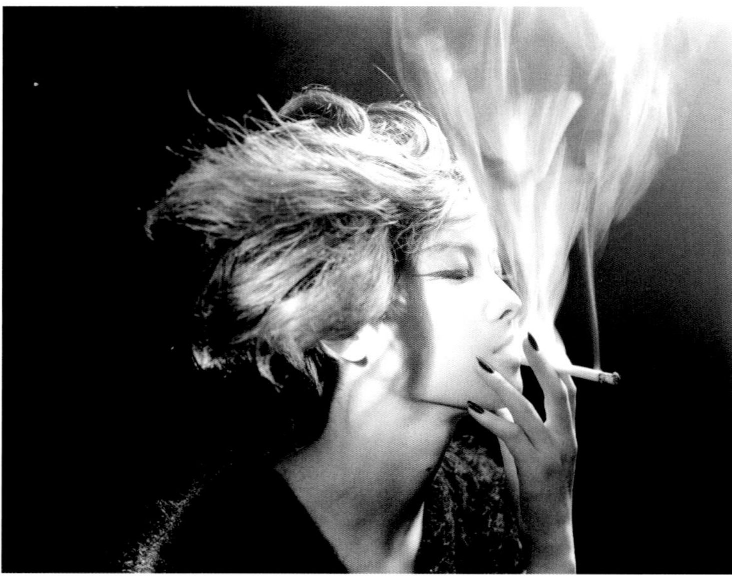

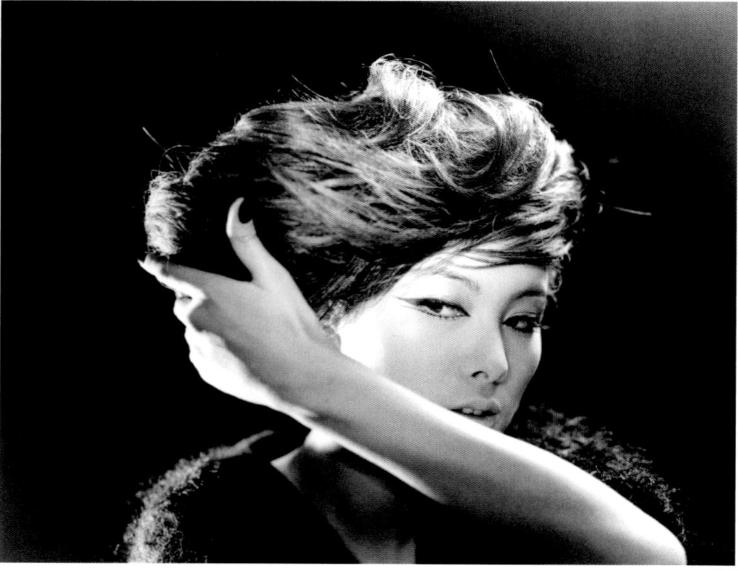

Page 38:
Ophelia, 1960

Previous page and this page, top to bottom:
Model and North Wind,
1961

Never has Ophelia looked so playful. In Hisae Imai's 1960 *Ophelia*, the character blooms not as Hamlet's betrothed but as a Japanese girl, tinted blue, patiently stuffing leaves into her mouth. Her hair, curling in the wind, looks alive. Her nails are bejeweled. "Poor Ophelia," the King laments in Shakespeare's *Hamlet* when Ophelia, having gone mad, drowns in a brook, "divided from herself and her fair judgment." In Imai's visual renderings, this division is not within Ophelia but in how we might interpret her face and expression. Is that two dabs of glitter on her cheek, or a tear? Are we interrupting the most unthinkable time in a life—the necessary solitude of the seconds before death?

In Imai's recasting, we do not see Ophelia's long hair submerged into a brook—a moment of incapacity made exquisite in Sir John Everett Millais's 1851–52 painting of the same scene. Instead, shorn and ear-length, the hair and the petals seem to be simultaneously part of her. Her expression is opaque—partly because the image is in negative—and a form of beauty confounds the viewer's gaze. "After Ophelia went mad, she didn't believe anything, and wasn't afraid of death. I thought that must've been a lovely place," Imai once wrote. It is this lovely calm that Imai's many pictures of women transmit, amid the blurring of human boundaries. They appear still and absorbed elsewhere, feeling the breeze rather than confronting a gale, seemingly listening to a song we cannot hear.

Imai's life and work embodied a kind of imaginative ambiguity. Her story reveals the most intimate seams between artifice and longing, ecstasy and tragedy. Throughout the late 1950s and the 1960s, she produced a staggering array of experimental imagery, for both personal projects and fashion commissions, establishing herself as the young darling of Japan's avant-garde photography scene. Born in 1931, in Tokyo, she studied painting at Bunka Gakuin College, becoming entranced by Surrealist art during her studies with designer Souri Yanagi and through conversations with the prominent Surrealist Shuzo Takiguchi. Other giants of the movement, including Man Ray and Jean Cocteau, would also influence her. Imai began casually working with photography while still in art school, after being given a Rolleiflex camera by her father, who ran a photography studio. By her mid-twenties, she was his apprentice and had converted her small room into her personal studio. In 1956, she opened *Daydreams*, a solo exhibition at Matsushima Gallery, located in Tokyo's Ginza area, where she presented evocative images of vases, photographed through burlap and buffeted by wind, edges fraying, suggesting otherworldly forms. The show drew the acclaim and interest of prominent critics and artists who had also shown there, including the photographer Eikoh Hosoe, then a pivotal figure. (Hosoe would marry Imai's sister.)

Imai surrounded herself with young, cutting-edge artists. She developed a friendship with Shuji Terayama, the famous theater and film director known for leading the *angura* (underground) movement, and she was in close proximity to the short-lived but groundbreaking VIVO cooperative, which included Hosoe, Ikko Narahara, and Shomei Tomatsu, among others. The group emphasized the role of subjectivity over the medium's ability to objectively portray reality. Imai would also take part in a 1962 group exhibition organized by the art critic Tatsuo Fukushima called *NON*, which stood for "non-tradition, non-section," at the Matsuya Ginza department store, featuring VIVO members and highlighting new approaches to photographic expression.

We can feel the sensibility of her peers, and the bold, experimental ethos of the era, in Imai's use of double exposure, mirrored bodies, and collage. But her photographs stand out for their unique approach to the depiction of the female body, often fragmenting and abstracting form. Her series *Memories of Summer* (1958) includes

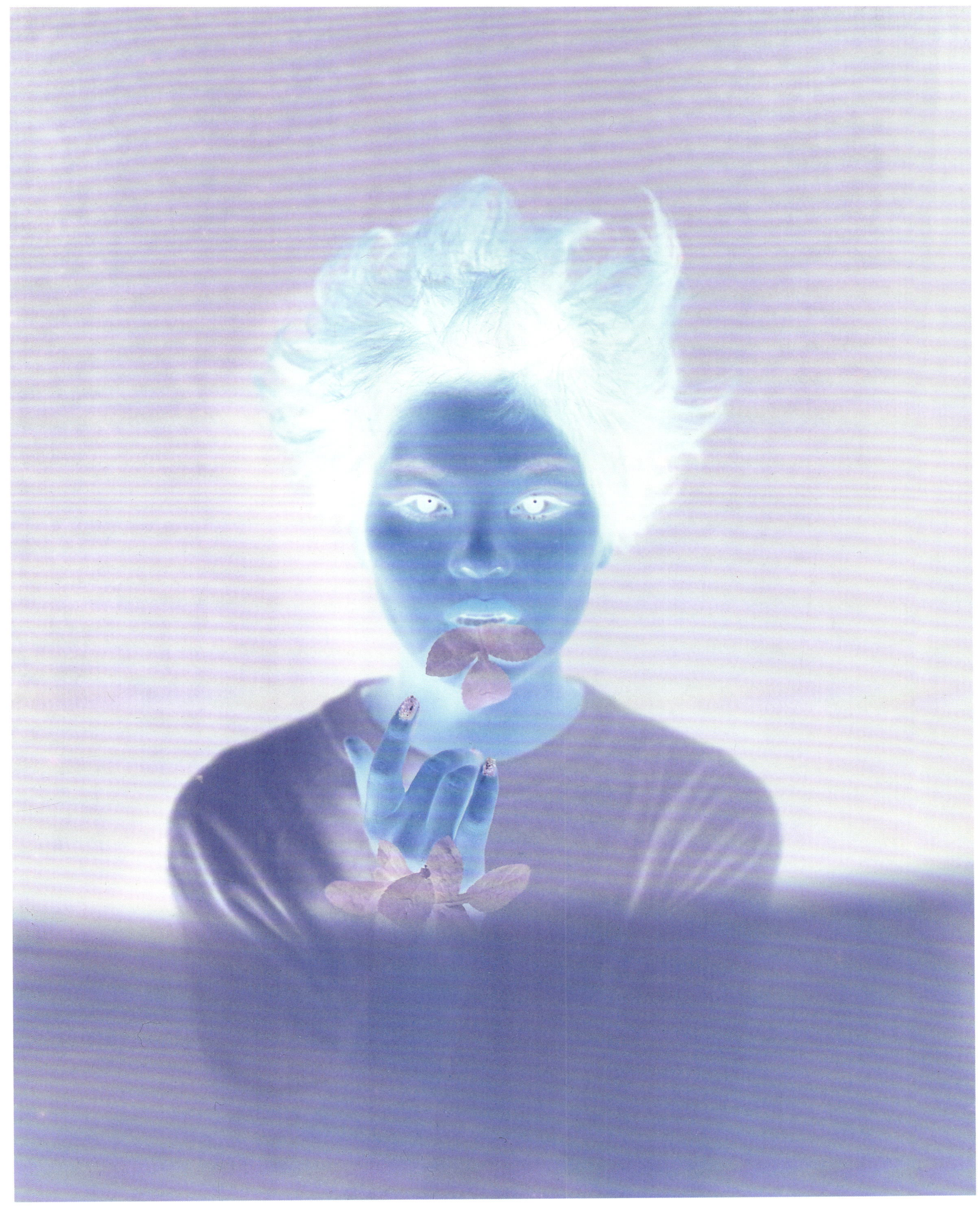

Ophelia, 1960

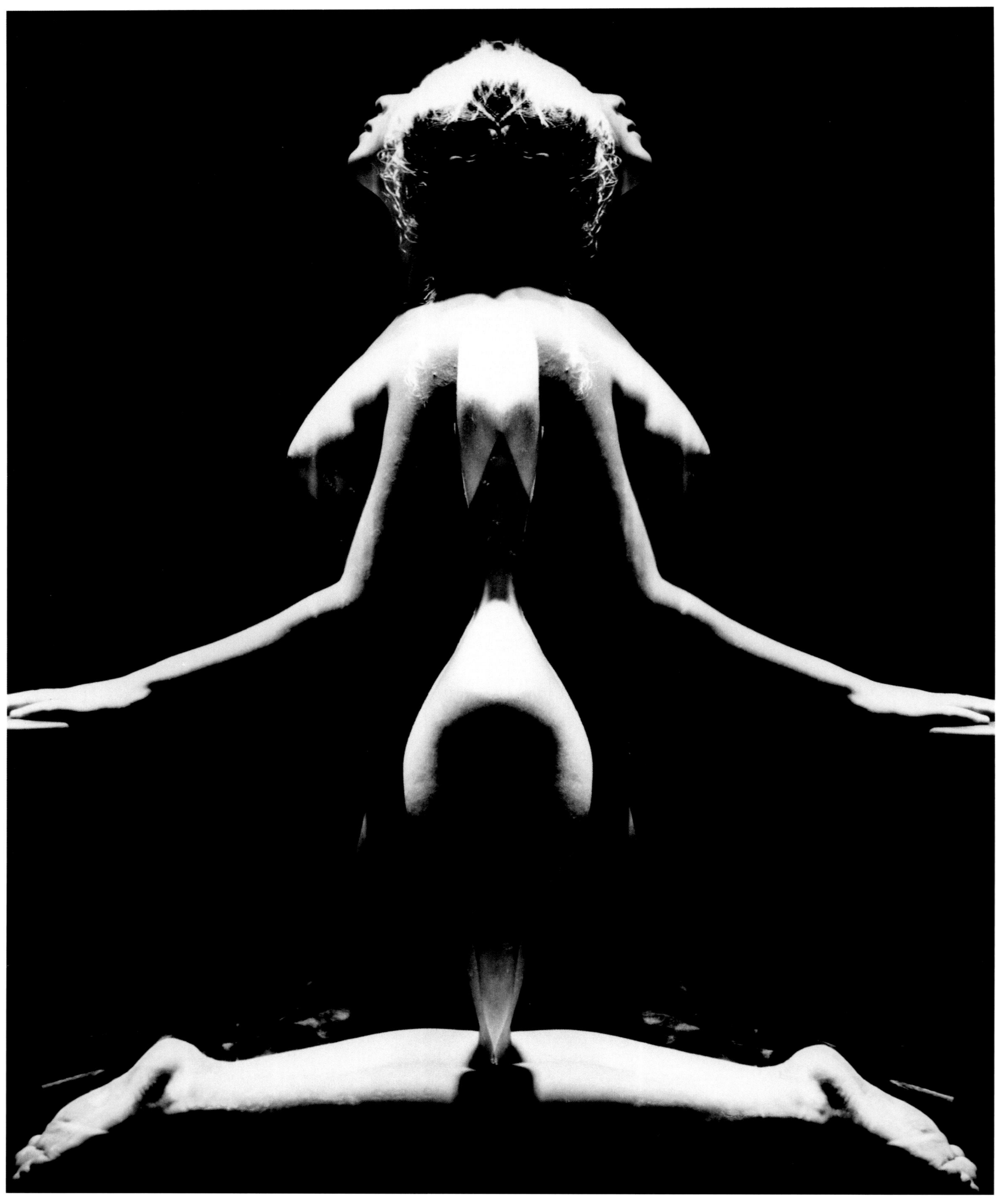

*A Donkey, the King and
Myself*, 1959

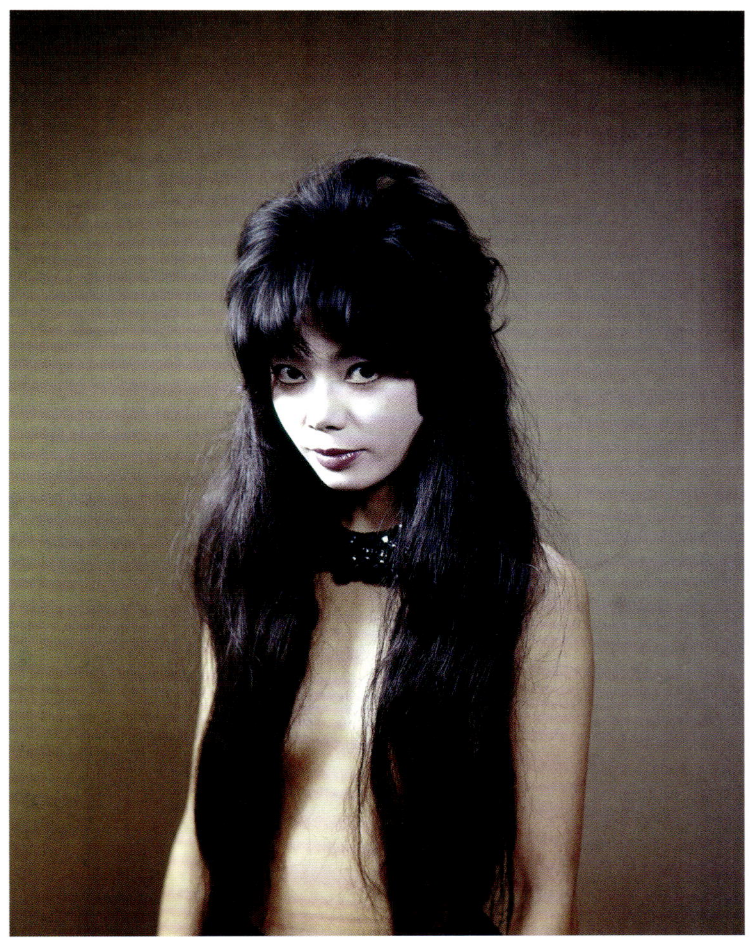

Imai's photographs stand out for their unique approach to the depiction of the female body, often fragmenting and abstracting form.

a torso with ample breasts. In one photograph, the figure is made out of thin bark, curling and peeling; in another, it is carved out of wooden blocks; in yet another, it is formed from tendrils of hair. The figures resemble a mannequin, doll, or robot in the process of being dismantled or slowly torn apart. Three years later, she would return to this idea, the split female body—but one that is no longer headless—in a solo exhibition at Gekko Gallery in 1961, titled *Model and North Wind*. The series appears to shift from considering what the models are—taking apart the women and seeing what they are made of—to considering where they exist, which is somewhere pitch-black. These figures float in fields of darkness, immaculately made-up in thick-winged eyeliner, split from context or even clothing.

At this time, Imai was building a successful career in fashion and her photographs were regularly published in magazines. The "fashion," however, in many of these images seems to be the models' hair, styled to dramatically undulate, reflect, and absorb light. Hair appears as both a living organism and a person's dead, ornamental boundary. "Always her hair grows thick, like an unknown plant," the poet Shuntaro Tanikawa noted, writing about Imai in the June 1961 issue of *Camera Mainichi*. "Today, as ever, the wind wafts in spores of dreams."

The strong desire to present women in vivid, almost unearthly ways is also visible in Imai's 1962 photographs of the lingerie designer Yoko Kamoi, who was pictured as a sorceress in a solo exhibition called *Sea-born Fantasy*. Kamoi had revolutionized women's lingerie in the 1950s, encouraging Japanese women to wear color instead of white, to be bold, to flaunt themselves. She championed the idea of transforming underclothes from simply practical things— to support, to shape, to cover the body—into garments of feminine pleasure. Kamoi was interested in not simply showcasing the female form but considering the gendered assumptions behind notions of use and uselessness, frivolity and practicality. Imai shared the same spirit. In the stills from the film component of *Sea-born Fantasy*,

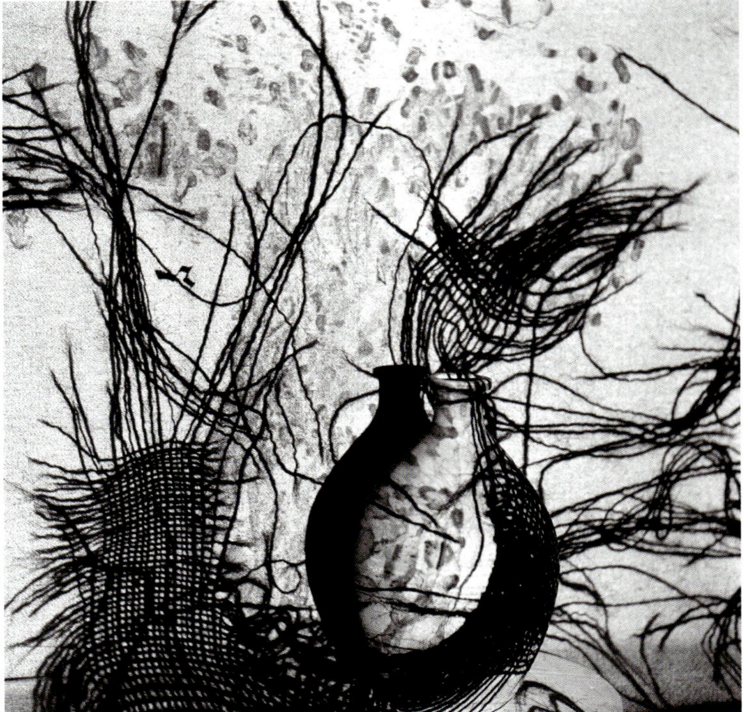

Kamoi is surrounded by discarded wigs and beheaded pink doll heads; in another, she compares her height, perched on her tippy-toes, to that of a blond mannequin.

By the early 1960s, Imai was ascendant. A profile in the fashion magazine *Soen* crowned her "No 1. of female photographers." The article offers every telltale touch of potential for this rising prodigy. Then, one day in the late spring of 1962, all of that changed in an instant when a taxi Imai was in crashed headlong into traffic. For nearly a year, she was blind. Her life entered a tunnel, and the world of artistic ambition fell temporarily dark. The details of this year are scant, but she would eventually recover her sight—and the traumatic accident would significantly alter her life and career trajectory.

In a photograph from the series *Fantasy: Eyes and Teeth* (1963), made during her recovery, we see, through the shadow of an outstretched hand, what looks like an X-ray, or a plaster cast, of a clenched jaw with a string of beads held between its

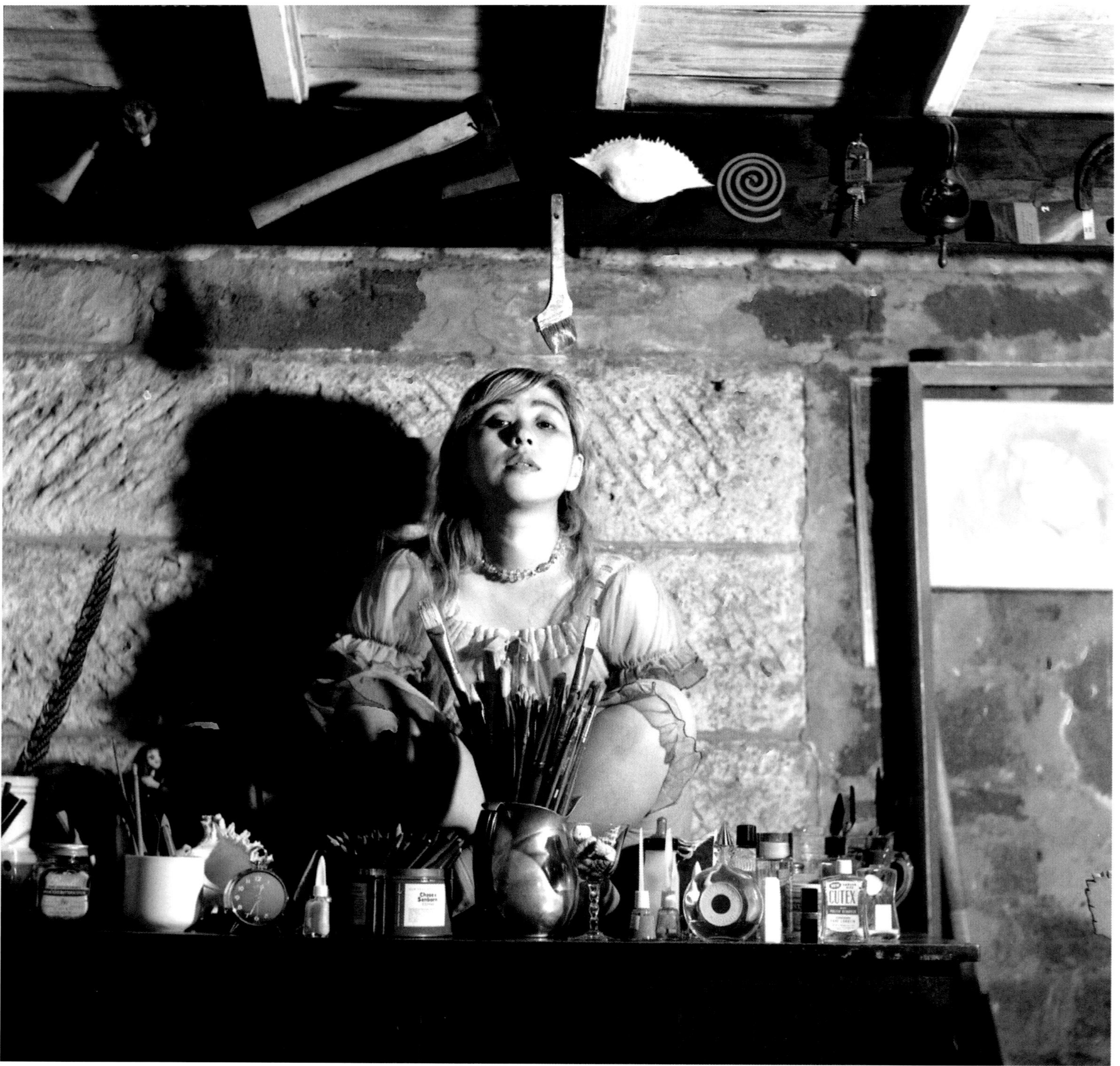

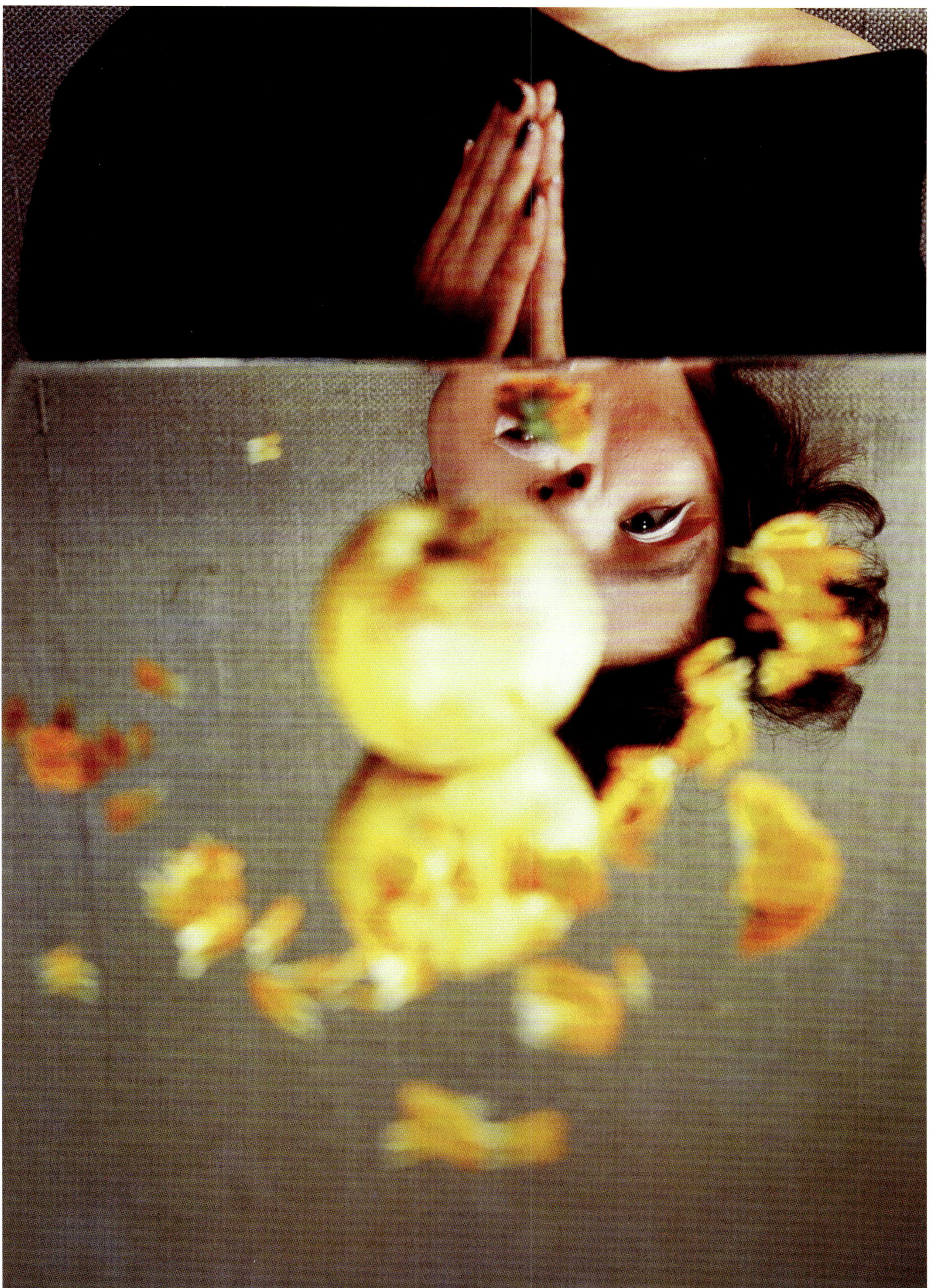

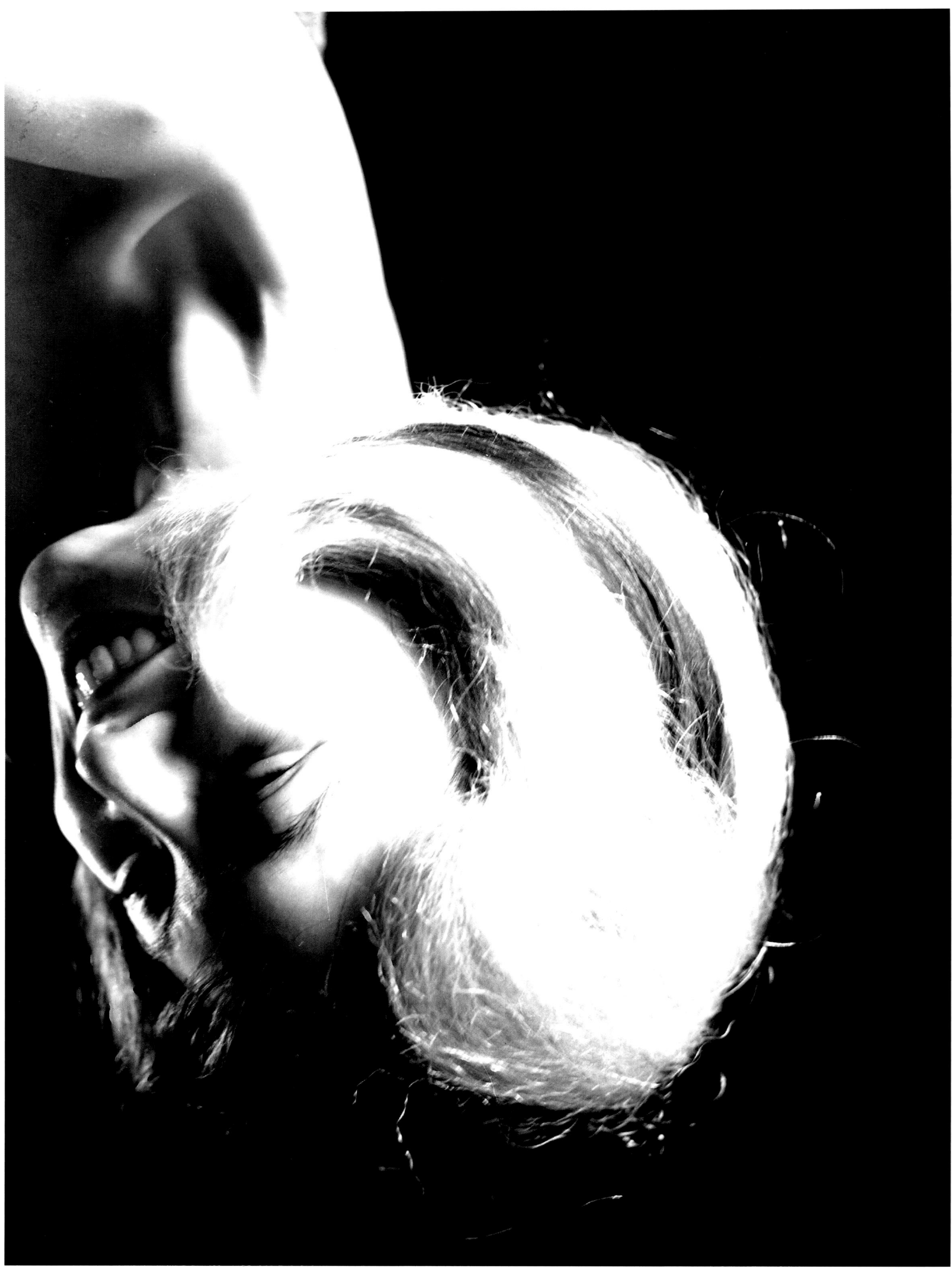

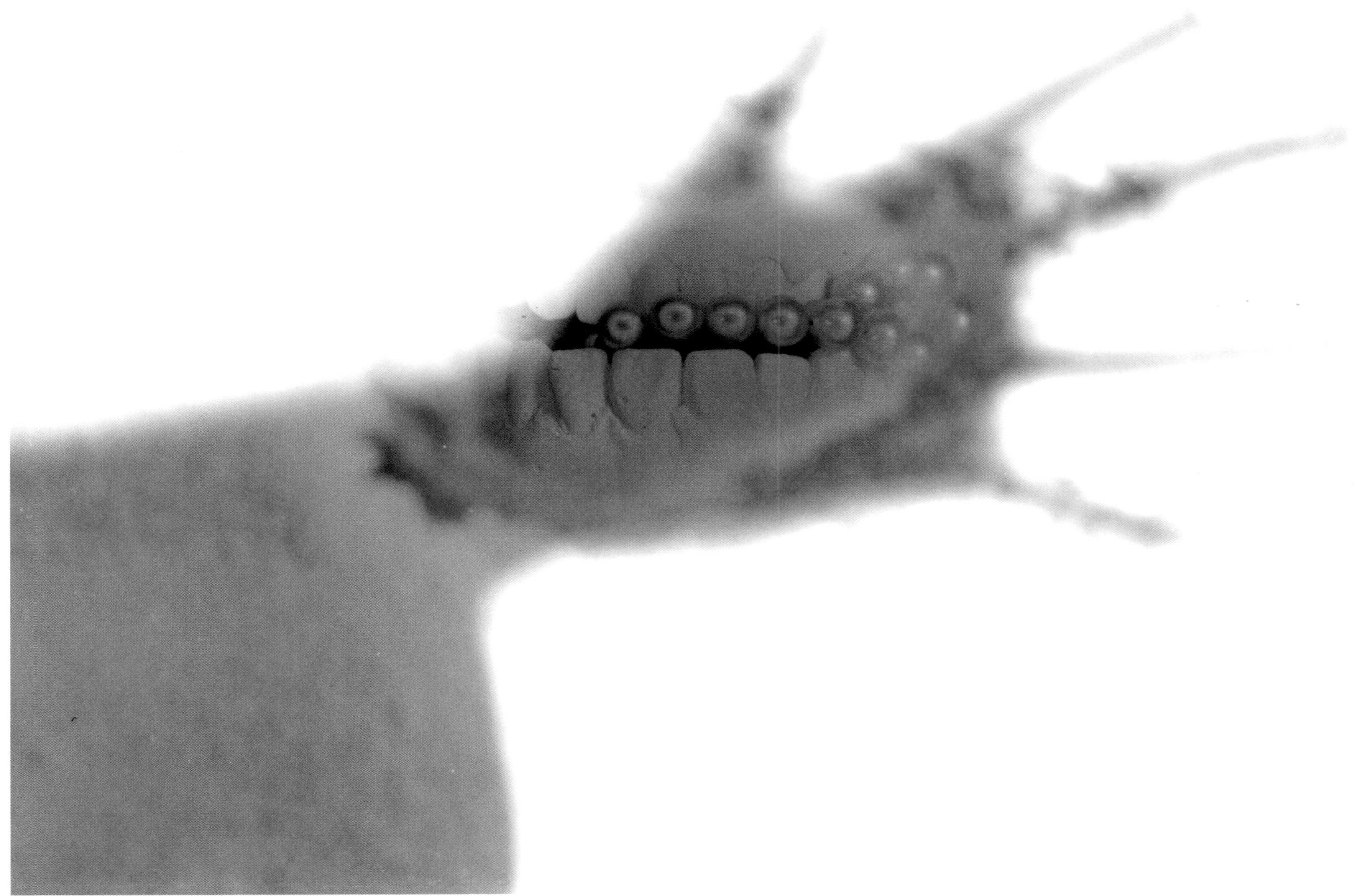

This page:
Fantasy: Eyes and Teeth,
1963; opposite: *Model
and North Wind*, 1961;
following spread: *The
Season of White Flowers*,
1965–75
All photographs © the artist
and courtesy the Third
Gallery Aya, Osaka

After her accident, the human body would concern Imai less and less, replaced by a newfound interest in the natural world.

teeth. The scholar Masako Toda, who has researched and written extensively on Imai, asks us to pay particular attention to the physicality of these photographs, which deliver a visceral charge. "There is probably a close relationship between her experience of almost losing her sight due to the accident and these painful-looking works of eyes and teeth," Toda writes. "This series of photos is very physical, and possesses an intimate feel." What is most affecting is not just the clenched jaw, or the forensic feeling, but the addition of the beads—the decorative ornament added, or grasped for, right when the X-ray turns a person into an image of yet another body to be operated on.

After her accident, the human body would concern Imai less and less, replaced by a newfound interest in the natural world, horses in particular. The story goes that on a bright day in 1963, her vision finally restored, Imai walked into a movie theater and watched David Lean's *Lawrence of Arabia*, the three-and-a-half-hour epic in which the most prominent four-legged animal is a camel, not a horse. But there was something about the horses featured in the film that stirred her; she left her photography studio behind to work in stables and open fields.

"Do I go out to see horses because it hurts to wander around, so aimless?" Imai asked in her 1977 photobook *Hippolatry: Enchanted by Horses*. For the last forty years of her career, trekking from Hokkaido to the Isle of Man, Imai would relentlessly, and

beautifully, photograph racehorses. She became a visual poet of
jockeys emerging from a haze, of the starched rituals and clamor
of a race track, of the curve of a foal's neck. She immersed herself in
the rush and quiet of a life lived among horses. For her, the animals
represented not the primal overcoming of a frontier, like they do
in a Western, nor the pedigreed lure of cultural capital, as they do
in Ralph Lauren advertisements, but the evocation of a threshold,
the feeling that they can bring us over to another world. In one
photograph, a white horse angles out of pitch darkness—in another,
horses are brown dots racing against a sky of yellow grain. To these
images, she added odd textures and color—not glitter or shine
or rose petals, as she did to her female figures. Here clouds are
streaked, variegated into pinks and blues. Manes are tinted with
color and mists evoke an otherworldliness that Imai must have felt
they contained.

Her photographs, through all their range and experimentation,
dare viewers to consider what it means to have a second life, and
to consider the selves that can be discovered in dreams, summoned
in solitude, or encountered outside in the world. The gallerist
Aya, of the Third Gallery Aya, who recently exhibited Imai's work,
emphasized in a conversation with me the importance of the
"after," such as in *After Ophelia*. In a 1962 essay she wrote about her
collaborations with Imai, Kamoi asked: "Was her work a longing
for a glimpse of the afterworld, or was it a challenge or protest
against this world, the world of the living?" The women and horses
of Imai's photographs hover at this threshold and, in their lush
metamorphoses, ask how we might disentangle longing from flight,
the living from those who come after.

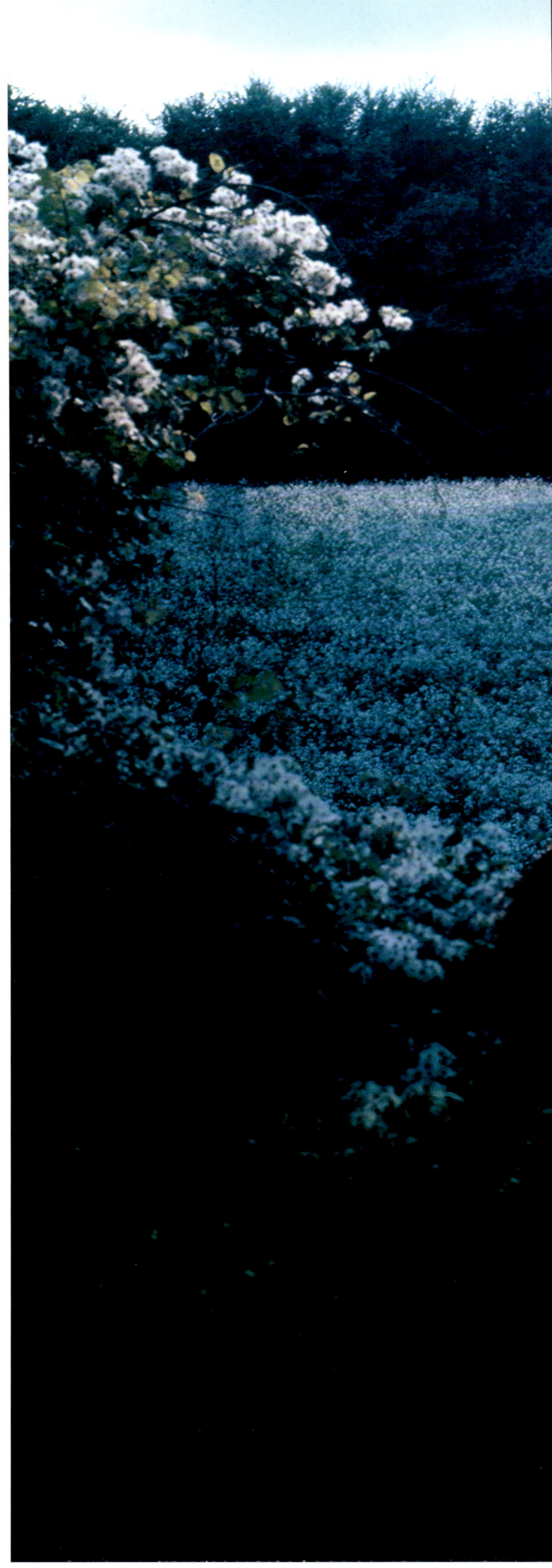

Moeko Fujii is an essayist and critic. Her
writing has appeared in the *New Yorker*,
Orion, and the Criterion Collection.

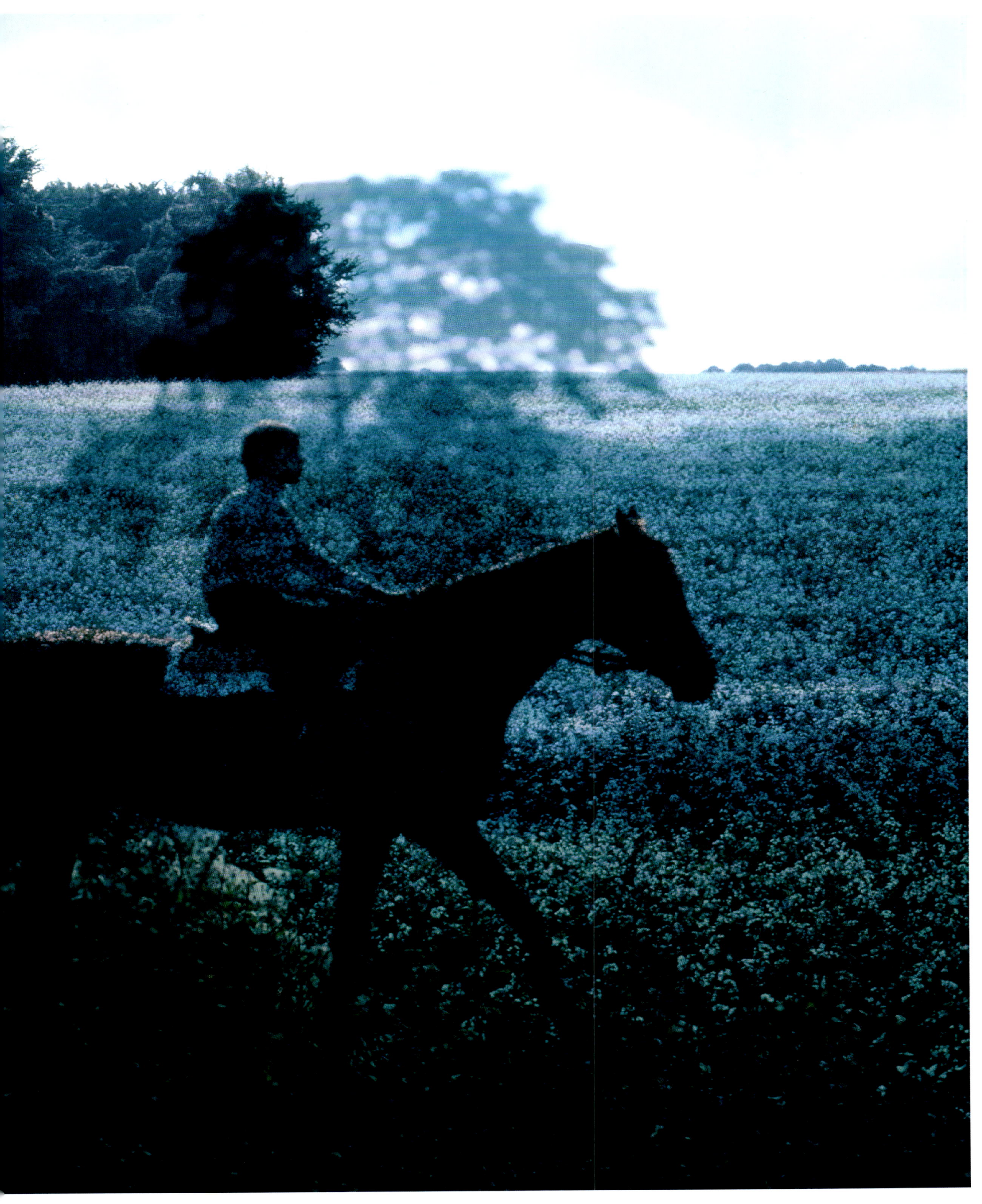

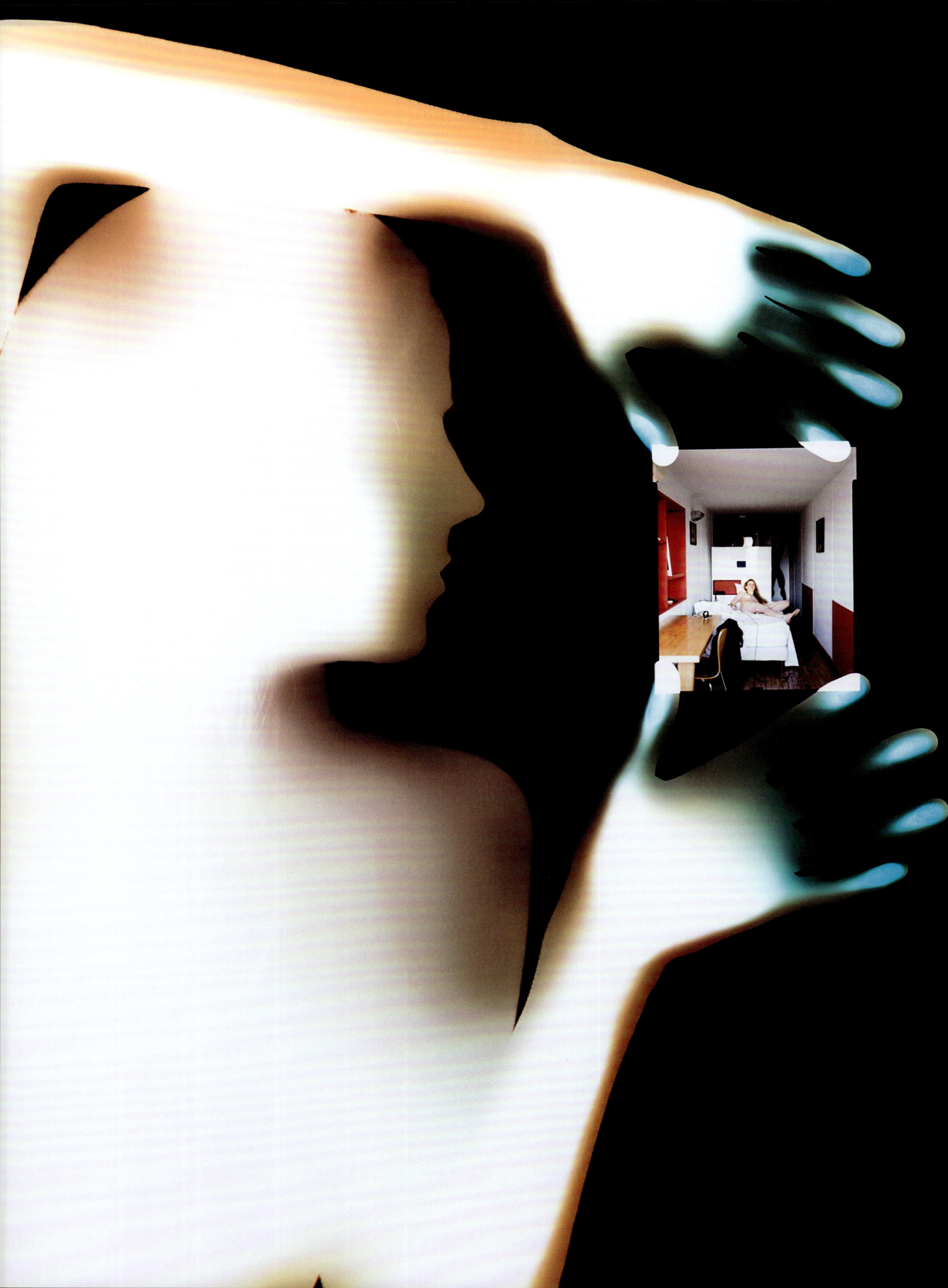

A generation of women photographers, drawing on feminist art of the past, reconsiders the dynamics of being seen.

She's Got the Look

Amanda Maddox

Sophie Thun, *Wild nights (desnuda) (Y82,3M18,3D-70F8T12m10,-153CA3B450)*, 2018
© the artist and courtesy Sophie Tappeiner, Vienna

Sometime around 1987, at the age of seven, I got caught looking. I was curled up on the sofa after school, watching MTV with the volume down low. The channel was all but verboten in our house at the time. At some point, the video for Madonna's "Open Your Heart" came on, featuring the singer herself as an exotic dancer who—spoiler alert!—ultimately escapes from the peep-show theater in which she performs. I was immediately entranced. I turned the volume lower still, ashamed but unable to avert my eyes. And then, just as Madonna pranced across the screen clad in a black satin bustier complete with gold nipple caps and tassels, my mother walked into the living room. "What are you watching?" she asked, somewhat dismayed to find me mesmerized by the sexualized performance playing out before us. Before I could change the channel, she turned off the TV and proceeded to the kitchen.

Decades later, I still love this music video, which seems rather tame in hindsight. Released amid the Reagan administration's antiporn campaign, the video was banned by a few channels and became a lightning rod for feminist debate. Some critics viewed Madonna's portrayal of a sexualized woman subjected to the male gaze as retrograde. Others believed the video helped to destabilize the hierarchy of the gaze, with Madonna unafraid to return the lascivious stare of unsightly, sleazy male patrons. Perhaps the divided opinions in my house mirrored this split among critics. Looking back now, I wonder about my mother's response. Did she believe I was too young to view anything with an erotic charge or subtext? Should a child not be allowed to conceive of a woman as

Talia Chetrit participates in the act of looking while presenting herself as the sight to be looked at.

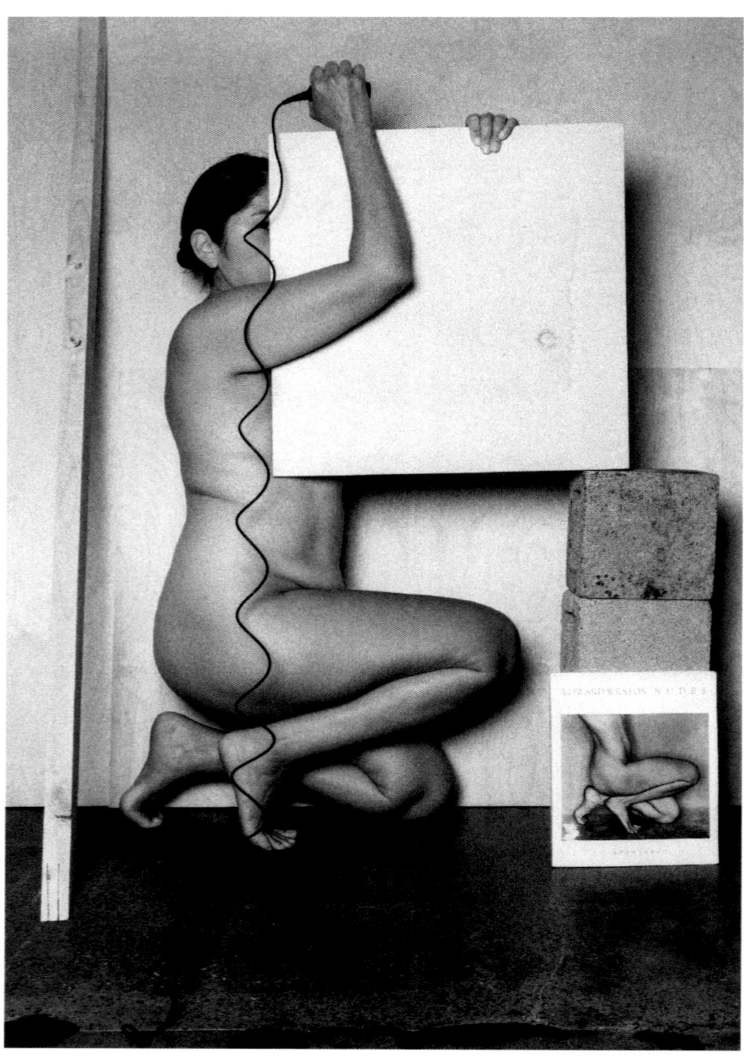

a sexualized figure, or even as an object of desire? And why had I felt ashamed? Was there some corollary between me and the innocent "presexual" boy in the video, who lingers outside the theater and plays one-way peekaboo with a nude female on a pinup poster until Madonna emerges and skips off with him into the sunset?

This line of inquiry ultimately invites a larger question: Who gets permission to look?

I found myself asking this same question in 2016, upon my first encounter with the New York–based artist Talia Chetrit's work. Shown as part of the AIMIA | AGO Photography Prize exhibition at the Art Gallery of Ontario (AGO), in Toronto, the opening wall displayed a provocative diptych: at left, an image of Chetrit's camera on a tripod held between her bare legs, suggestively angled toward her crotch (which was presumably exposed, but not included in the frame); at right, an image of her lower body, naked from the waist down except for a pair of "invisible" jeans (effectively a waistband with the seams of the excised denim pant legs still attached). I watched the room to see how other visitors were engaging with her photographs, feeling as if I'd unwittingly stumbled into a video store that only stocked adult films. No one else appeared fazed.

Another photograph by Chetrit, *Plastic Nude* (2016), which I came across later in her 2019 book *Showcaller*, further complicates the question at hand. In this image, Chetrit photographed herself from head to toe with the aid of a mirror—which, in its reflection, reveals that she is dressed in transparent overalls. While Chetrit's see-through garment leaves virtually nothing to the imagination, it's not exactly titillating by default. Perhaps this image is an evocation of the striptease, which, as Roland Barthes characterized it, "is based on a contradiction: Woman is desexualized at the very moment when she is stripped naked." Then again, is Chetrit nude? As she leans back against a piano, her plastic-wrapped torso and legs all but open to be viewed, I can't help but be reminded of the beguiling woman dressed deceptively in a flesh-colored body stocking that E. J. Bellocq photographed a century earlier. In each case, the viewer must look closely to determine if the nudity is an illusion.

In *Plastic Nude*, Chetrit's body remains encased in some kind of PVC layer, akin to a work of art displayed behind glass. Her outfit ultimately says: You can look, but you can't touch. With this work Chetrit embodies the oft-cited idea that the film theorist Laura Mulvey described in her groundbreaking 1975 essay "Visual Pleasure and Narrative Cinema": "The determining male gaze projects its fantasy onto the female figure, which is styled accordingly. In their traditional exhibitionist role women are simultaneously looked at and displayed, with their appearance coded for strong visual and erotic impact so that they can be said to connote to-be-looked-at-ness." And yet, holding a camera in front of her face, she simultaneously reminds the viewer that she—the artist *and* the sitter—participates in the act of looking while presenting herself as the sight to be looked at.

Since my visit to the AGO, I have noticed something of a vogue among a small but sharp crop of contemporary photographers—all of them women born within a decade of forty-one-year-old Chetrit—for whom self-representation functions as an exercise in "to-be-looked-at-ness." On the face of things, this is not new. Within the history of photography, there is a rich tradition, particularly in the West, of women photographers' work disrupting the structures of looking. As the noted art historian Griselda Pollock wrote in 1982, arguing for feminist rethinkings of art history, "creativity has been appropriated as an ideological component of masculinity while femininity has been constructed as man's and, therefore, the artist's negative." Looking across the twentieth century, one can find interwar women photographers such as Gertrud Arndt and Claude Cahun, who made pictures of themselves that countered conventional and patriarchal ways of

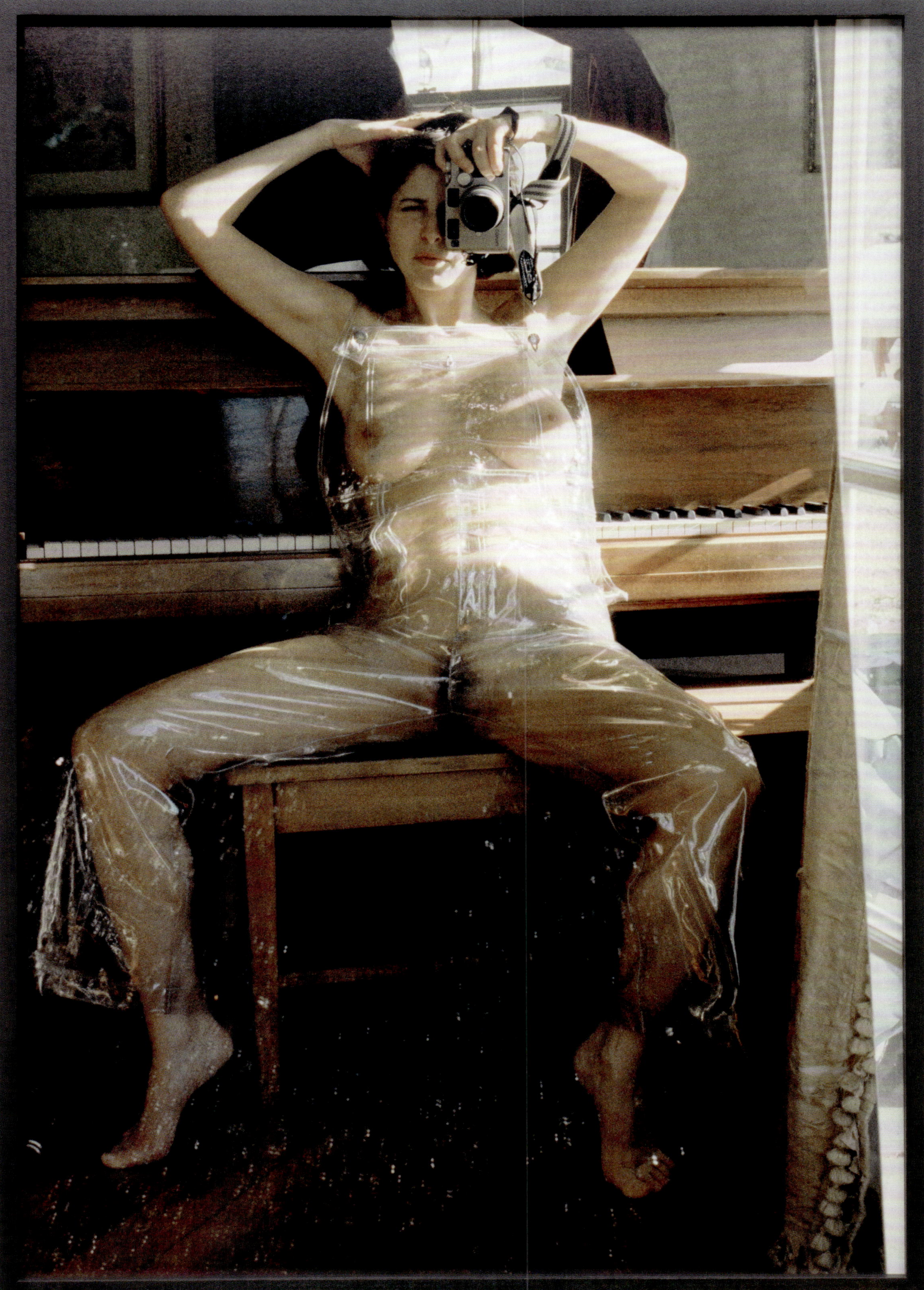

seeing women. In the 1970s, a particularly fertile moment in this
history, feminist practitioners like Jo Spence and Hannah Wilke
generated self-representational work that further complicated the
objectification of women and addressed what Pollock referred to
as "the signification of woman as body and as sexual." Emerging
in their wake in the 1980s, another wave of groundbreaking women
photographers—Laura Aguilar, Jeanne Dunning, and Catherine
Opie among them—made work depicting bodies (their own)
that further deviated from art-historical norms and contemporary
conventions of beauty and femininity.

Chetrit and other midcareer photographers consciously
deploying self-representational forms today are certainly inspired
and informed by this history. Some were even formally educated
by women who helped to shape it. But beyond their placement,
chronologically speaking, as part of its continuum, how do they
relate to the tradition of female photographic self-representation?
And how does this seeming trend of soliciting, welcoming, and
approving "to-be-looked-at-ness" relate to the present moment
in which it unfolds?

By the 1980s, several decades before this latest wave of
practitioners began their careers, feminist issues and theory had
reached the mainstream, and criticism had strengthened its focus
on the problem of "woman-as-image," as identified by the art
historian Abigail Solomon-Godeau. With discussion around the
representational politics of gender and the power relations of
looking already well underway, younger contemporary photographers
have entered into the conversation midstream, arriving with
different agendas.

For some, inclusion in the canon of photography and the
visibility it brings—the understanding that their bodies will
most certainly be looked at—is part and parcel of the impulse to
photograph oneself. The Peru-born, Oregon-based photographer
Tarrah Krajnak models this approach in her 2020 series *Master
Rituals II: Weston's Nudes*, wherein she poses in the guise of Edward
Weston's female sitters but, given her Latin American background,
challenges what she describes as "the ideal of white female beauty
central to Weston's work and its historical appreciation." Krajnak
incorporates direct references to her predecessors, such as Weston's
one-time wife and model Charis Wilson, by including Weston's
images of them within the scenes she stages, ultimately generating
distorted mise en abymes.

Nydia Blas, raised in the predominantly white city of Ithaca,
New York, employs photography as a means for creating spaces that
celebrate multiracial bodies like hers, which historically have been
discouraged if not prevented from representing themselves. In a
photograph of her midsection and upper thighs, titled *My Body
Has Been Colonized* (2022), Blas reveals a tattoo in Spanish—the
language of her father, which she can't speak fluently—and stretch
marks. She subtly obscures the latter while maintaining her modesty
with a handkerchief covered in flowers native to Panama, her
father's birthplace. "Is it possible to reclaim something like sexuality
in a photograph where you don't have clothes on?" Blas asked
when I spoke with her recently. "How can you still maintain
power?" She admits that while she doesn't have an answer, there is
strength in reclaiming something for oneself in self-representation,
in part because, as any photographer knows, it's devilishly difficult
to photograph yourself.

Two other photographers, Iiu Susiraja and Whitney Hubbs,
despite the marked differences in their work, both mobilize the
trope of the feminine pinup and its associative baggage, employing
humor to neutralize it. Hubbs, born in 1977 and based in Syracuse,
New York, mocks her own ability to adapt this fetish, partly
given her age. Wearing protective knee pads while balancing a
watermelon on her back or reclining topless while supported by
a chair pad, Hubbs's stagings evoke something like the grotesque

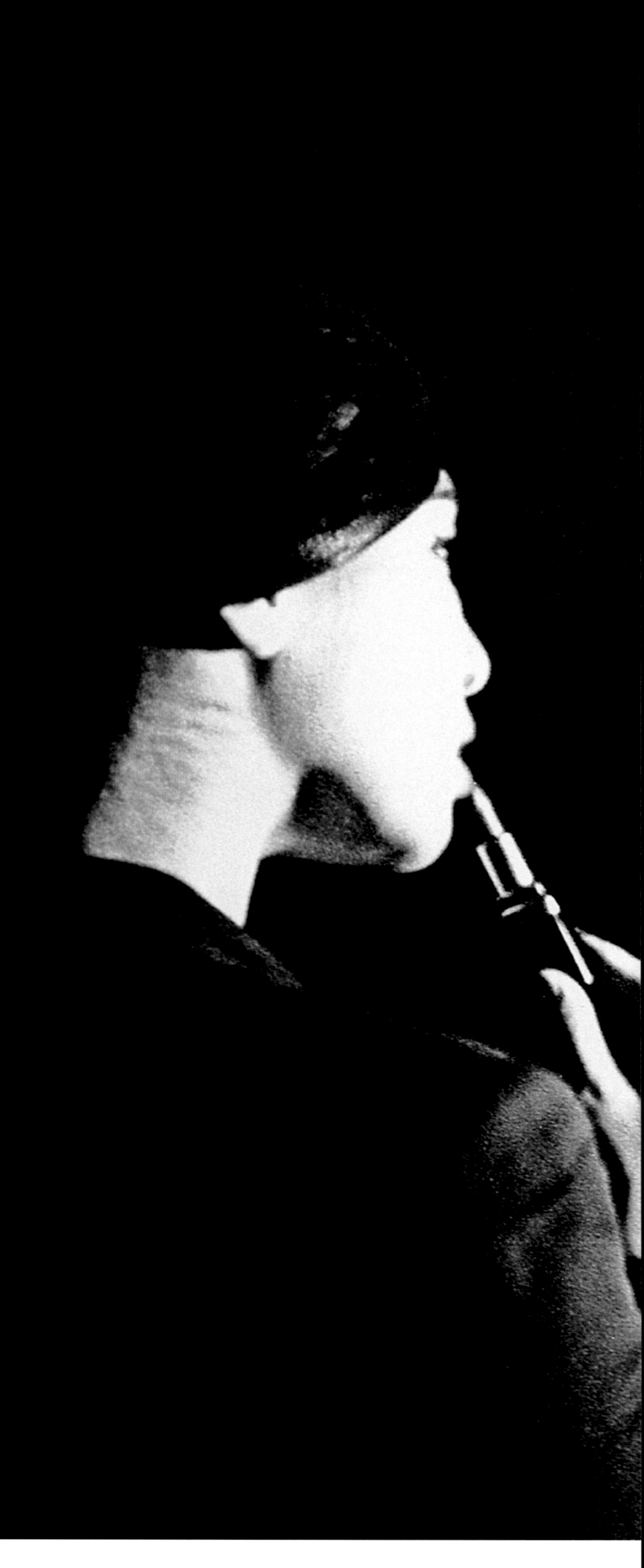

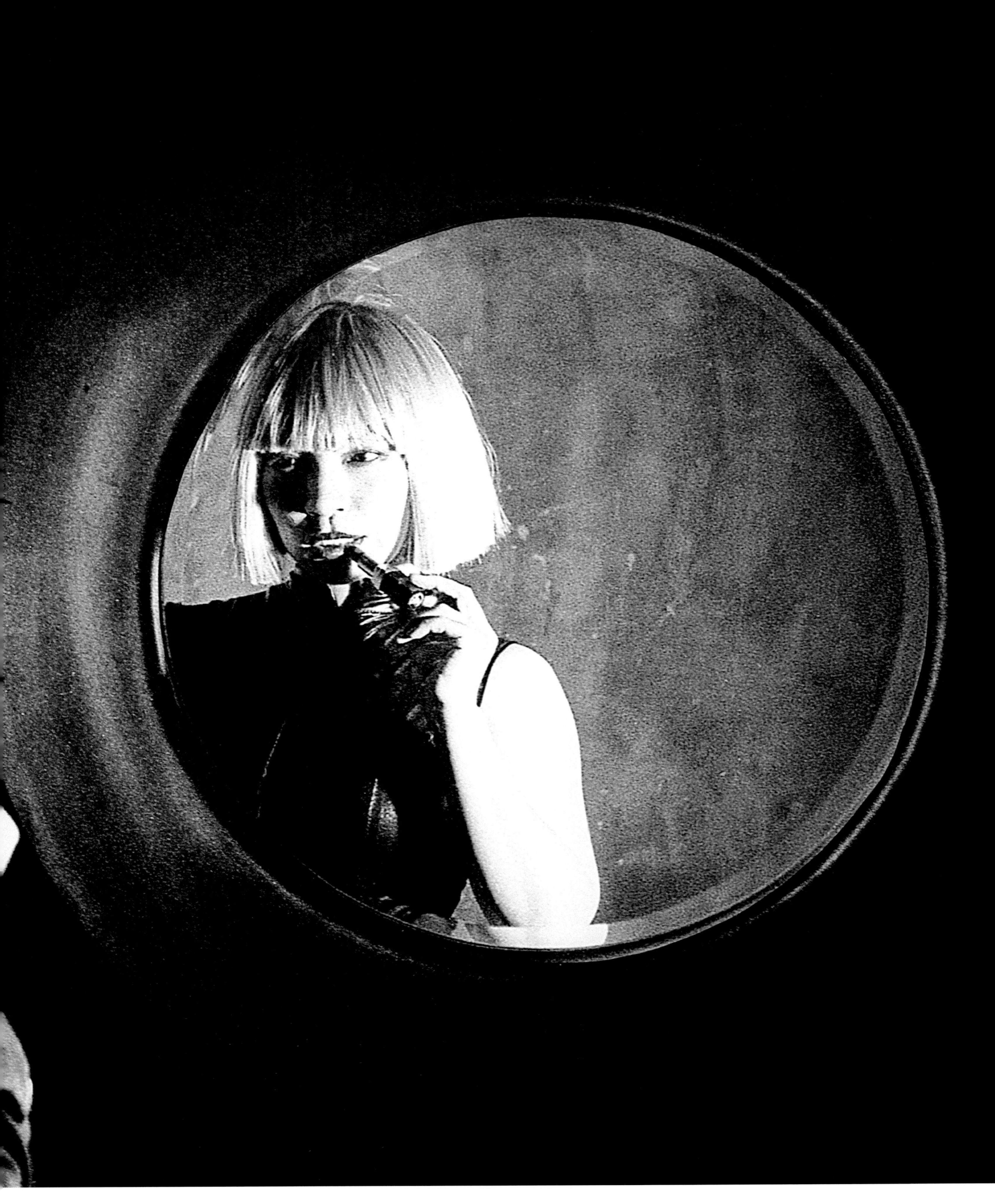

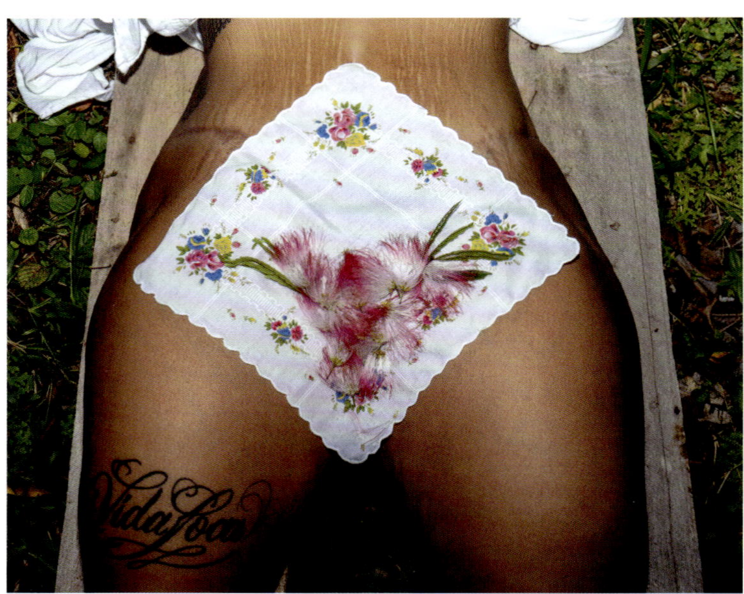

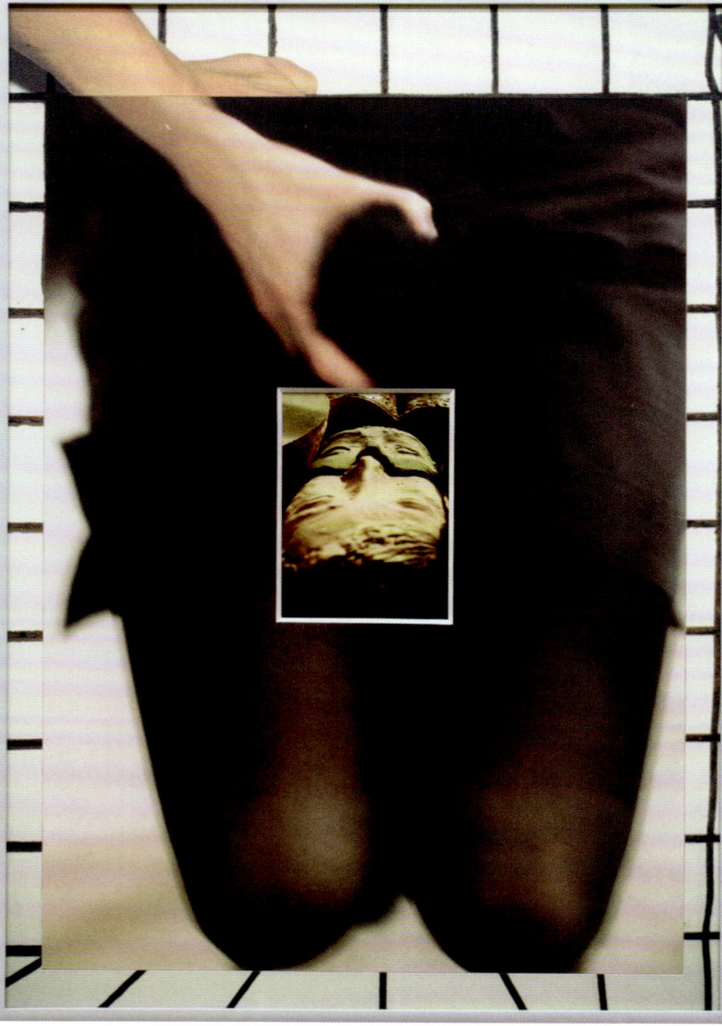

or carnivalesque. In the case of Susiraja, absurd props, occasional bruises, and a deadpan style confound conventional expectations around viewing an image of a seminude body, if not to simply desire, consume, or covet it. According to Susiraja, who lives and works in Turku, Finland, the prospect of acceptance partly fuels the public dissemination of her photographs. In a 2022 interview, she likened her interest in seeking approval through self-representation to how people utilize social media: "I believe when you put self-portraits to Instagram, you look for acceptance and love."

How should we think about the apparent increase in self-representational tactics used by women artists today? Can it be seen as a consequence of selfie culture and its aspirational, branded aesthetic? It bears noting that in the past ten years, the decade during which much of the work discussed here was made, social media flourished. Its platforms produced, disseminated, and censored notions of femininity and masculinity, as well as sex and gender. Around 2013, gender-based double standards that permitted censorship of female breasts on social media prompted an advocacy campaign called Free the Nipple. In her series *The Greece Piece*, from 2019, the Dominican-French photographer Karla Hiraldo Voleau gives a nod to these policies, making self-portraits where she exposes her breasts, which she then covers up with tape on her prints. Gender-based exclusionary practices, likewise, informed the photographs in her contemporaneous project *Hola Mi Amol* and its eponymous book, which show Voleau close-up and clothed alongside her hypothetical male paramours in the Dominican Republic, whose bodies almost always appear seminude or nude. By way of explaining her motivation to make the project, Voleau asks, "Why couldn't women stare, gaze, observe, desire, objectify, and look at men the same way they were looked at?"

Despite her best efforts to shift the power balance between the seer and the sight to be seen, Voleau understands the limitations of her strategy. She remains "woman-as-image" to some observers, acknowledging as much in *Hola Mi Amol*. The book closes with an image of her lying recumbent in bed, fully clothed, staring back at the reader. Beneath the photograph, she poses the question: "Have I been transformed into the character I was pretending to be?"

In *The Desire to Desire*, a 1987 book about Hollywood films and female spectatorship, Mary Ann Doane reinforces this sort of conclusion. "It can never be enough simply to reverse sexual roles or to produce positive or empowered images of the woman," she writes. Photographers Tokyo Rumando and Sophie Thun, another unlikely pair, share an ability to recognize this limitation. Both assume the existence of a putative male gaze whose powers they mock, and try to undermine by assuming the position of the spectator (presumed a man) within their images.

An erstwhile model for the provocateur Nobuyoshi Araki, widely known (and recently publicly derided) for his explicit depictions of women, the Tokyo-based photographer Rumando reprises the position of subject in *Orphée*, a series published in 2014. Here, though, Rumando takes control of her representation. She depicts herself beside a round mirror—a proxy for her camera's lens—that doesn't directly reflect her likeness. Instead, the mirror acts as a portal that presents another version of Rumando (she plays twenty-six unnamed characters in the mirror, some of them styled to resemble famous figures such as Marilyn Monroe or the writer Yukio Mishima) to enact fantasies, desires, and memories. In an interview published in 2017, Rumando divulged that "the mirror and I are not facing each other directly, which means that the encounter is not a confrontation. Instead, it's like I'm watching from afar." Assuming the role of spectator within the composition, she attempts to displace or redirect the gaze of additional viewers who exist beyond the frame. Between these various depictions of Rumando, which collectively function like the reflections in a funhouse mirror, where are we supposed to direct our attention?

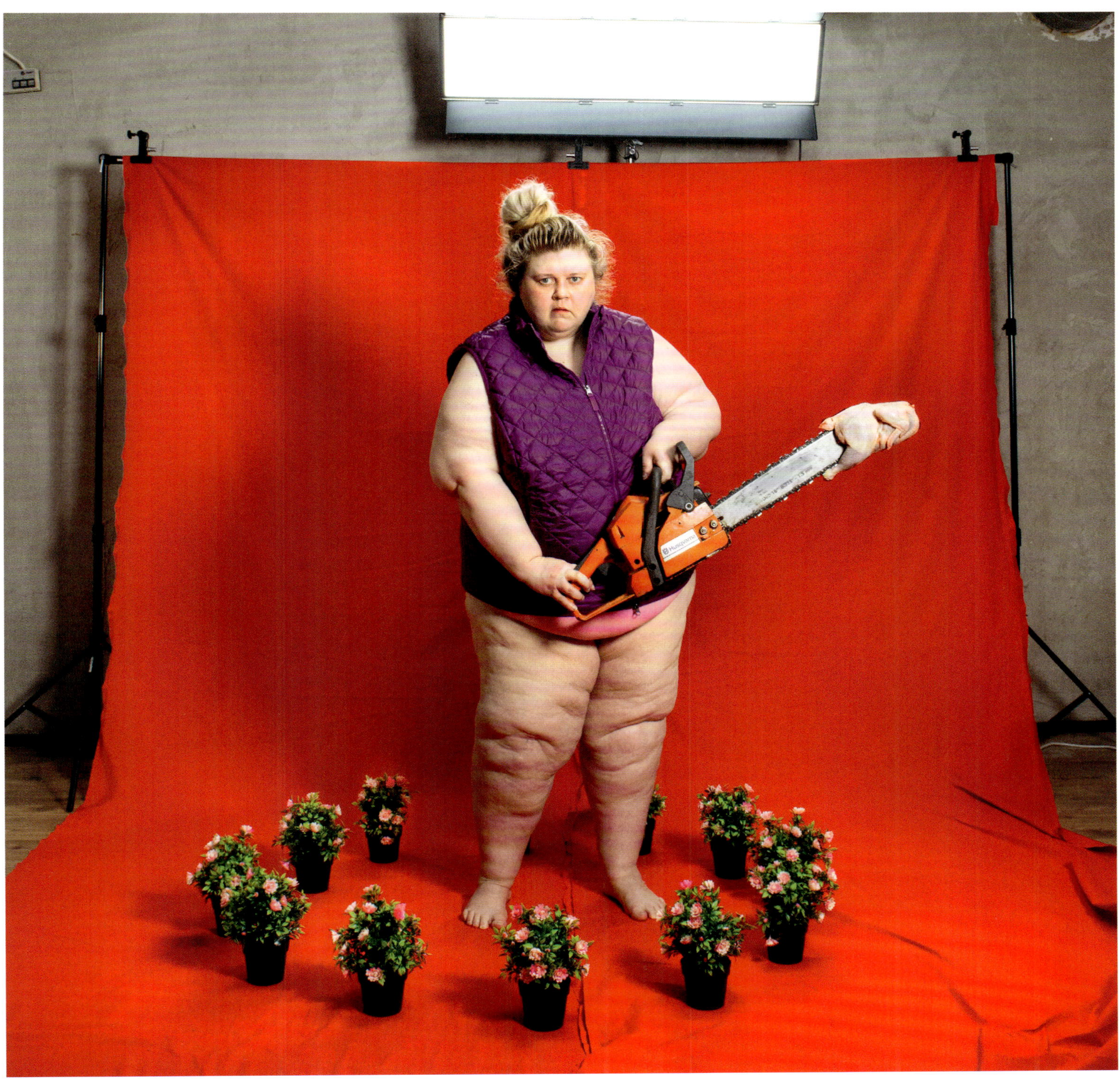

Iiu Susiraja, *Lovely Wife*
(Ihastuttava vaimo), 2018
© and courtesy the artist

Based in Vienna, Thun parlays jobs assisting male artists by utilizing the hotel rooms she occupies during those gigs to create her ongoing series *After Hours*. This premise allows Thun to unpack notions of "hierarchy and interdependence, because these artists depend on me in a technical capacity, and I am dependent on them financially," she says. Turning these rooms into makeshift studios at night, she photographs herself naked and, most crucially, often collages her pictures so that she appears twice in the composition, usually in positions that suggest she's having sex with herself. Like nearly all the other photographers mentioned here, Thun uses a film camera and employs a cable release to photograph herself. The visibility of her devices is essential, communicating her technical skill and, by association, her authority: this is what knowledge and control look like. They are active, as is her body, which refuses to play the art-historical part of passive object of desire. As viewers survey her work, they are confronted by Thun and her double, who address Thun's camera with an unflinching gaze. But to invoke

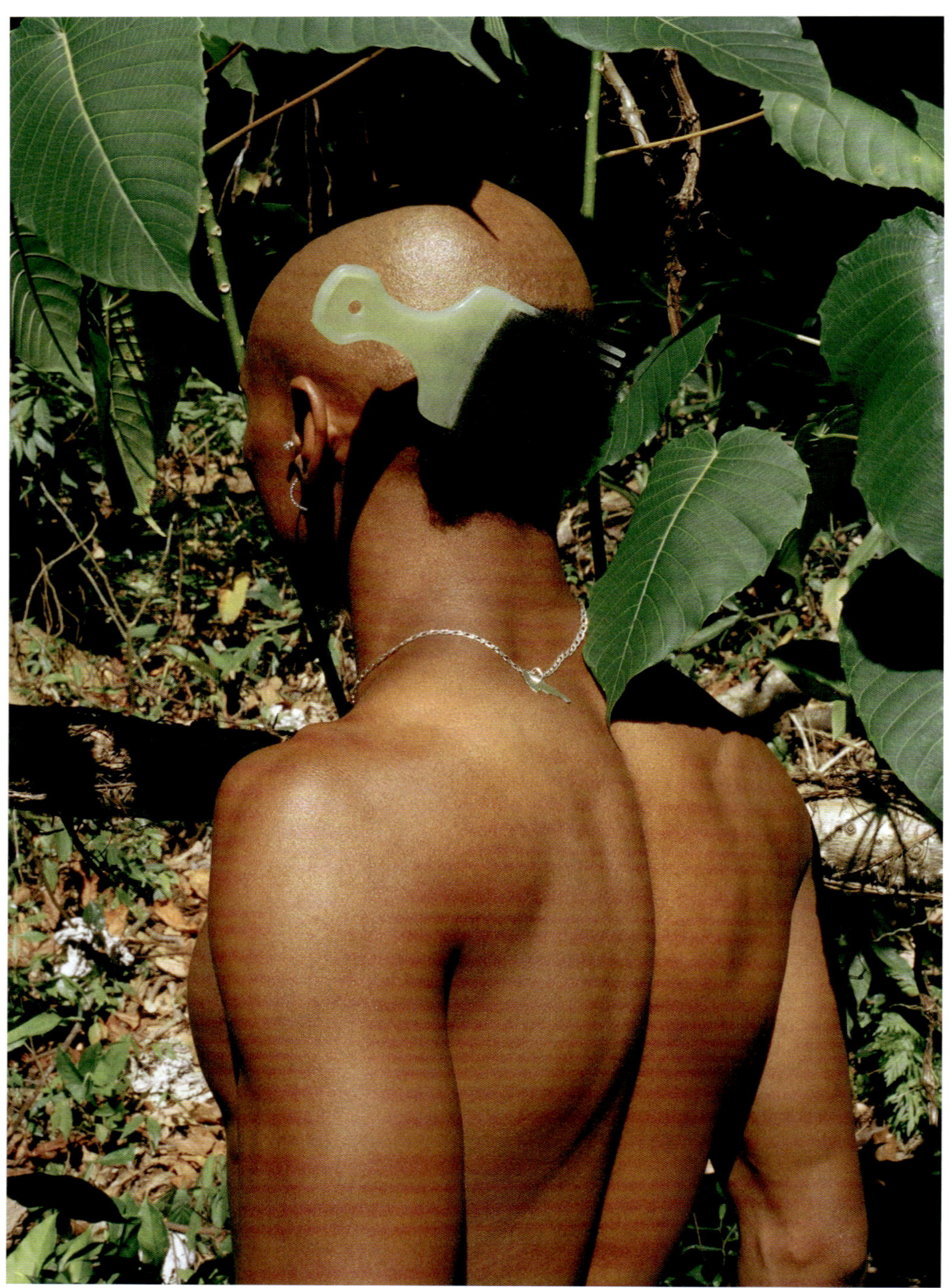

Doane again: Is that enough of a power play to expose or disturb the status quo?

What if the quality of work that invites looking and commands a certain "to-be-looked-at-ness" also actively chafes against the instinct to gender the body? What if the bodily form in the photograph defies identification within the categories of male, female, or nonbinary? The photographs of the Chicago-based artist B. Ingrid Olson—who identifies as female but appreciates the mystery and possibility of androgyny afforded by her first initial—explores this terrain. In an interview on the podcast *Modern Art Notes*, she confesses to "making images that allow you to see yourself in the image or make yourself more aware of being a body in front of an image." But she's resistant to labeling her work as self-portraiture; indeed, as Solomon-Godeau has noted, self-representation is not always self-portraiture. Olson's face never appears in her pictures, while the rest of her figure appears so fragmented as to become defamiliarized and nearly inscrutable; it's difficult to pinpoint what crevice, orifice, or limb she has photographed. To understand what you're looking at, you have to keep looking.

"It's okay to look and like looking," Whitney Hubbs remarked after I told her about my long-ago moment with the Madonna video. "I had a similar reaction while watching [the 1983 film] *Flashdance*. It was arousing." It strikes me that this admission reflects another potential rationale behind the rash of self-representational photographs that Hubbs and others are making today: just as there's often a need for women to talk to one another for their voices to be heard, there's an enduring need for us to see each other, too, in all our multiple, complicated selves. In a political climate when women are increasingly losing control over their own bodies, such self-made forms of visibility fulfill a particularly useful function. They encourage what the authors of *Caught Looking*, a book on feminism and pornography, identified as "free discussion of sexuality and its representation [which] is essential to our feminist vision." They reveal what we otherwise ingest without thinking. They make us want to keep looking.

Amanda Maddox is the lead curator at World Press Photo.

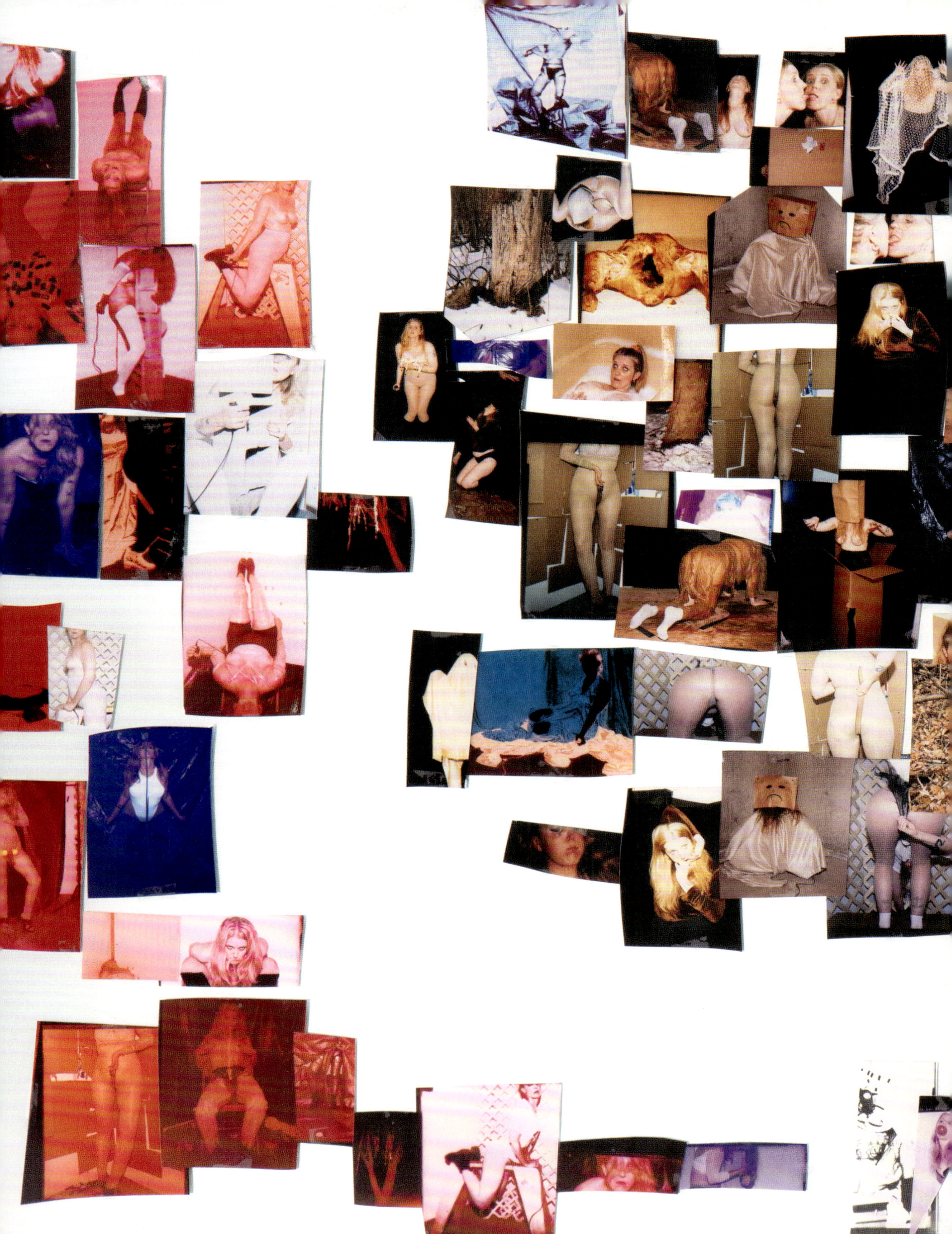

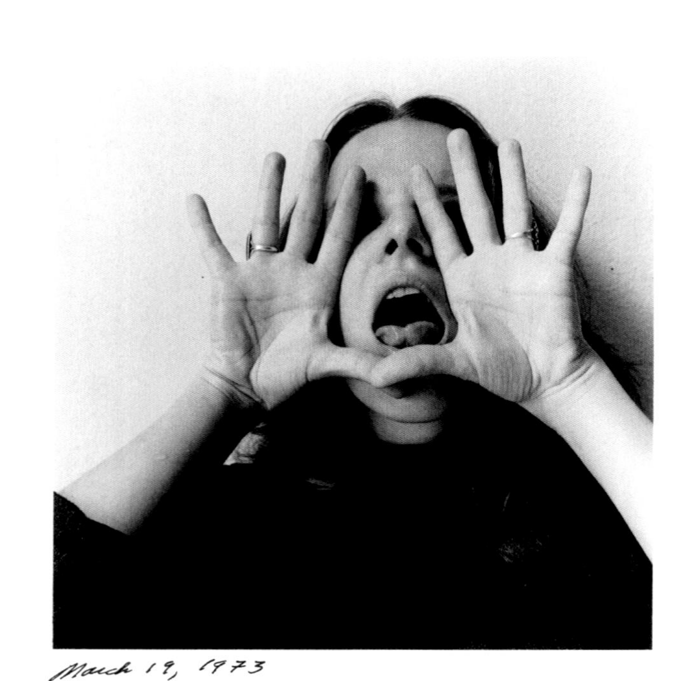

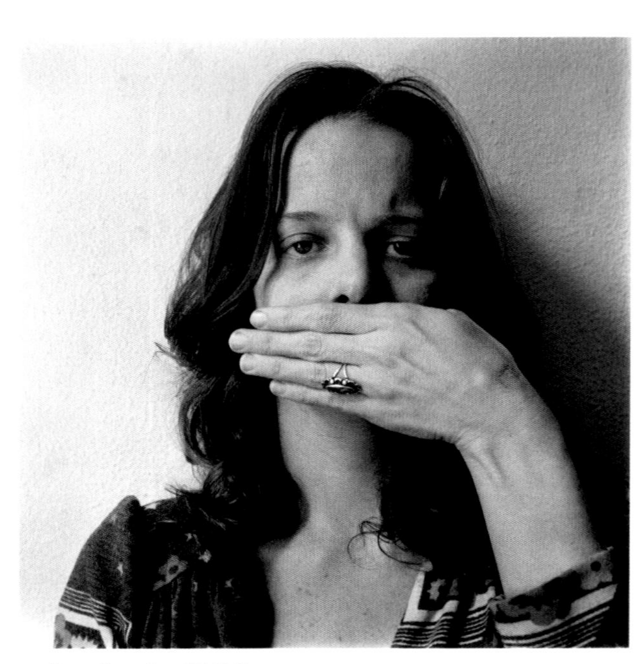

More Real Than a Memory
Melissa Shook

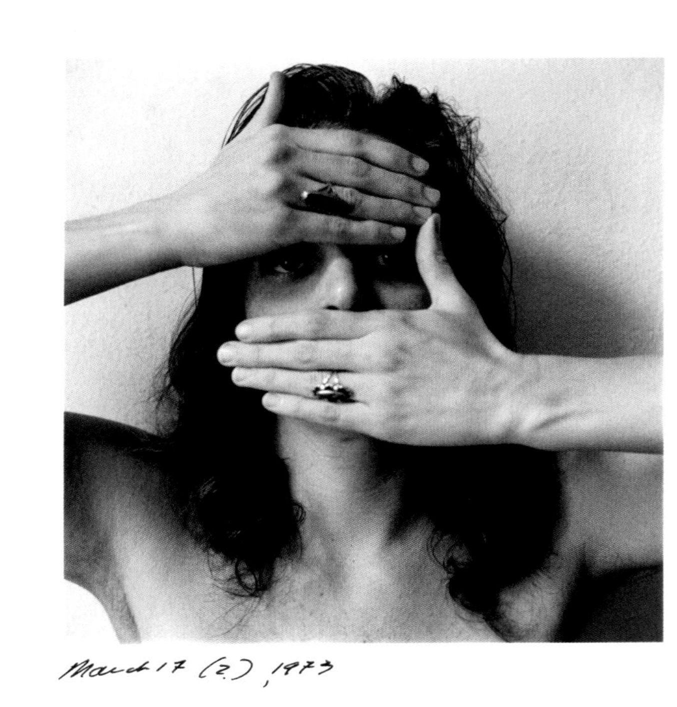

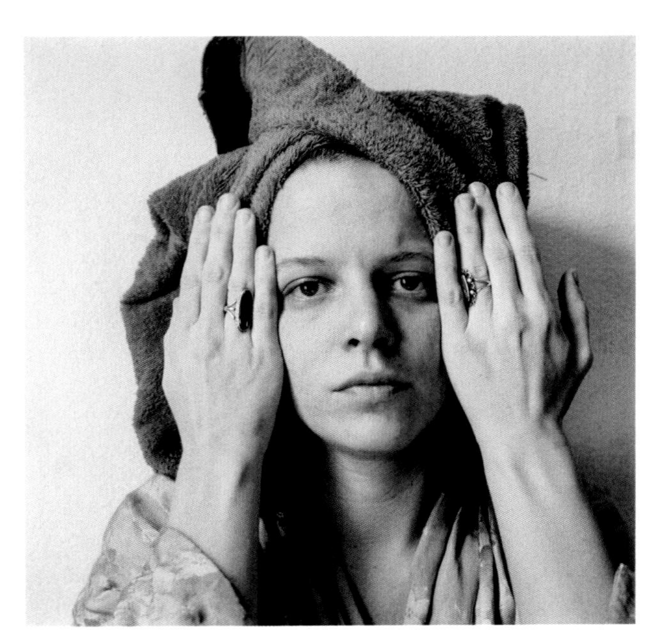

The photographer's rigorous self-portraits show the longing and sensuality of a woman inventing herself every day. Fifty years later, new audiences are discovering her work.
Lucy McKeon

In December 1972, the photographer Melissa Shook found herself stuck at home in her apartment on Manhattan's Lower East Side nursing a toe infection. Removed from her usual busy routine, she began to take daily self-portraits. In a diary from that month, she notes what she photographed each day, along with domestic details and increasingly involved meditations on loneliness and abandonment, the struggles of being a single parent, difficult family dynamics, and her ambitions as a photographer: December 5, "A romantic shot of me with the avocado plants." December 7, "2¼ me, nude, alone in sunlight. Terrible sadness at how detached I am. Real sorrow at not loving anyone, the wall of fear." December 30, "It was a lovely and incredible day. It's very difficult to write about—if I do I commit myself for me to read again, make more real than a memory."

Shook was thirty-three and would continue taking pictures almost daily until August 1973, by which time her young daughter, Kristina (called Krissy as a child), joined or replaced her in the

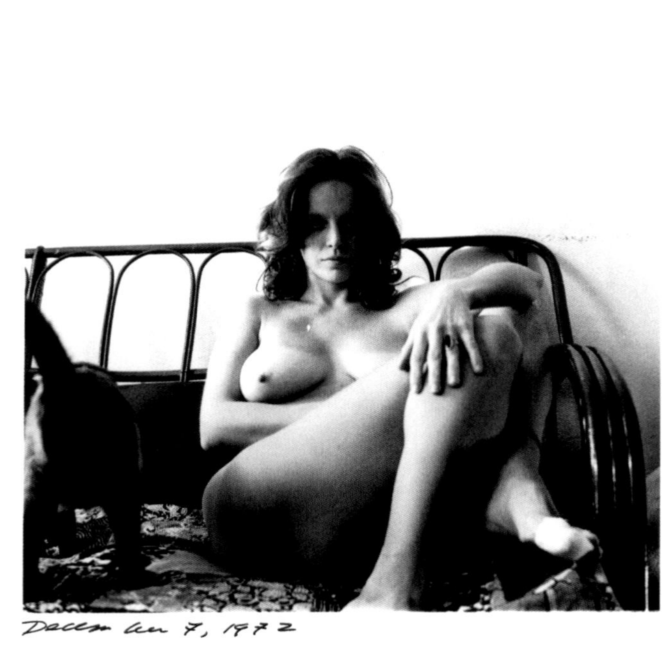

Shook's pictures evoke the kind of domestic landscape of dreams— familiar, but with an uncanny sense that something is different.

photographs. Her devotion is to the process. In each image— some playful, sensual, slightly sinister; others melancholy, sociable, abstracted, masked—Shook's artistic presence is felt. "She didn't hide," Kristina told me recently. In these self-portraits, Shook meets what emerges each day, even when clarity is elusive. What makes the series remarkable is its exploration of the self as something familiar and yet removed, unknown. And in some ways, it was. "I was interested in when I would forget that I had committed myself to this project," she later wrote of the series that became *Daily Self-Portraits 1972–73*. "The obsession with forgetting has been central."

Born in 1939 in New York, Shook was twelve when her mother died. She was left with few memories of her and a foggy sense of childhood, at best. Her father, who was an alcoholic and refused to speak of his late wife, gave Shook her first camera, a Pentax, for her twentieth birthday. Photography became a way for her to try to make sense of what had been lost so early. "Losing my memory means so much because I lost myself," Shook wrote in her 1972 diary; the daily photographs helped "to maintain, or more accurately to establish a sense of internal identity."

Taken mostly against a white wall of the tenement apartment Shook shared with Krissy, the pictures evoke the kind of domestic landscape of dreams—familiar, but with an uncanny sense that something is different. Where the logic of the quotidian might normally reign, here psyche is the primary author of experience. Shook uses a wide frame in some images to show a bed, a chair, several potted plants against the white wall. Others capture at close range Shook's face—fingers curled around eyes like glasses or outstretched to frame mouth and tongue—or her nude torso, breasts, bush, body, blurred in motion.

The process, according to Shook, was instinctual: "It was important to let my unconscious, rather than my intellect, dictate the progression. For reasons I don't entirely understand, being nude became part of the project early on." Some critics at the time saw her photographs as "co-opted by the male vision of the nude female posing against a wall," Shook wrote, which she believed was "to some extent . . . correct," but missed the satire and subversion conveyed by the series as a whole. One might be reminded of charges against Hannah Wilke's nude self-portraiture as narcissistic, frivolous, antifeminist; Wilke and Shook, who both used their young bodies in their early work, would also document their failing bodies, overtaken by cancer, later in life. In *Daily Self-Portraits*, Shook considers the confines and conflicts of beauty, desire, and womanhood, exploring physicality and performance to painful, even wicked, effect. Carole Kismaric, founding editor of the Time-Life Photography Series and editorial director of the Aperture Foundation from 1976 to 1985, was an admirer of Shook's work. Some of the *Daily Self-Portraits* images were published in 1973 by *Camera 35*, edited by Jim Hughes; the next year, John Szarkowski acquired more than thirty prints for the Museum of Modern Art, New York, some of which were shown in its 1976 exhibition *Photography: Recent Acquisitions, 1974–1976*. Around this time, Shook became self-conscious, her momentum disrupted. The spell had been broken.

While Shook had conceived of the series as a project to be shared, she was also "always ambivalent about the self-portraiture as a public work," Sally Stein, an independent scholar of photography and a longtime friend of Shook's, tells me, and Shook's diary confirms this. In an essay for a forthcoming monograph, which coincides with an exhibition at La Patinoire Royale in Brussels, Stein argues for expanding the historical record of that era to include Shook's project of sustained self-imaging—not overlooked at the time but largely forgotten today. Before Cindy Sherman's self-portraits as film stars in the late 1970s and 1980s, before Carrie Mae Weems's landmark *Kitchen Table Series* (1990), Shook began her

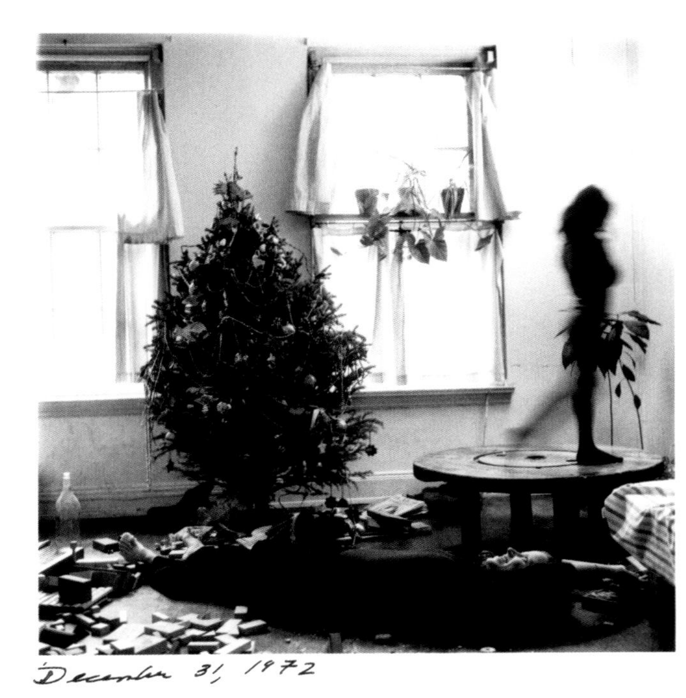

December 31, 1972

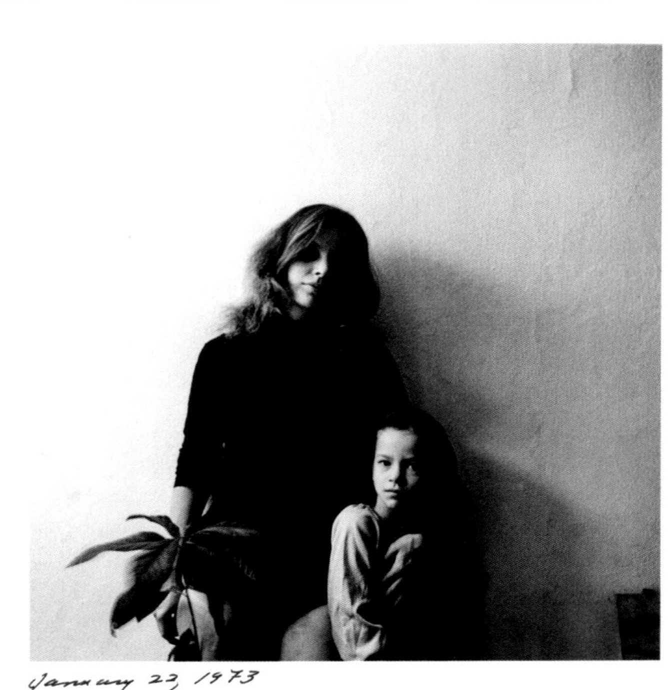

January 22, 1973

daily practice taking pictures of herself at home—amid second-wave feminism's radical inventory of gender roles and inequality.

The domestic, and the labor that went on there, was a critical site of inquiry; as Silvia Federici, the scholar, activist, and author of *Wages Against Housework*, would write in 1975, "To say that we want wages for housework is to expose the fact that housework is already money for capital, that capital has made and makes money out of our cooking, smiling, fucking." Shook was an artist following her instincts, but her personal inquiry can also be seen as a political one. For the male-dominated and still burgeoning field of fine-art photography, the domestic was not widely considered a suitable subject. In Dorothea Lange and Daniel Dixon's 1952 essay for *Aperture*, "Photographing the Familiar," they distinguish between the familiar they champion and the domestic: "The photographer need not suspect the familiar for fear of the domestic. The two are not the same. Nobody likes to look at dull photographs; boredom, in the end, is as outlandish as outrage." Stein argues that Shook's

self-portraits were invested in the balance between the everyday responsibilities of a single mother struggling to support her family— Shook taught at the private Dalton School and led small workshops—while making time for herself as an artist. "Melissa's work is essentially saying, 'But, of course, it's going to be boring some of the time!'" Stein says. And in this plain fact, one might see existential depth. Other times, "explosive surprises" arise—as in the bodily contortions, ghoulish and amusing, like a deranged ballerina—out of images taken April to May 1973. Mistaken for the innocent maiden, Shook reveals herself a clownish sage, an avant-gardist reminding us all of the absurdity of our own mortality.

There's a wisdom to Shook's playful and sincere improvisation— a claim on her own time and bodily autonomy but also a recognition of the losses and loneliness of womanhood, motherhood, the struggle toward selfhood. Critically, she also explores the mother-daughter relationship, a dynamic she had no memory of as a daughter but was remaking as a mother. "Not remembering meant,

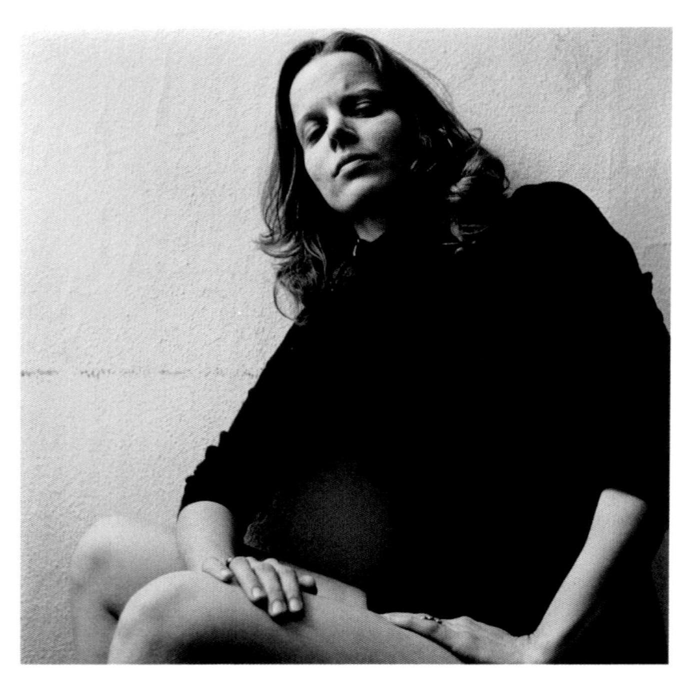

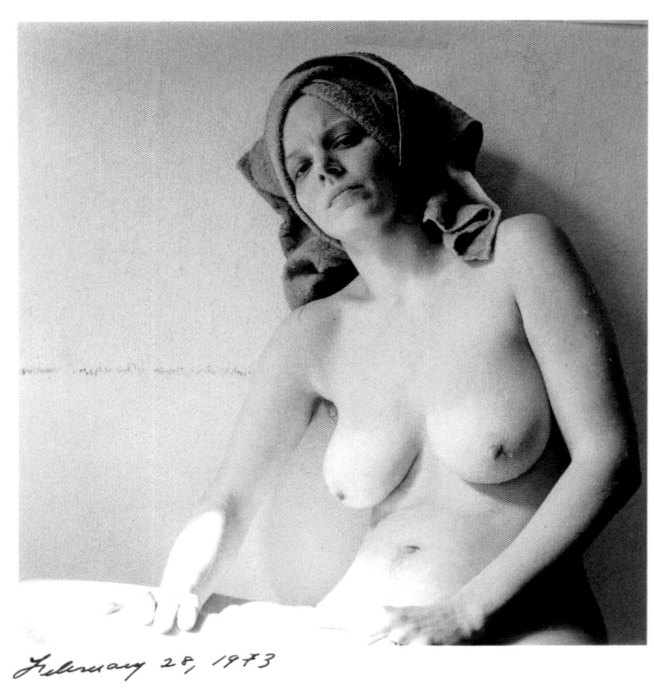

to some extent, having to create a self without the foundation of remembering much about those first twelve years," Shook wrote, "and trying to raise a daughter without remembering having been a child." Shook documented their lives through sustained exposure; the incorporation of the camera into daily reality was, in itself, a radical gesture.

"My mother had a third hand; the camera was always there," Kristina Shook tells me. Shook had met Kristina's father, Darryl Clegg, at Bard College, where they were studying literature and art, respectively; he eventually went west, leaving Shook to care for Kristina on the Lower East Side. "I grew up mixed. I never thought anything about it," Kristina says. "One of my closest friends, Naima [the daughter of the late jazz singer Jeanne Lee], was the opposite of me in terms of having an African American mother and a white father." There is a lovely picture of the two of them on a stoop, Naima's arm around Krissy, one of countless photographs Shook took of her daughter over the eighteen years following her birth in 1965.

"When I look back at these pictures, she was recording our life," Kristina says. "I really have proof that this is what I remember." It was an unconventional, bohemian life, where kids played freely; single mothers, interracial couples, and artists abounded and struggled for money; and the community looked out for one another. It was beautiful, in Kristina's telling, yet not without difficulty or danger. "My mother had to photograph our life—to prove that we were there."

During that time, Shook was deeply influenced by Paul Byers, a Columbia University lecturer whose anthropological view of photography emphasized the importance of the photographer's subjectivity. Will Faller, a neighbor and editor of *Photograph* magazine in the 1970s, was also influential—he taught Shook how to use the darkroom. Shook's friendships with Faller, his ex-wife Marion, also a photographer, and their son, Little Will, were central to her and Krissy's life in New York and to Shook's photographic education.

In both the series of Krissy's childhood and in Krissy's appearances in *Daily Self-Portraits*, Shook's daughter is a natural before the camera. "I forgot it was there," Kristina explains. In one photograph, Krissy stands naked on a wooden chair, arms outstretched as if addressing what appears to be a melon rind on the floor below. Here is the full-throated embodiment of childhood, a world in which Krissy is king. Slowly, over the course of the series, the valance of girlhood descends. Krissy poses ironically for the camera: modeling dresses, bikinis, and costume jewelry. The torture of having her hair brushed. Reading quietly, flanked by stuffed animals. Arms folded behind her back or slung around her knees.

Shook's close observation of others took many forms. Kristina remembers her mother as a curious person, more likely to ask after others than to talk about herself. She interviewed photographers, including Harry Callahan and Steve Szabo, for *Photograph* magazine and other publications. An illuminating and amusing conversation with Roy DeCarava, published in 1983 but conducted primarily in 1977, spans masculinity and money, his signature prints, racism in photography, and the origins of the Kamoinge Workshop, a collective of Black photographers. One has the sense of both a mentee consulting a mentor and two friends chatting over dinner.

Around the time of this conversation, Shook had recently relocated herself and Krissy to Boston for a job teaching photography with Minor White at MIT's Creative Photography Laboratory, where she stayed for three years before moving to the University of Massachusetts Boston's art department. She taught photography with dedication for more than thirty years, most of them at UMass Boston, and might have recognized herself in DeCarava's words: "In teaching you have a serious relationship toward your students, no matter what level it is. It's stimulating. I feel I'm not wasting my time and I think I'm doing some good."

Teaching may have been one way for Shook to look toward the future, through the eyes of her students, a respite from the instinct to look back to the childhood she could not remember. That same 1973 summer of daily self-portraiture, Shook returned to Port Washington, Long Island, to the house of her aunt Marion, which was next door and almost identical to her mother's home, where Shook grew up. There, she tried to re-create scenes from her childhood. These photographs, some of which were featured in the Time-Life Books series in 1975, are quieter than those in *Daily Self-Portraits*; Shook, Marion, and Krissy variously inhabit the space like three generations of ghosts. Shook would continue to photograph herself in several regular yearlong series until her death in 2020 from a brain tumor. Later in life, she became increasingly interested in documenting aging (her own as well as that of family members) and, finally, her experience of cancer, exhibited as *Clutter* at Boston's Atlantic Works Gallery in April 2019; she also used Instagram as an artful, diaristic medium.

"When I look at these photographs, I see a young woman, trapped in a body too attractive for her to manage, much less enjoy, who was battling depression and struggling like the devil not to reveal the pain she was in," Shook later wrote of *Daily Self-Portraits*. Miyako Yoshinaga Gallery, which represents Shook's estate, holds one complete set of these prints; the Nelson-Atkins Museum of Art, in Kansas City, has the other existing set and is planning an exhibition of them in 2024. In these remarkable images, one can observe the pain Shook was reluctant to reveal—but there, too, that sense of searching and slow revelation. In 1972, Shook wrote in her diary, "I can't dislodge the past . . . I'm more aware now that that's specifically what I'm working through and using in my work—the source of it—the source of my depression also, but a coin which won't flip over and let me free myself."

Shook's approach as a photographer began largely in response to the absence left by her mother's death. But by chasing memory, searching to recover a sense of self, Shook was making herself in the process. With the daily self-portraits, she began to flip the coin, and we see in the uncertain movement a map of difficult discovery. That the work is gaining new audiences today, fifty years later, is a testament to its honesty. Through disappointment, longing, fear, frustration, determination, sadness, sensuality, and boredom, nothing is hidden. And there is new relevance to Shook's insistence that her and her daughter's lives—the care and care work, the artful and the demanding, all of it pictured at home—warranted close looking. Kristina wants to be sure her mother's photography is not forgotten. Seeing these photographs now, through the eyes of others, Kristina observes, "I keep discovering her."

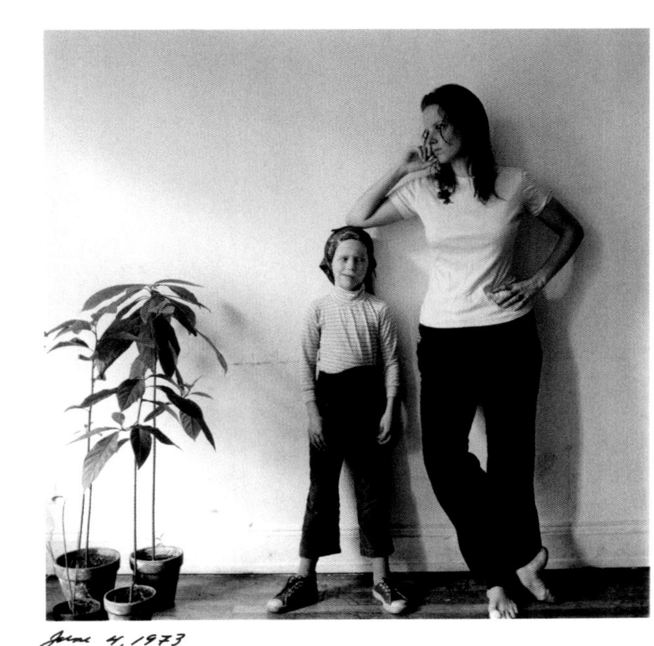

June 4, 1973
All photographs from the series *Daily Self-Portraits* 1972–1973
© Kristina Shook and the Estate of M. Melissa Shook, and courtesy Miyako Yoshinaga Gallery, New York

Lucy McKeon is a writer and editor based in New York.

Nakeya Brown
Black Beauty Still Lifes

Lovia Gyarkye

Nakeya Brown began making still lifes in 2012, after her baby was born. Motherhood changed Brown's relationship to time, forcing her to fit a practice into fragmented days and corners of her home. In arranging the Afro pick in *Nu-Vogue* (2022) or the eucalyptus stem in *Native-Accents* (2020), Brown wrestled with her thoughts and stalled time. Staging these vivid, polychromatic sets became an exercise in control.

That Brown, a Maryland-based photographer, works with objects of Black beauty is a consequence of maternity. Children invite reflection. Searching the banks of her memory, Brown returned to hair-care rituals and other aesthetic rites of passage in Black girlhood. She explored their attendant ideas in *The Refutation of "Good Hair"* (2012), a series of portraits (and some still lifes) in which Black femmes masticate on bundles of Kanekalon. It's an early example of how Brown's work cannibalizes desire, interrogating aspirations for and expectations put on Black hair.

Did she need the bodies? Brown is a Black working mother without a studio (an under-discussed privilege among artists), and her days are structured by another person's needs. As she cared for her child, she wondered: Could she experiment without models, which come with the fuss of schedules and ateliers? In the series *X-pressions: Black Beauty Still Lifes* (2020), Brown ditches the figures and plays, exclusively, with objects. These works are her "solitary space," the necessary realm bell hooks argued—in "Women Artists: The Creative Process," an essay Brown cites as foundational to her practice—that women need for dreams and visions.

The images are a form of world-building. Within each frame, Brown stages dramas of desire and Black femininity. They are performed by spirits of the archive. You can't see who owns the pick in *Nu-Vogue*, but you can feel her presence. She is a version of Brown, a woman reveling in community and nostalgia. The Afro pick leaning against the green wall connects her to a broader African diaspora, as do the colors (red, green, and black) of the set. Copies of a style magazine, issued by the Black-owned hair and cosmetic company Dudley's, rest underneath a crimson calla lily. A cassette of the iconic 1990s R&B group En Vogue stands upright. The objects are arranged by height, a formal decision that creates a cascading effect, encouraging viewers to follow an invisible trail with their eyes.

Native-Accents responds to white, Eurocentric norms of beauty and emphasizes the labor of Black hair. An undated copy of *Native Accents Braids* magazine, a braiding style guide, sits next to an instructional pamphlet. Their coupling underscores the technique and skill required to perfect certain hairdos and offers a counterimage to the popularity of silk presses and perms. *Like Natural* (2020) shares similarities to *Native-Accents*, but here Brown has built a shrine to the diversity and range of cuts and coiffures available for Black femmes.

Brown culled these archival materials from her own collection. They are gifts from friends, wares sourced online, and half-forgotten products from her own drawers. They hold secrets and evidence of past lives. When Brown plays with them—leaning photographs against planters in *BBBShow* (2022), or angling rollers just so in *Afro-Curls* (2020)—she assumes the role of director. She reanimates the quotidian and reclaims their rituals.

Lovia Gyarkye is a writer based in New York.

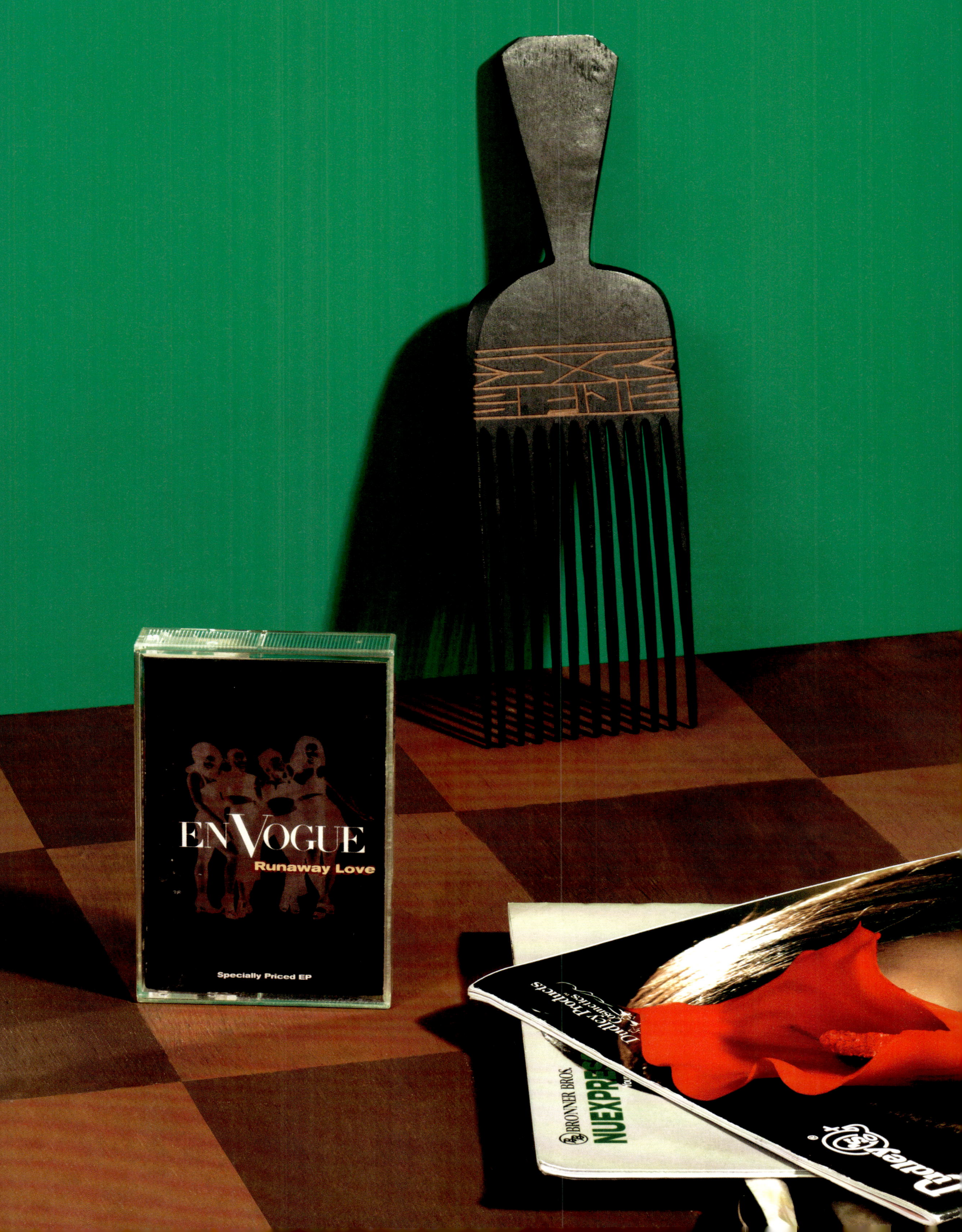
ENVOGUE
Runaway Love
Specially Priced EP
BRONNER BROS.
NUEXPRESS
Dudley Products
cosmetics
Duke

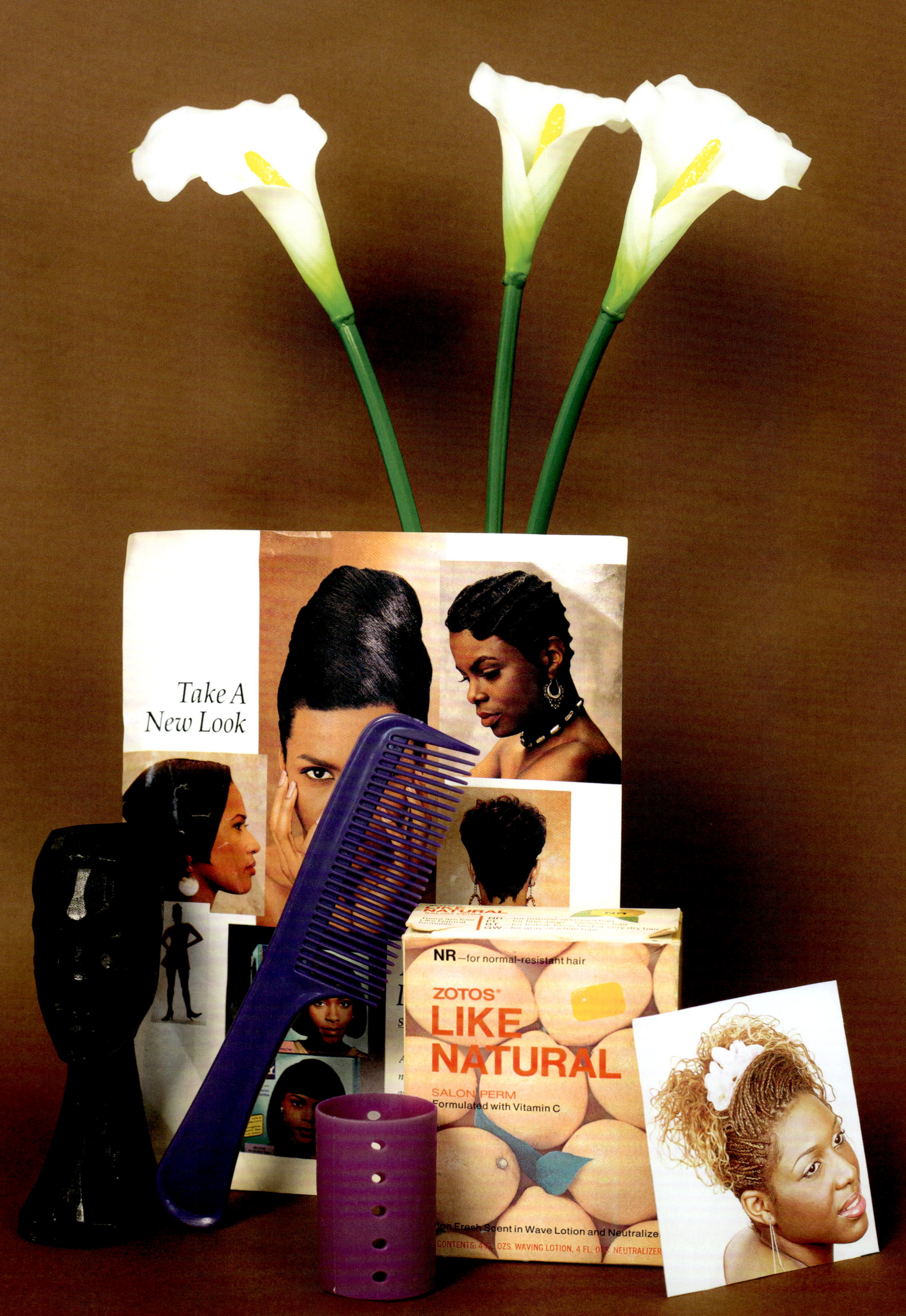
Take A
New Look

NR—for normal-resistant hair

ZOTOS
LIKE
NATURAL

SALON PERM
Formulated with Vitamin C

Fresh Scent in Wave Lotion and Neutralize

CONTENTS: 4 FL. OZS. WAVING LOTION, 4 FL. OZS. NEUTRALIZER

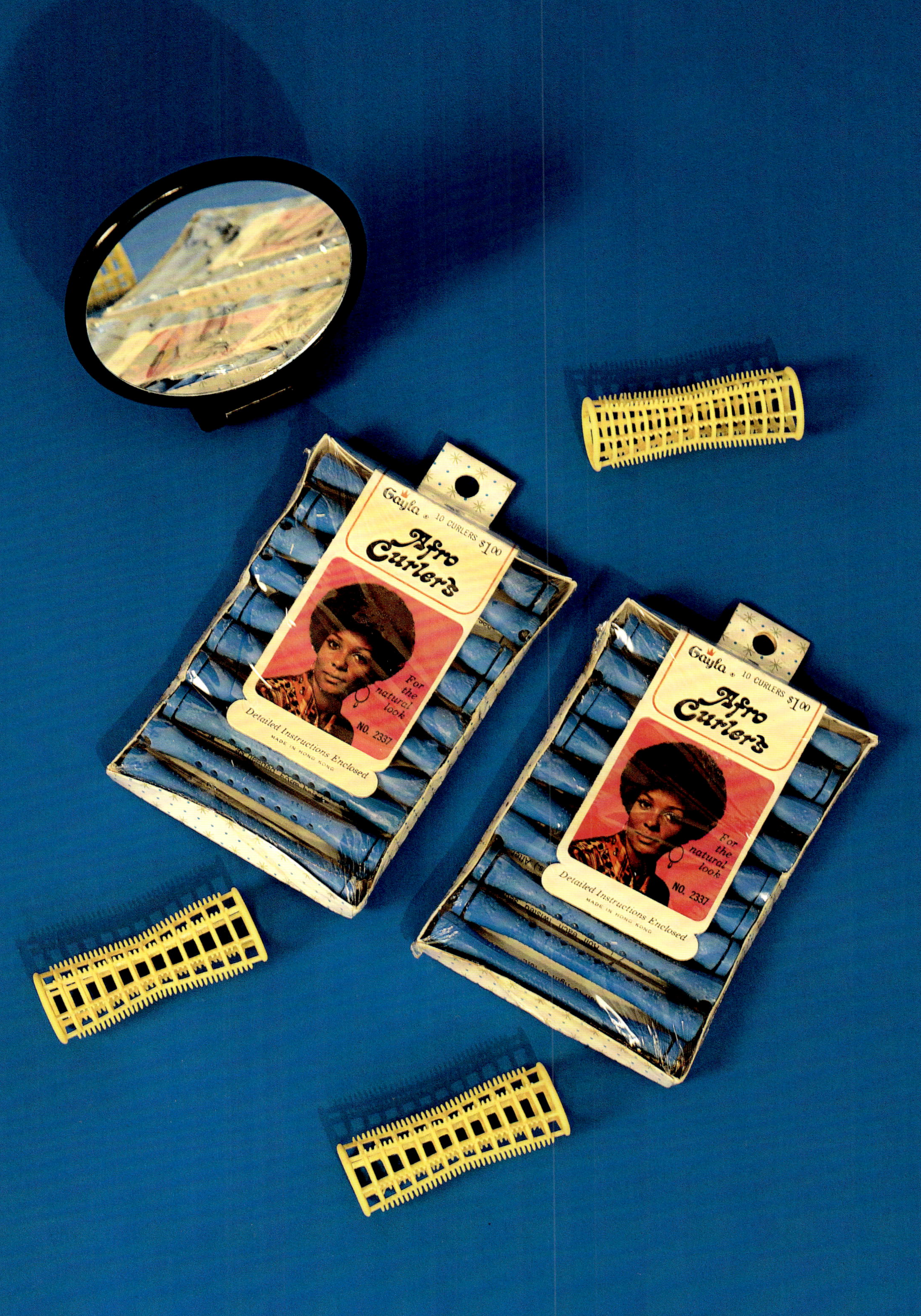

Gayla   10 CURLERS $1.00
Afro
Curlers
For
the
natural
look
NO. 2337
Detailed Instructions Enclosed
MADE IN HONG KONG

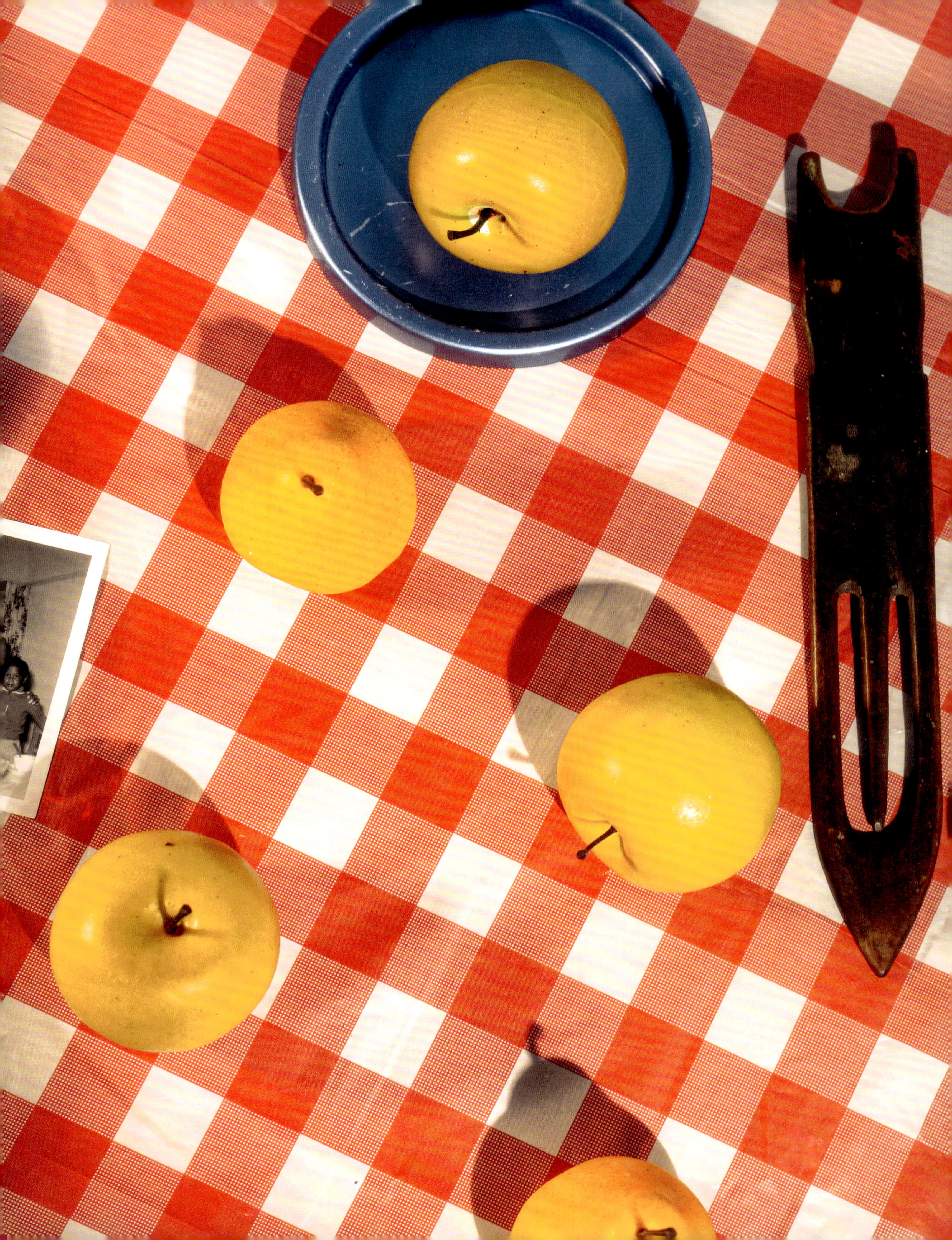

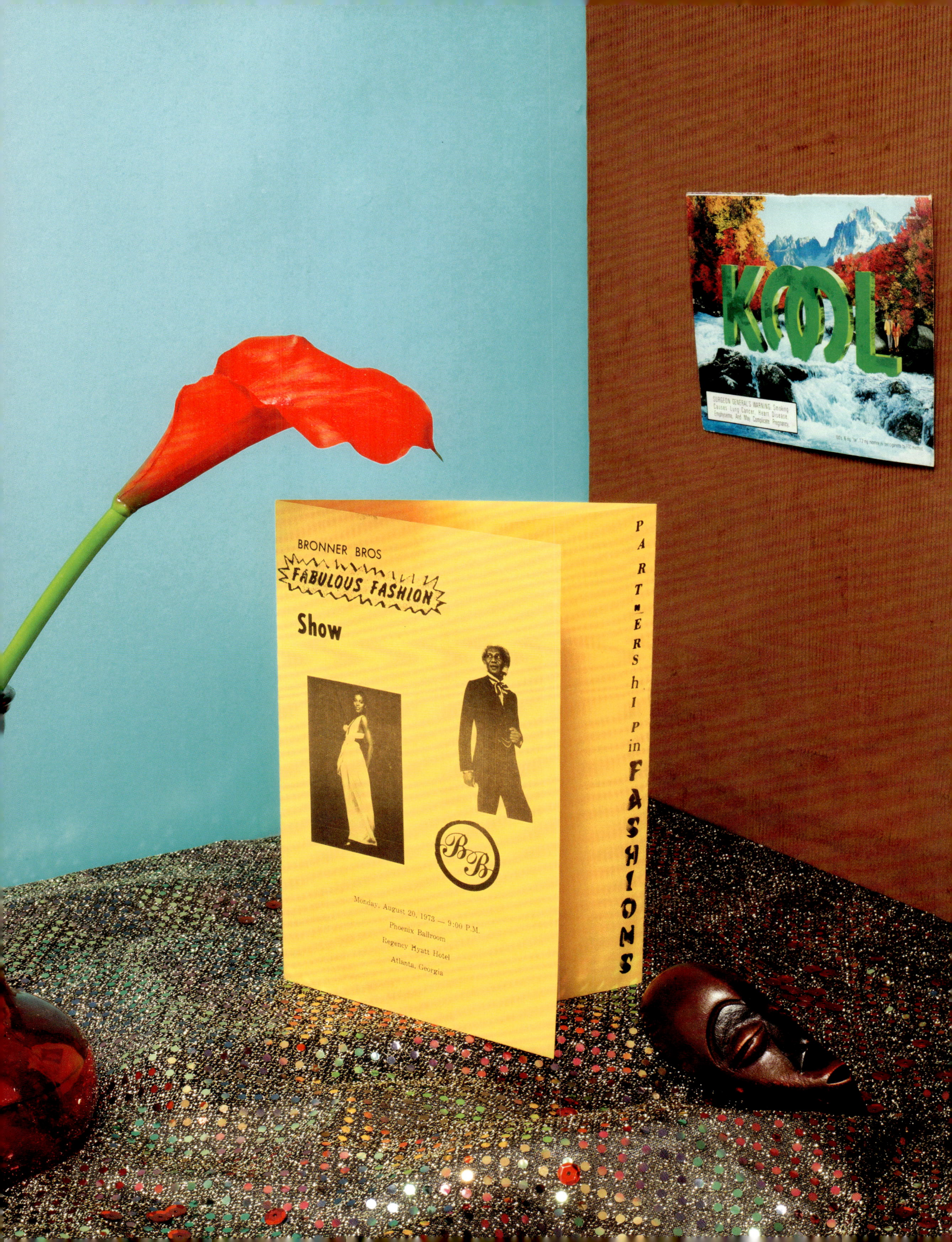
BRONNER BROS
FABULOUS FASHION
Show
BB
Monday, August 20, 1973 — 9:00 P.M.
Phoenix Ballroom
Regency Hyatt Hotel
Atlanta, Georgia
PARTNERSHIP in FASHIONS
KOOL

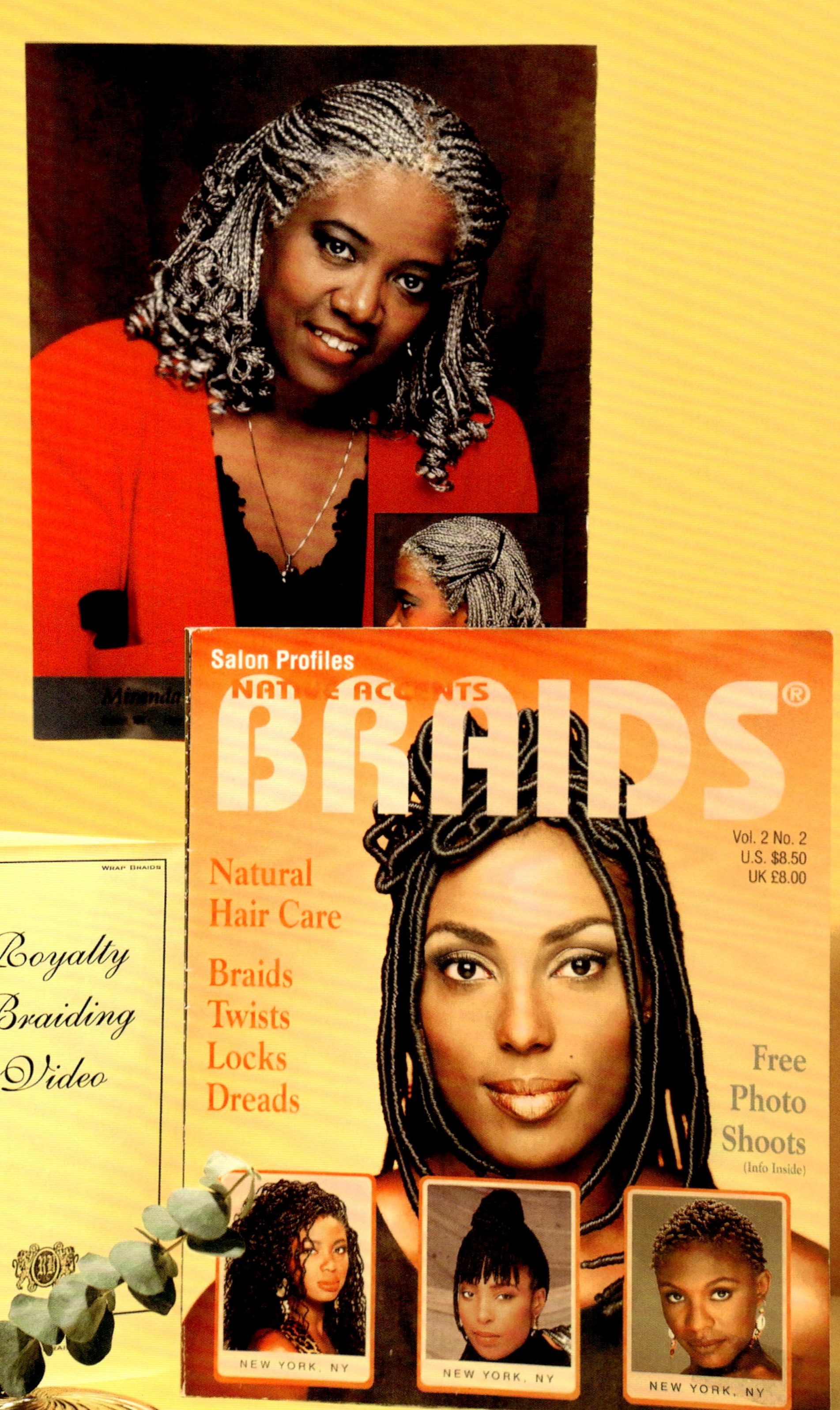
Royalty
Braiding
Video
WRAP BRAIDS
Salon Profiles
NATIVE ACCENTS
BRAIDS®
Vol. 2 No. 2
U.S. $8.50
UK £8.00
Natural
Hair Care
Braids
Twists
Locks
Dreads
Free
Photo
Shoots
(Info Inside)
NEW YORK, NY
NEW YORK, NY
NEW YORK, NY

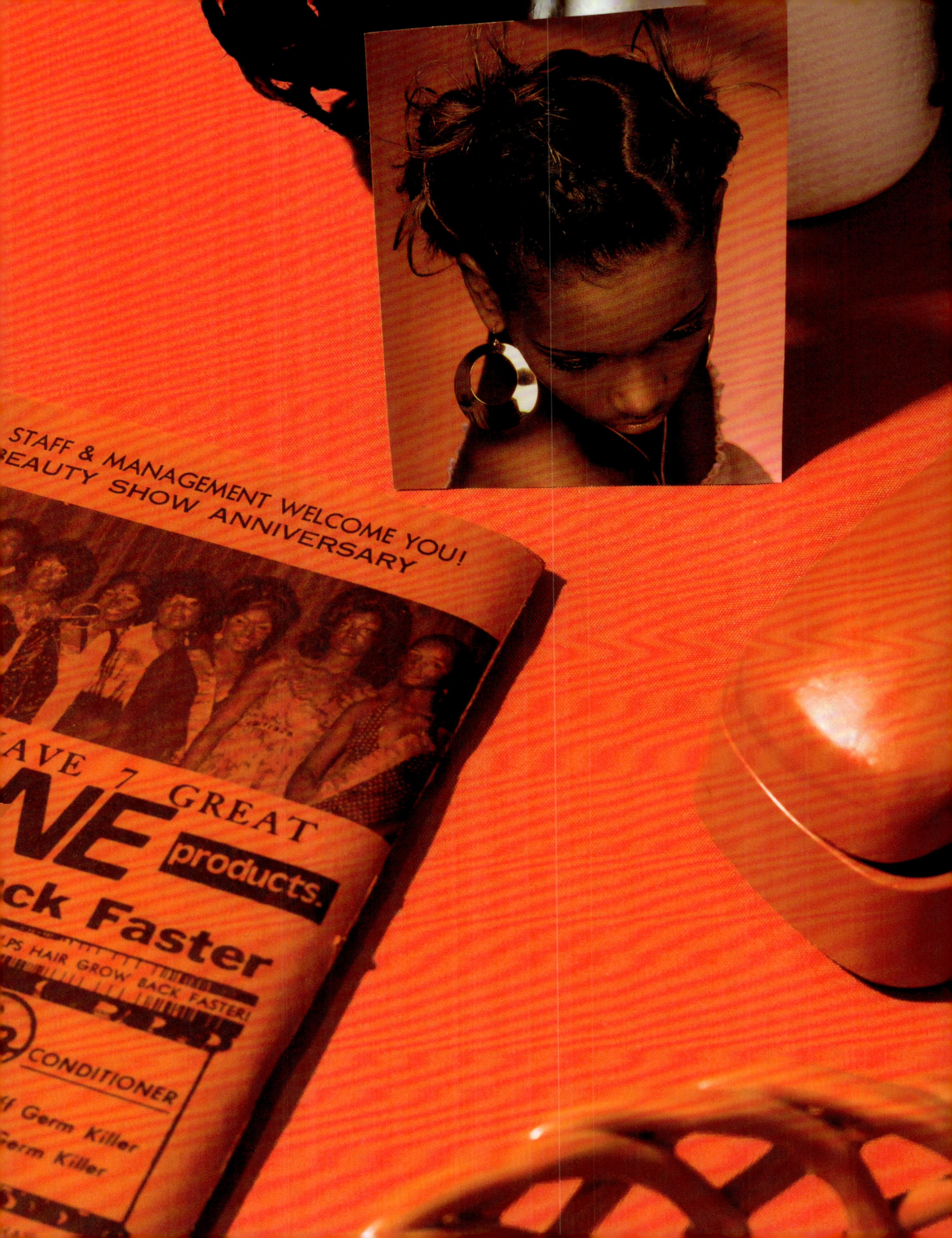
STAFF & MANAGEMENT WELCOME YOU!
BEAUTY SHOW ANNIVERSARY
HAVE 7 GREAT
VE products.
ck Faster
HELPS HAIR GROW BACK FASTER!
CONDITIONER
Germ Killer
Germ Killer

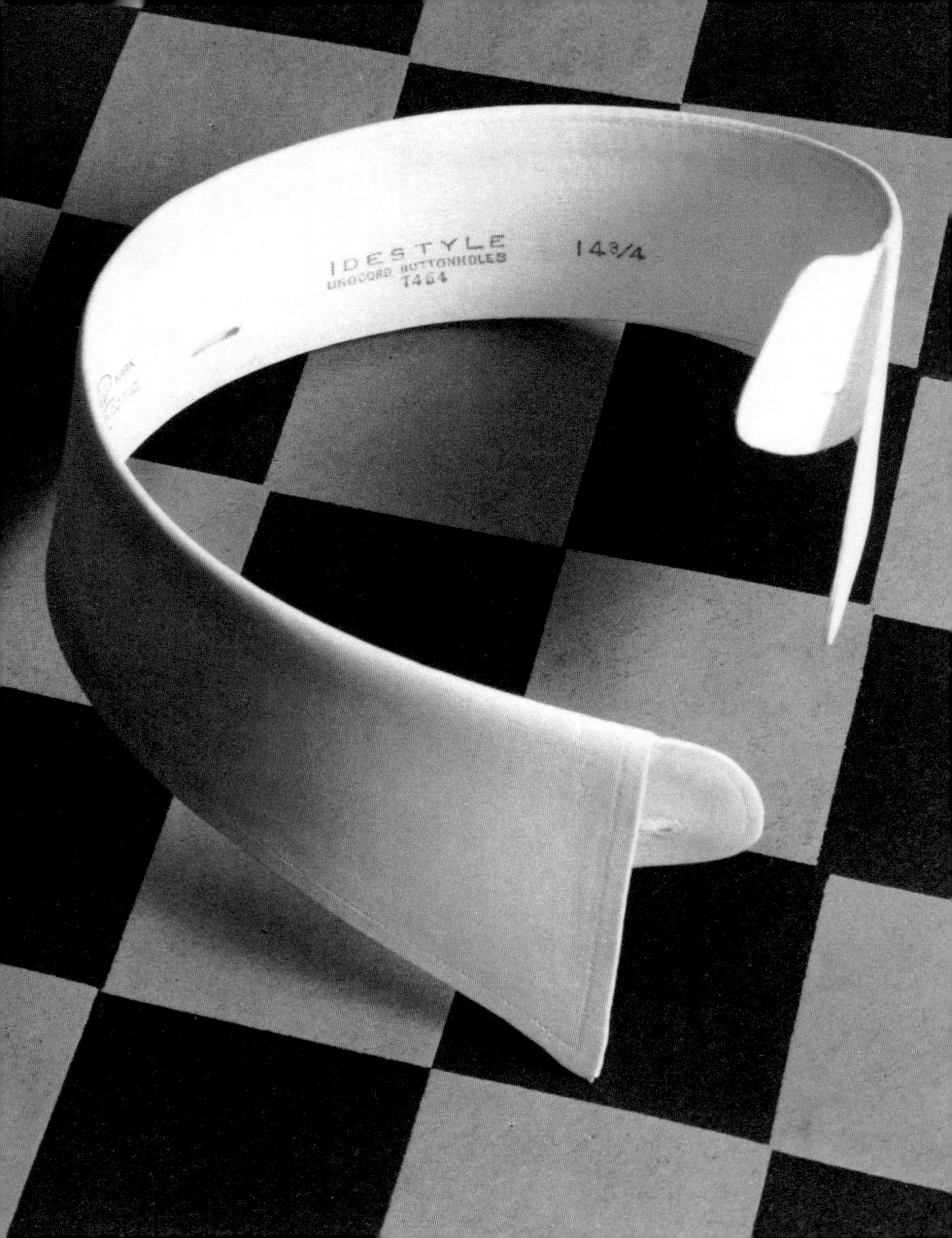

IDESTYLE
UNCORD BUTTONHOLES
T464
14 3/4

Everything Shines

When it comes to advertising, great photographers have always worked between art and commerce.
Brian Dillon

By turns luxe and austere, sometimes both in the same image, the work of Paul Outerbridge occupies a special vantage in the sleek, vexed space between modernism and Madison Avenue. In the black-and-white *Ide Collar* (1922), which was made the year he began photographing for *Vogue*, a detached white shirt collar—a svelte size fourteen and three-quarters—sits alone on a checkerboard surface. The picture is part New Realist severity, part found object or readymade (Marcel Duchamp tacked a copy on his studio wall), and wholly expressive of the venerating isolation that has been essential to product photography since its inception in the 1850s. In Outerbridge's later advertising work, especially the color carbro prints for which he is now best known, a busier style of composition dominates. But objects still float in opulent detachment; in a series of advertisements for "petal soft" Scott toilet paper from the late 1930s, the product unrolls among jewellike flowers on plain-colored backgrounds.

Outerbridge is one of the few photographers working in the early twentieth century to be featured in the exhibition *Objects*

Is it still possible for a photographer to take advertising as a subject when advertising has blurred into social media?

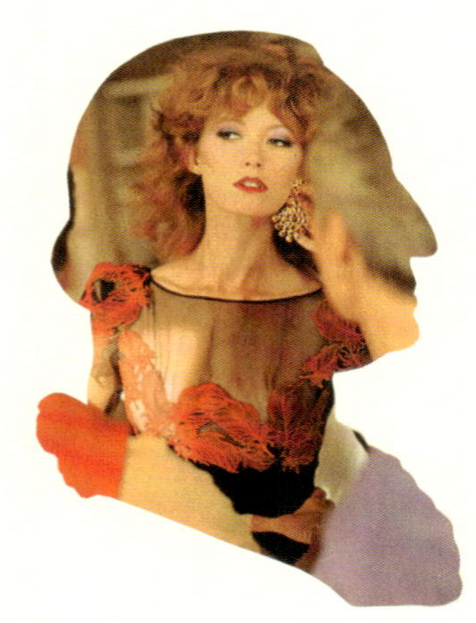

of Desire: Photography and the Language of Advertising, curated by Rebecca Morse, that ran in the fall of 2022 at the Los Angeles County Museum of Art (LACMA). As a mostly US-centric survey of, or argument about, relations between art and advertising from the 1970s onward, the accompanying catalog acknowledges some earlier critiques of commercial photography and its motives: Pop art, the Independent Group, the near-poetic analyses of advertisements in Marshall McLuhan's book *The Mechanical Bride* (1951). (All of which may also be said to be half in love with the imagery they borrowed or analyzed.) Among the most energetic pieces in the show was Pat O'Neill's 1964 film *Bump City*: a four-minute color portrait of LA as a circus of headlights, neon, and billboards depicting lurid and monstrous foodstuffs. For the most part, however, Morse's focus is more explicitly critical (and theoretically informed) photography of the decade following, when, as she puts it, advertising "became a generative source for material, conceptual framing, and physical output."

There are some familiar images and artistic maneuvers in *Objects of Desire*—beginning with the *Pictures* exhibition at Artists Space in New York, in 1977, and the associated artists who may, or may not, have actually been in that show. Morse organizes her material according to "formal qualities, content, sites, and systems of production." Appropriation and recontextualizing are key: in Richard Prince's rephotographing of Marlboro cowboys, in Sherrie Levine's montage of a fashion model and George Washington's silhouette for *President Profile I* (1979), or in Victor Burgin's coolly distanced black-and-white studies of the texts and textures of America in *US 77* (1977). Burgin, alongside artists such as Barbara Kruger and Mitchell Syrop, introduces a verbal element that (as Morse notes) drew on recent translations of Walter Benjamin and Roland Barthes—the advertising caption being repurposed as self-aware critical tool. The larger narrative at work here tells us that photographers (unlike painters) only really began to make

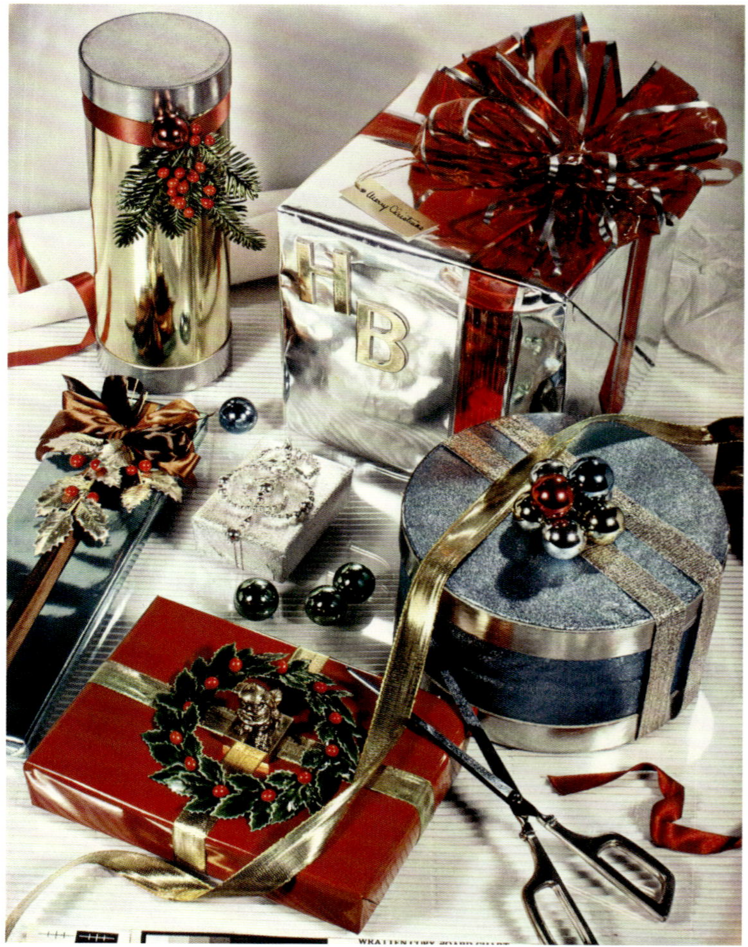

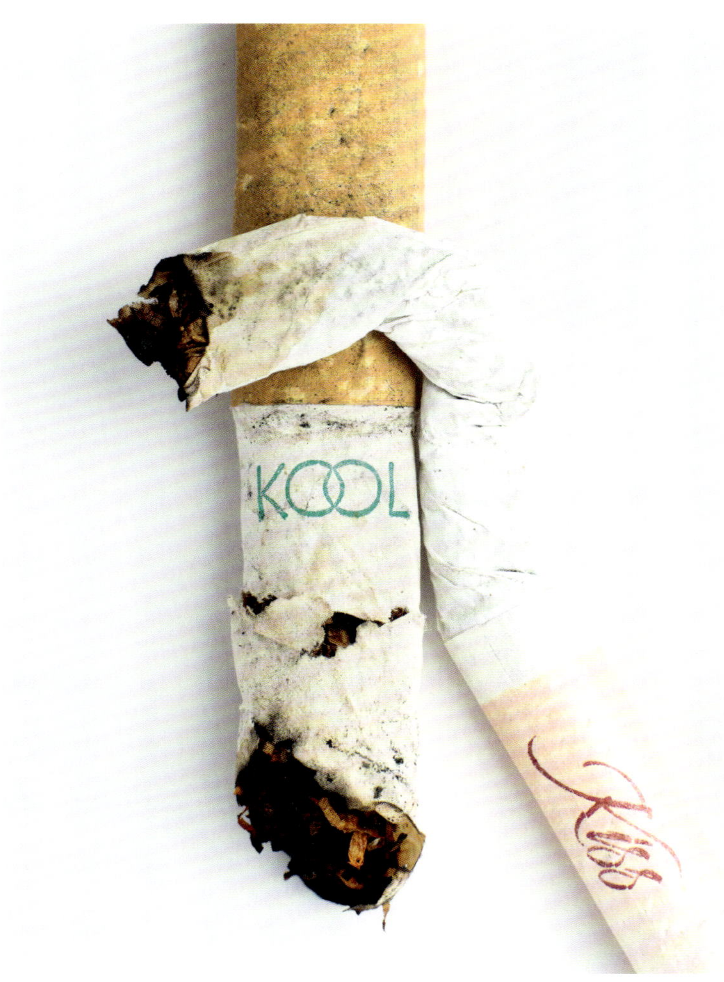

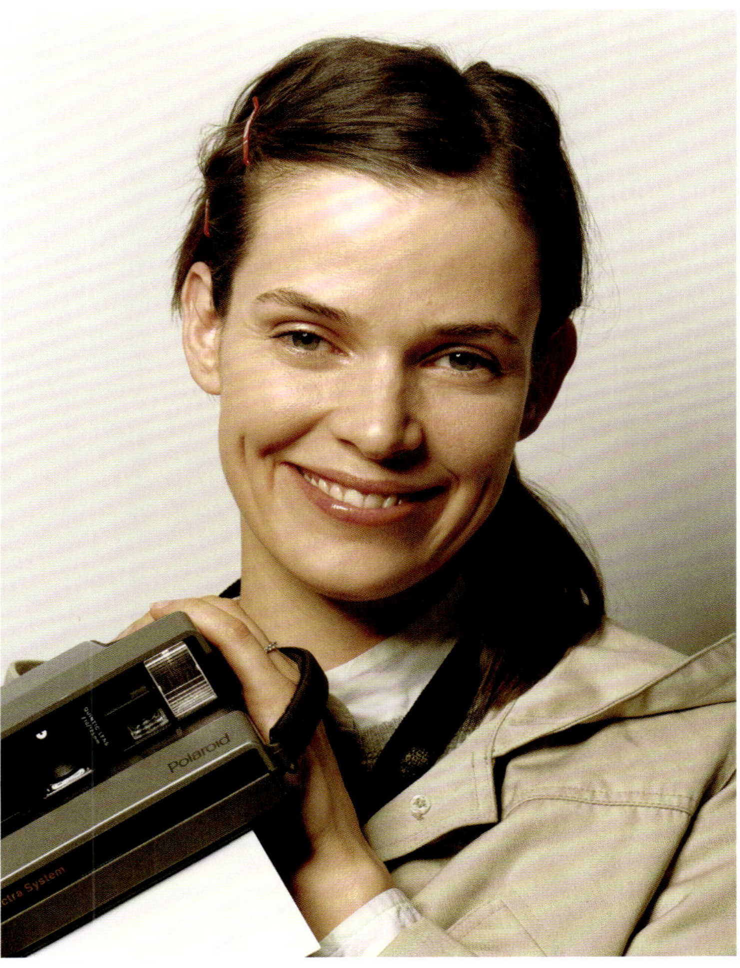

This page, left:
Natalie Czech, *Kool Kiss/*
***Cigarette Ends*, 2019**
Courtesy Kadel Willborn,
Düsseldorf

Right:
Roe Ethridge, *Nancy*
***with Polaroid*, 2003–6**
© the artist and courtesy
Andrew Kreps, New York

images along these lines when advertising photography was already well over a century old.

Where does the output of an artist such as Outerbridge fit in this story about photography's belated reflexivity when it comes to advertising? Do he and his contemporaries really occupy an era of naivety or moral blankness about how their imagery affected its publics? On the one hand, Outerbridge simply illustrates the obvious fact that great photographers have always moved easily between art and commerce, and a picture like *Ide Collar* can be excerpted from its original context to sit alongside what Morse (surely begging the question) calls more "personal" work. But something in Outerbridge's images, and in the wider history of advertising photography, pushes at, or worries, its commercial context too—and always has done, in ways both artists and audiences have understood. (This is very clear in the photography of cosmetics and makeup—pushed to a deliberate extreme in the long and daring history of Shiseido's advertising campaigns, for example.) And this quality, which can't be reduced to commercially minded aesthetics, is quite missing from the categories broached in *Objects of Desire*. It has something to do precisely with texture, with an allure that often verges on obscenity or disgust.

Consider, for example, Outerbridge's *Christmas Gifts*, the first picture of a sequence published in *House Beautiful* magazine in December 1936. As Morse points out in her catalog text, the photograph has already detached itself from the usual run of seasonal advertising and editorial pointers to yuletide gift ideas—instead, it advertises the very idea of giving. The absence of specific products is part of its appeal, or supports its real import, which is that here, in the weeks and days before the holiday, *everything shines*. There isn't a single object—ribbon, bauble, scissors, or wrapping—that isn't aglow and agleam with festive promise. So much so that the image seems somewhat in excess of its purpose, and enters into that realm of early color photography where things

have taken on an unearthly glow. Outerbridge's Christmas gifts
have the bizarre, slightly sickly texture and hues pursued in
the portrait and advertising photographs of Madame Yevonde
in the United Kingdom, another master of the carbro process in
this period.

There is a strain of post-*Pictures* photography in *Objects of
Desire* that addresses this textural glamour. At its subtlest, it's
present in Roe Ethridge's *Nancy with Polaroid* (2003–6), where the
model and her Spectra camera have the neutral tones of the more
tasteful end of 1980s or early 1990s advertisements—hard not
to linger on the slightly too-muted tones of lipstick and raincoat,
which signal too hard their sophistication. The knowingly unsubtle
version is Jo Ann Callis's series *Cheap Thrills and Forbidden
Pleasures* (1993). Drawing on the kind of color food photography
that goes back to the work of Nickolas Muray in the 1940s, Callis
made fifteen images of store-bought desserts against more or less
plush surfaces. Cream puffs, pear tarts, doughnuts, éclairs: they
advertise their own lusciousness in an overstated fashion that
is already familiar from advertising rather than being satirically
exaggerated. (A relatively unexplored theme in *Objects of Desire*
is the way such work responds not to photography but color
television, where foodstuffs, especially, took on a kind of monstrous,
gelid life.)

Where does this textural aspect of advertising, also of earlier
examples that appropriate and repurpose advertising, live in
contemporary photography beyond the selections of LACMA's
show? The overloving attention to the surface and color of things
that one sees as much in Callis's images as in those by Outerbridge
is abjectly present in Natalie Czech's *Kool Kiss/Cigarette Ends*
(2019). An obvious reference point is Irving Penn's 1970s series
of detailed anatomies of the dead cigarette, exhibited as exquisite
platinum-palladium prints, quite as if they were uptown portraits
or sumptuous still-life studies. For Penn's delicate black-and-white
tones, Czech substitutes dusty pinks and greens and orange
backgrounds that rhyme with the brand names printed on filters
and butts: Kool, Kiss, High Life, Fact, True, Select, Heritage, Lord,
Prince, King. The isolated object against its flattering ground is
drawn from the long history of advertising and product photography,
but the textual element is grubby, decayed, a pathetic promise of
liberty or prestige.

A modest but charged instance of the kind of isolation within
profusion that is necessary to advertising can be seen in pictures
of storefronts and interiors across Latin America by the Mexican
photographer Pablo López Luz. The storefront, of course, is the
space, or the image of sorts, in which products advertise and project
themselves. As David Campany points out in López Luz's 2021 book
Baja Moda, the shop window has been a subject for photographers
since at least the time of Eugène Atget's early twentieth-century
records of disappearing Paris. In 1958, for *Fortune* magazine, Walker
Evans's series *The Pitch Direct* depicted New York sidewalk displays
as lavishly low-key arrangements of color. What links Atget, Evans,
and López Luz is the sense of a localized and provisional holdout
against the larger forces of corporate takeover, gentrification, and
advertising itself as it separates from the place and time of exchange.
There are no store owners or customers in López Luz's clothing
and shoe stores, just the things themselves against their improvised
backdrops—frail promises of humble luxury.

Is it still possible for a photographer to take advertising as
a subject when advertising has blurred or dispersed into social
media? The globalized-glamour version of this subtler intrusion
into everyday screen life is certainly there in the work of Sara
Cwynar, whose 2017 film *Rose Gold* was included in the LACMA
show. In a sense, "rose gold" is the very definition in recent decades
of the way a product—in this case, a 2015 iteration of the iPhone
and, subsequently, the many products meant to mimic it—may

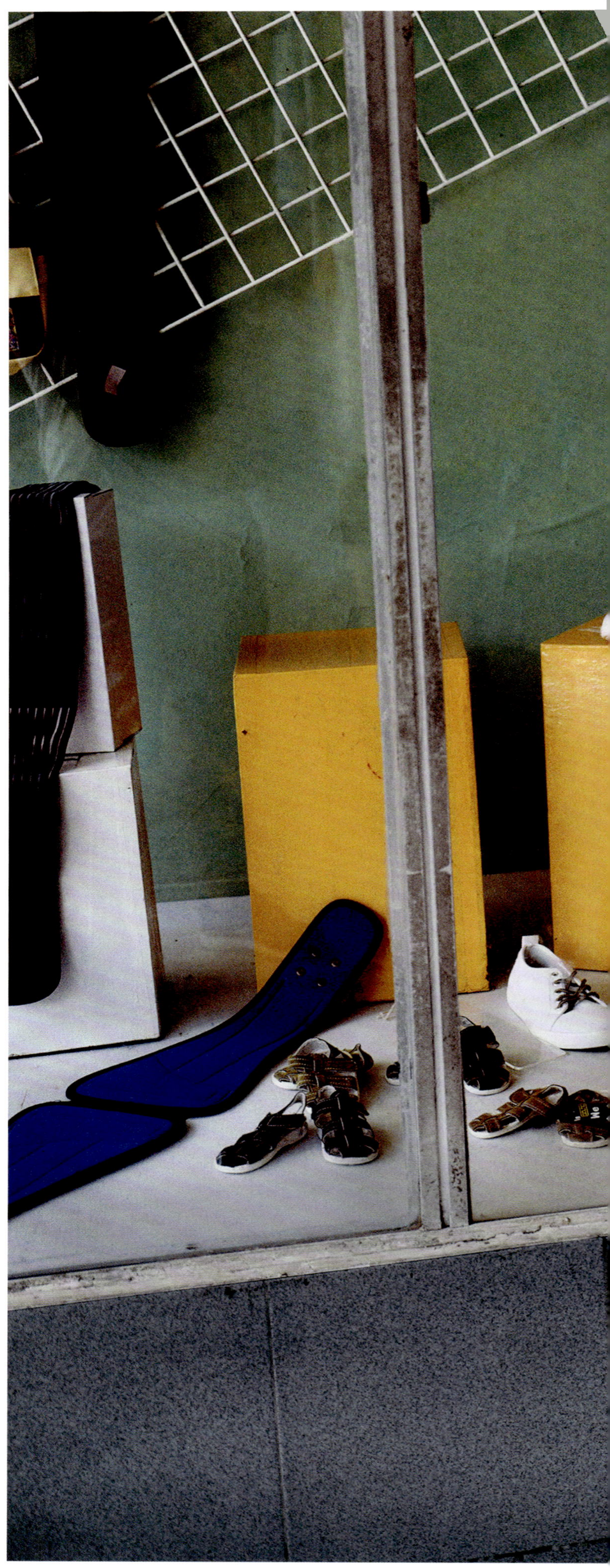

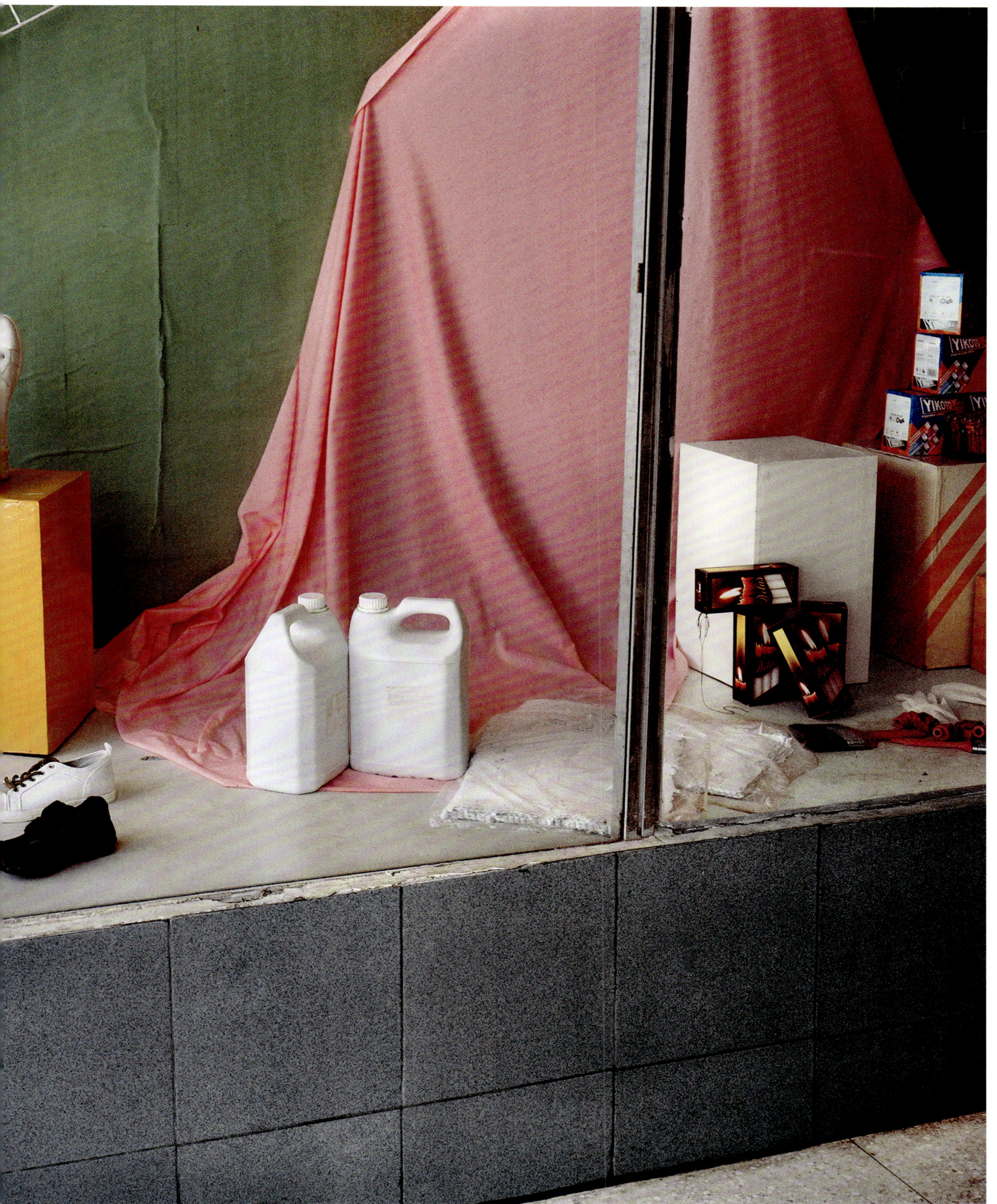

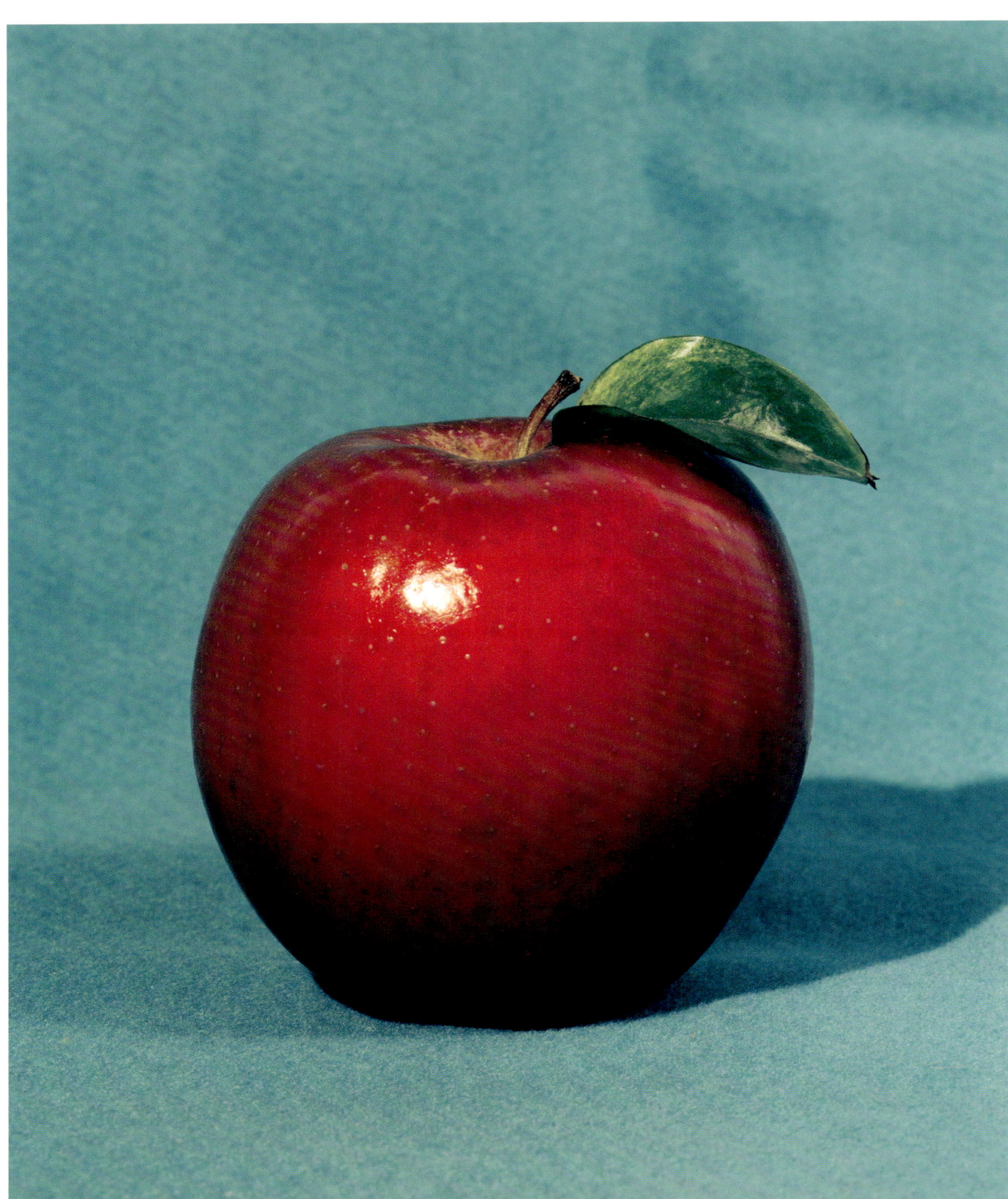

overstate its visual presence on the screen, on the page, or in reality.
(The color seems new but dates, at least, to the jewelry of Peter Carl
Fabergé in the nineteenth century.) Cwynar has explored in later
moving-image works, such as *Glass Life* (2021), the decades-long
profusion of online imagery, our laborious curatorial approach
to the pictures leached from our own lives, the corporeal advances
and regressions involved in gestures of swiping and pinching.
But there are ghosts in her art, too, of the kind of unreal isolation
to which advertising photography such as Outerbridge's once
subjected the object. In *Apple for Scale (After Steve Jobs)* (2022),
an apple is modeled after one in a framed photograph behind Jobs
in a 1977 portrait. Cwynar's too-bright, too-red apple looks as if
picked from another of Outerbridge's *House Beautiful* spreads—
a Thanksgiving scene in which everything is austerely itself and,
at the same time, far too much.

Brian Dillon is the author of *Affinities: On Art
and Fascination* (2023).

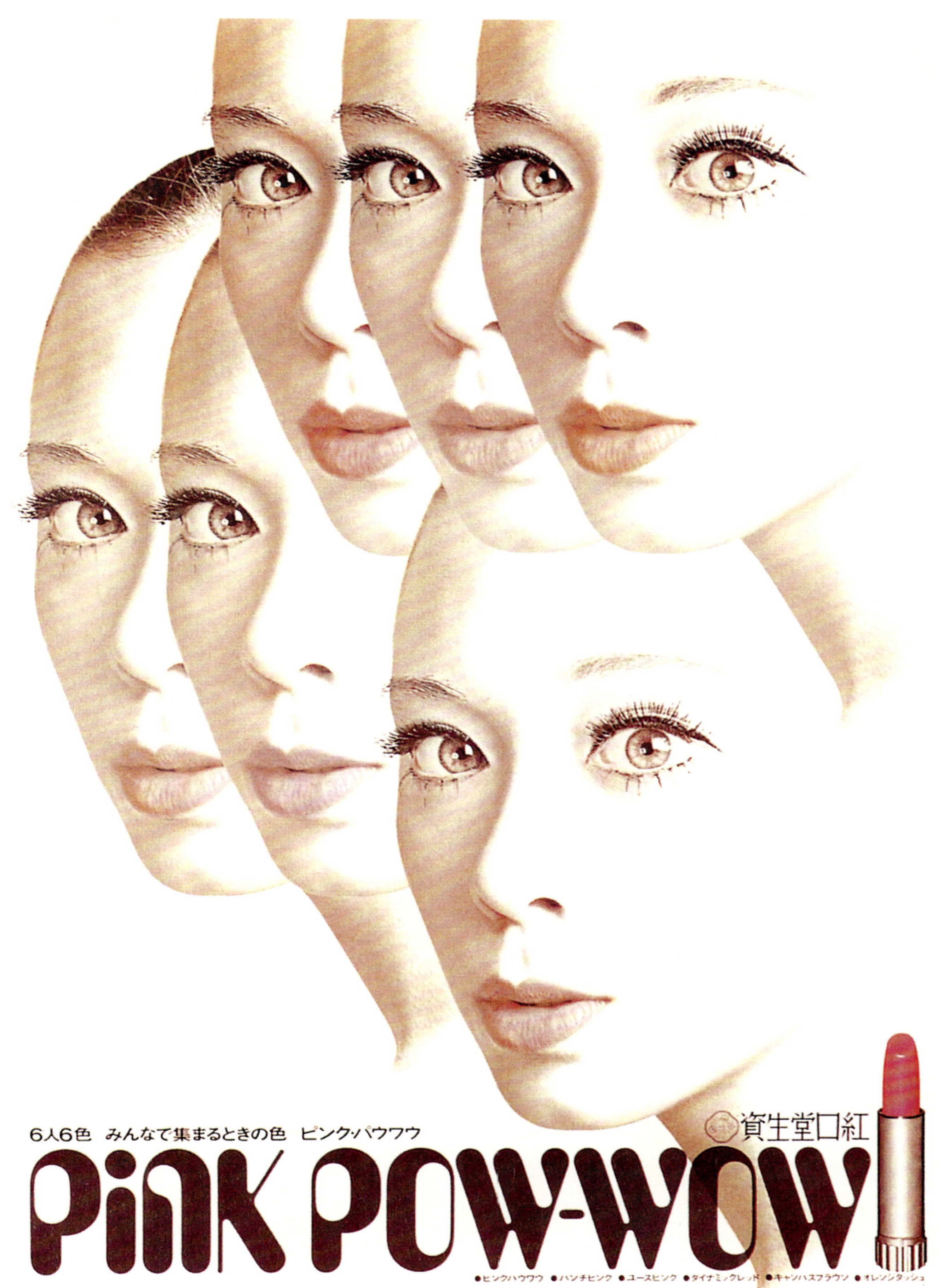

Poster for Shiseido Pink Pow-Wow, 1969, from *Creative Works of Shiseido* (Kyuryudo Art Publishing, 1985)

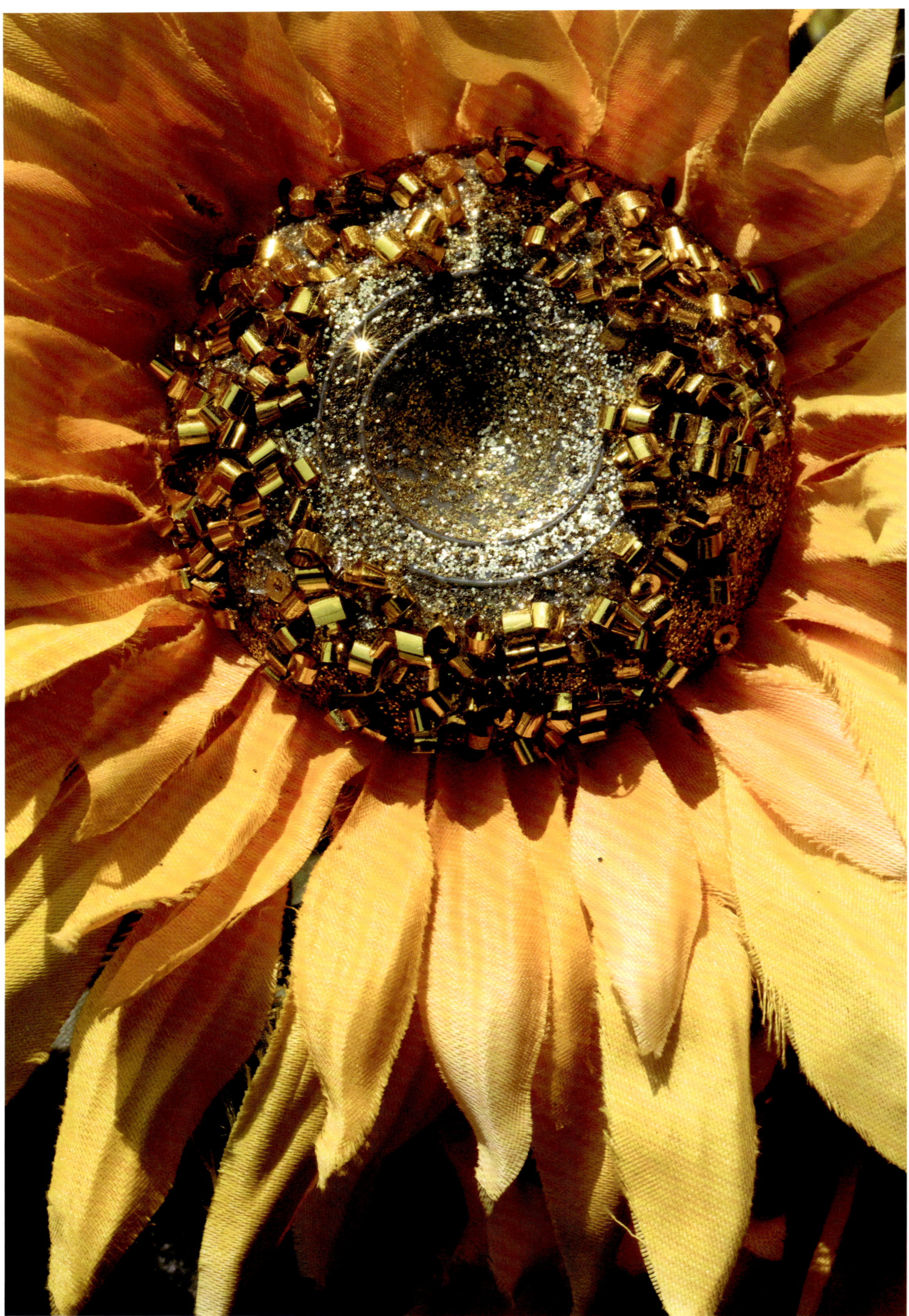

In the spring and summer of 2020, as COVID-19 restrictions halted travel and kept millions of people indoors, cities began to get wild again. Deer grazed in the streets of Nara, Japan, and dolphins were spotted in the canals of Venice. Nature seemed to be taking back control. Yet when the photographer Oto Gillen wandered the avenues along the west side of Manhattan, where he was born and raised and still lives today, he noticed a very different kind of super bloom: crops of fake flowers, their too-bright petals fashioned from synthetic fabrics and plastic, sprouting from the sides of bars and restaurants or emerging from real dirt in sidewalk planters. Overnight, grimy corners became kitschy Instagram backdrops designed to attract outdoor diners. Gillen sensed something more sinister in these cheerful garlands, which may take centuries—if not millennia—to decompose. They're emblematic of the human tendency to aestheticize nature by the same means our species is destroying it. Surely enough, when the lockdown ended, the dolphins fled; perennially, the fake flowers remain.

The photographs in *This Odor*, Gillen's solo exhibition at Lomex Gallery, in New York, earlier this year, magnify to larger-than-life scale artificial blooms that the artist spotted on the street. Made with a digital camera and a 200mm prime lens, they are startling for their extreme detail; like a bee's vision, his camera picks up details that would evade a human eye, including errant cigarette ash and stray hairs. Gillen was inspired by the botanical studies of Karl Blossfeldt, a leading photographer of the New Objectivity school, whose crisp close-ups of plant forms, taken in the early decades of the twentieth century, focus attention on organic geometries. Gillen's work also references Bernd and Hilla Becher's photographs of industrial architecture. Like the pair's typological studies of the 1960s to 1980s, Gillen's crisp images have an unusual amount of human pathos; their glitter and polyester belong on a drag queen's décolletage. At the same time, the flowers' soiled edges feel relatably fatigued.

New York's streets have always been Gillen's primary subject. His breakthrough presentation in the 2017 Whitney Biennial, *New York* (2015–2017), comprised a black box slideshow of nearly eight hundred digital photographs, many depicting NYPD guns, barricades, and surveillance cameras—an easily overlooked but foreboding presence in an increasingly gentrified and militarized city. Gillen grew up in the meatpacking district, a former industrial zone famous for public sex that in recent years has become a banal destination for Sunday brunchers. He is particularly sensitive to signs of urban change. A 2022 solo exhibition at Löwengasse, in Cologne, Germany, featured dozens of photographs of the gasoline-powered generators that run New York hot dog carts and halal stands. Parked on curbsides, their flatulent presence is surprisingly easy to miss. Captured in high resolution, they look like dirty shrunken heads, spirits of an environmental degradation that we ignore at our own peril.

For the last few years, Gillen has been transferring his digital photographs to dye-sublimation prints on custom-built aluminum panels. On a practical level, the panels are designed to absorb rather than reflect light, so they can be easily photographed without glare in a gallery. Yet their industrial medium also mirrors their message. As objects, Gillen's photographs are as artificial as the subjects they depict, pointing to the ways photography itself has changed in the age of global warming. There can be no return to nature in the Anthropocene, and no nature photography without the polluting marks of human presence. "There's something really sad about the cliché of flower photography," Gillen says. "It kills a living thing by isolating it in time, but it will never attain the power or sensation of it." There's no escaping the ecological anxiety of his flower portraits, or the sense that they show us what we're in the process of losing. Polyester is an ugly substitute for a petal, but it will remain, forever fresh, as the world around it continues to decay.

Oto Gillen
This Odor

Evan Moffitt

Opposite:
sunflower, 8th avenue, may 11, 2023; page 84: *morning glory, hudson street, march 30, 2023*; page 85: *plum blossom, 7th avenue, may 17, 2023*; page 86: *daffodil, macdougal street, may 22, 2023*; page 87: *daisy, perry street, march 18, 2023*
Courtesy the artist

Evan Moffitt is a writer and critic based in New York and London.

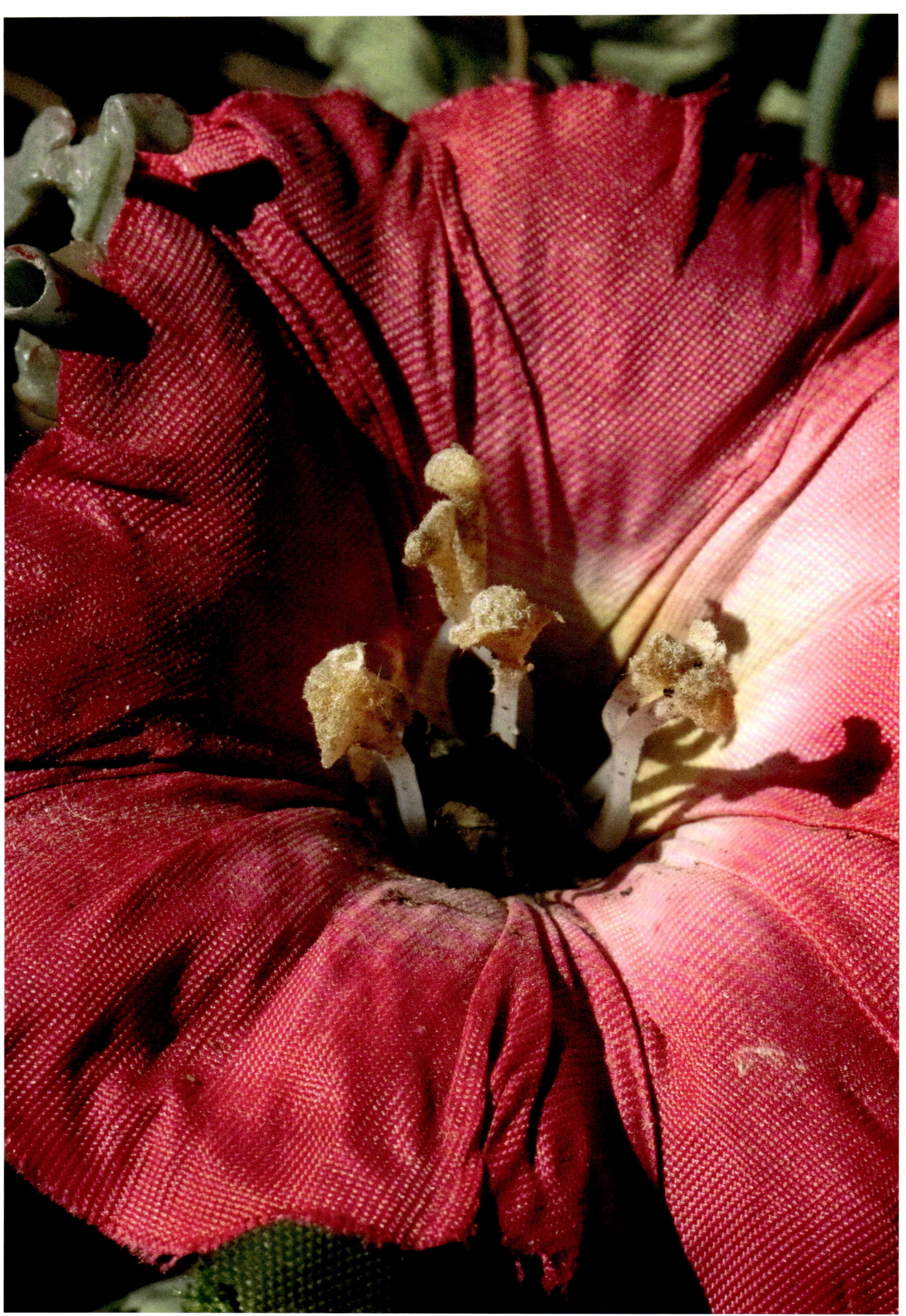

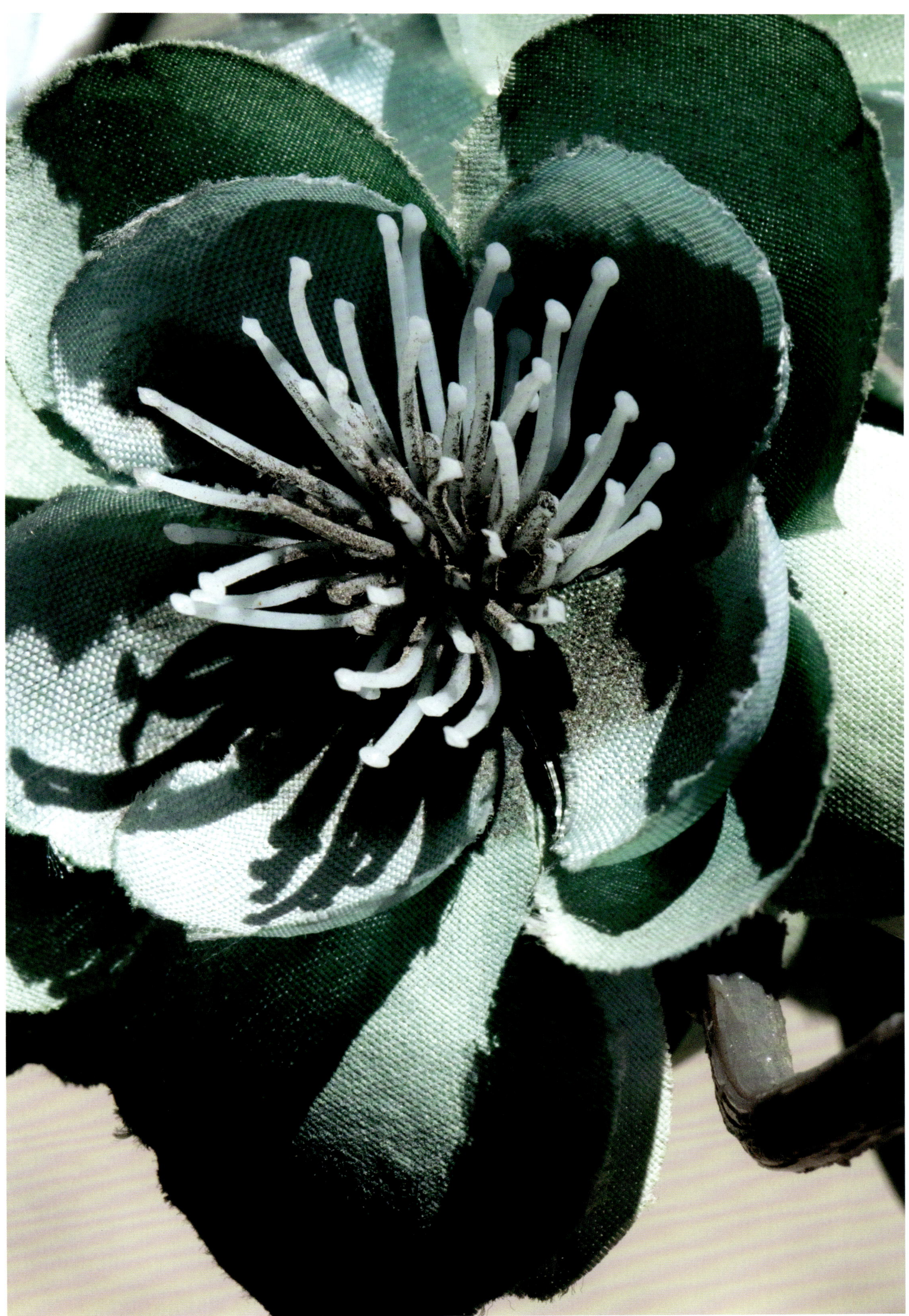

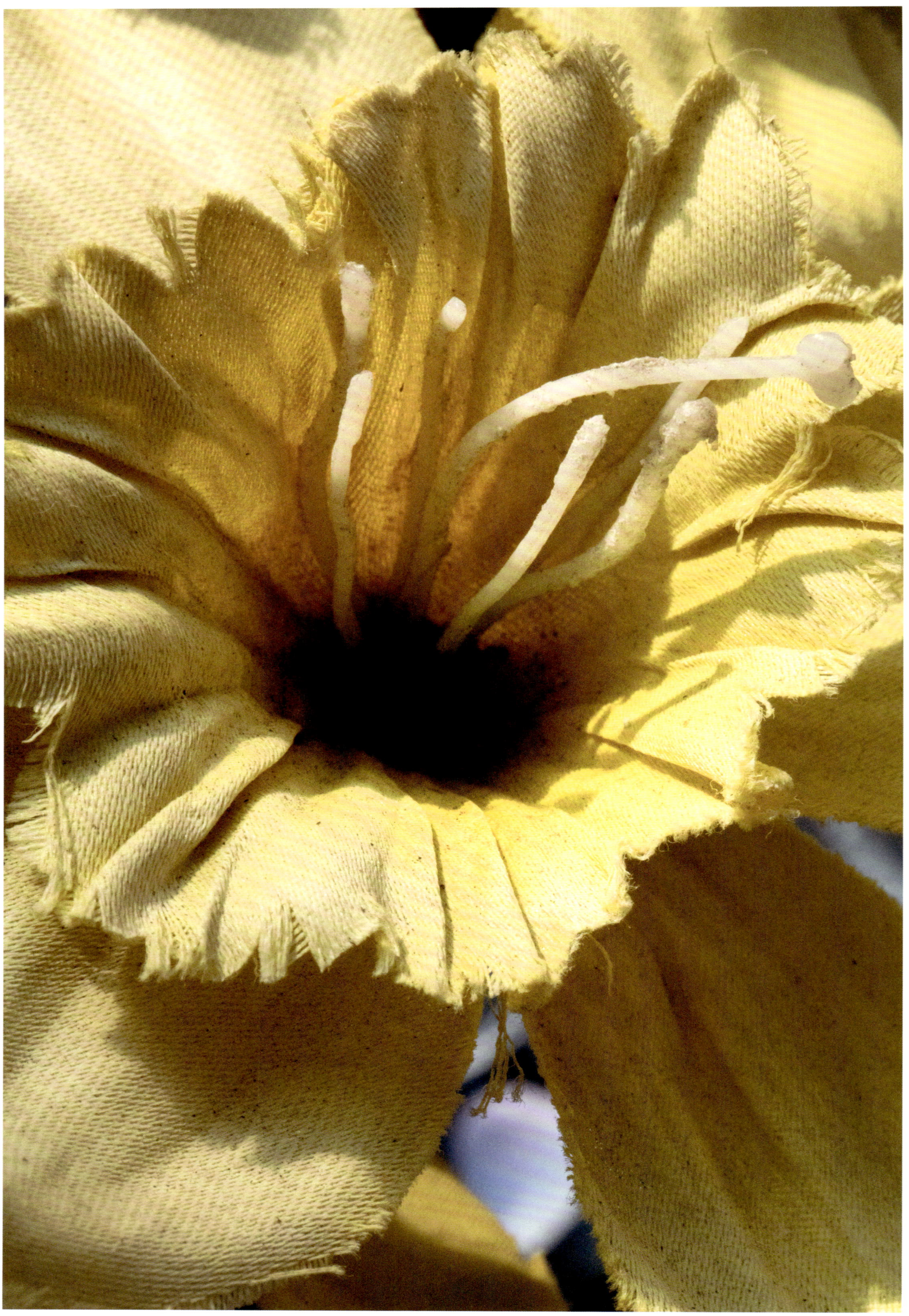

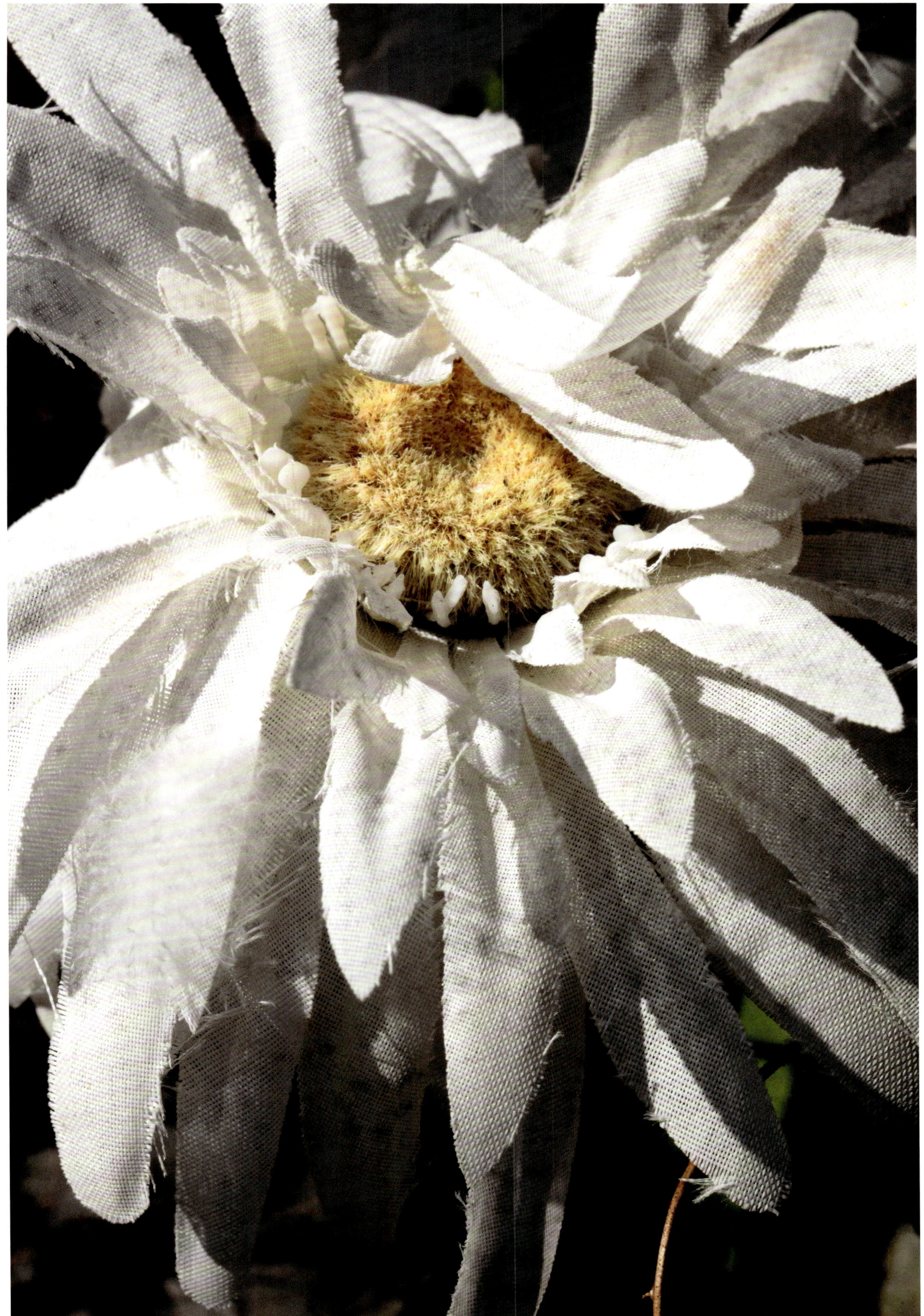

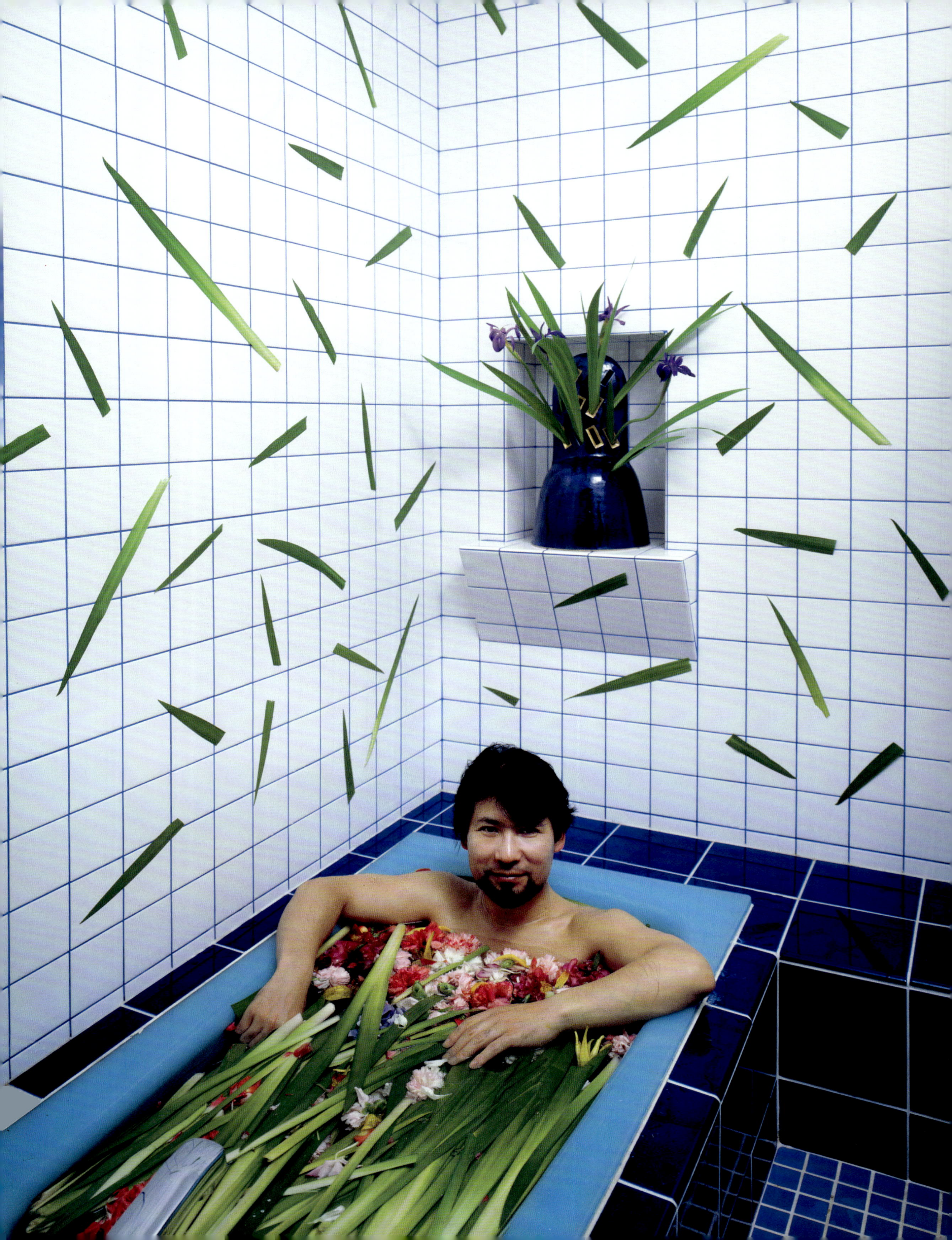

Inspired by jazz, improvisation, and conceptualism, the ikebana artist has created playful works that merge disciplines.

Kosen Ohtsubo's Flower Planet

Daniel Abbe

For nearly fifty years, Kosen Ohtsubo has run roughshod over the idea of ikebana as a stately practice of arranging flowers in a vase. He is known for using vegetables, when he sticks to plants at all, and he often sets his compositions in unconventional containers. His 1984 work *I Am Taking a Bath Like This* was arranged in his own bathroom. On one wall, a cobalt vase in a small alcove holds some flowering irises. But this is only an accent within the wild gaiety of the entire piece, in which iris leaves have been plastered across the tiled room and gather neatly in the tub below, next to an array of flowers including roses, yellow lilies, and hydrangeas that just cover the bare chest of a man lying in the drawn bath. That's Ohtsubo himself, with a faint but devious smile playing across his face. Is Ohtsubo's own body also part of the "arrangement"? His knowing gaze, which lures the viewer into the scene, is directed toward the camera, operated in this case by Koichi Taniguchi, a photographer employed by the ikebana school to which Ohtsubo belongs. Recently, Ohtsubo has exhibited his ikebana in the form of photographs. He collaborates with other photographers, most often Taniguchi, though he sometimes operates the camera himself.

    Now in his mid-eighties, Ohtsubo lives in Tokorozawa, a suburb of Tokyo, in a house that also serves as his studio and

I Am Taking a Bath Like This, 1984

Ohtsubo has taken a gleefully unorthodox approach to ikebana, a practice of flower arrangement that emerged in Japan roughly six hundred years ago.

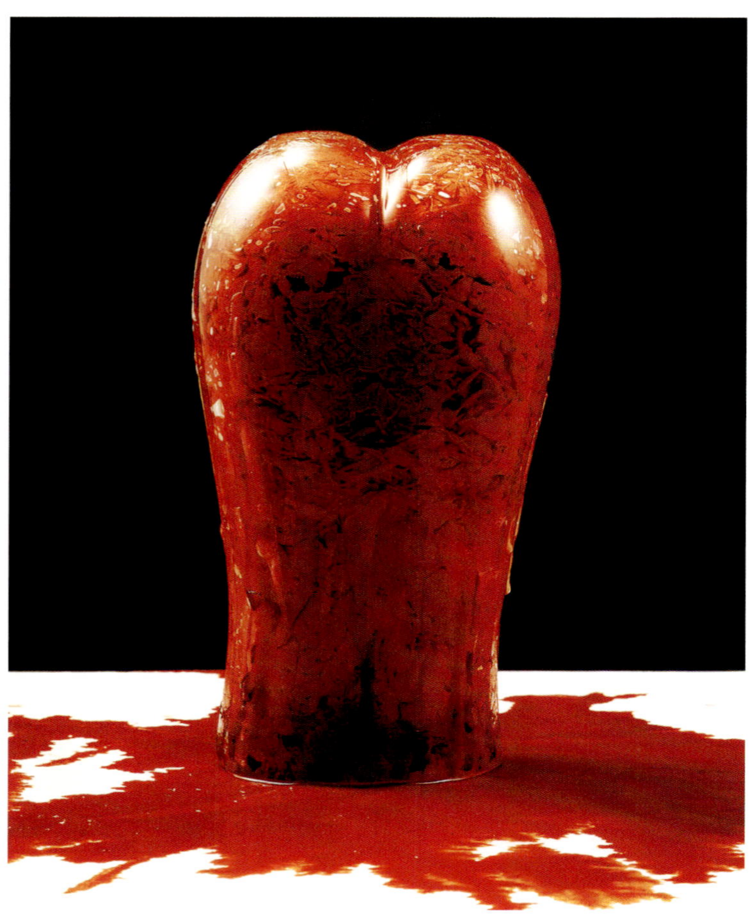

classroom. The building's exterior is clad in ruddy steel plates that call to mind Richard Serra, but, by contrast, a charming, goofy sign that reads "Flower Planet," in colorful and playful letters, hangs above the door. When I visited Ohtsubo in late 2022, he greeted me warmly and invited me to lunch before we started speaking about his work.

Ohtsubo has taken a gleefully unorthodox approach to ikebana, a practice of flower arrangement that emerged in Japan roughly six hundred years ago. Since then, various methods of displaying plants in vessels have been developed, discarded, and revived. In its modern form, the study and exhibition of ikebana are largely administered by various schools, to which almost all artists belong. Ohtsubo is no exception; for many years, he worked as one of the top teachers of the Ryuseiha School, and even in retirement he continues to serve as a special advisor to the school's headmaster. Ohtsubo's having such an esteemed position is somewhat ironic: when I spoke with him, his eyes lit up as he talked about how he wanted to produce work "with the goal of destroying ikebana." Against the more rigid aspects of ikebana, Ohtsubo sought to introduce the rambunctious energy of free jazz, which he listened to eagerly as a teenager. In 1971, he caused a stir with his contribution to the Ryuseiha's annual exhibition: he gathered up plant clippings and trash left behind by other artists who were preparing their ikebana on-site, threw everything into a large canvas bag, and put *that* on display. The act drew excitement and scorn in equal measure.

Submitting a sack of botanical trash to an official exhibition was a deliberately provocative gesture. Since then, Ohtsubo has continued to poke at the limits of ikebana; he titled one 1988 composition *Is a Vegetable Stir Fry Avant-Garde Ikebana?* It is, in fact, a vegetable stir fry, not so much arranged as *plated* in a large dish. But Ohtsubo is no simple jester: the work forces the viewer to consider what separates plating from arranging, cooking from ikebana. To prod the discipline in this way recalls the gestures of conceptual artists from the 1970s, whom Ohtsubo watched carefully. For example, he was deeply impressed by *Between Man and Matter*, a large 1970 exhibition in Tokyo in which Arte Povera and Mono-ha artists were shown alongside each other. Highlighting the Greek artist Jannis Kounellis in particular, Ohtsubo tells me that he was drawn to conceptual art for the same reason that he liked free jazz—it "rejected a traditional aesthetic, and tried to take an attitude toward material itself." In other words, these practitioners of different disciplines—music, ikebana, contemporary art—are linked by a shared desire to go beyond the accepted structures of art.

Even so, Ohtsubo is also capable of working in classical modes. Take *Rikka of Lotus* (1993), in which three lotus flowers run straight down the middle, while their leaves extend outward with the slight asymmetry that corresponds to classical ideals of beauty within ikebana. The entire composition curves thrillingly through space, describing a gentle arc to the left, while the top leaf returns back to the central axis. The arrangement is placed in a studio, and here the photograph seems to be more clearly about recording the plants at hand. "Photography is not able to completely grasp the content of ikebana," Ohtsubo says. Looking at this photograph, I can only imagine the smells and spaces that the picture cannot contain.

Perhaps for this reason, the relationship between these two forms has not always been friendly. The avant-garde ikebana artist Yukio Nakagawa, a precursor to Ohtsubo, also engaged extensively with photography, using techniques gleaned from the famed Japanese photographer Ken Domon. Nakagawa also swore off traditional materials and vessels. His most famous work, *Flowery Priestess* (1973), shows nine hundred carnation petals stuffed into a blown-glass vase, which has been turned upside down so that the paper below is stained with a red liquid that has spilled out. This could not possibly be stored in a museum—audiences today

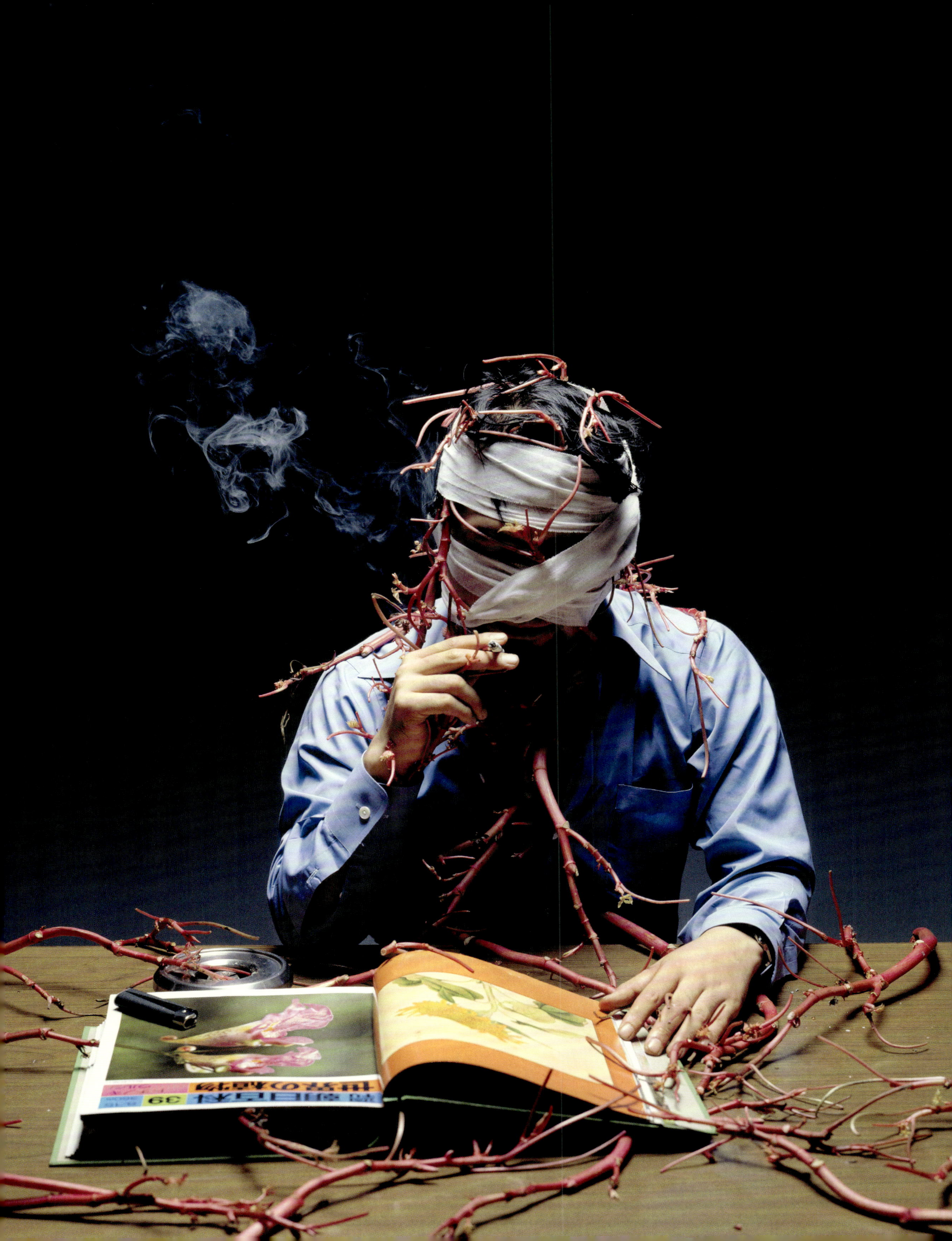
39

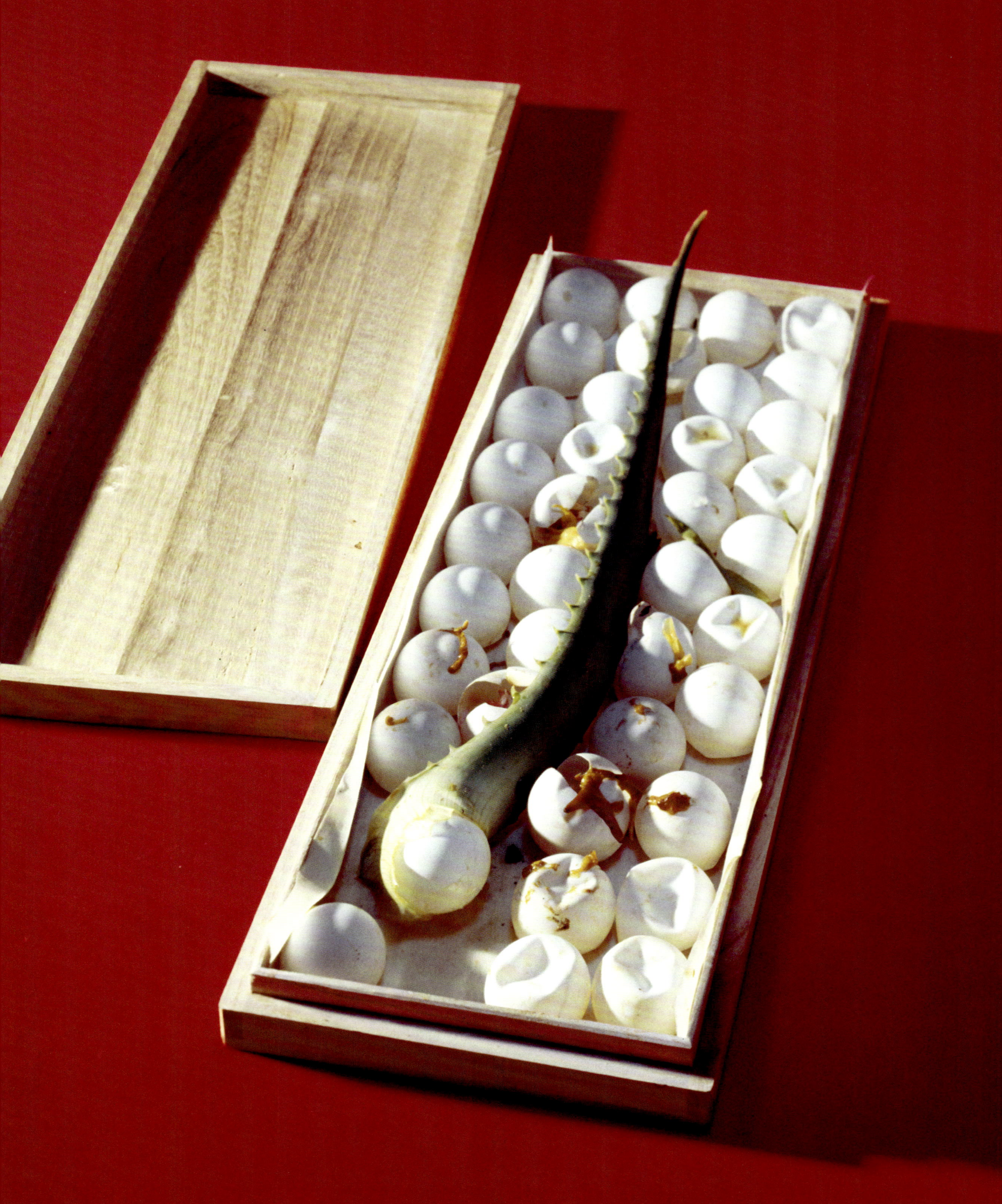

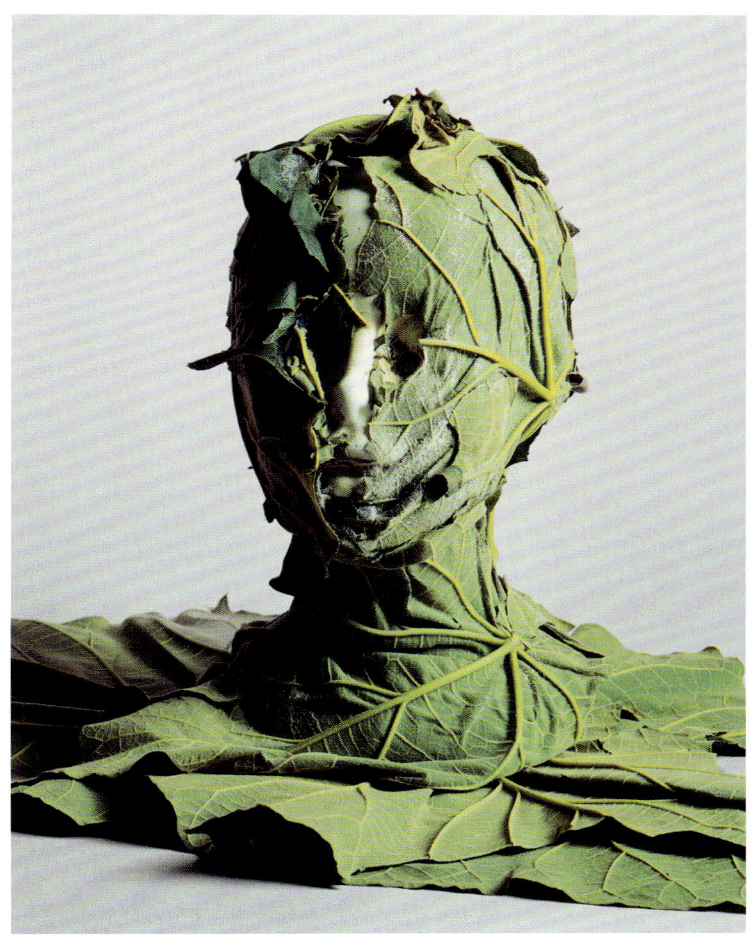

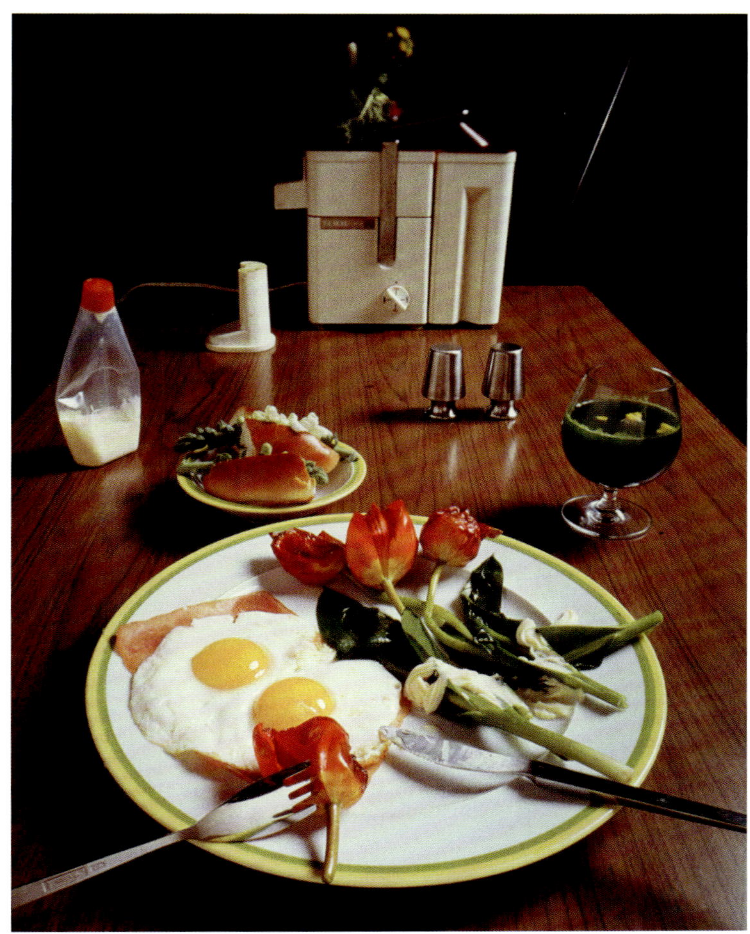

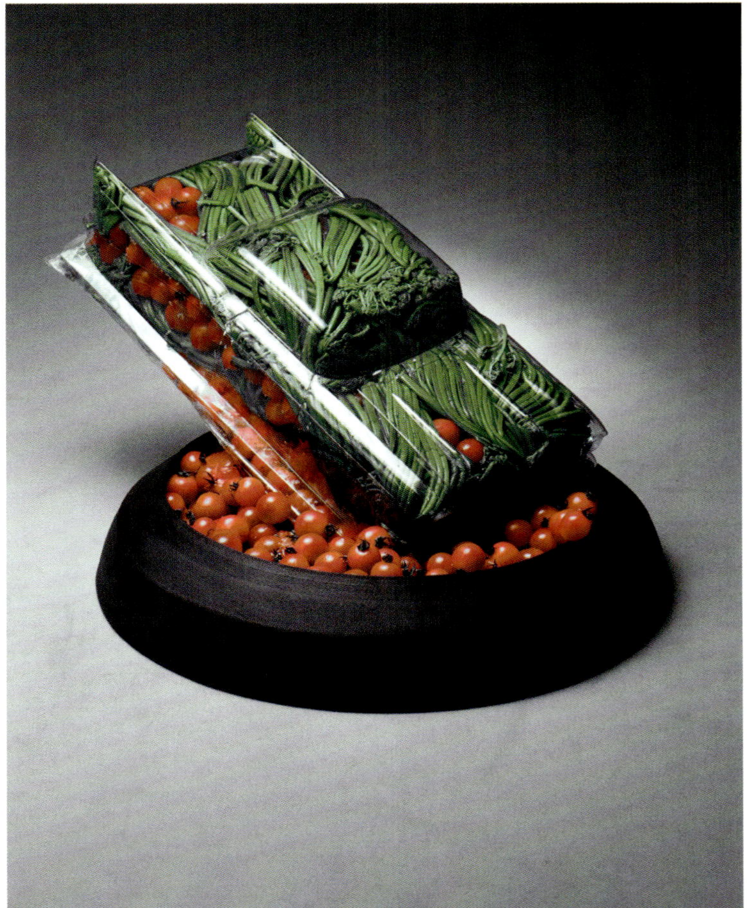

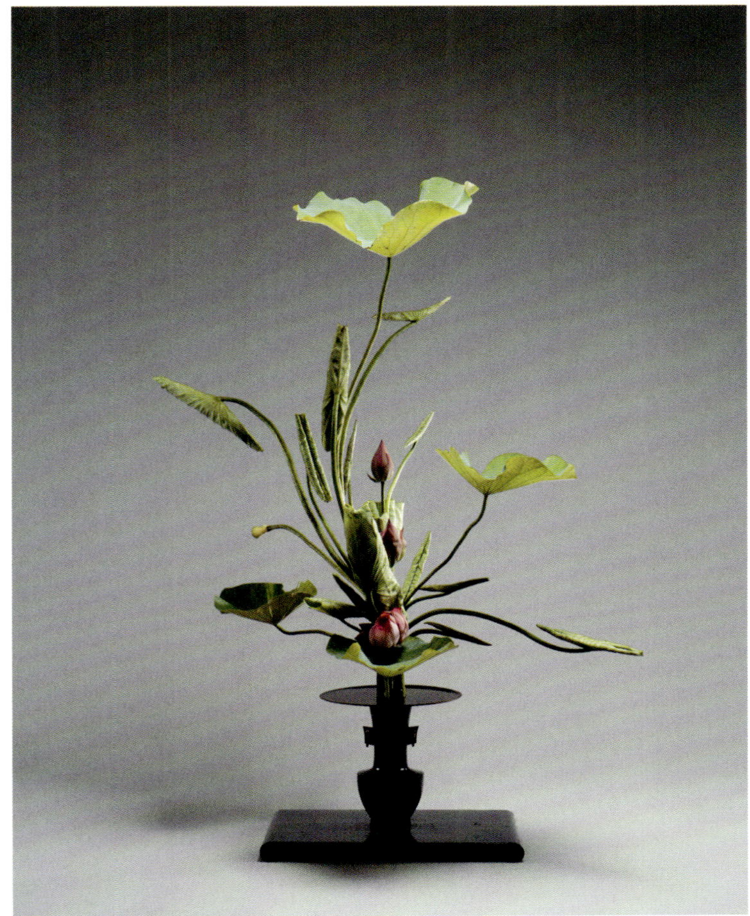

Opposite:
Like an Umbilical Cord,
1974

This page, clockwise
from top left:
Keloid Man, 1976; *Mr. O's
Breakfast,* 1973; *Rikka of
Lotus,* 1993; *Car Crash,* 1996

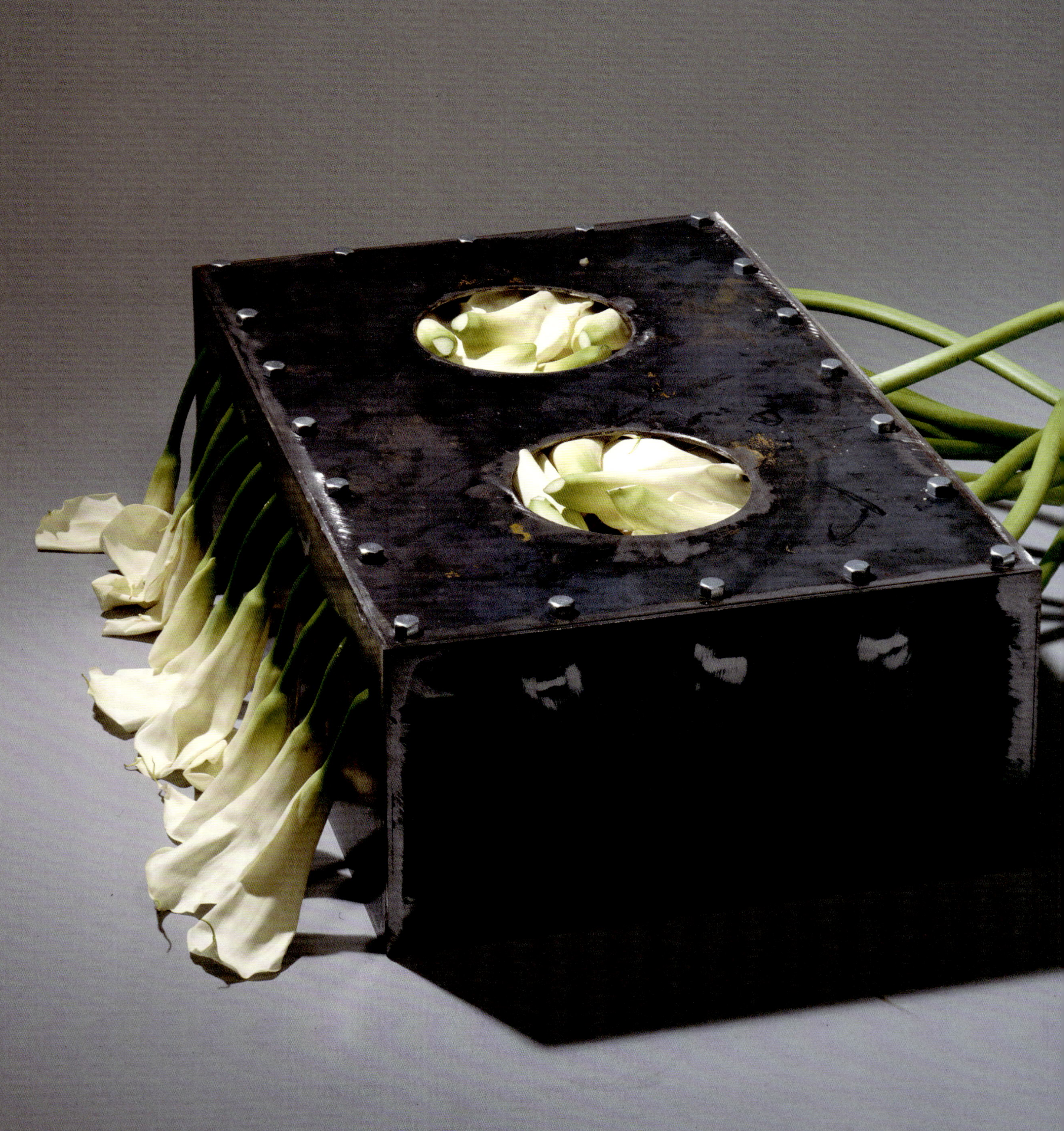

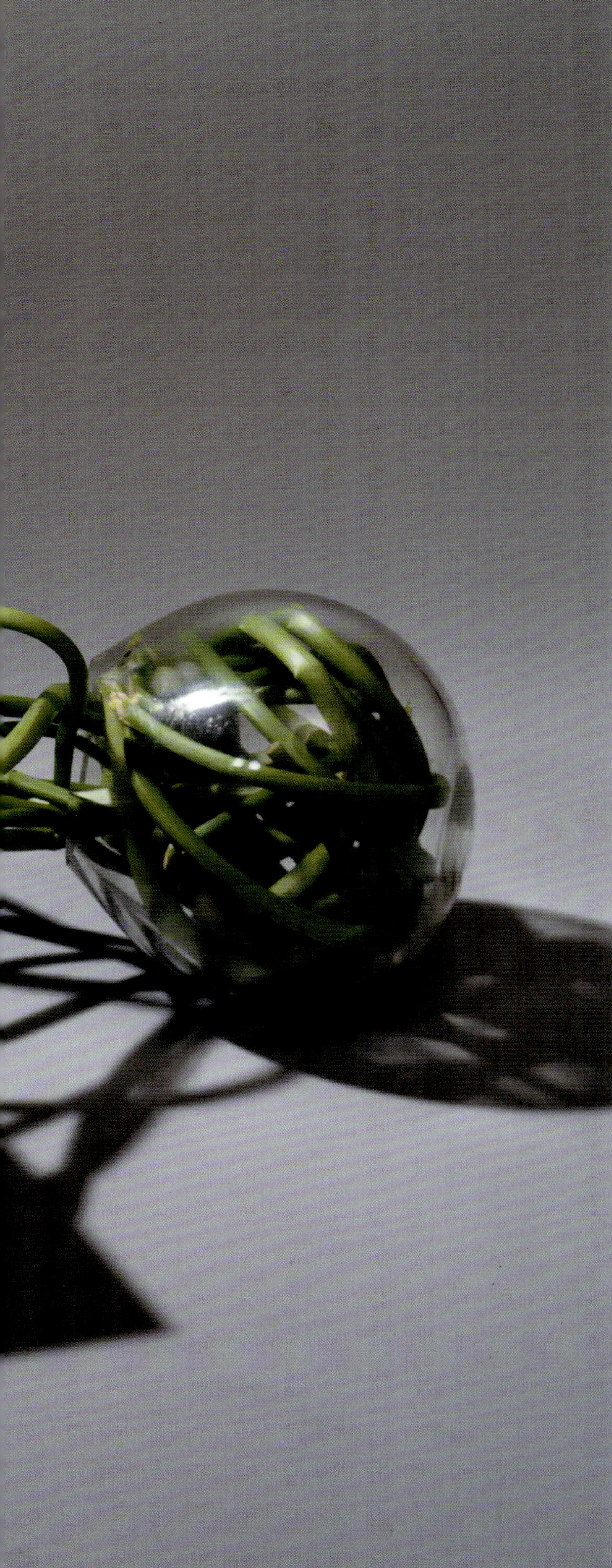

know it only as a photograph. And yet, in an interview from 1974 that dealt specifically with the relationship between ikebana and photography, Nakagawa argued for the former's greater importance: "The main subject is the flowers that I arrange," he said. "I do not arrange them for the purpose of being photographed." The interviewer pressed a bit further: Couldn't the photographs that result from his work be shown as photographs in their own right? Nakagawa offered a terse reply: "No. This is my *ikebana*."

Ohtsubo is less tied to these disciplinary boundaries than Nakagawa, perhaps because of his more mischievous approach—after all, Nakagawa never jumped in the bath with his flowers. "I do believe in the power of photography," Ohtsubo says. "It can bring out really important aspects of ikebana. In that sense, I have hopes for fantastic photographers." Perhaps ikebana *needs* photography in a way that sculpture does not, for the simple reason that plants wither away. Even in *I Am Taking a Bath Like This*, as soon as Ohtsubo stands up he will have disturbed the carefully laid out flowers at his chest. Histories of performance are often told through still and moving images, and the ephemeral aspects of Ohtsubo's work, which go above and beyond the simple decaying of plants, both draw him to photography and place him within a broader tradition of performance art.

In *Botanical Man* (1978), Ohtsubo again puts himself in the arrangement, to such an extent that he seems to merge with the plants. He strikes a studied pose, looking over a series of bound magazines with a cigarette held lightly between two fingers. Purplish castor oil bean plants crawl up the table and intertwine with his own body, held in place by white fabric resembling a bandage. I try to press Ohtsubo about why he included himself in this image, but he is keen to play down his role. He tells me that the castor oil bean plants had been assigned to him by an ikebana magazine as a prompt. "I tried a few things, and they weren't working," he says. "In the course of putting things together, I thought that it would be better to have the plants wrapped around me than using a vase—that's all!"

Ikebana, photography, or performance? Ohtsubo relishes in leaving such questions unresolved. His work thrills by consistently, and exuberantly, mixing disciplines, leaving them all a bit refreshed—like they just went for a bath.

Strange Callas II, **1978**
Unless otherwise noted, photographs by Koichi Taniguchi. Courtesy the artist and Ikebana Ryuseiha

Daniel Abbe is an art historian living in Kyoto.

In Polk County, Florida, Nabil Harb arranges his calendar around nights when the light turns green at dusk, how the shadows look blue in spring, or how the cicadas start to hum as the temperature reaches a hundred degrees. To live here is to know the feeling of humidity enveloping you like a duvet in July. To know in what oak hammocks you'll find butterfly orchids blooming by May. And to count the seconds between lightning strikes and thunder in August. More than five and you'll be fine.

Then, come September, Polk County's creeks, rivers, and trickling branches of sweet water swell. The Green Swamp at the northern edge of the county collects the remnants of the afternoon storms before that water moves south into the Peace River as it wends its way into the Gulf of Mexico. For Harb, those veins of water that course through Polk County, alongside 554 lakes, form a map he's been tracing all his life. With a camera, he's started to draw his own maps, as did William Faulkner in his fictional Yoknapatawpha County, William Christenberry in Hale County, or Zora Neale Hurston next door in Orange County.

Harb left his hometown three times, living in Boston, New York, and New Haven. And like many Southerners, he returned home three times—putting stakes down between the urban sprawl of Tampa Bay and the edge of the Everglades' headwaters just south of Orlando. "I moved back because I don't like being that far from my concerns," he tells me. Often, folks told him, "You're gay. You need to move to New York," as if he couldn't be himself at home. "I hate that," he says.

Here, everything is growing, green as ever, always. The live oaks are ancient, the sites of treaties, lynchings, and produce stands. Bends in the river call up Indigenous history, archaeology, and colonialism. In making a photograph, Harb wants you to feel how wet it is, the fog of mosquitoes, the mist rising off the ground. He wants people to better understand what rural places once were and are becoming, to know there's good and bad in Bartow, taciturn and queer in Eloise, this and that in Frostproof. He wants others "to actually see this place, rather than the stereotypes or easy metaphors." Beneath the headlines generated by lawmakers' political ambitions, past the policies that target the most vulnerable and most vital minorities in Florida, Harb gives a nod to the deep well of mystery here, to a place full of people as hopeful as they are complicated.

His parents, both Palestinians who left Nazareth, made lives together in Lakeland, Florida, but for Harb, who was raised there, the roads and rivers now seem bound up in his bones. Growing up brown, Muslim, and queer in central Florida set him apart from the good ole boys, but, he states softly, "I am just as much a part of this place."

A year after the 2016 murder of forty-nine people at the Pulse nightclub in Orlando, Harb started photographing his local gay bar in Lakeland. The work he made there was the product of questions, or a way to ask them. But as he explains, you arrive with one set of questions and leave haunted by another. These photographs, which began in earnest six years ago, have become inextricably, although not deliberately, engaged with what's happening in Florida and throughout America today.

And as in the photographs he was making all around Polk County—say, the bugs at dusk in the Green Swamp, or his friend Clay in the cab of a truck painted in mud—he focused on the quieter details inside the bar, capturing gestures, the sense that life was being lived and celebrated. His life. Here were the queens who formed the heart of the performances, but here, also, were the people sitting at the back of the bar, his friends, the ones who lent this building and this part of America its character. As he tells me, "You should see the people."

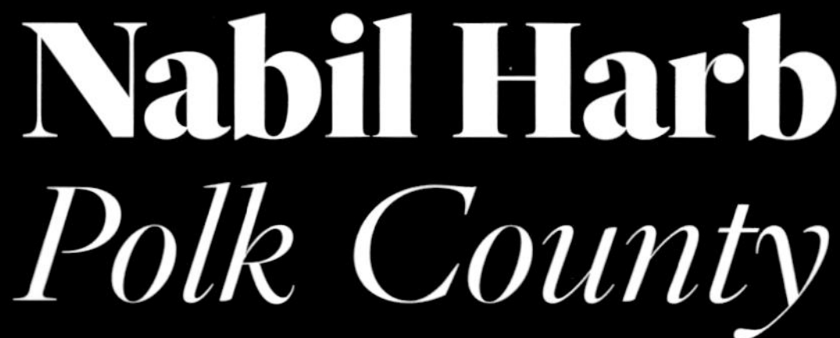

Nabil Harb
Polk County

Michael Adno

Dani, 2018

Michael Adno is a writer and photographer who lives in Sarasota, Florida.

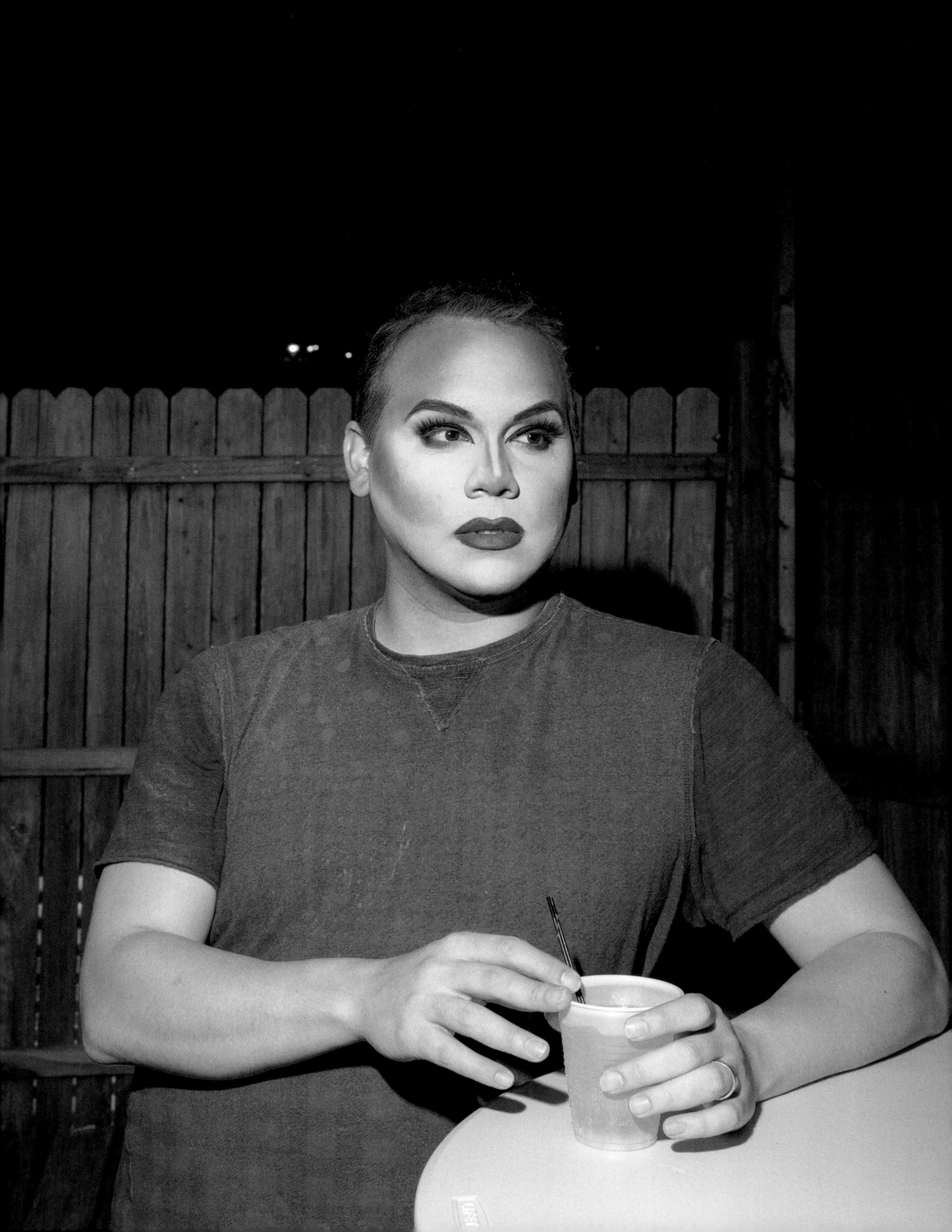

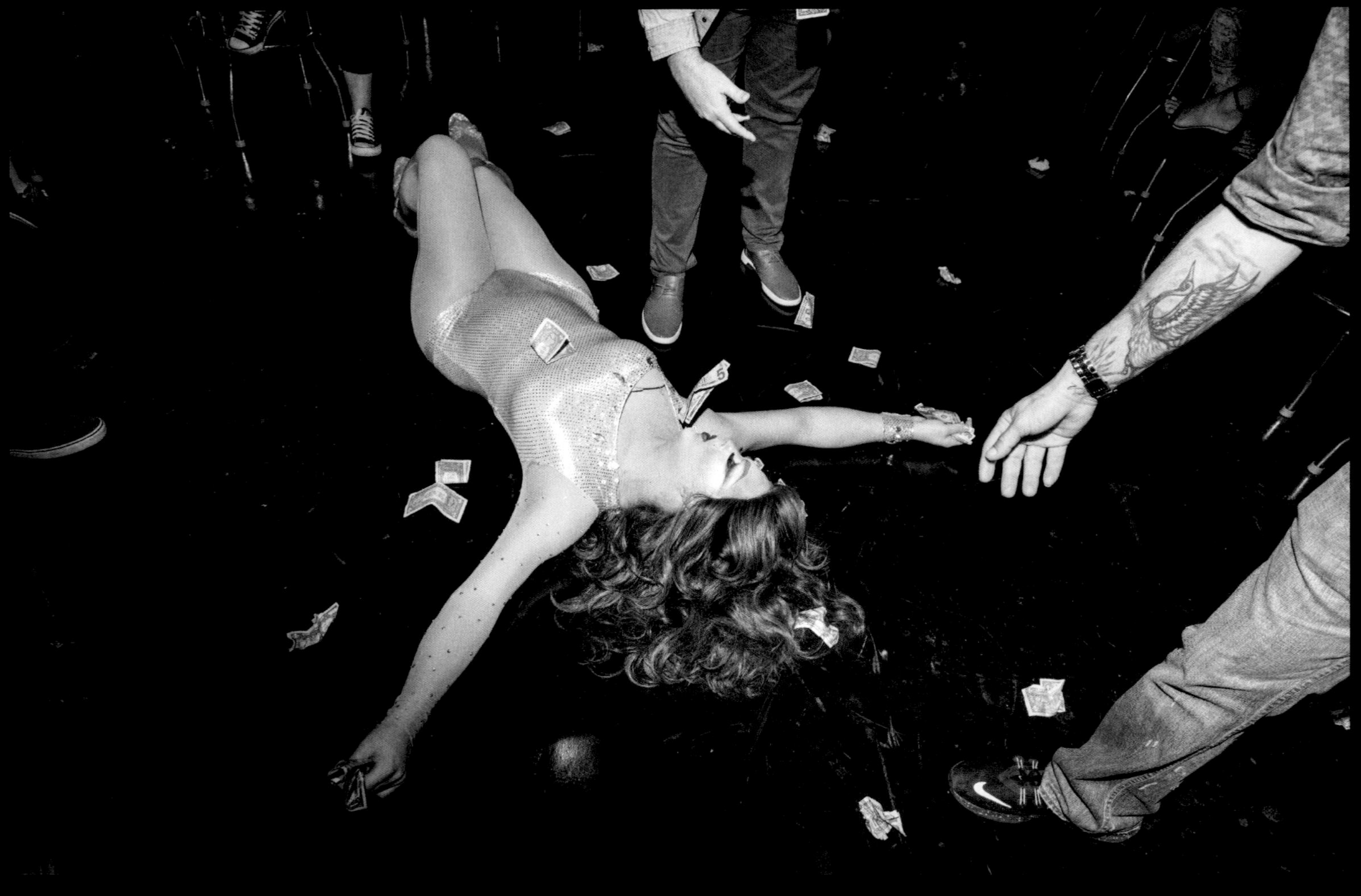

Allegra, 2019

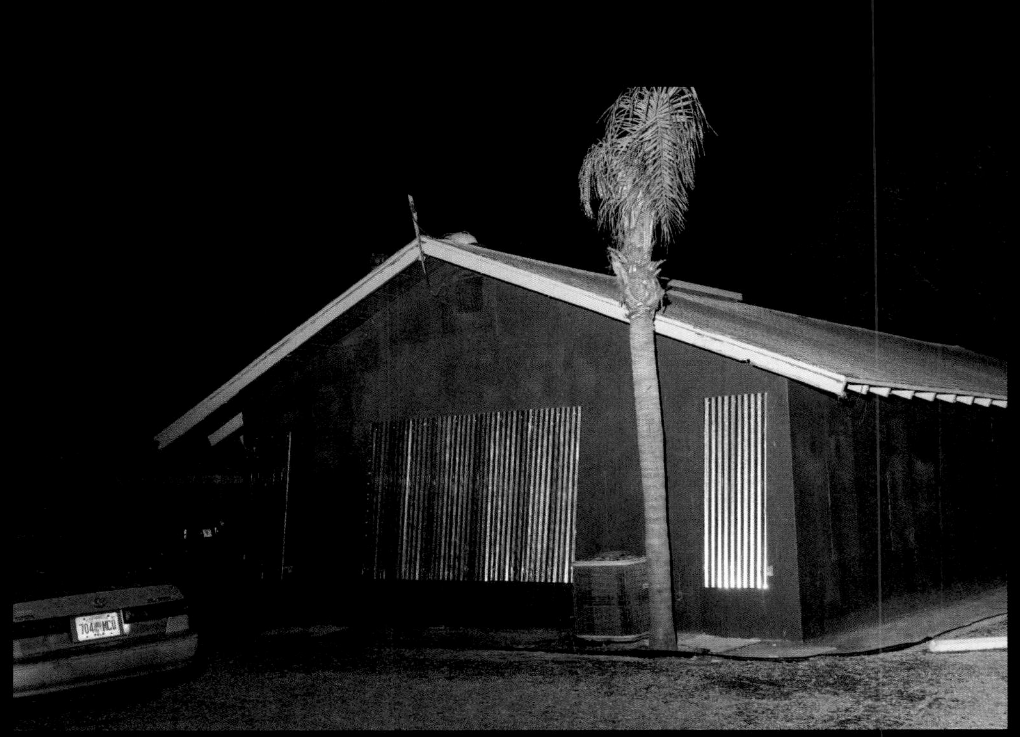

Pulse Exterior (Lakeland), 2019

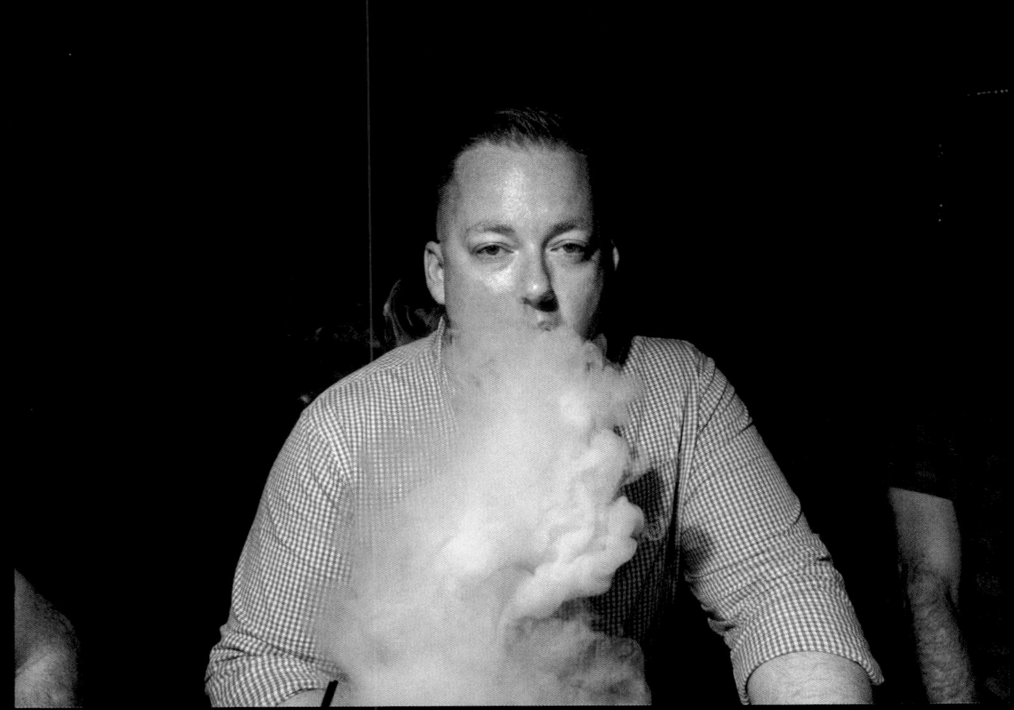

Vape, 2021

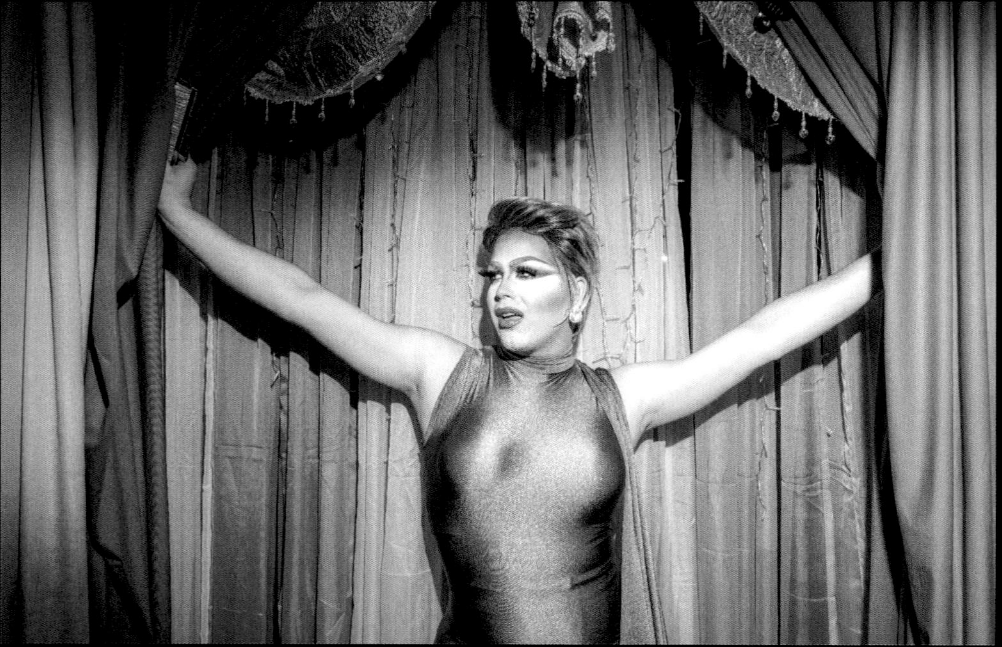

Allegra, 2020

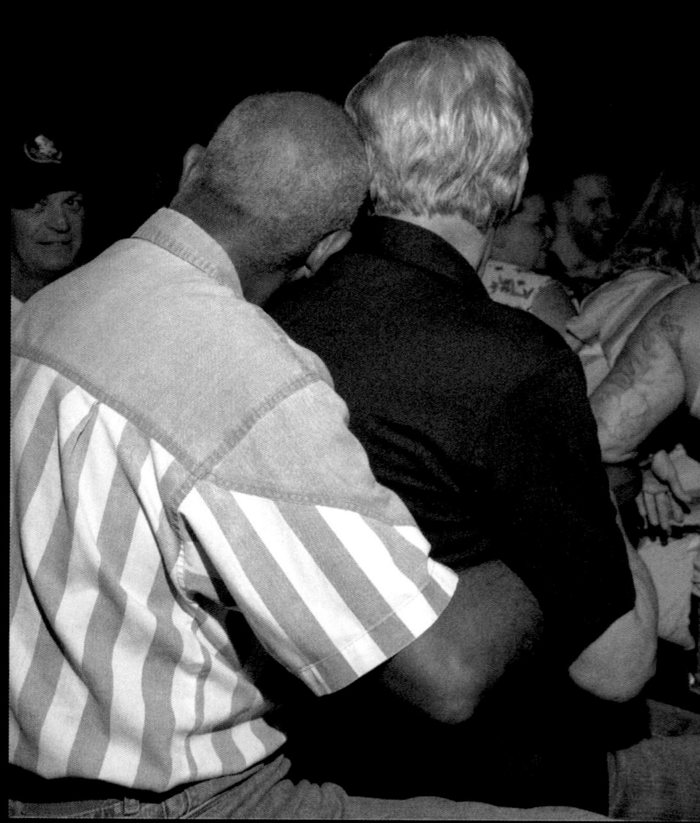

J & J, 2019

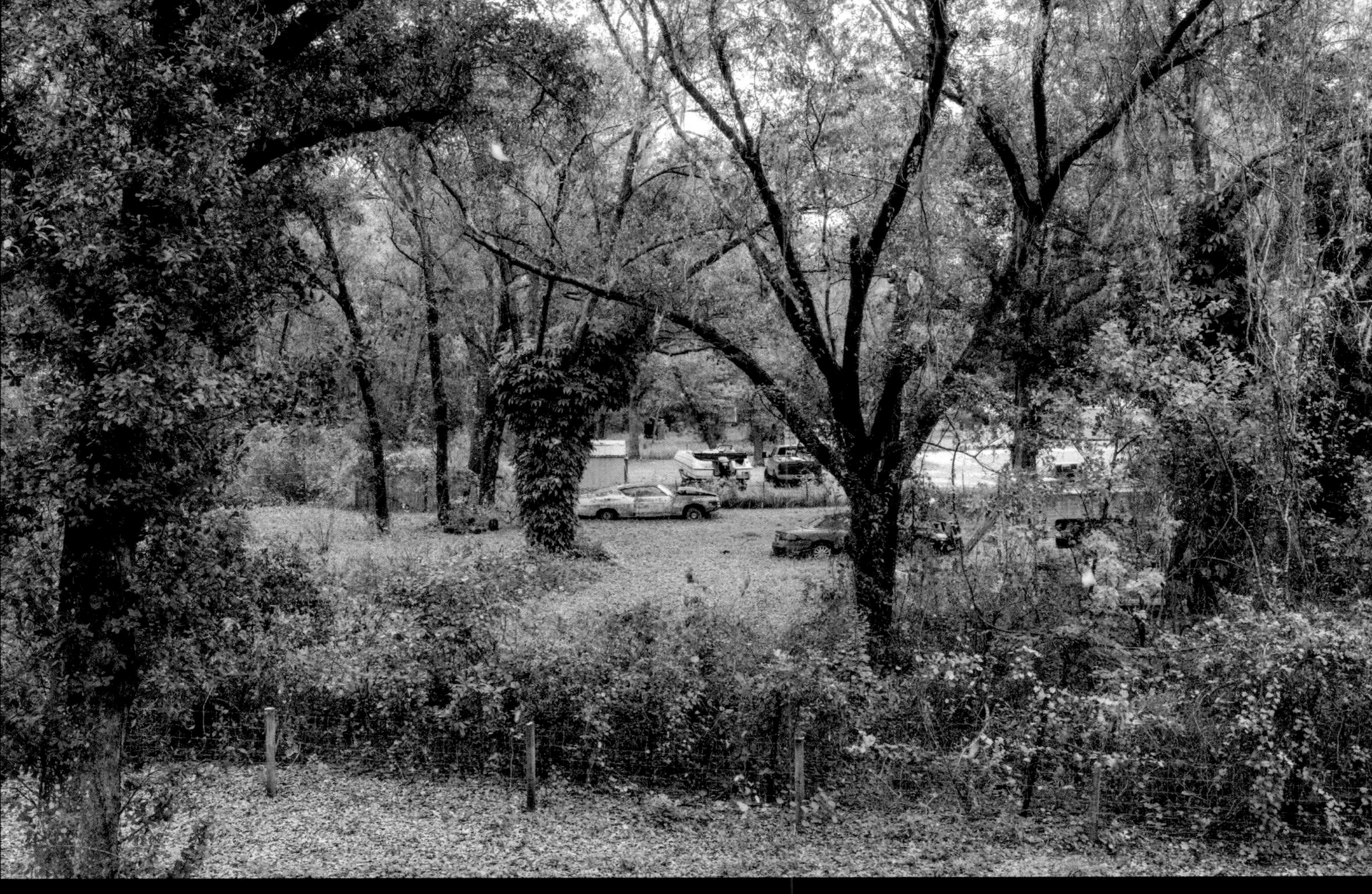

Northside, 2020

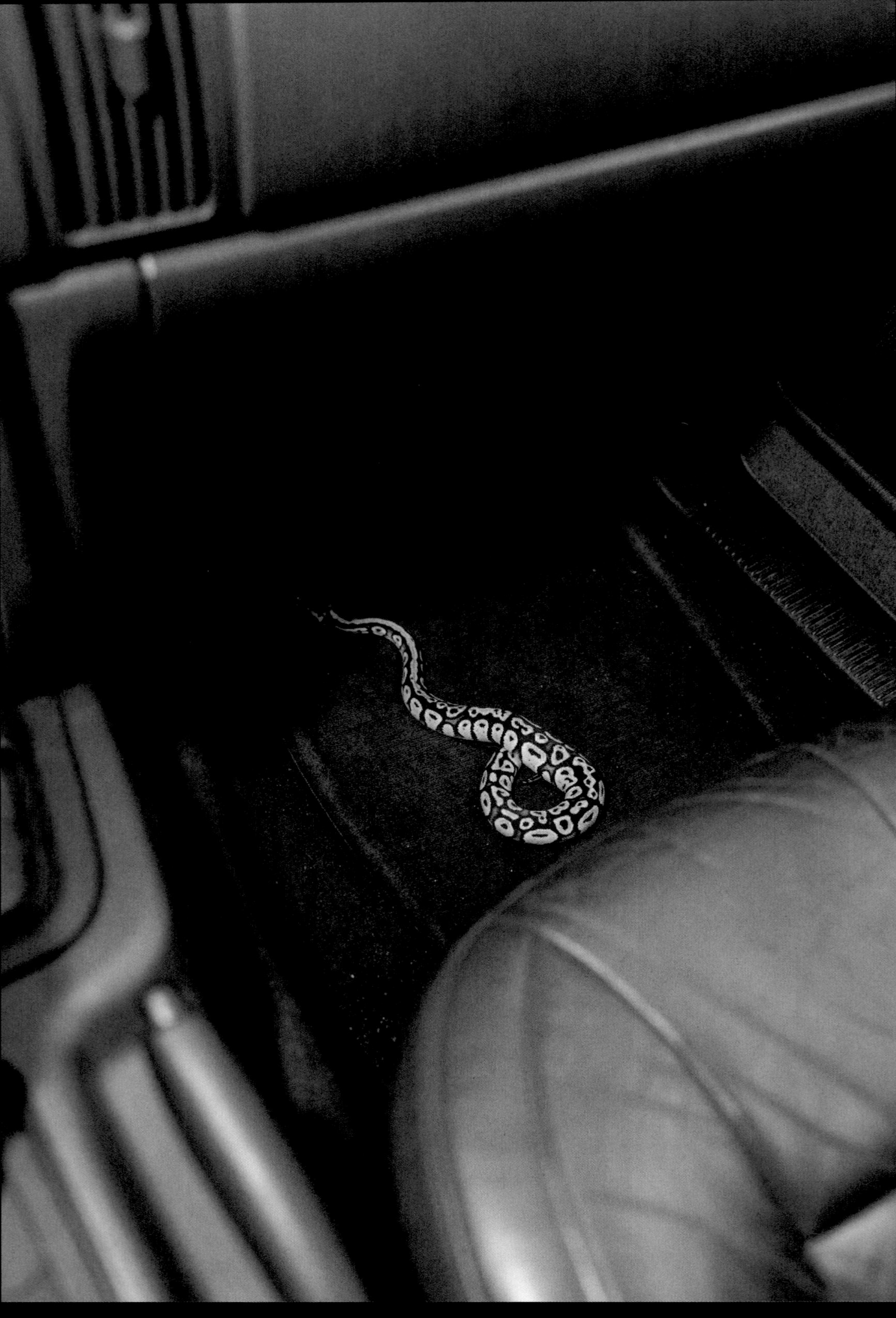

This page:
Python, 2022; opposite: *Carter Road, 2019*
Courtesy the artist

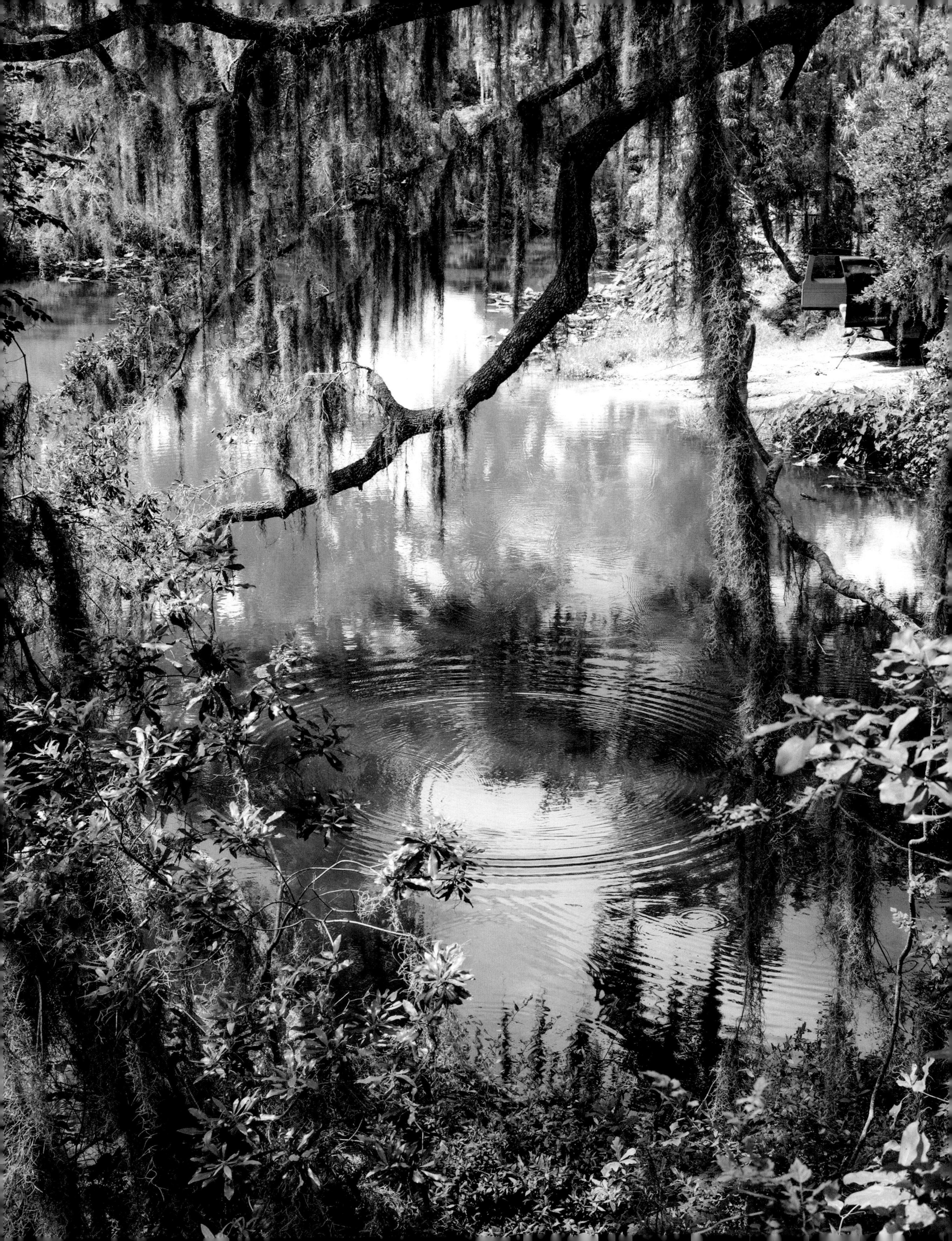

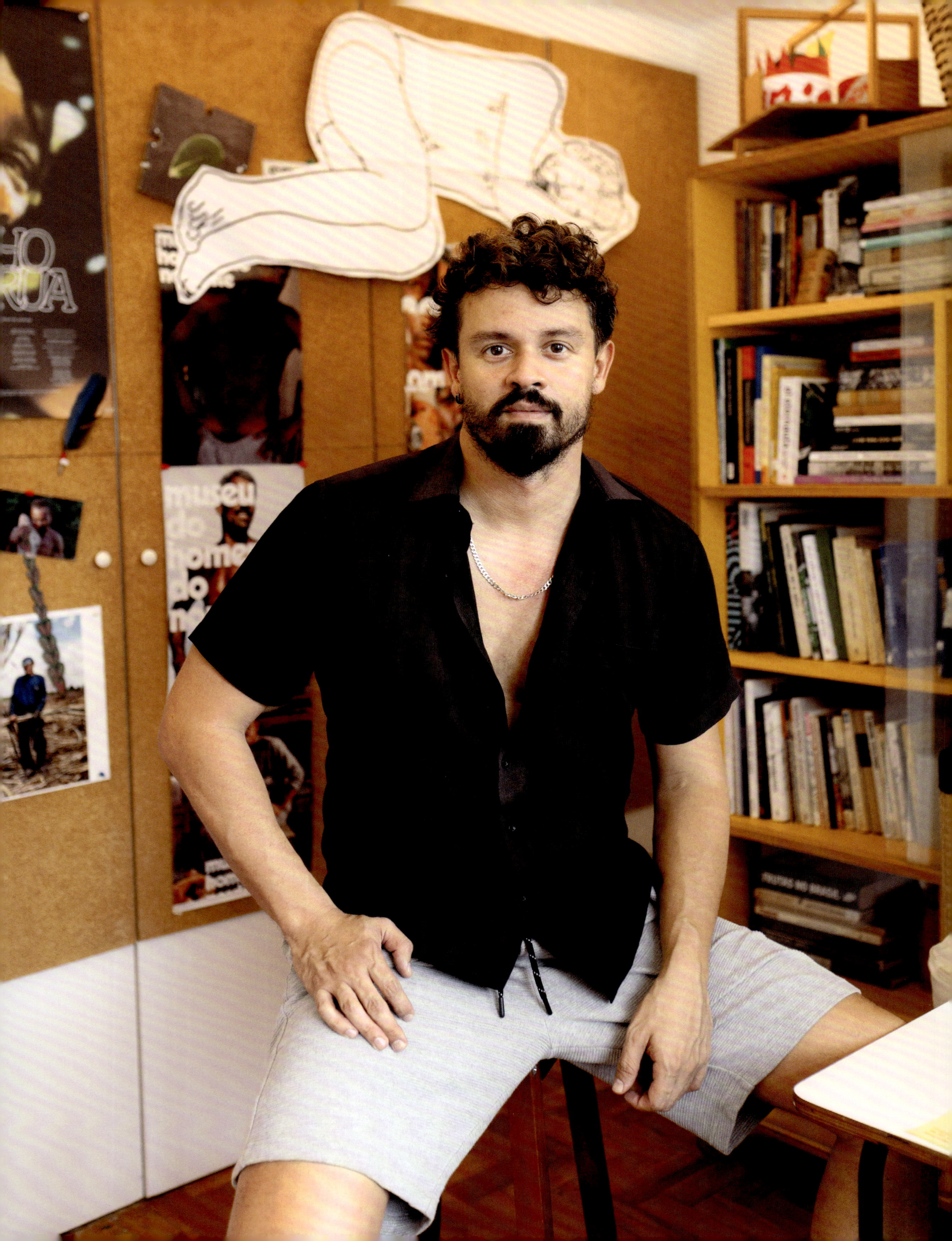

Jonathas de Andrade

The Spark

The renowned Brazilian artist's work is energized by sexual tension and the possibilities of intimacy between men.
Silas Martí

A cool breeze blows in from the wide-open windows on both sides of the artist Jonathas de Andrade's modernist flat in Recife, a city in the northeast of Brazil. It's June, the end of autumn in this part of the world, but it feels more like the peak of summer. "Ventilation is gold here," he says, adding that it's not just because of the humid and intense tropical heat of the region, but because otherwise everything would go stale and grow mold. Water hangs heavy in the air and drops without ceremony everywhere, in buckets of sweat, and sometimes as tears.

It's no wonder that de Andrade—one of the most celebrated contemporary artists in Brazil, an art-world darling graced with survey shows across the globe, from Chicago to Paris, including a stop in Venice, where he represented Brazil in the last Biennale and premiered a new video, *Knot in the Throat* (2022)—renovated part of his living room to build a shower massive enough to fit a football team. "This is where I shower every morning," he says, gesturing toward what almost appears to be a sauna, which opens onto a room where minimalist midcentury furniture is in harmony with a hammock, tables, and sculptures sourced from Indigenous artists all over the country.

This contrast is not just a detail in decor but a driving force behind de Andrade's work in video, photography, and installations. His vision is anchored as much in the rigorous geometry of tropical modernism as to the men of Brazil's northeast, dark-skinned, brown, Black—and beautiful, as he portrays them. Spotless right angles, he seems to suggest, have never clashed with the overcharged eroticism he finds in the subjects inhabiting his art.

Tropical Hangover (2009), the piece that catapulted him to fame, shows this sensibility under a sweet, uncanny light. The installation, which was later published as a photobook, displays loose excerpts from a journal found in the trash in 2003 and photographs of Recife's run-down modernist mansions and apartments. These are forgotten structures in what he portrays, along with aerial views of the city over the years, as a splendorous kind of decomposition, from the massive floods that scarred it decades ago to the construction of the port that locals blame for both the destruction of coral reefs and the invasion of sharks, closer than ever now to shore. The narrative in the journal speaks of trivial goings-on in the city's landmarks—the cinema, the beach—but also of sexual encounters in motels and parking lots, fleeting relationships, life itself, carved into a modern-era cityscape designed to repel blood, salt, and sweat. In the photographs he takes and those he appropriates, such places for living, meant to be cool and removed, foreign to the terrain, crumble and give in, succumbing to life's unstoppable violence.

De Andrade now lives in a building that could appear in his photographs. His outlook on the city he has called home since the beginning of his career always integrated the tensions of its streets and alleys. Even after achieving fame and critical recognition, de Andrade did not hide his attraction to working-class and dark-skinned men, the subjects who animate these urban constructions. "Desire is a really strong thing, and it has social, racial, and class components," he tells me in his Jeep as we drive around Recife, seeing the places he has pictured in his works. "It's like a spark going off close to a barrel of gunpowder. It's risky, explosive, and, at the same time, super powerful."

In 2002, de Andrade moved to Recife to study advertising, after dropping out of law school in the southern coastal city of Florianópolis. He has described the energy of Recife as a vortex of contradictions. "This is a territory in dispute with a background of revolutions, built on social fault lines and fractures, where every exchange of glances, eye to eye, echoes the history and scars of violence. But it is also the place where desire operates like a dance, where every brush against somebody is also a fight," he says. This kind of attraction, he has come to understand, is not the straightforward wanting of someone else. His interest is located somewhere at the crossroads of sex and curiosity as he explores not just the body but also the social identity of his subjects, those maybe once unfamiliar to him and now closer and closer to the way he sees himself in the mirror—not a fully white man in Brazil but a brown, darker man who has somehow stepped out of the closet, or the shadows.

It's not something he takes lightly. "With the current political temperature and the racial debate in the country, if I announce myself as a brown man, everything I say will have to go to justify this

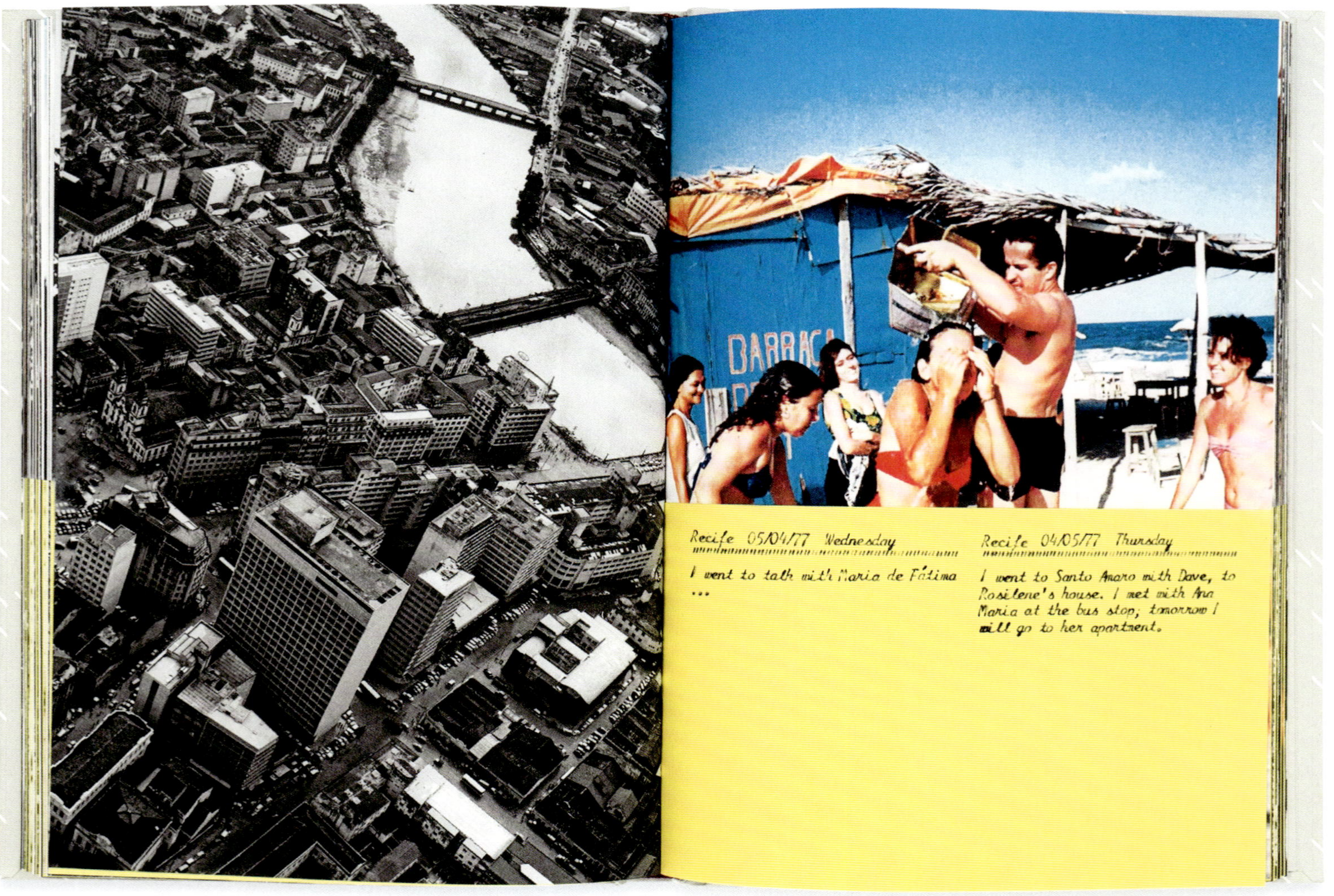

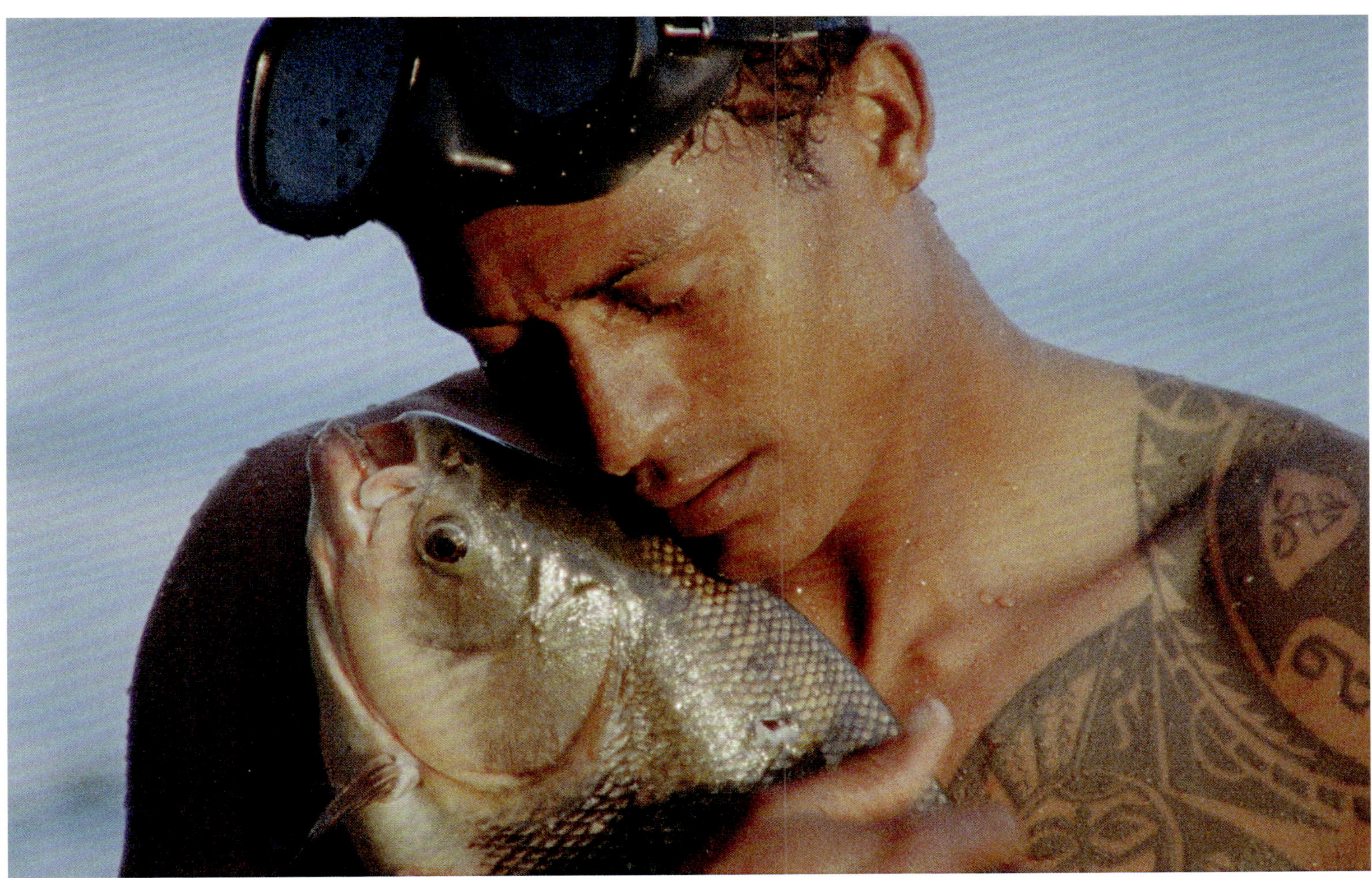

brownness," he says, "and I don't want to be mistaken for someone taking advantage of his skin color to have some kind of legitimacy." He is referring to the deep polarization that has split the country apart in the last decade, along with the turmoil brought about by the pandemic and the last four years under the former president Jair Bolsonaro, a government so violent toward minorities that the racial and gender debate heated to the point of boiling. "If we think of whites in Brazil as those with privilege, the ones that won't go hungry, that will live well, and study, and have a voice," he continues, "then maybe I'm white, because I never experienced racism; even if in São Paulo, I'm not that white, and in Europe, they see me as a full-on Latino."

These shades of white, brown, and Black have become clearer to the artist. During a 2023 presentation of his work in Recife, de Andrade was confronted with concerns about exploitation. The retrospective, *Na Cidade da Ressaca*—a Portuguese play on words that doubles as "in the city of hangover" or "the city at the edge of the sea in tumult"—was held at the Museum of Modern Art Aloisio Magalhães, a former nineteenth-century palace. In its three-month run, the show sparked fierce debate. But for de Andrade, it was a homecoming, the first time his work was shown exactly where it was made, with the overflowing life and energy of the old city pulsating all around it.

Posters for the Museum of the Man of the Northeast (2013), a towering installation and one of de Andrade's most well-known series, hung above the stairwell of the building. The piece depicts construction laborers, drivers, and shopkeepers. De Andrade first tried to attract his models with personal ads in local newspapers, putting out a call for a "strong dark man, a worker, handsome or ugly." The choice of words—intentionally dated, the way men would speak of workers as *men*, never women—reflected the social norms of old Brazil, the northeast especially. Those who showed up, however, were interested in a real job, not an artistic performance,

De Andrade's vision is anchored as much in the rigorous geometry of tropical modernism as to the men of Brazil's northeast.

His subjects would become the models on posters for a fake museum with the same name as a real one: the Museum of the Man of the Northeast.

so de Andrade took to the streets in search of guys who fit the description, exchanging glances and then proposing a brief photo shoot in which his subjects would become the models on posters for a fake museum with the same name as a real one: the Museum of the Man of the Northeast, an anthropology institution in Recife that tries to tell the story of this region built on sugarcane plantations, the slave trade, and overwhelming savagery.

De Andrade tells me about what he nicknamed the "soap hour," the time of evening when workers leave their jobs to go home to their wives after having just showered at the factory, the smell of lotion clinging to their skin as they board the crowded buses at dusk. The counterpoint to that particular fragrance formed *Working Up a Sweat* (2014), a collection of 120 sweaty work shirts he acquired from men on the street in Recife, buying or swapping on the spot for a brand-new piece of clothing, and draping them on floor-standing wooden supports. They might be seen as a fetishization of labor, but as the sculptures take different formations in various exhibitions, the piece also considers the rituals of movement around a city. "This is the thing about lust, it allows for risk as much as the possibility of an encounter," he says. In short, de Andrade targets in these pieces the inescapable, raw sense of possibility that underlines intimacy between men.

Before this sexual tension exploded with undeniable clarity in his more recent pieces, the cruelty that can mark even the most passionate moments appeared in the video *The Fish* (2016), one of his most admired works. De Andrade filmed fishermen who cradle their prey, fish just poached from the water that twitch and agonize in what is depicted, despite their dying in those arms, as a loving embrace. The animals' gasps preceding death clash with the warm gestures of the men, who hold them close to the chest, their bodies

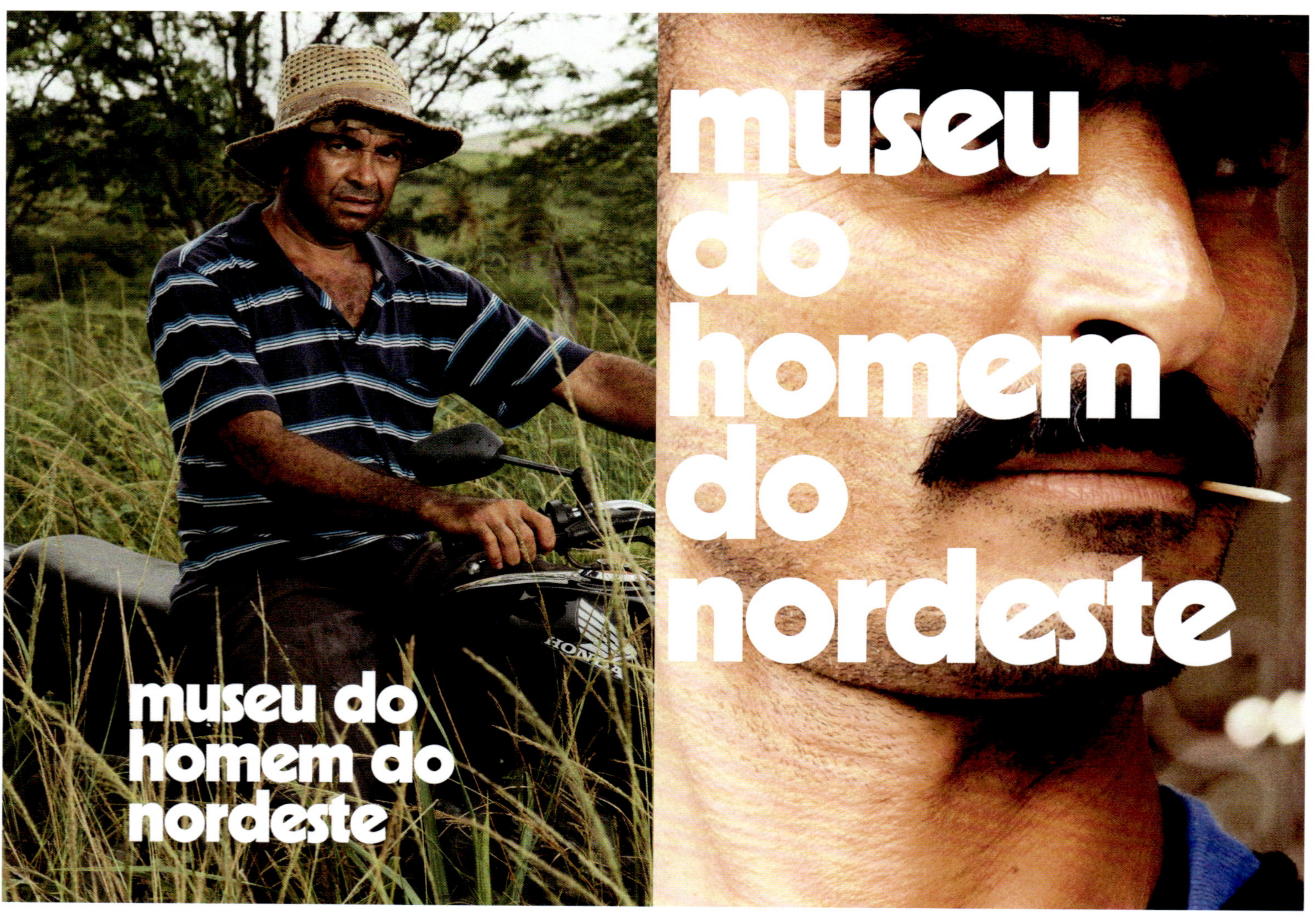

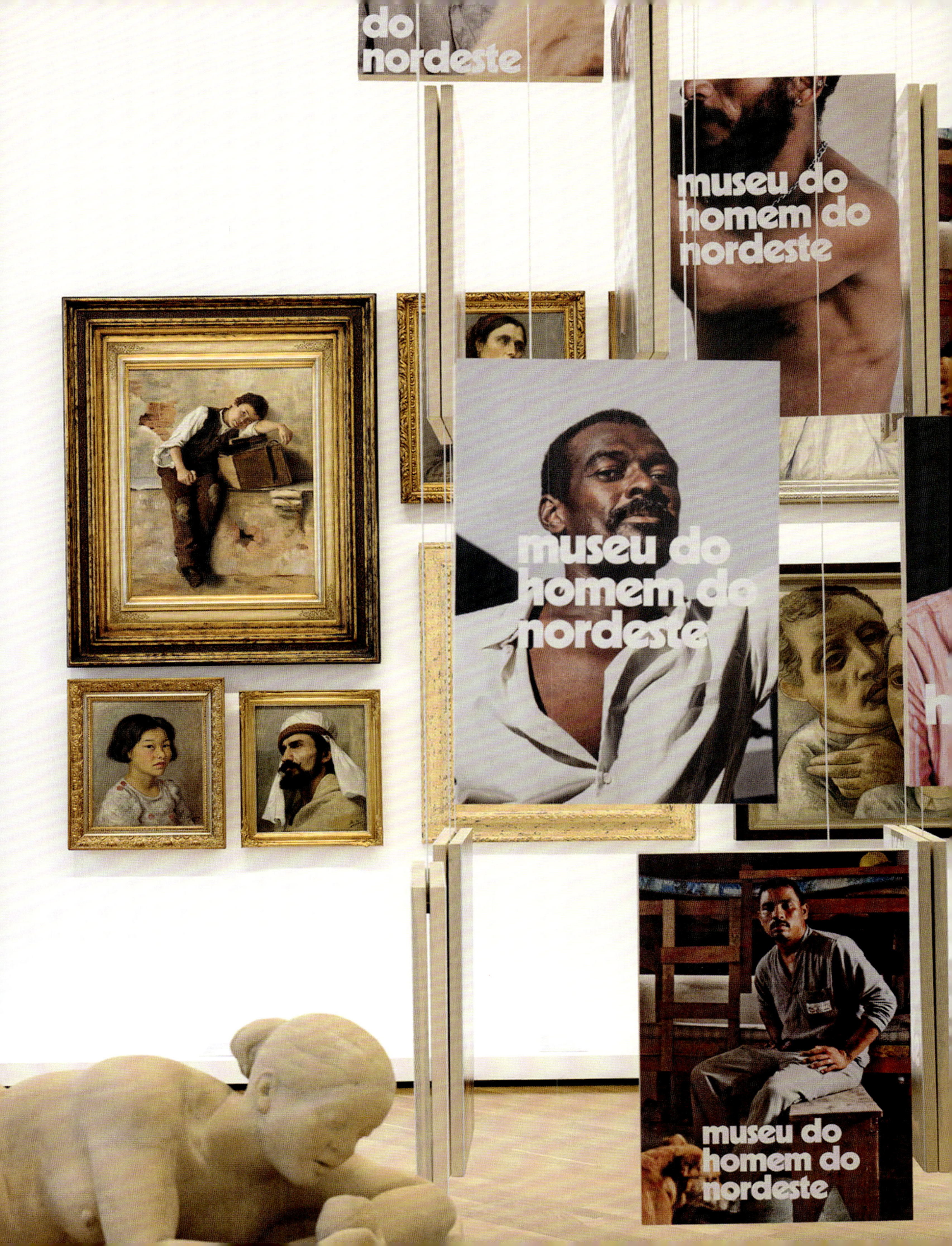

do
nordeste
museu do
homem do
nordeste
museu do
homem do
nordeste
museu do
homem do
nordeste

wet under the sun, as lustrous, sticky, and viscous as the fish. De Andrade equates here the aggressor and his victim in an act of love laced with ultimate danger, as if extracting from desire its unshakable component of despair.

De Andrade's work, in the end, is as much about hot and heavy attraction as it is a social commentary on class divisions in a country split at the seams between the miserable and the superrich, with a narrow layer of middle-class bourgeoisie trapped in between. Recently, he has faced criticism for works that once were received with acclaim, a side effect of the changes in public opinion regarding race and gender in Brazil. His choice of words and erotic depiction of Black and brown men have become the target of activists who see pieces such as *Posters for the Museum of the Man of the Northeast* as exploitative. Another work, *40 black candies for R$ 1.00* (2013), a series of Risograph prints about a fictional banana plantation factory, which de Andrade has decided to no longer show, came under fire for its title in Portuguese, *40 nego bom é um real*, which states that forty pieces of a sweet called "nice negro" cost just one *real*, the Brazilian currency. He tells me the title referred to how undervalued these lives have been in the country, from the time of slavery until now.

At the beginning of his career, de Andrade worried that stepping onto the art-world stage as a gay man would restrict him to the shelf of queer art, a label he dislikes, even though his artwork has always navigated queerness. "This ambiguity has always seemed very powerful to me, but it also had to do with me being from a generation that couldn't announce itself as gay publicly, so I thought it was important to be more open-ended, to let the works speak for themselves," he says. "I have to deal with this now, though, and how difficult it is. I need to put myself on the line all the time."

That requires coming to terms with what it means not only to be a man in the northeast of Brazil but to face today's decaying modernist narrative in Recife. In a broader sense, de Andrade looks through the lens of thinkers such as Gilberto Freyre, whose writings romanticize the melting pot of races at the core of Brazilian identity, in order to turn those ideas upside down. The artist turns romance into friction to make art that—despite all contradictions, blurred lines, and blind spots—is essentially about lust, love, and affection, and the barbarity these feelings sometimes carry with them.

In *Eye – Spark*, a solo show presented earlier this year at the Museum of Art, Architecture and Technology in Lisbon, he finally found a way to describe this rather electric sensation—two words, *olho* (eye) and *faísca* (spark). At his suggestion, the catalog's cover has them printed in big, bold black letters against a yellow background. It's subtler and less violent than *4,000 Shots* (2010), for which he photographed random men on the streets of Buenos Aires. That was a work rooted not so much in the latent homoeroticism of cruising but rather on a hot-tempered consciousness of a history marked by dictatorships in Latin America, where anyone deviating from the norm would automatically become a target.

Between then and now, he made *Looking for Jesus* (2013), combing the alleys of Amman, Jordan, searching for a look-alike of the son of God—not the blond, blue-eyed, long-haired white man who became a poster child for the Renaissance, but a guy that could be de Andrade's own stunt double, someone who could pass for white, Black, and Indigenous at the same time—a common perception in Brazil, where anyone of mixed race is labeled *pardo*, or light brown, exotic by Eurocentric standards but normal by his own.

His latest work leaves no doubt as to the nature of this quest. Literal and almost minimalist in its construction, *Eye – Spark*, the 2023 series for which the exhibition is titled, is an installation that neatly displays the used underwear of de Andrade's former lovers, lost pubes and all, perhaps in an attempt to protect not just an object

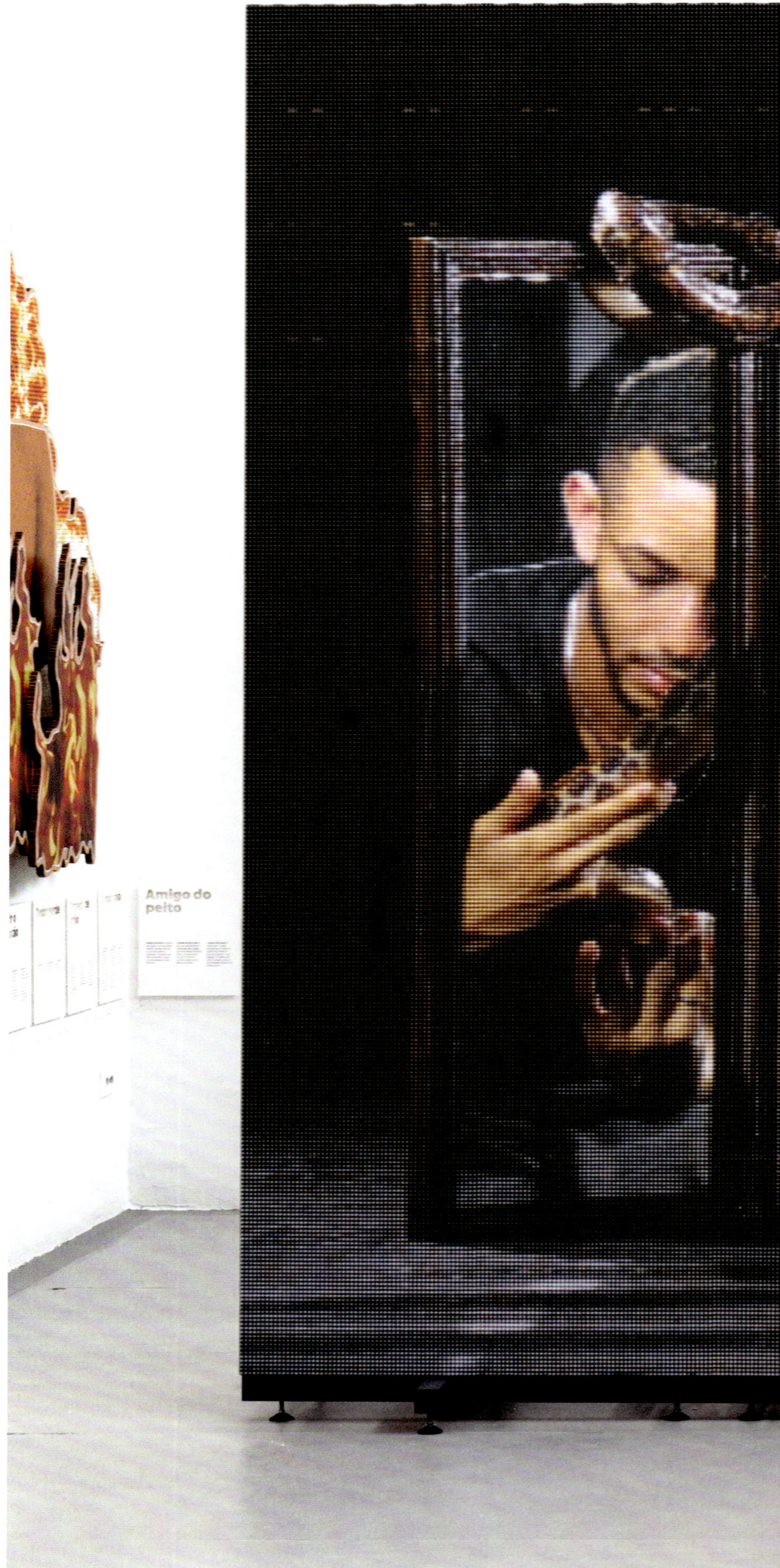

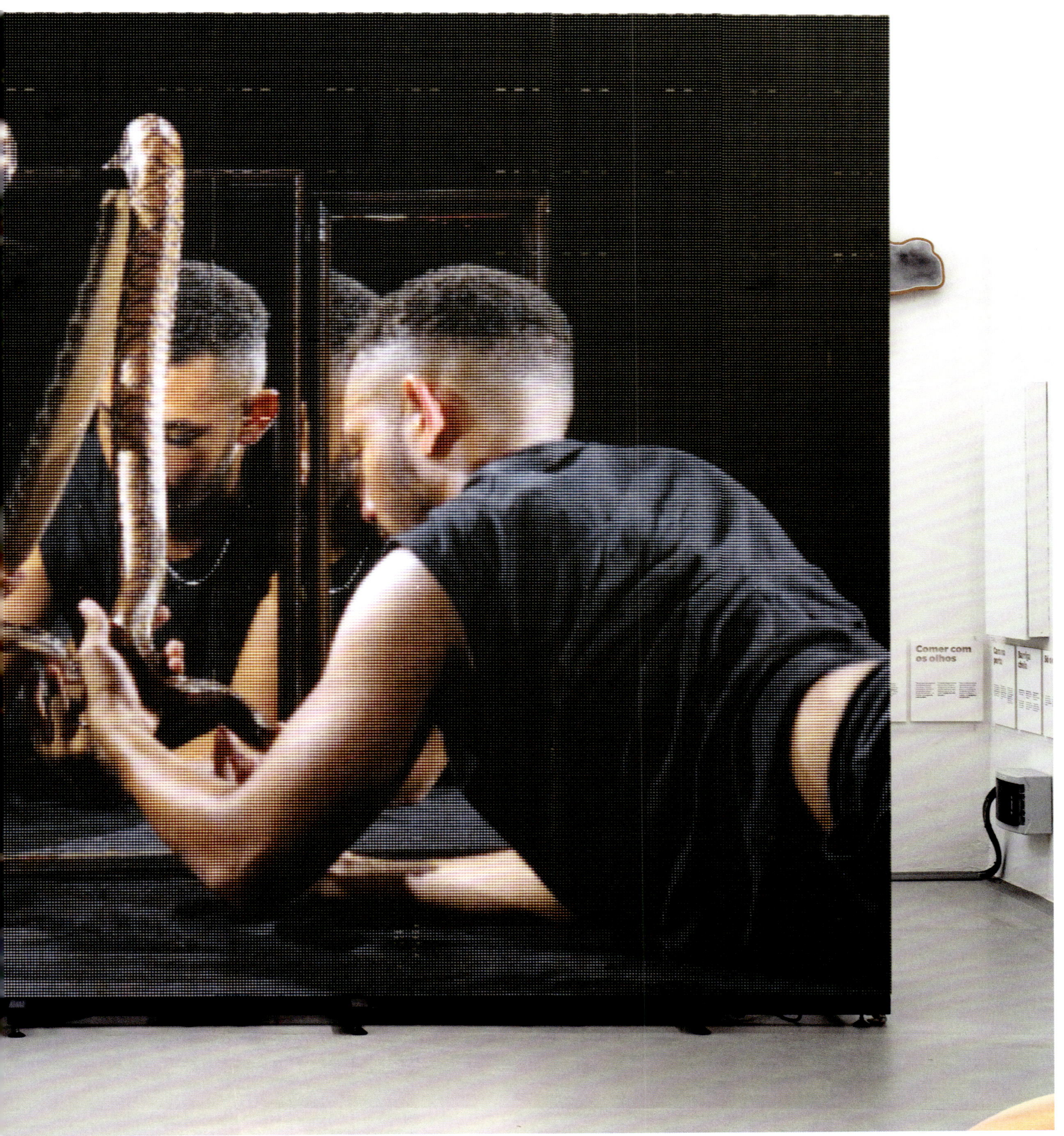
Comer com
os olhos

De Andrade has often traced the impulse in bodies of water toward forbidden desire and the thrill of discovery.

but a memory, an experience. Despite its deceptive simplicity, this is a work that hits a spot for those who have, against all the odds, enjoyed a liberated gay lifestyle in a very macho setting. It is striking to see this piece, a collection of trophy undies, presented proudly and without shame.

Lost and Found (2020) is an installation of forgotten swimsuits de Andrade collected from the male locker rooms of public pools in Recife, from his college years to where he swims, close to his flat, today. They now dress oddly shaped ceramic sculptures of men's groins, pieces commissioned by de Andrade from local artisans told to imagine a man's body in a swimsuit, curves and all, discreet and indiscreet. The piece was also shown last year at the Pina Estação, one of São Paulo's most important art museums, and at the Art Basel Miami Beach fair, where it resonated with the beach-going queer community.

De Andrade tells me all about the work as we drive out to the biggest pool in town, the heart of the public university's massive sports club. His eyes sparkle, and he remembers all the twisted-gut feelings drowned by laps timed more to match naked rush hours in locker rooms than any logical schedule. "It's all about flirting, feeling the chill down your spine," he says. "It was the realm of sexual fantasy that would most of the time go nowhere, but there is a beauty in that too."

De Andrade has often traced the impulse toward forbidden desire, and the thrill of discovery, in bodies of water. Before used shirts, underwear, and swimsuits, there were the rigid, stark white lines of an abandoned yacht club, a 1960s construction pictured

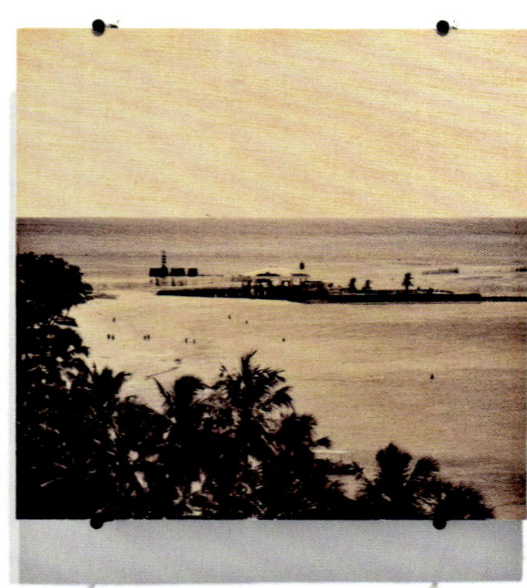
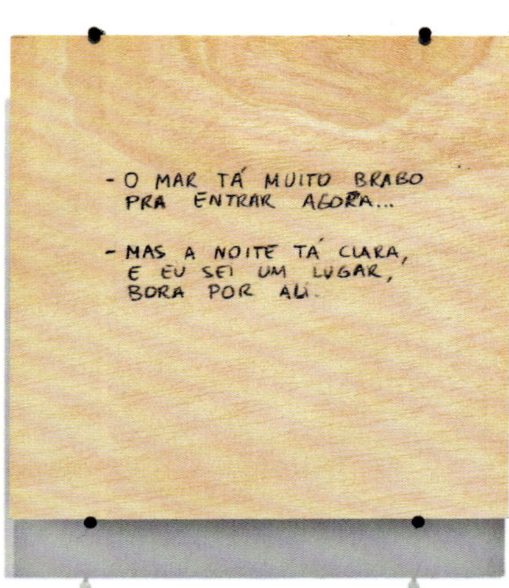

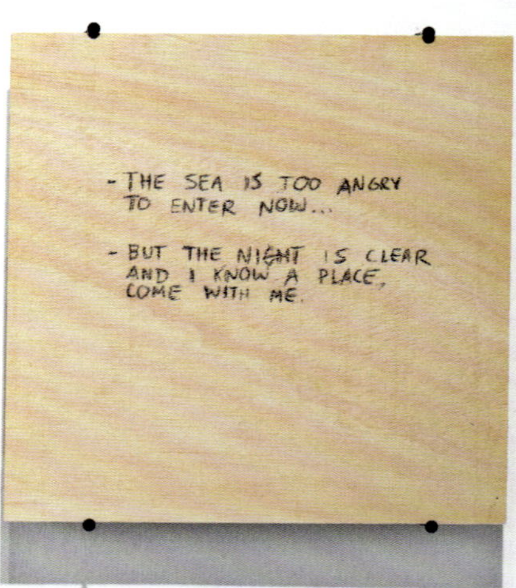

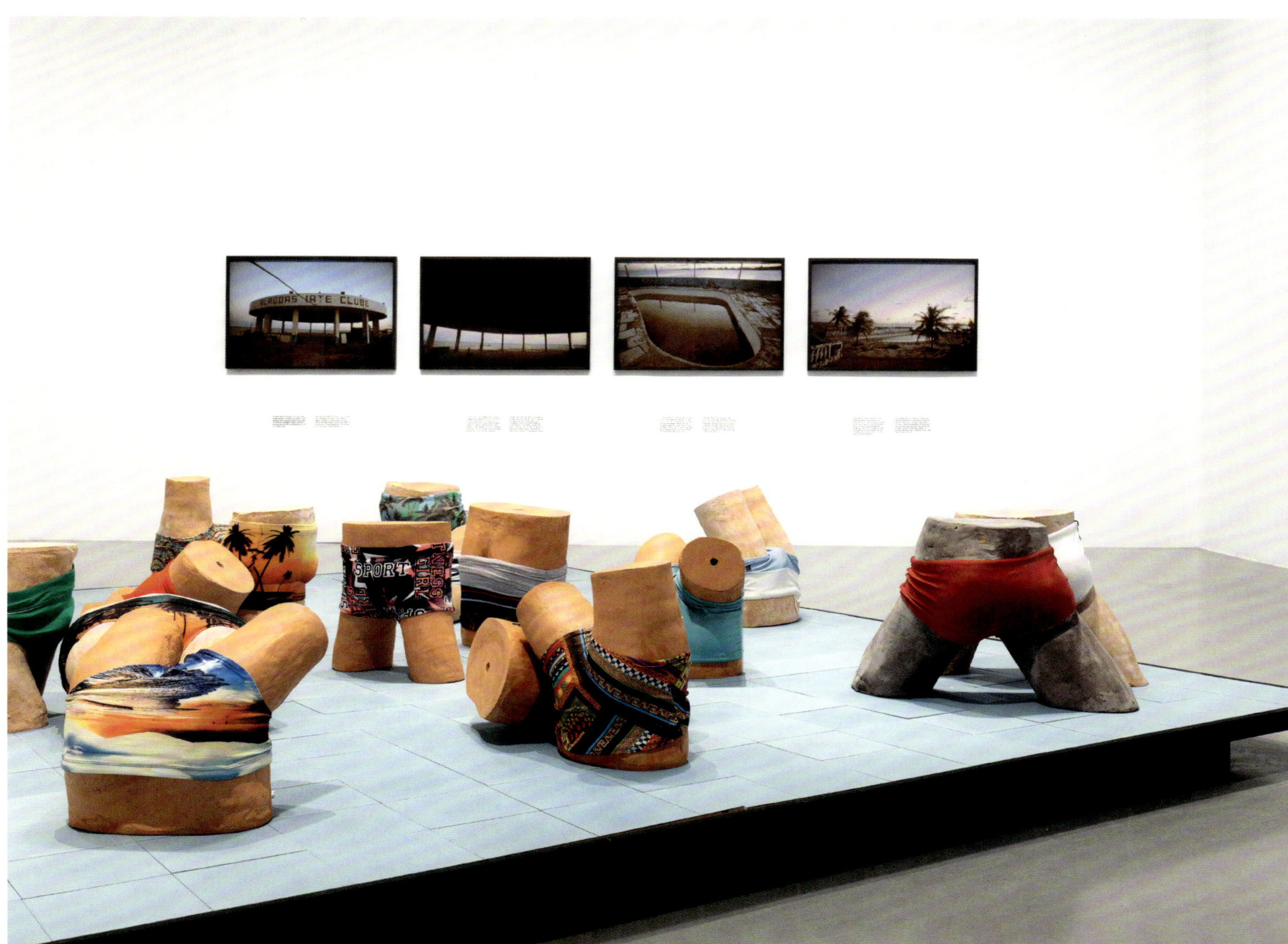

Lost and Found, 2020.
Clay sculptures and
speedos found in
swimming pool locker
rooms. Background: *The
Club*, 2010. Installation
view at Museum of Art,
Architecture and
Technology, Lisbon,
2023. Photograph by
Bruno Lopes
All works courtesy the artist
and Alexander and Bonin,
Galleria Continua, and Nara
Roesler

in one of his earliest works, *The Club*, from 2010. The building was
once a hangout for the moneyed elite of his native Maceió but now
appears as an empty ruin, a festering, fertile ground for clandestine
sexual rendezvous between men, a cruising spot rooted in an urban
wound, a trace of long-gone glory. We don't see sex but, instead,
the decaying ledges and pillars that embraced a marginal form of
love and lust.

"Ruins are a place of power, filled with the sadness for
something that was lost, but also a place of regeneration, a place
to fuck," he says. "Those ruins and the sea filled me with hope,
the salt, the heavy air of the beach, all this showed me I could live
my sexuality. My art somehow became this, a day at the beach,
this melancholy drive, sweet and lazy, the erotic dimension of
life itself."

Silas Martí is a writer based in São Paulo and
an editor at the newspaper *Folha de S.Paulo*.

Marcelo Gomes
Things, Moments, Multitudes

Jesse Dorris

The remarkable story of the photographer Marcelo Gomes begins in northern Brazil, near the equator. It was wet there. When he was twelve, his parents took him to a concert by the Brazilian musician Caetano Veloso, a cofounder of the avant-pop psychedelic movement Tropicália, who had been exiled from his home country during its military dictatorship. For Gomes, who grew up in a smaller city, it was a transformative, visceral experience, an introduction to how art could move people. As an adult, in 2016, he took Veloso's picture at a concert at the Inhotim art gallery in Minas Gerais. I asked Gomes in a recent conversation what he wanted from such portraits of his heroes. "To preserve them," he says. "There's a dream where I'm from, a dream of Brazil that sort of dies with him, in a sense, which will be very sad."

Gomes, who now lives in Paris after years in New York, came to the United States to attend the University of Iowa on a full basketball scholarship. Team sports resonated, he explains, because of the surrender, the subsuming of one's self into a composite. "There's something really beautiful about the fact that you're a collective of very disparate upbringings and cultures and geographies," he says. "There's something really nice about just sticking these people together and letting them figure it out. And if they do figure it out, the odds are that they will be much better than the individual."

Photography is an individual pursuit that often relies on team collaboration. Gomes makes evocative work entirely for himself but also dips into the fashion world. Lately, he says, the two are blending further, as he's permitted to use personal work in commercial contexts. His images for Editions de Parfums Frédéric Malle feature red rectangular forms, like an olfactory Rothko canvas. He trades traditional advertising's aspirational charge—*buy* this so you can be this—for expressions of beauty that are expansive yet found mostly in closely observed moments and things.

A bubble becomes, in its bursting, a portal. A fig beads with ooze. In the end, natural splendor depends on submission. An image from Hydra is all cerulean swoon, but accessible only because someone built a ladder of bent metal and stuck it in the sea. The water is still, but we know those waves. They can pool like the wooden beard Gomes cropped from a large statue he saw in Paris, its ostentatious masculinity virile and swirling. The image is grainy; it could almost be chewed. Gomes calls his world of texture a "sweetened reality." It's bigger and beautiful. What more could one want?

Untitled (New York), 2017

Jesse Dorris is a writer based in New York and a frequent contributor to *Aperture* and the *New Yorker*.

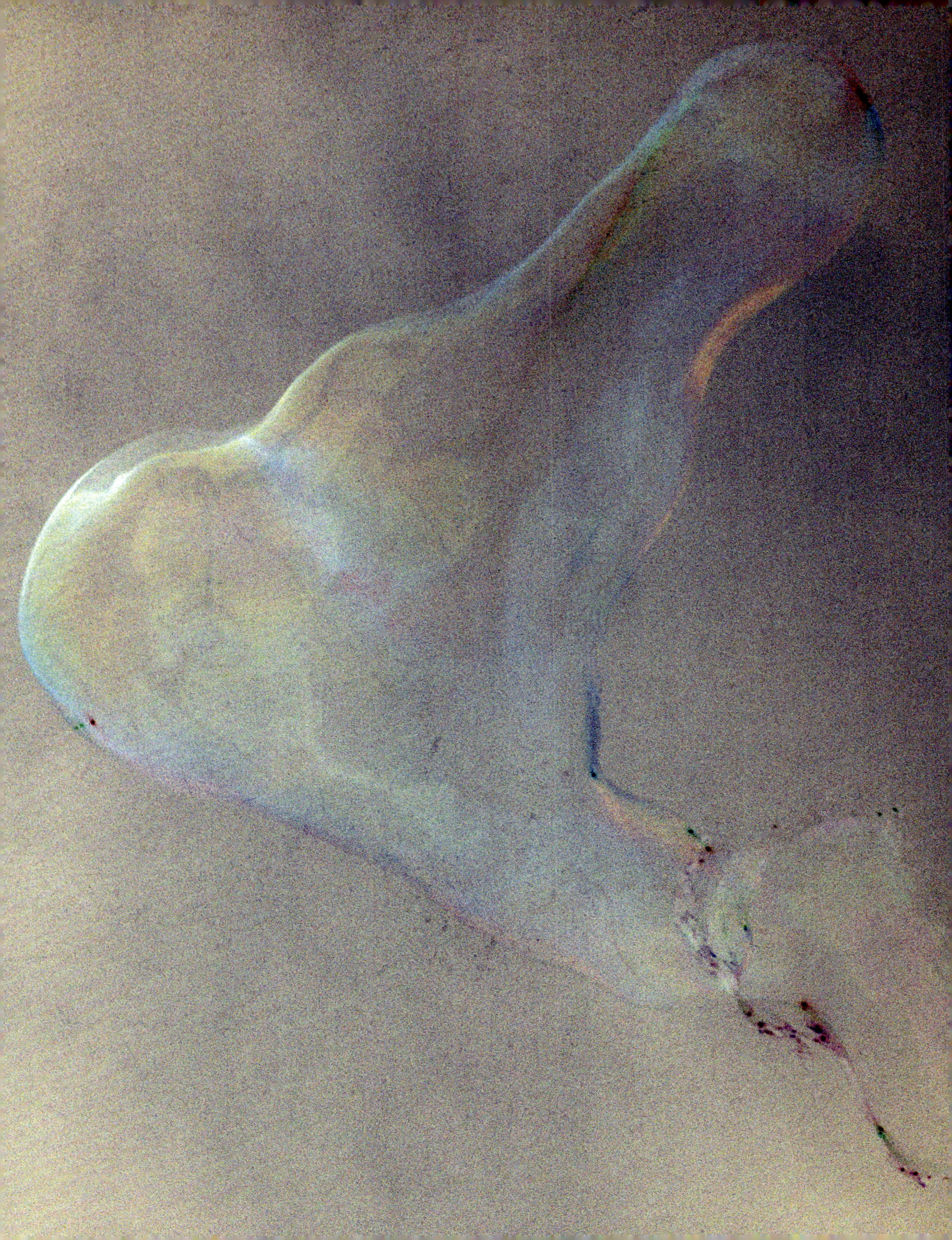

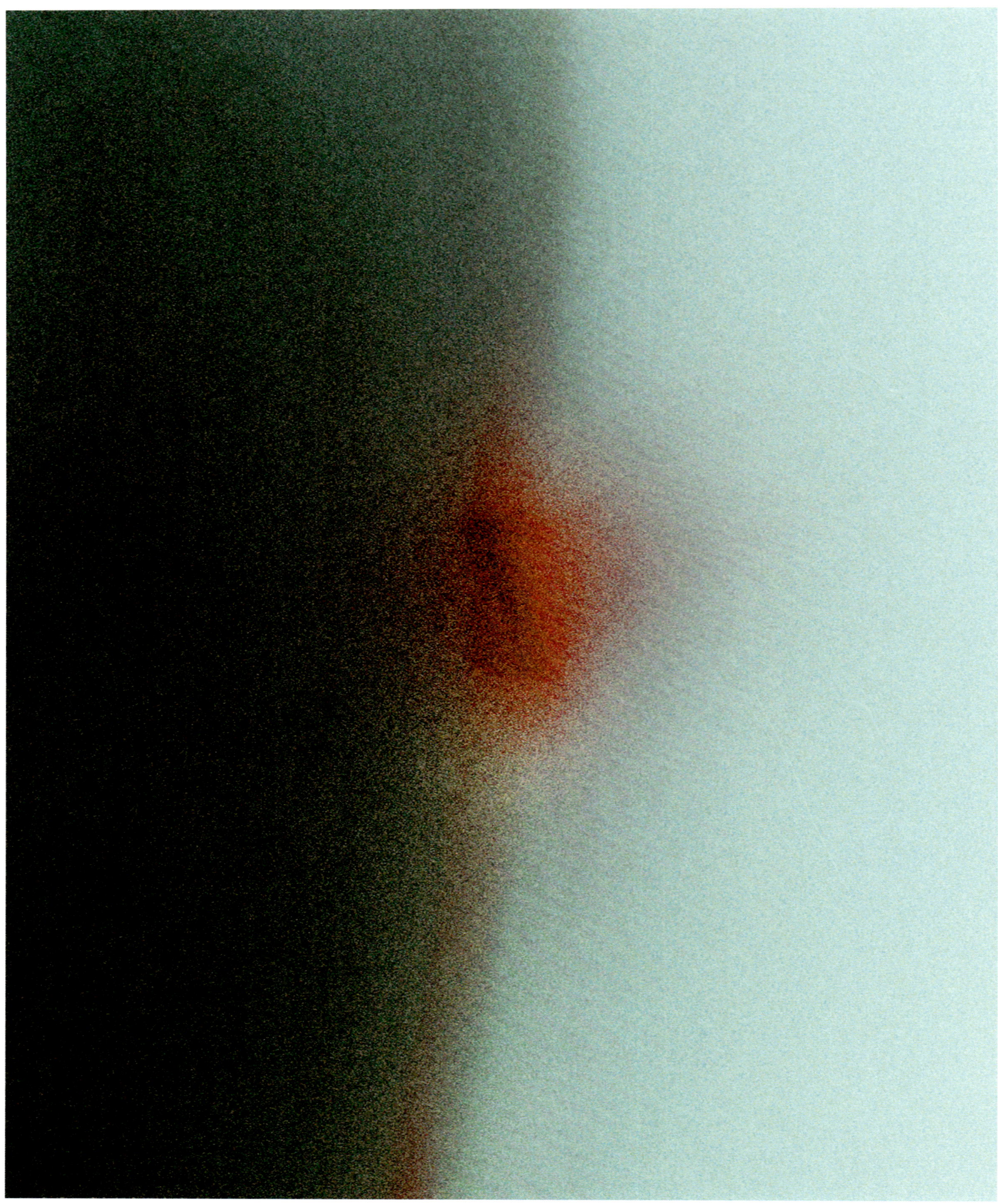

This page:
Untitled (After Durer,
New York), 2017; opposite:
Untitled (Fig, Paris), 2017

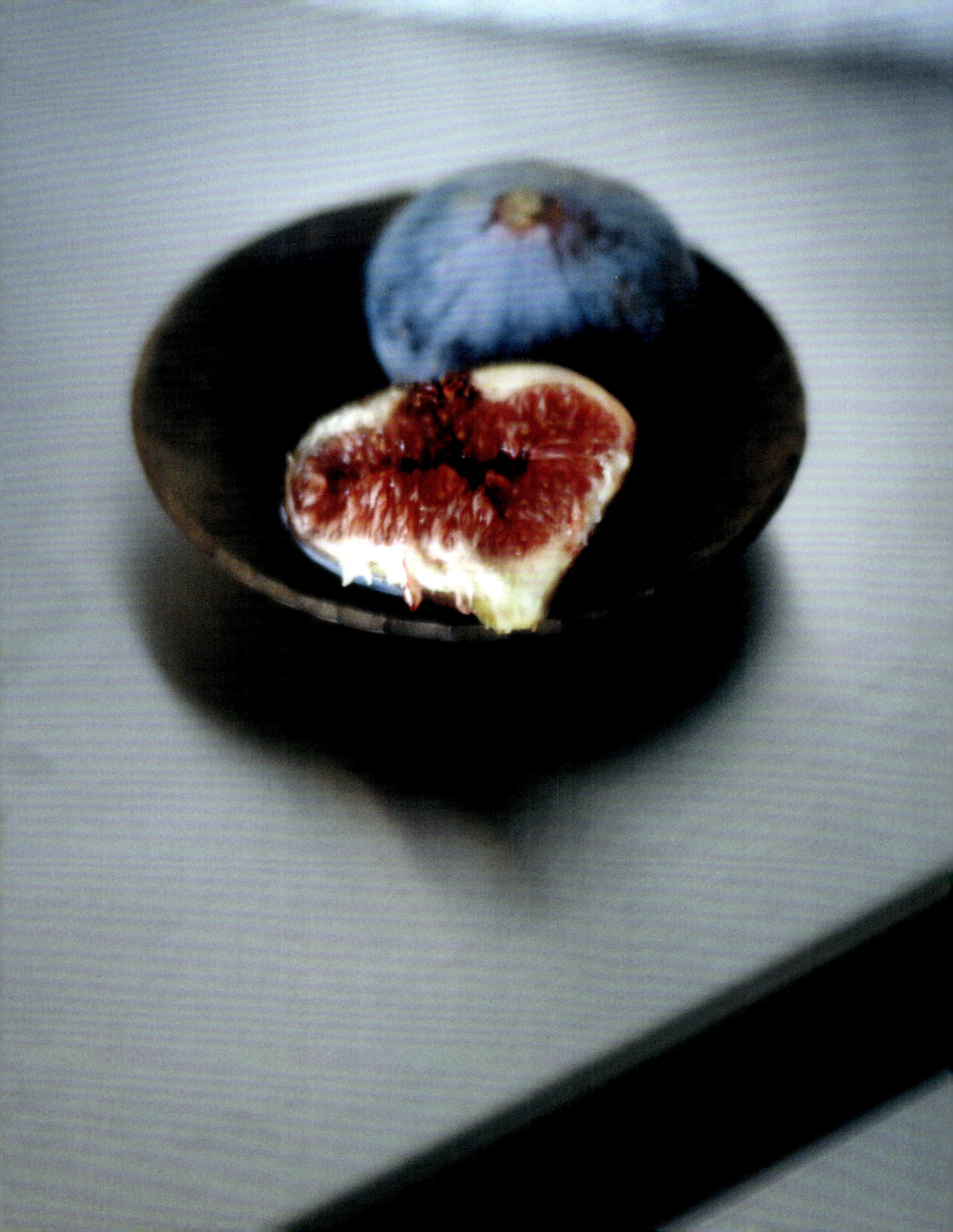

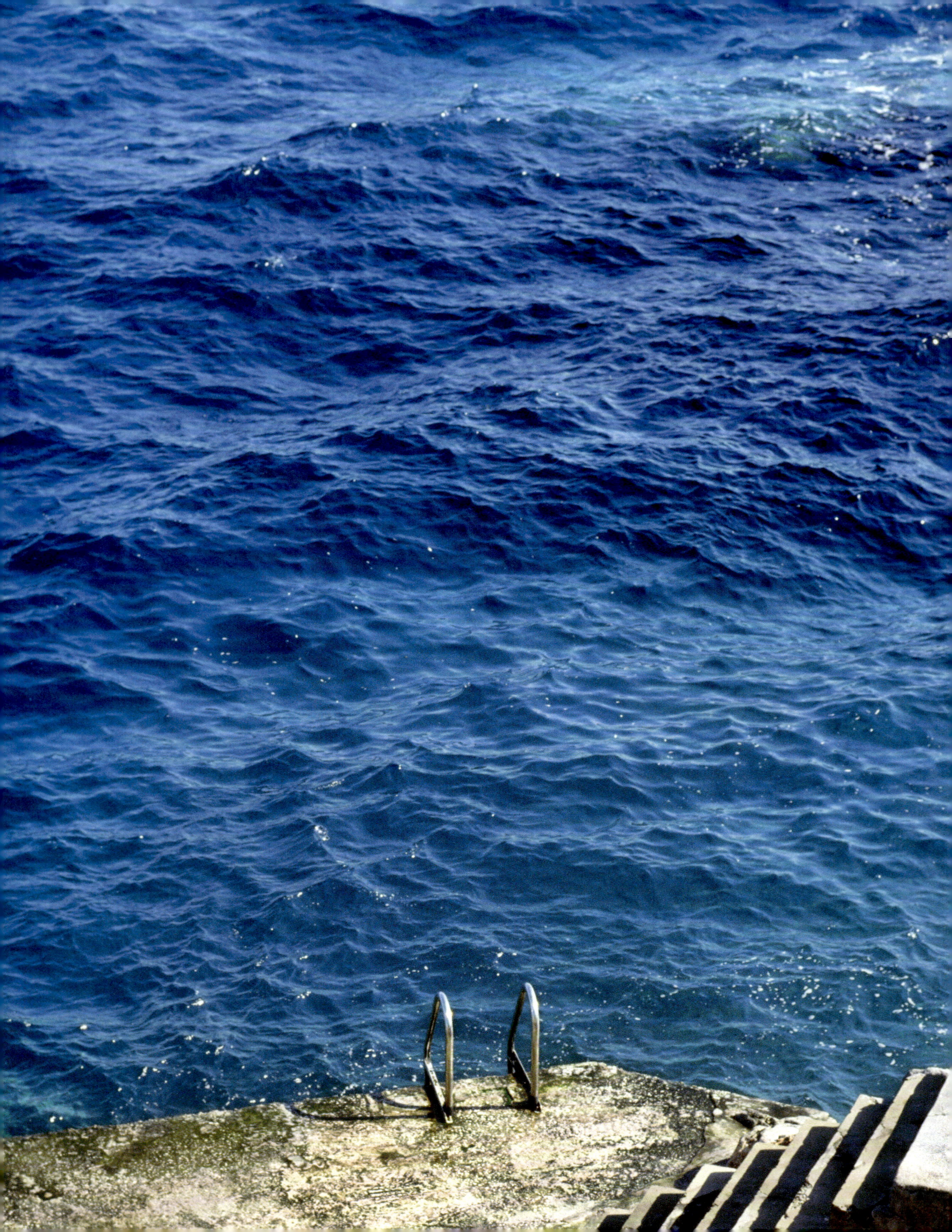

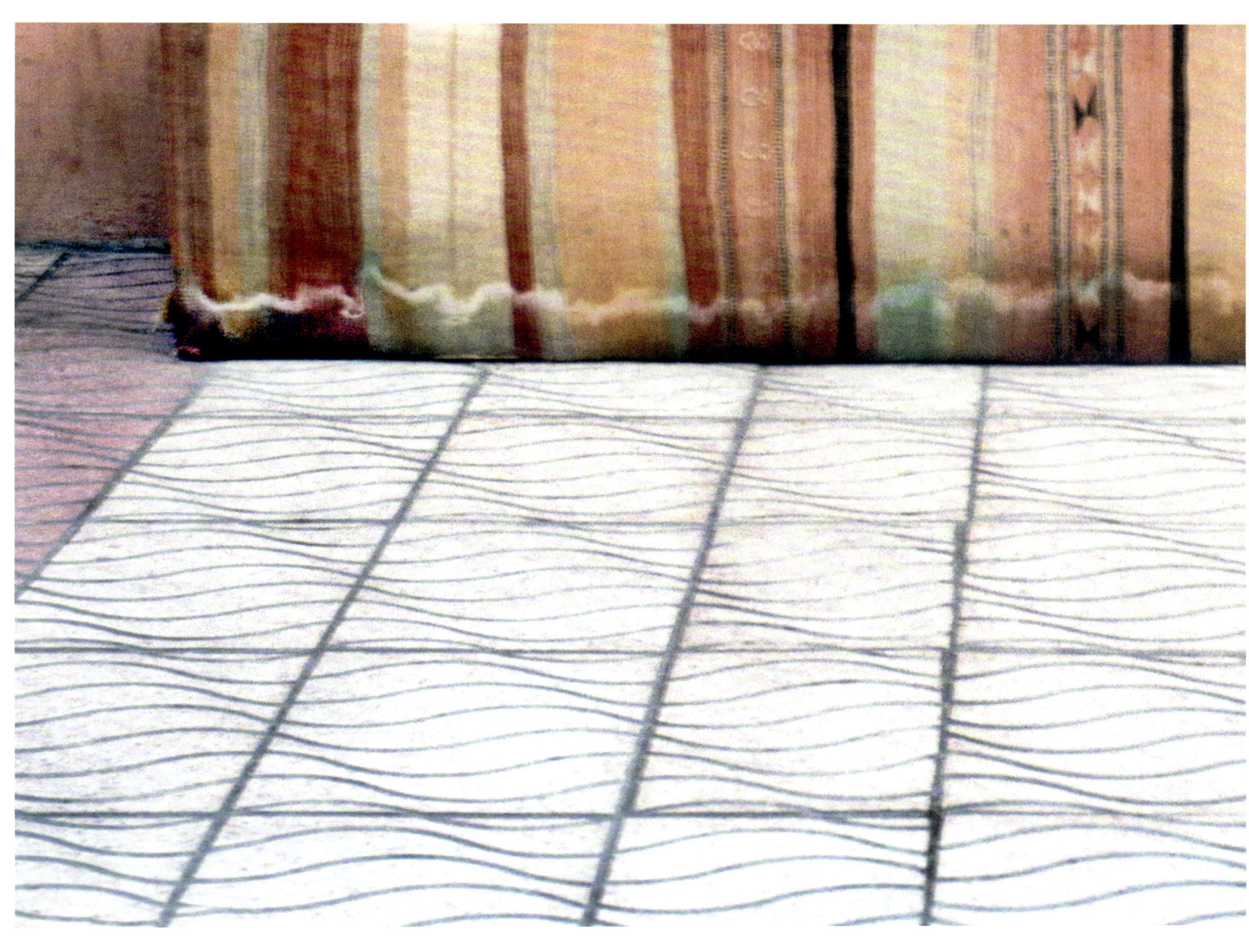

This page:
Untitled (Marrakesh),
2020; opposite: *Untitled*
(Hydra), 2020

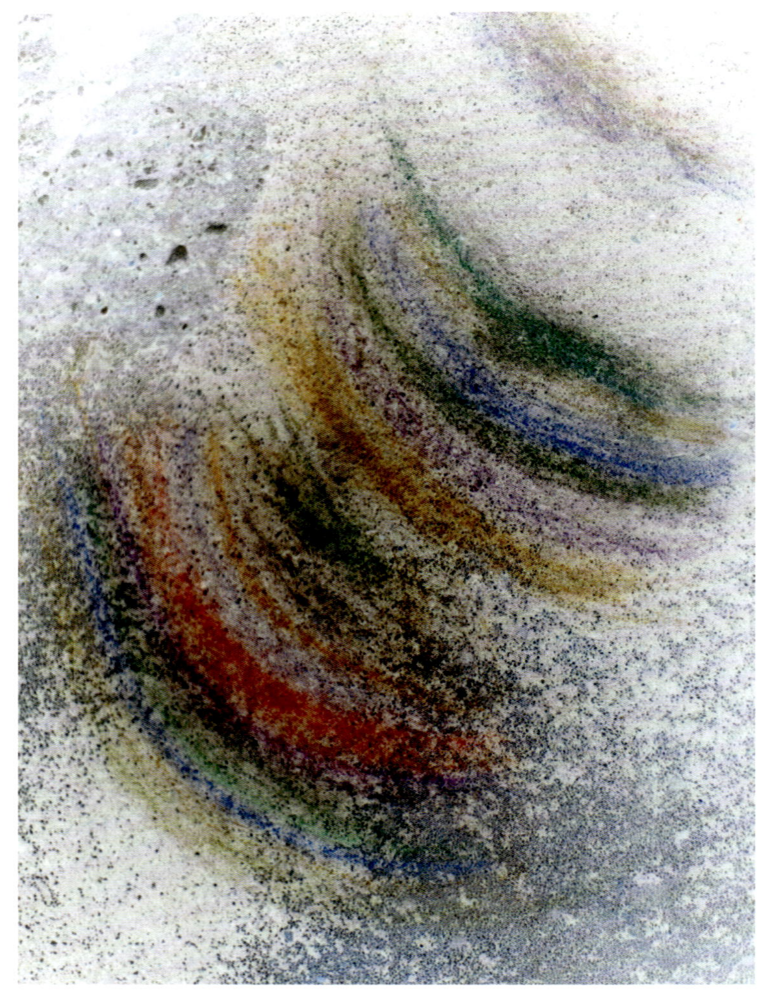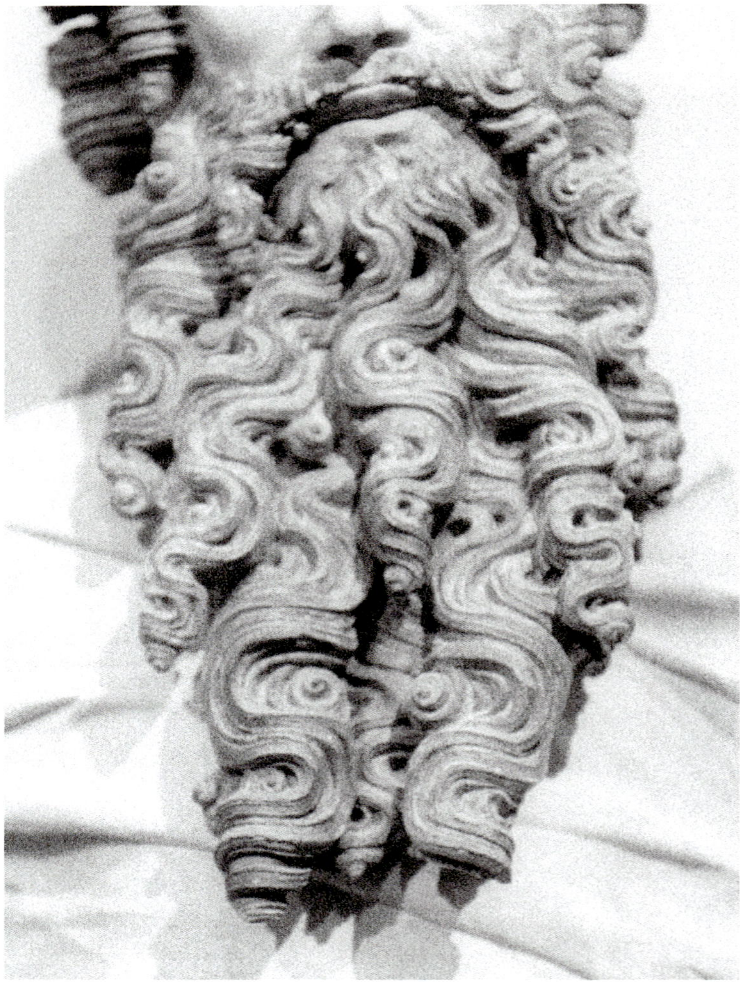

This page, left:
Untitled (Milan), 2016;
right: *Untitled (Paris)*,
2022; opposite:
*Untitled (Flower Study,
Paris)*, 2020
Courtesy the artist

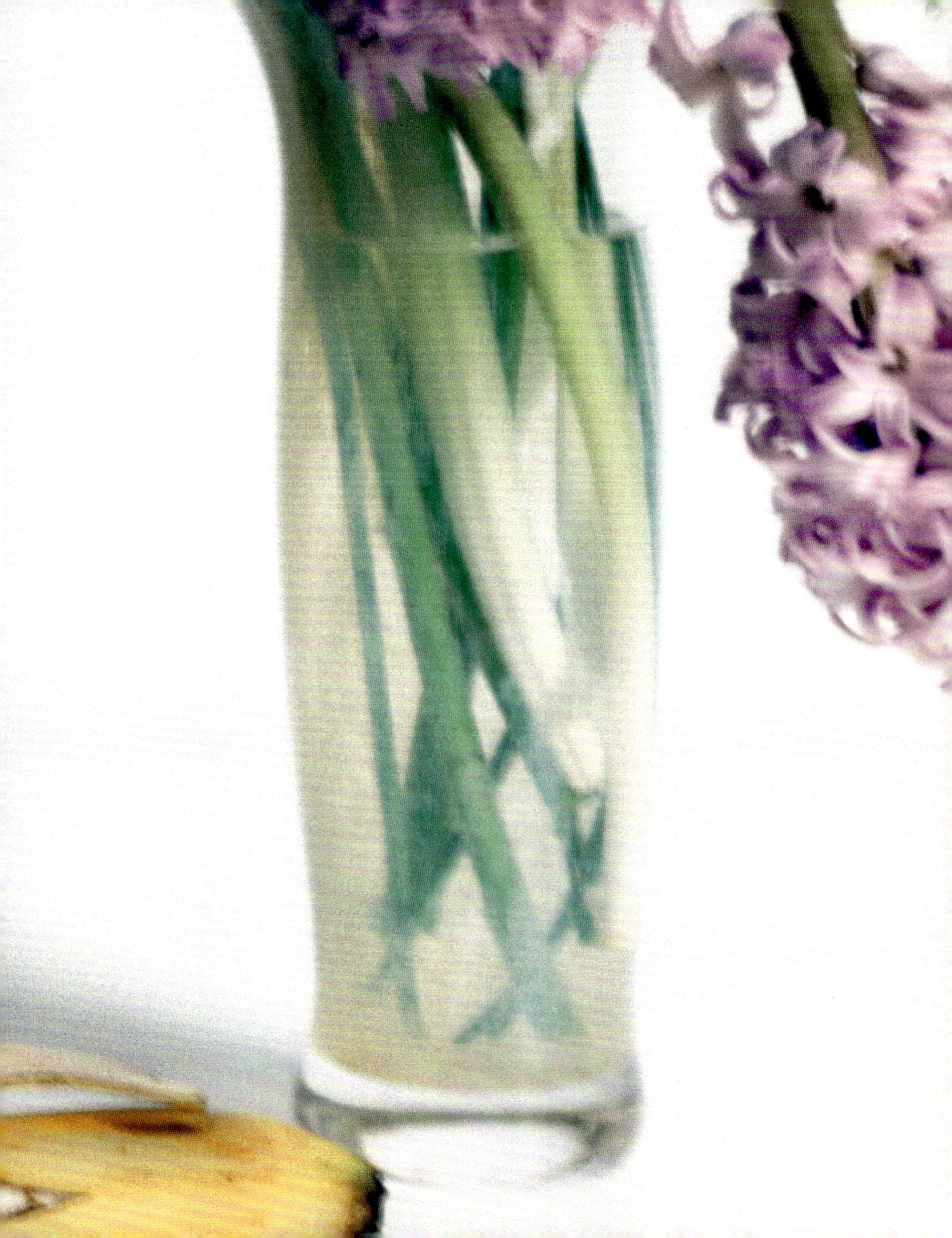

Ishiuchi Miyako

For decades, the esteemed photographer has delved into personal and social histories with vigilant attention, revealing how something as physical as a home, a body, or a loved one may be dispossessed of us at any time.
Andrew Maerkle

The Afterlives of Objects

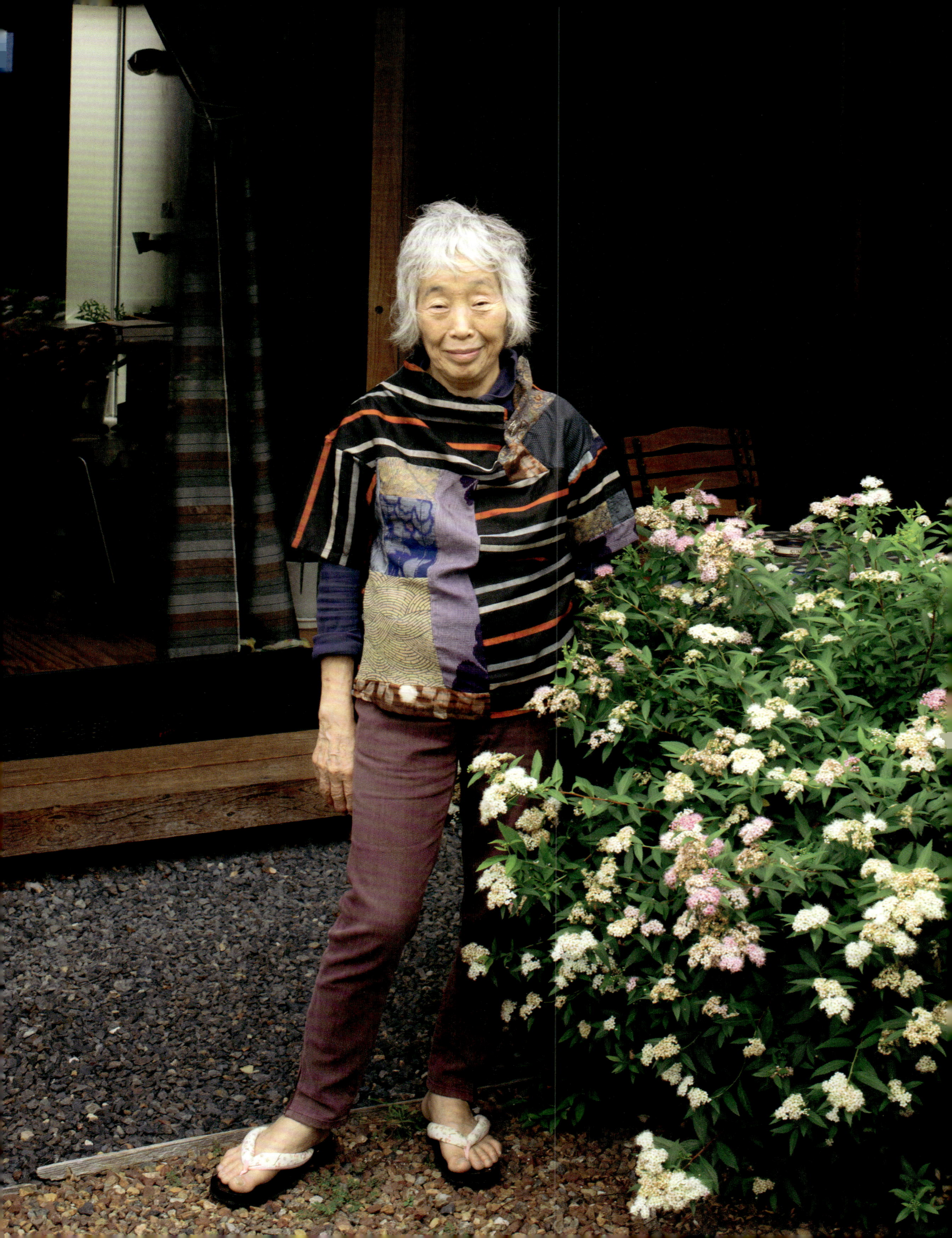

Ishiuchi has been one of Japan's foremost photographers practically from the moment she first picked up a camera.

Maybe it's just because it's our first meeting, but Ishiuchi Miyako frequently deflects from herself when she speaks. She relishes asserting, several times over the course of the afternoon we spend together at her home in Kiryu, Gunma Prefecture, about two hours by express train north and inland from Tokyo, that she's not really a photographer. Yet she's been one of Japan's foremost photographers practically from the moment she first picked up a camera, after receiving some equipment from a friend, in the mid-1970s. Ishiuchi insists that she doesn't take many photographs and that, when she does, she never fusses over composition. And she demurs that she's no writer, despite being a powerful storyteller whose 1993 book, *Monochrome*, a collection of reflections on photography, reads like a postmodern fiction in which the elements of her work—individual dots of black ink, a trio of vintage enlargers—function as characters in their own right, appearing as objects of desire, attachment, and relinquishment. Even Ishiuchi's name is an invention of a sort: at a certain point, she took her mother's full maiden name and dropped her given one.

Ishiuchi studied textile art at Tama Art University in the late 1960s before turning to photography, a field in which she is essentially self-taught. Steeped in the radical foment of that era, she has a bracingly independent mindset, unperturbed by the sanctities of what then was, and still is, a male-dominated field. Her investigations of the traces and markings of personal and social histories on the physical world, in everything from the built environment to the human body to domestic objects, have earned her sustained acclaim. She won one of Japan's highest honors for photography, the Kimura Ihei Award, at the start of her career in 1979, and more recently received the Hasselblad Award, in 2014.

She moved back to Kiryu, a historical center of silk production, in 2018. Although this is the city where Ishiuchi was born and spent

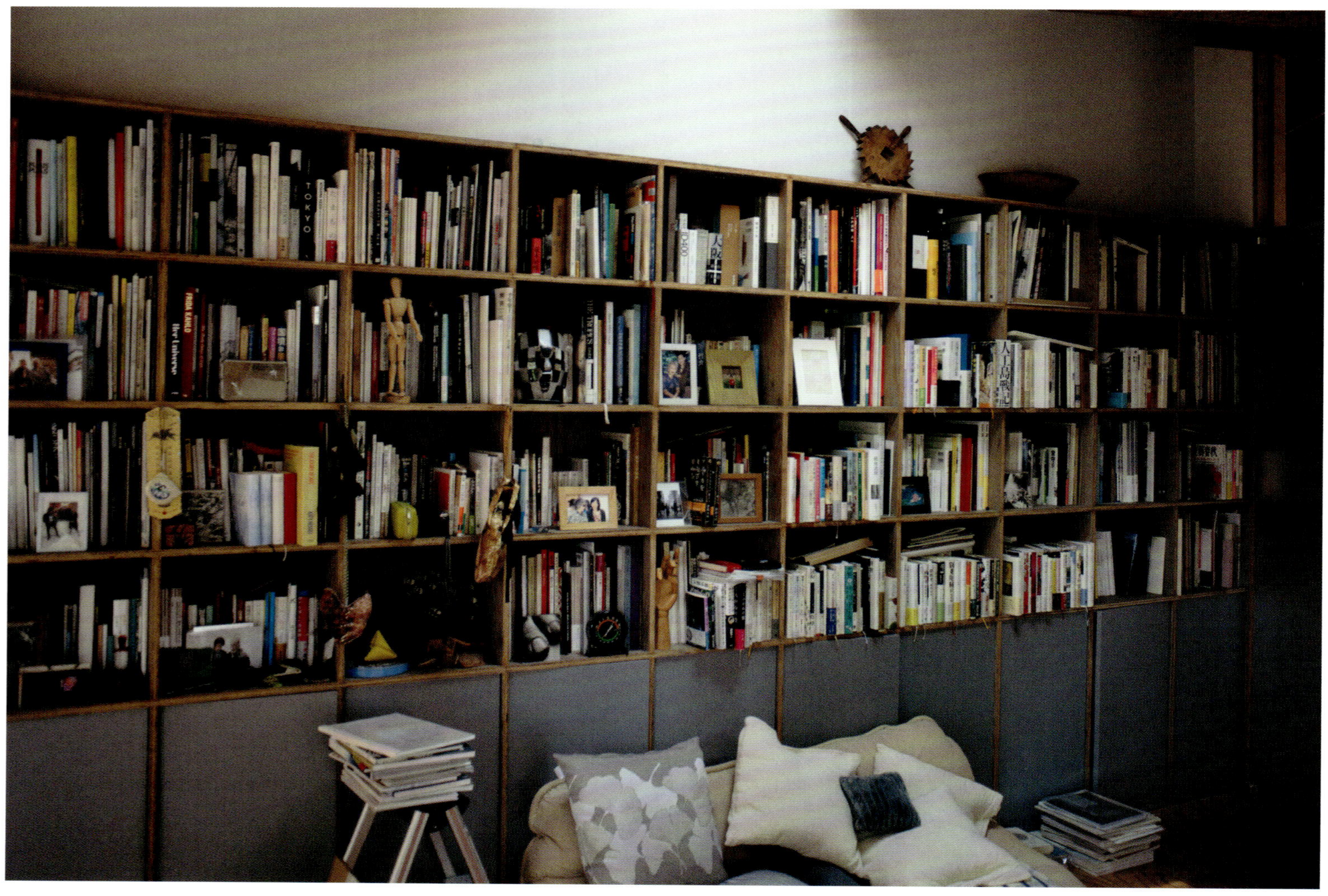

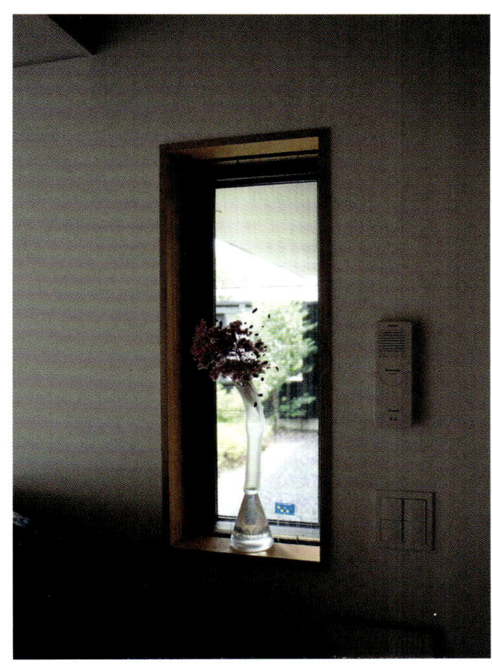
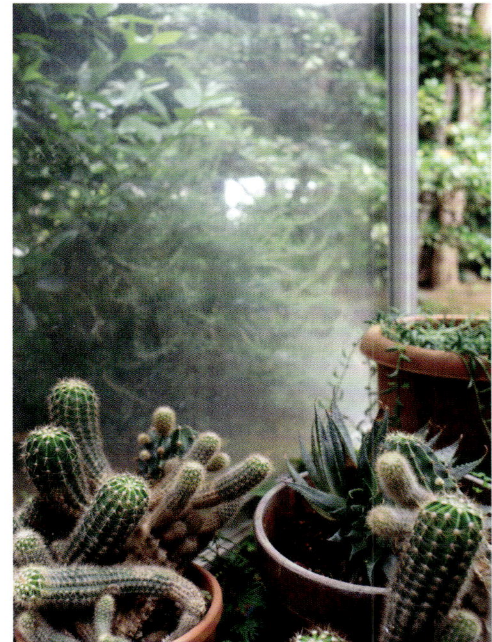
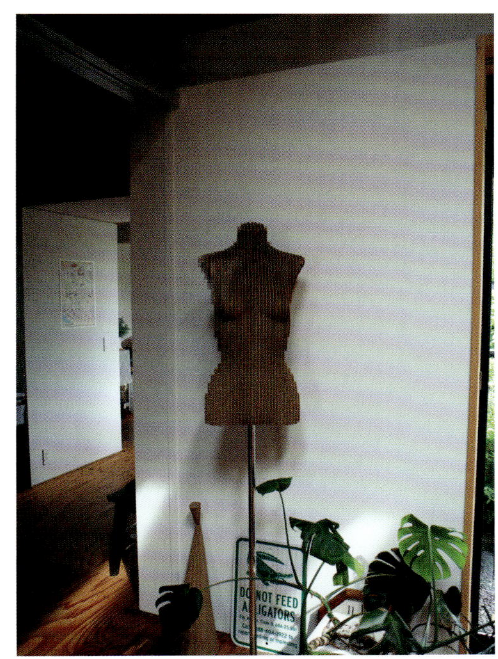
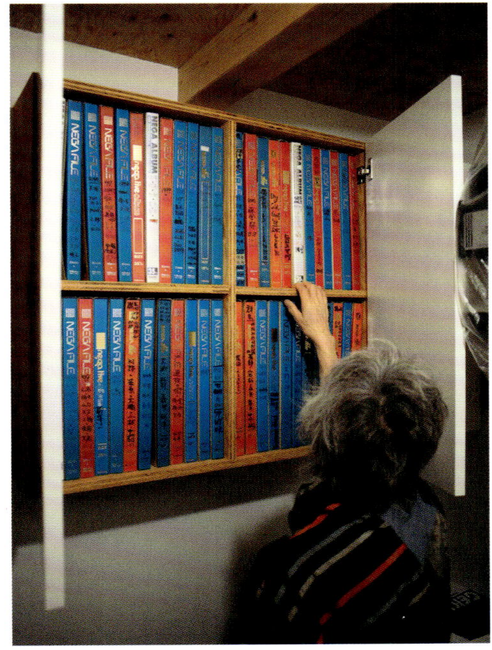
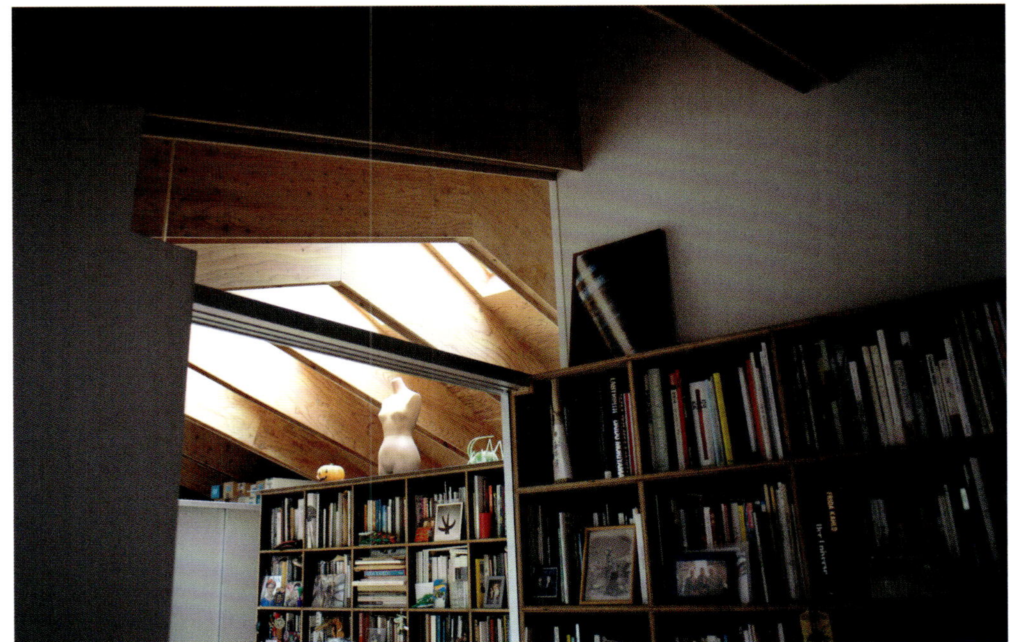
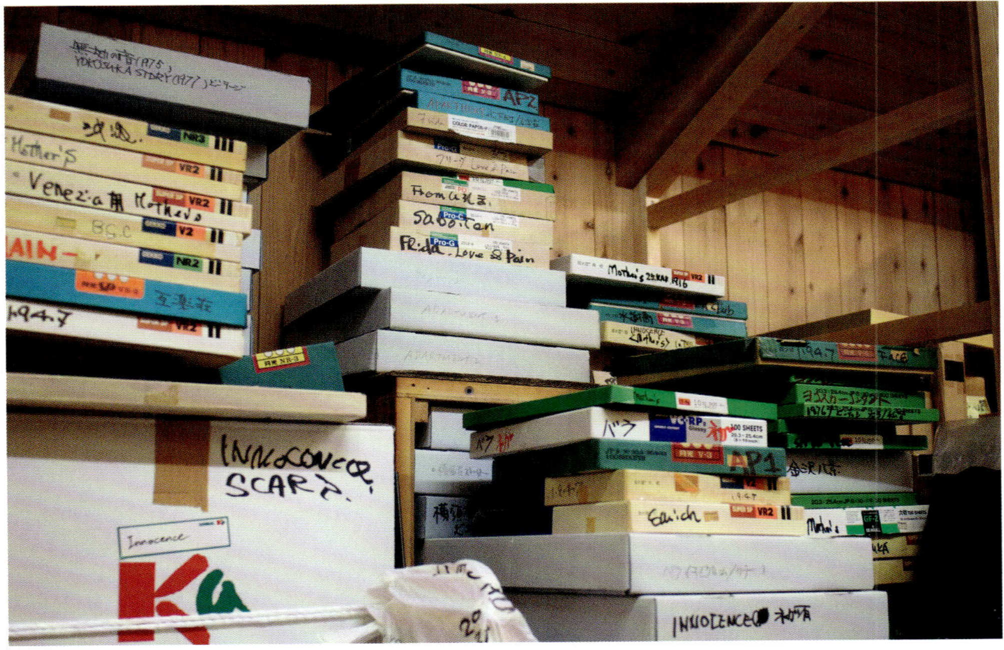
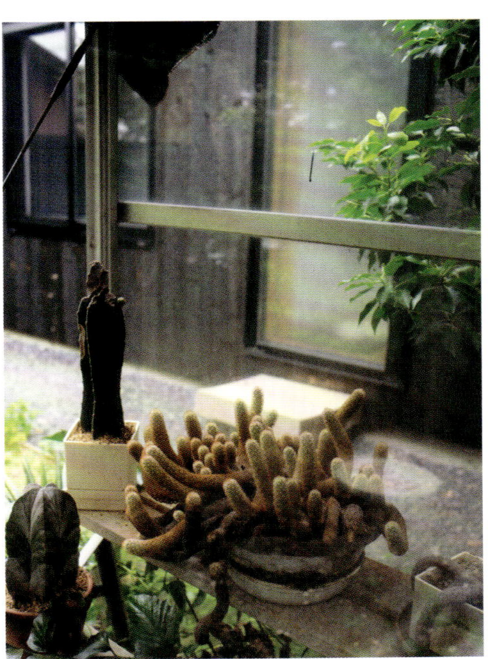

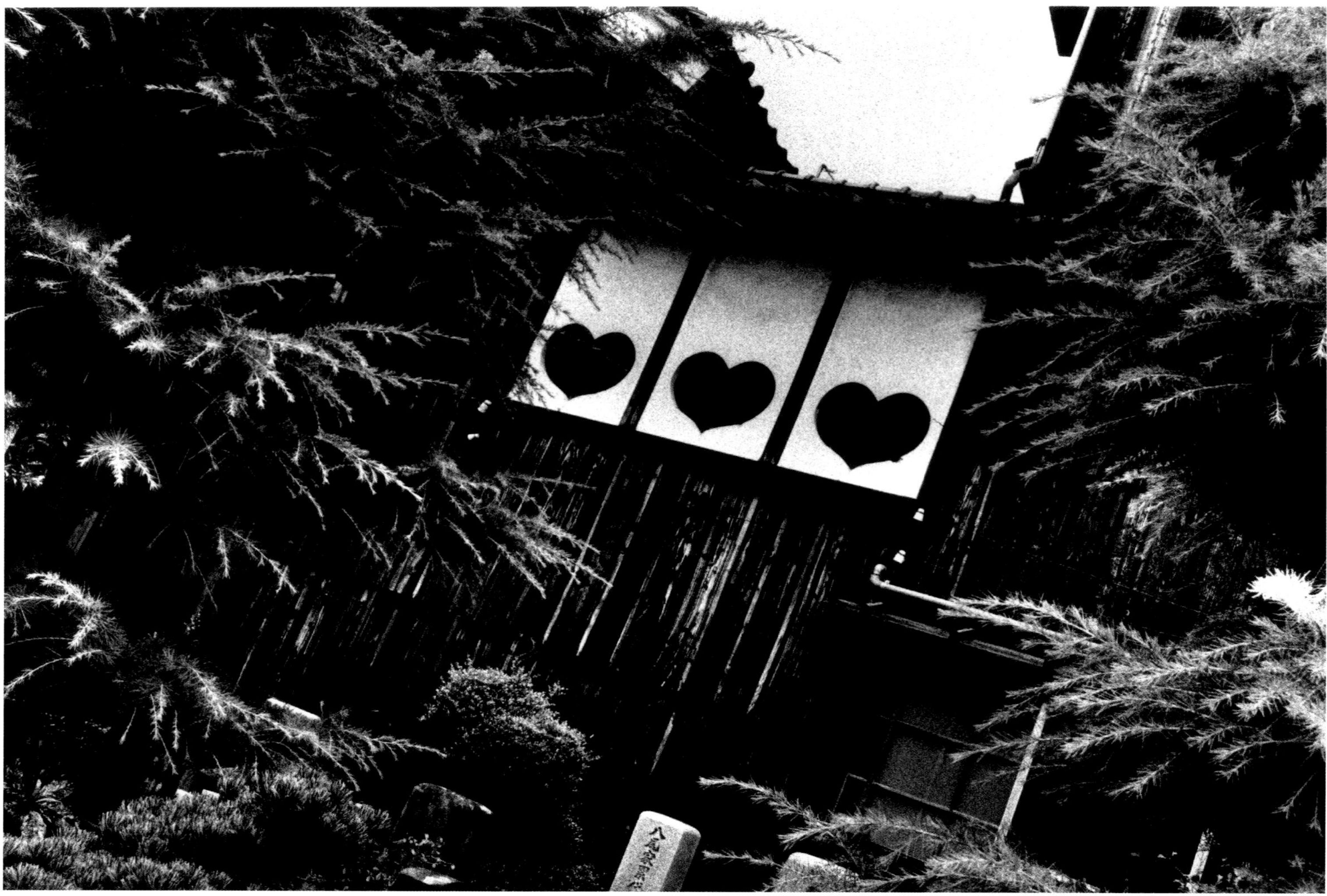

the first six years of her life, she surprises me again when telling me that she came here as an outsider, drawn not by family ties but rather the influence of three figures with local roots, all dead: Junichi Arai, the innovative textile designer; Eiji Okawa, a businessman and art patron whose collection forms the basis of his namesake Okawa Museum of Art, in Kiryu; and Shima Ryu, whose 1864 portrait of her husband is considered to be the earliest known photograph made by a woman in Japan. Ishiuchi now lives in a new house designed in the style of an airy modern bungalow, with skylights and sliding glass doors looking onto a garden.

Her main focus these days is preparing for an upcoming solo exhibition at the Okawa Museum of Art, scheduled to open in July 2024, which Ishiuchi informs me will be the first time the entire museum is dedicated to a single artist. When I visited, she had just decided the exhibition's English title, *Step through Time*, which nods to both the central staircase leading down to the museum galleries and Ishiuchi's view of photography as a means of "activating the past," as she writes in *Monochrome*. Yet, more than her photography work, she seems to be most excited about a current project with two younger, local partners in a clothing business to make jackets out of salvaged kimono fabric and obi sashes, reams of which get thrown out every year as an older generation of Japanese dies off and younger family members are suddenly confronted with inheriting a lifetime's worth of possessions. The jackets are fashioned in the style of *sukajan*, the souvenir garments commemorating US military deployments in the Asia Pacific through orientalized embroidered motifs.

The references in these textiles to the US military connect to her long-standing concern with US imperialism. An early celebrated body of photographs was made in Yokosuka, the port town at the entrance of Tokyo Bay, which since 1945 has been the base of the US Navy's Seventh Fleet. The postwar Allied occupation and the terms of the US-Japan Security Treaty, signed in 1951 and renewed in 1960 in the face of popular opposition, established populations of US military personnel in towns such as Yokosuka across the country, leading to quasi-colonial conditions for the surrounding communities. If the bases help sustain the local economies (the Korean War is credited with kick-starting Japan's postwar recovery) and contribute to cross-cultural exchange, they are also a source of tension over everything from sexual violence to environmental concerns.

Ishiuchi, who was born in 1947, grew up in Yokosuka from age six onward and later returned to photograph the city for *Yokosuka Story* (1976–77). Her haunting images made there feature skewed, black-and-white snaps of military installations, street scenes, aging cinemas, and pastoral vistas, all printed with characteristic grain. Even the sky often appears as a sandpapery field of particulate matter rather than mere negative space. Through these photographs and her subsequent series *Apartment* (1977–78), focusing on dilapidated low-income housing, and *Endless Night* (1978–ongoing), exploring former brothel buildings across the country, Ishiuchi evocatively traces the overlaps between her own biography and the nexus of "liquor, girls, and soldiers, sex and war" (as she puts it pointedly in one of her essays) that loomed over her childhood.

Making the work was not easy, and it required Ishiuchi to also confront her own objectification as a woman in a patriarchal society. For six months in 1981, she took over a former cabaret on Dobuita Street, the main drag outside the Yokosuka naval base, then notorious for its rows of boozy, seedy establishments, which, Ishiuchi writes, "stank of semen." She used the cabaret as a studio and exhibition space, capturing the environs, developing her photographs on-site, and then putting them on display. When I ask what gave her the confidence to pursue her practice in those early years, Ishiuchi replies with a grin, "I just imagined I was making the photographs for aliens, because obviously, they were never going to show up to see them."

As urban development accelerated amid Japan's economic surge in the 1980s, she continued seeking out buildings that were about to be torn down. Ishiuchi had a keen sense for quotidian sites inscribed with the history of Japan's turbulent twentieth century, such as the Gorakuso apartments in Yokohama, the industrial port city just up the coast from Yokosuka. Built as modern luxury housing in the wake of the devastating Kanto earthquake of 1923, the complex was requisitioned by the Japanese Navy during the war, and then briefly converted into a brothel under the Allied occupation before eventually being returned to residential use. She also photographed the remnants of the US Navy's Yokosuka Enlisted Men's Club, in its heyday a privileged zone offering American servicemen movie screenings and slot machines, among other diversions.

Ishiuchi states that she sees her photographs of buildings as portraits: "Those buildings were alive, and they felt all the more alive to me knowing they were about to be torn down." She used the printing process—manipulating contrast, the density of the ink, and the size of the prints—to heighten the sense of the spaces being organisms in their own right, paying particular attention to the teeming detail of paint flaking from the walls and ceilings or fields of debris scattered on the floors. The resulting images play on the spectral entanglements of photographer, setting, object, photograph, and viewer; the absence of multiple generations of former inhabitants and the inevitable obsolescence of the site loom equally large.

"A photograph is something I make in the darkroom," Ishiuchi declares. "It's not a document." Given her experience with textile art, an important revelation in her photography practice was the realization that the printing process is akin to the dyeing process. She tells me that developing her own photographs offered her an escape from reality. In *Monochrome*, she describes darkroom work

"A photograph is something I make in the darkroom," Ishiuchi declares. "It's not a document."

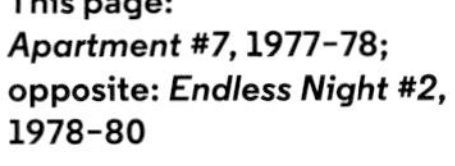

This page:
Apartment #7, 1977–78;
opposite: *Endless Night #2*,
1978–80

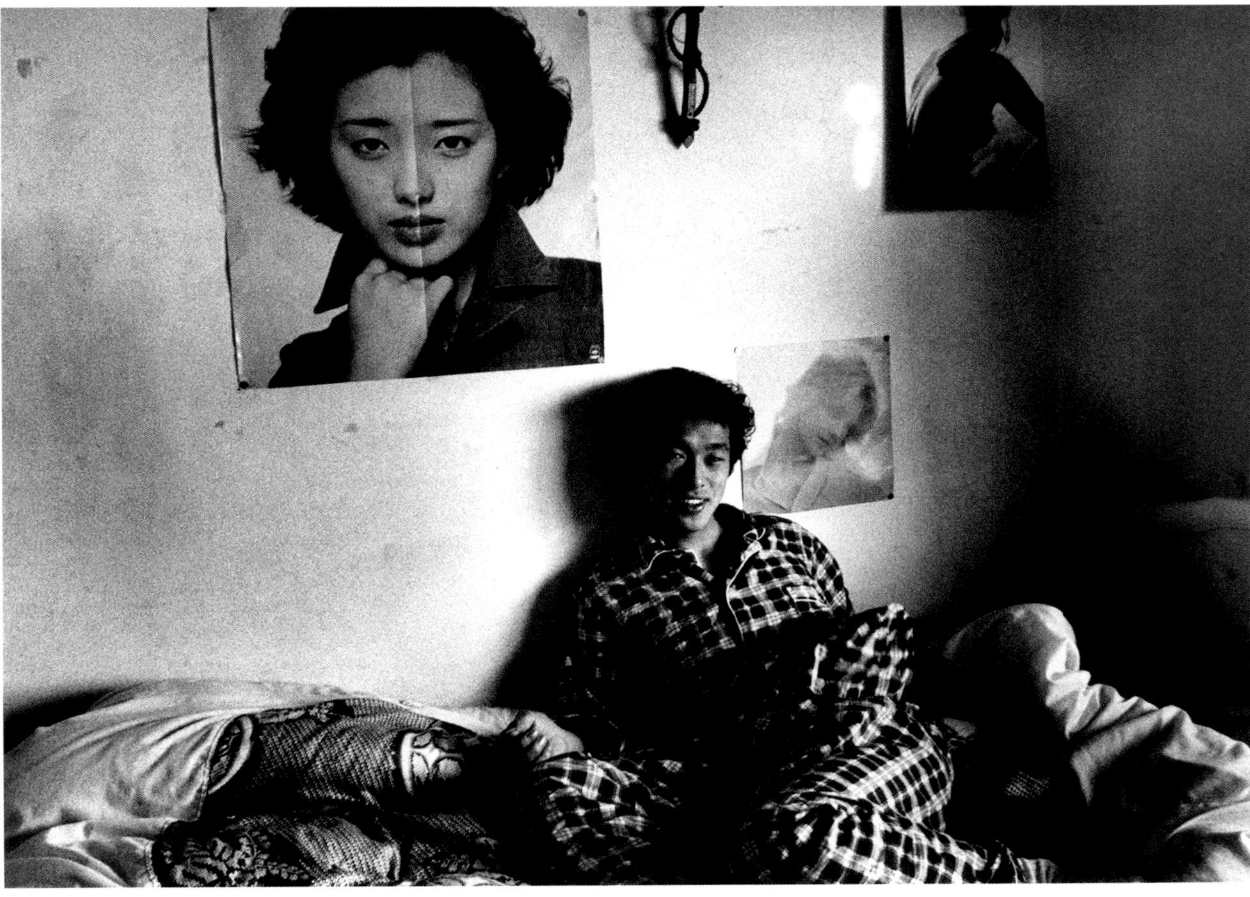

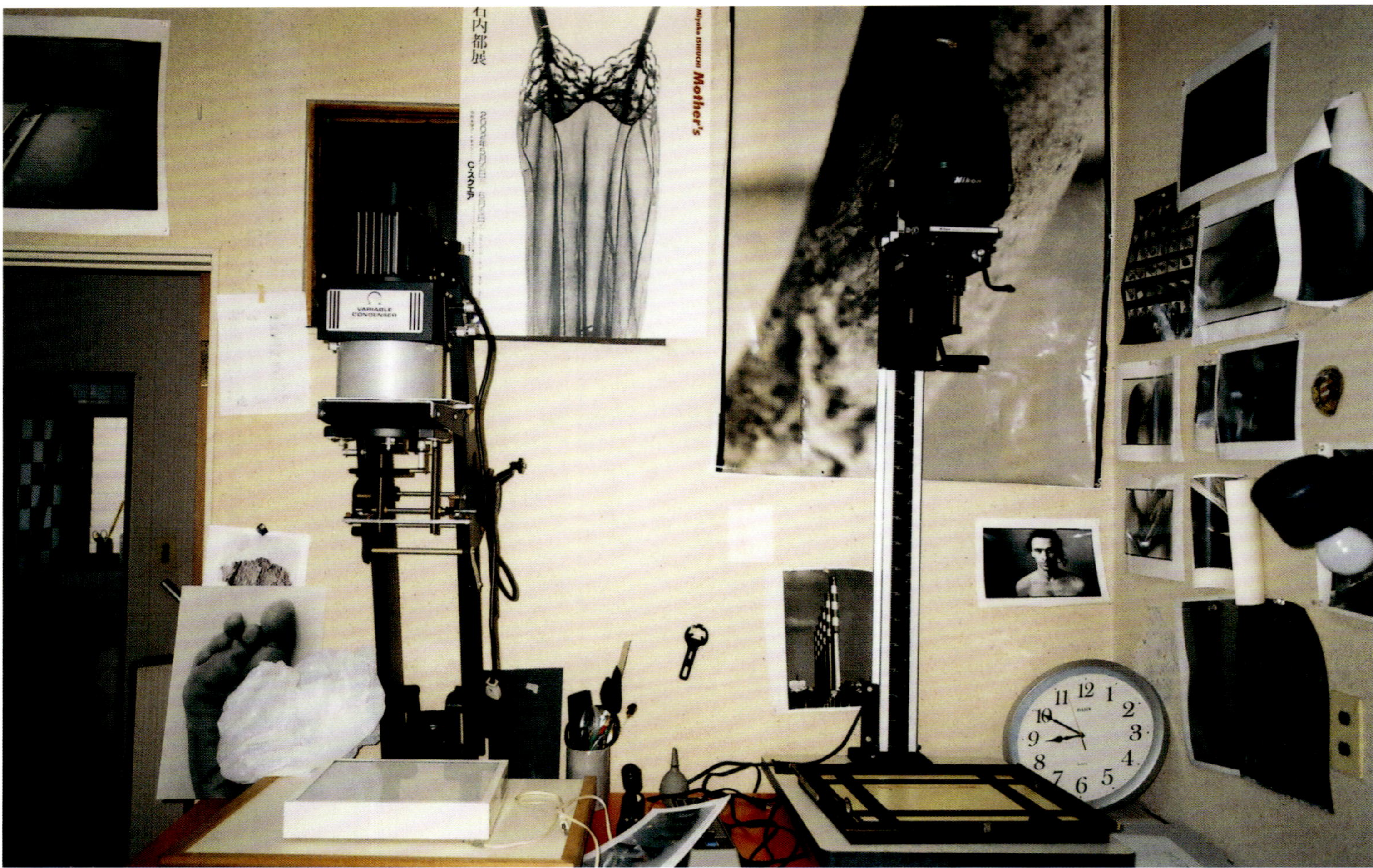

as being "close to sex," emphasizing the sensuality of the process and the smells and sensations that overtake her when she is at work alone in the humid darkness. But her declaration against documentation is not just an assertion of artistic bravado. It also comes from an understanding that you can never actually revisit the substance of a photograph. For all its realism, a photograph will, sooner or later, become a reference without a referent. "All photographs have a will to document. The stronger that will, the more the identity of the subject gets dispersed and diminished," Ishiuchi writes. "Until it gets obliterated in the photograph." That is, the more we try to fix something in place, the more it escapes us.

Due to health concerns, Ishiuchi stopped developing her work years ago. She now sends her film to a lab. This transition coincided with a shift to working primarily in color. "If monochrome is something I held tight to me, color brings distance," she says. Although she had to let go of her old way of working, over the past two decades she has found a new language for investigating the afterlives of objects. She has since pictured the possessions left behind after the death of her mother, the personal effects of victims of the atomic bombing of Hiroshima from the collection of the Hiroshima Peace Memorial Museum, and the former belongings of the artist Frida Kahlo held in a museum in Mexico City.

The series *Mother's* (2000–5) was exhibited at the Japan Pavilion during the 2005 Venice Biennale and was recently shown alongside work by the younger photographer Yuhki Touyama (who accompanied me on my visit with Ishiuchi), as part of the 2023 edition of Kyotographie, an annual festival in Kyoto. These images hold a visceral charge similar to that of the much earlier Yokosuka work. Depicting personal items that once belonged to her deceased mother, there's an oedipal frisson behind these color close-ups, enlarged to relatively massive proportions. Sticky red lipstick protrudes from its burnished metallic casing. Diaphanous lingerie

on a white backdrop, printed slightly larger than life-size, seems ready to float off the wall. Without revealing anything explicit about the nature of Ishiuchi's relationship with her mother, the images take on a life of their own, hovering uneasily between the allure of advertising, the macabre of a memento mori, and the banality of a product catalog. As with Ishiuchi herself, they refuse to be pinned down.

One of her recent projects, *Moving Away* (2015–18), represents a full-circle moment of a sort. These photographs depict the family home that Ishiuchi inherited on her mother's passing. This was the home where Ishiuchi set up her main darkroom and that served as a base for her early projects. Photographed in lucid color, the scenes she captures—a workspace with a pair of enlargers, curled black-and-white test prints tacked to the walls nearby; a developing sink with scores of colorful plastic pans—convey, with a detached, almost forensic eye, the density of years of accumulated habitation. By forging something new from the materiality of the past, these are quintessential Ishiuchi images. "Moving away" is an inevitable theme for someone who studies how the world continually, inexorably changes around us. She shows us how something as physical and fixed as a home, a body, or a loved one may be dispossessed of us at any time. Ishiuchi's photographs are so compelling because, rather than trying to hold a memory in place, they ultimately intend to set their objects free.

Andrew Maerkle is a writer based in Tokyo.

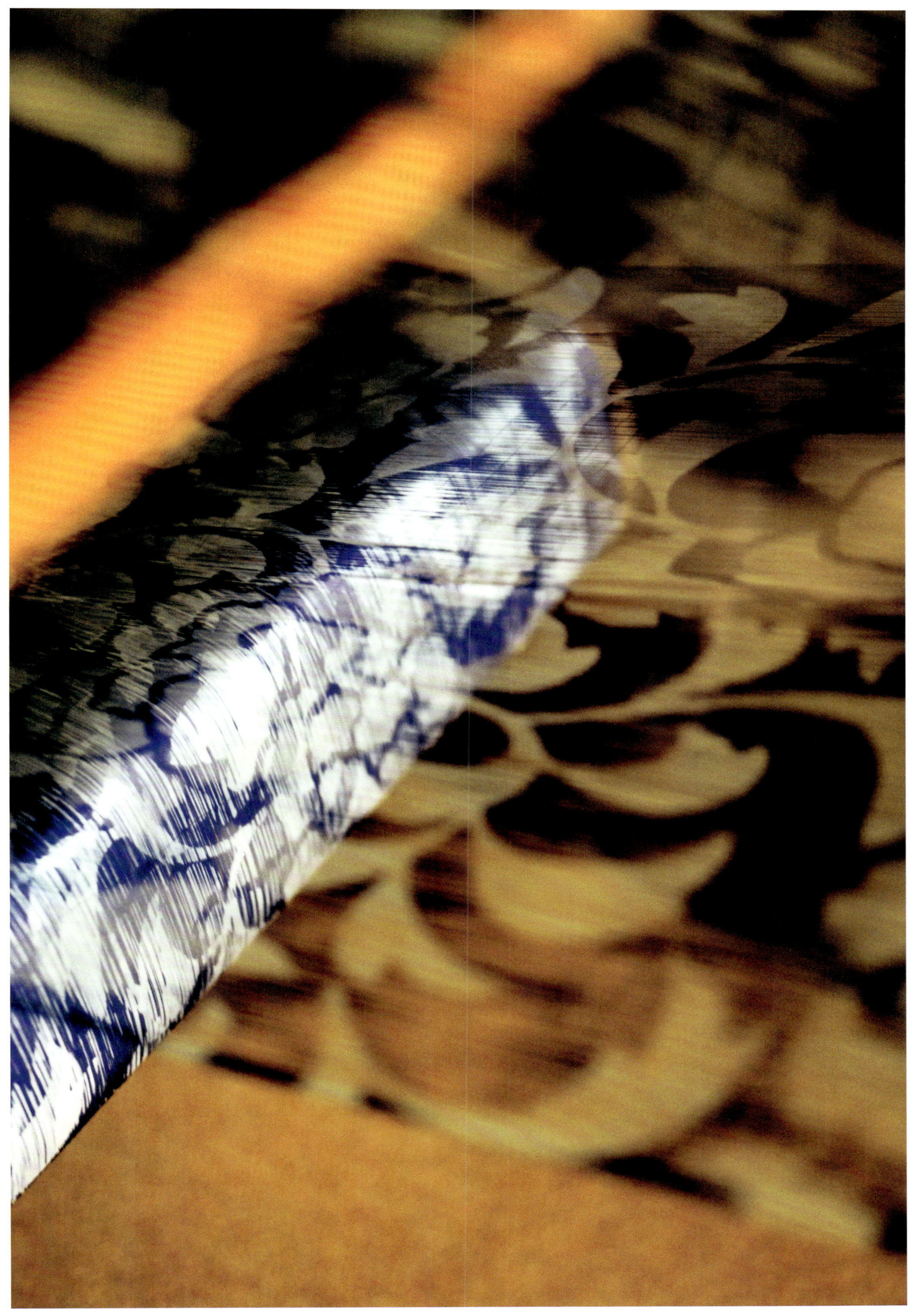

Opposite:
Moving Away #16, 2015–18

This page:
Silken Dreams #1, 2011–12

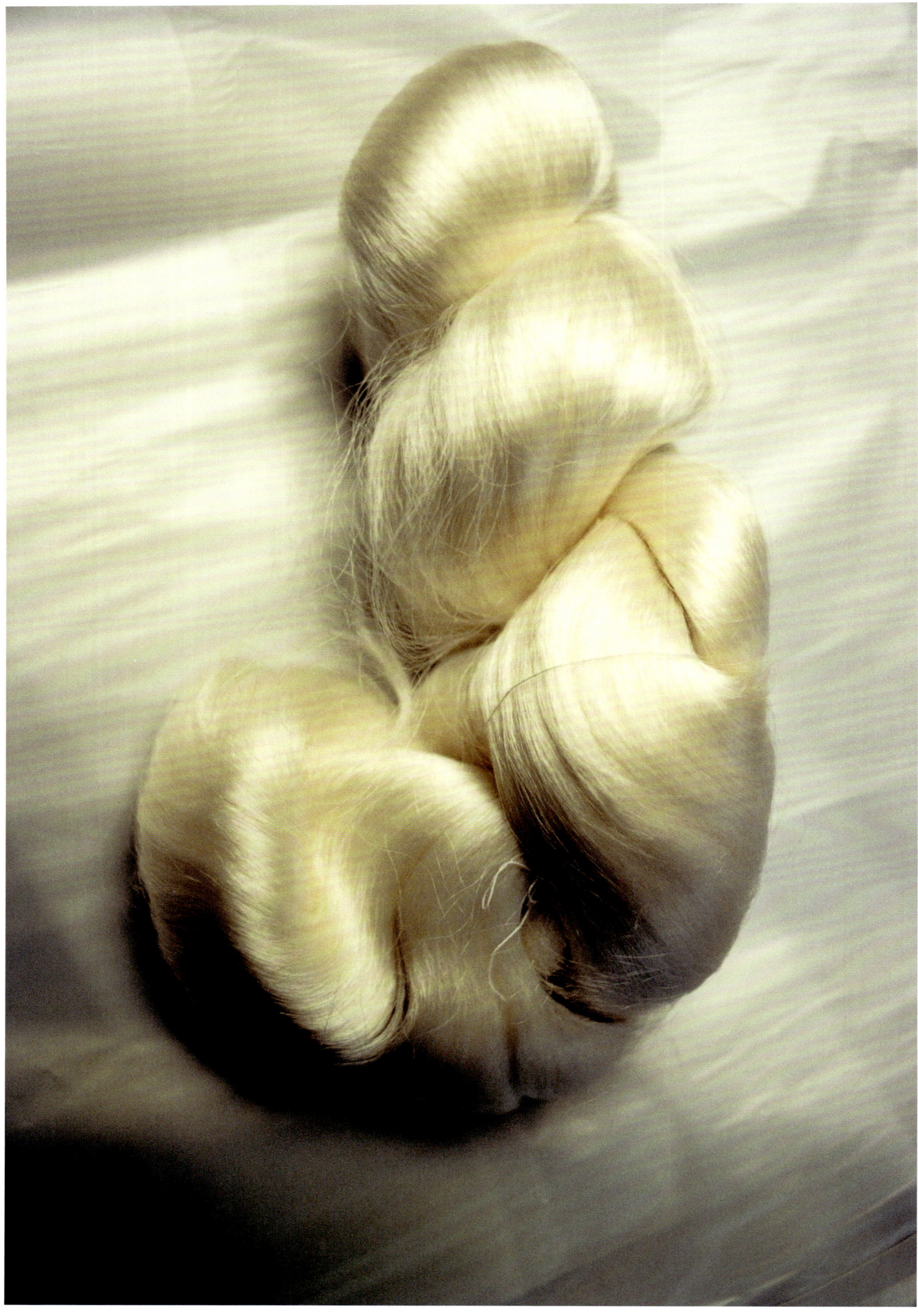

Silken Dreams #72, 2011-12

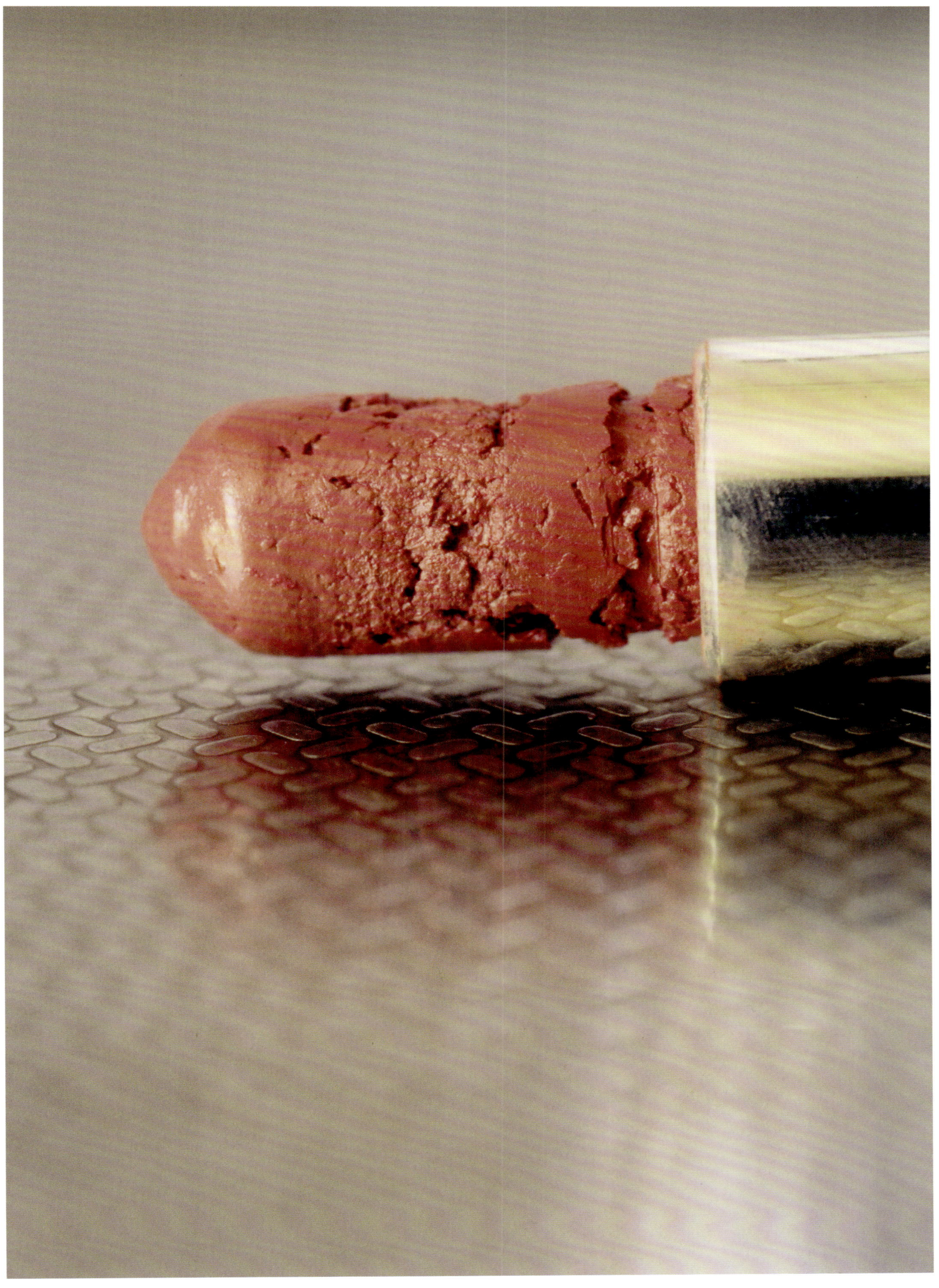

Mother's #35, 2000–5

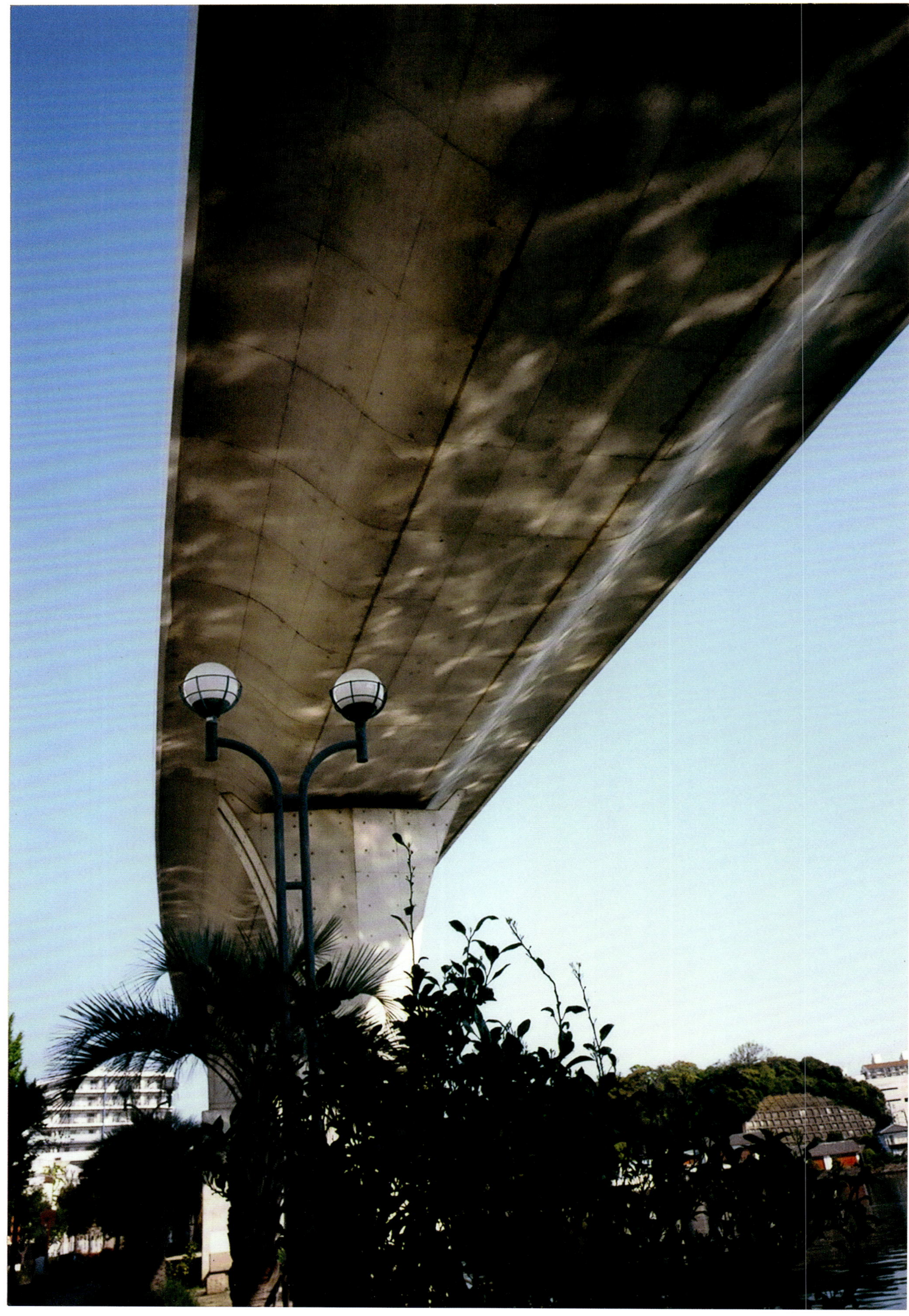

Moving Away #30, 2015–18

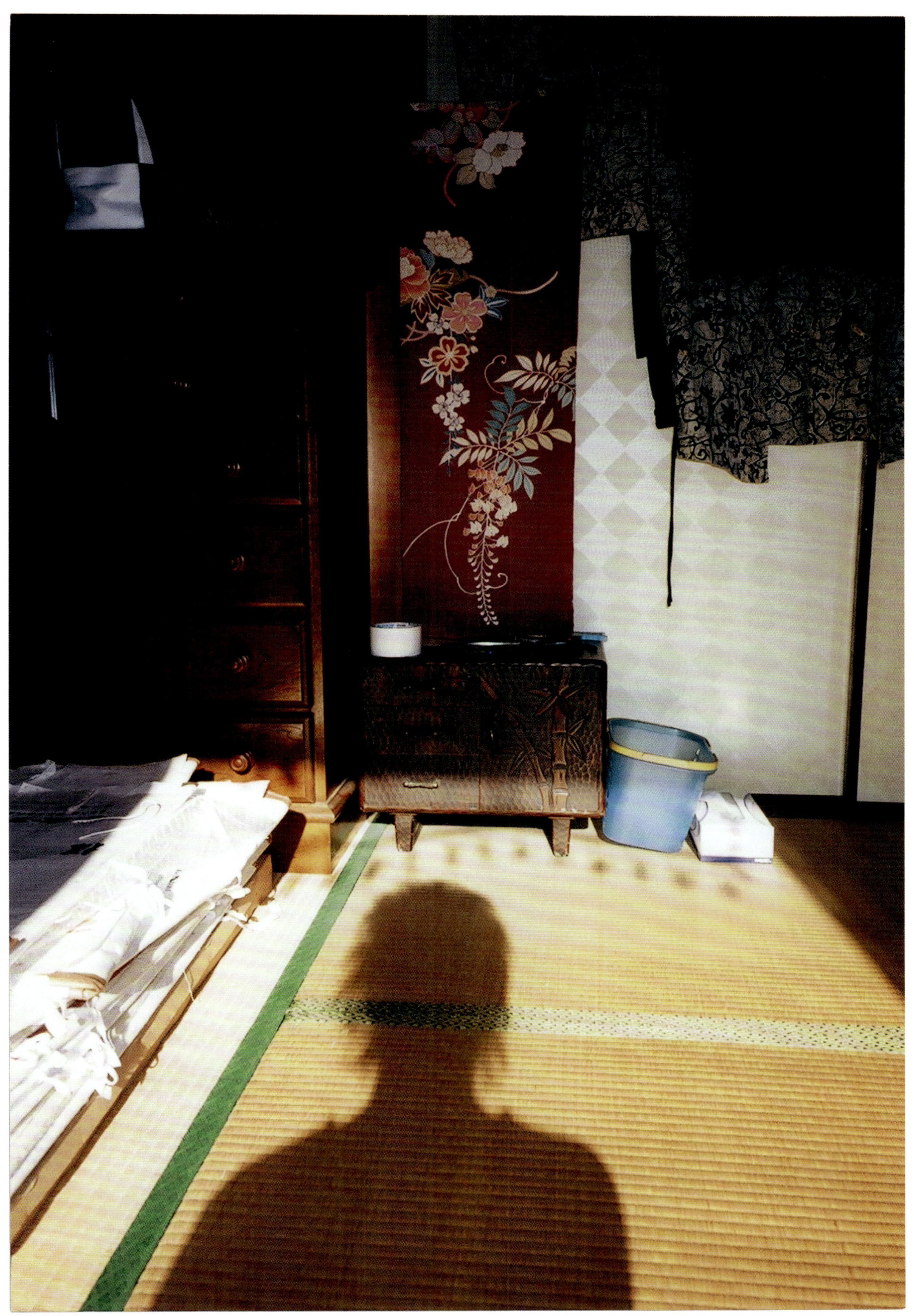

Moving Away #53, 2015–18
All photographs © the artist and courtesy the Third Gallery Aya, Osaka

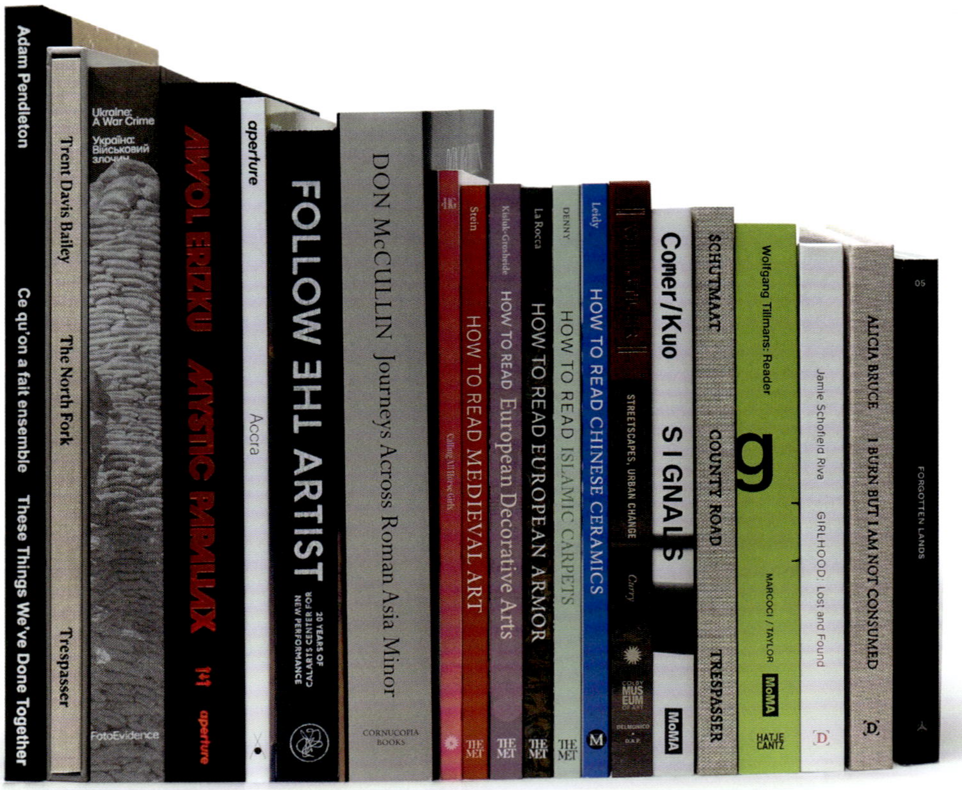

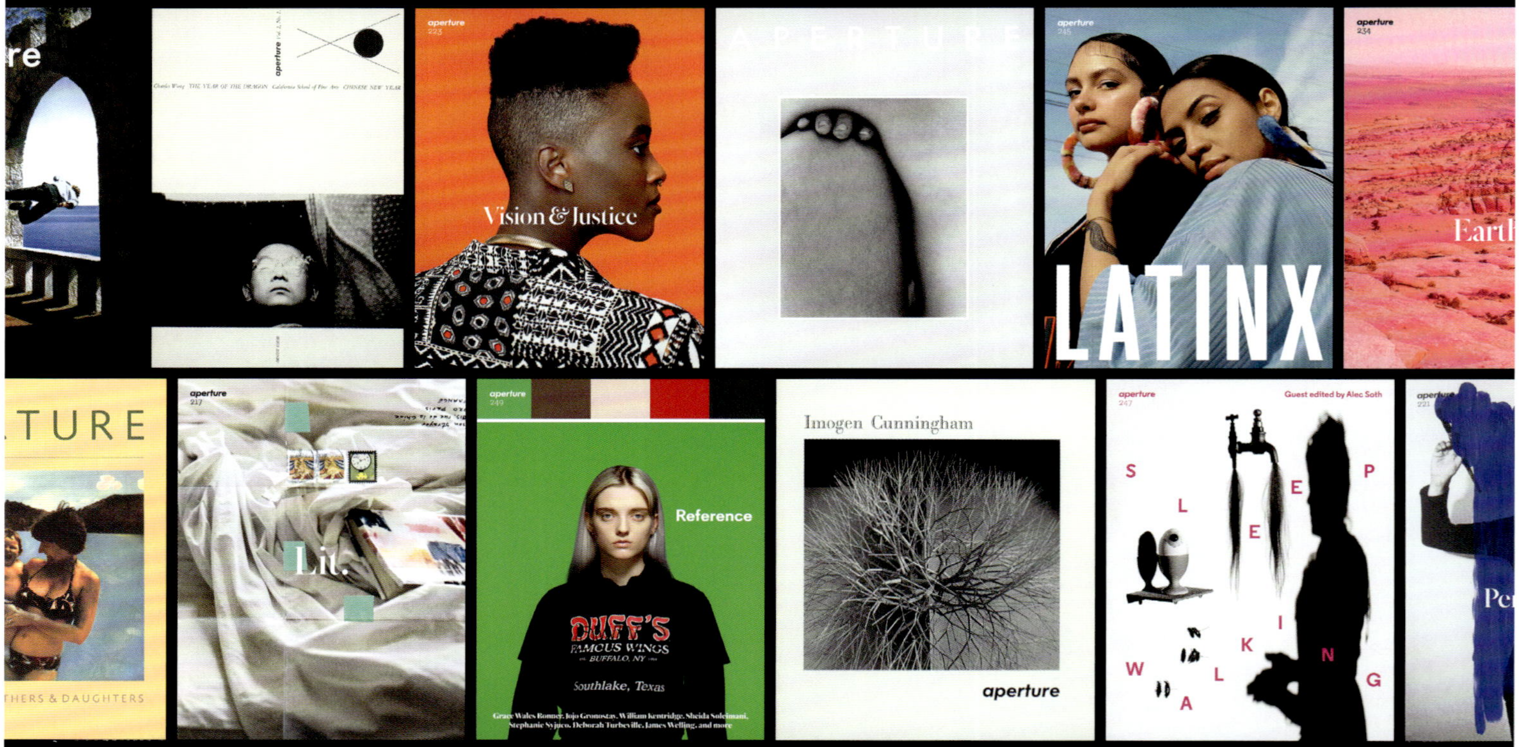

The PhotoBook Review

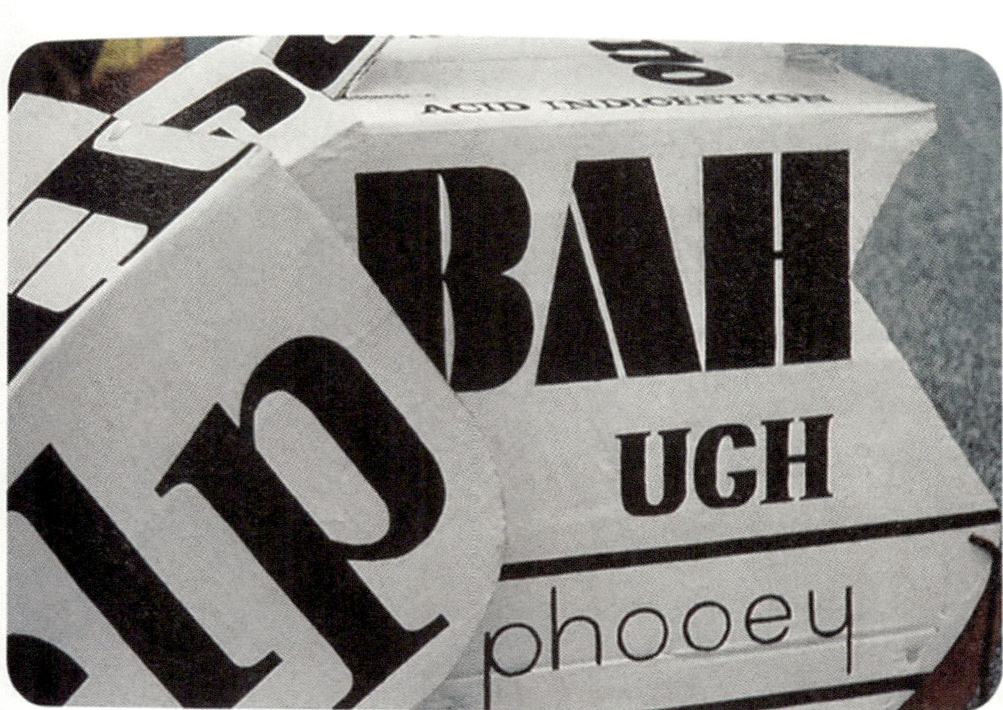

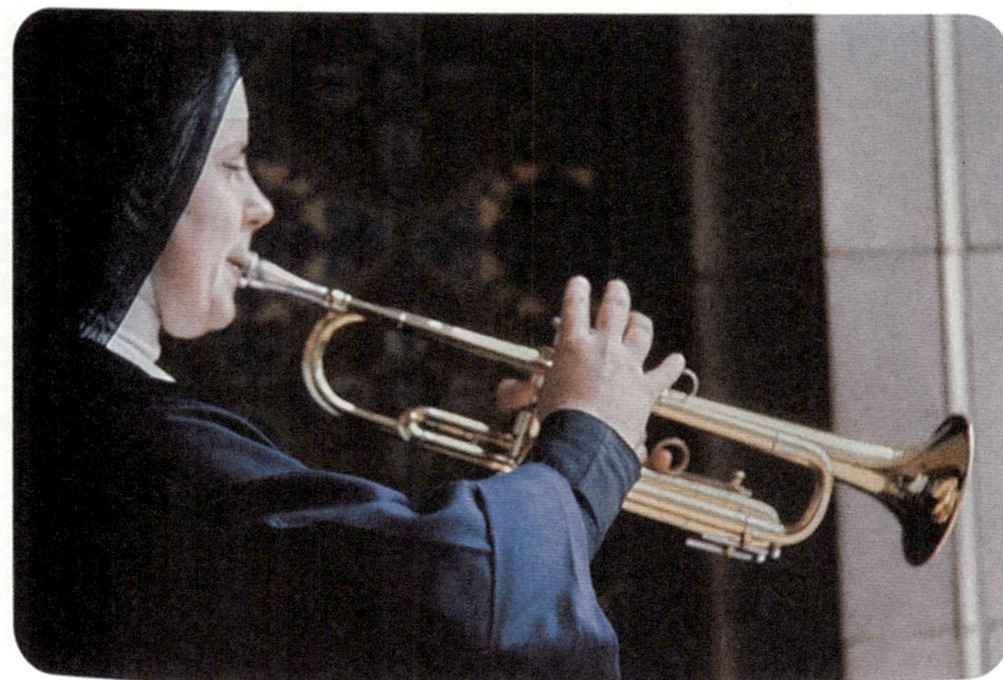

A Space for Everyone

How does the Metropolitan Museum of Art bring its vast book collection to life?

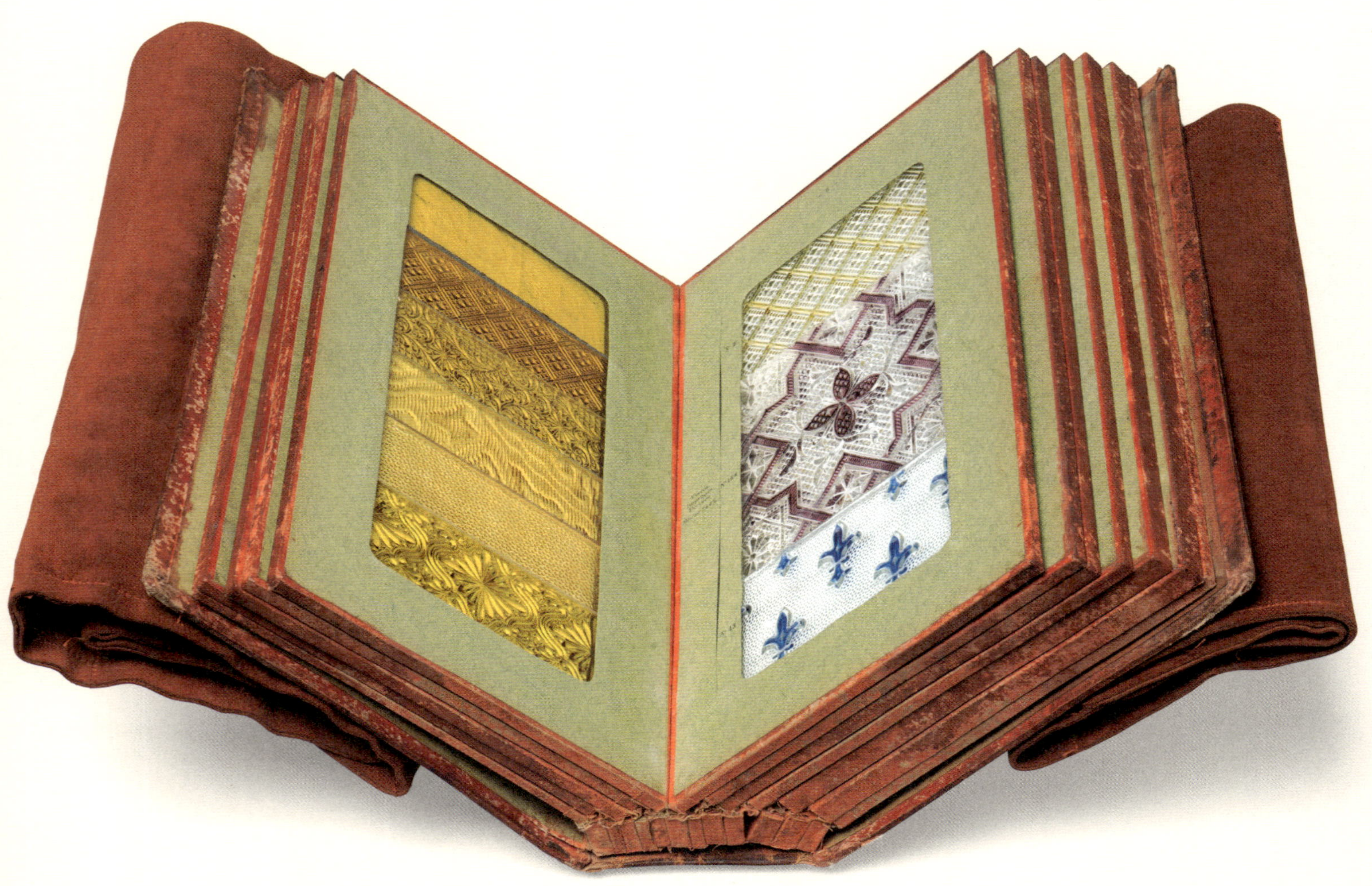

An experimental collaboration between a legendary Japanese graphic artist and novelist, a book of decorative glass panes, and another with a slipcase in the shape of a cigarette pack. The diversity of books at the Thomas J. Watson Library at the Metropolitan Museum of Art reveals the flexibility of the form, one that can accommodate endlessly inventive designs and meanings. Home to more than a million objects—which span centuries and include historically significant volumes, contemporary photobooks, and inventive artists' books—the library's shelves are full of surprises. As collections librarian, Jared Ash oversees its encyclopedic holdings and works with his team, online and offline, to create a wider appreciation for what a book can be.

—Russet Lederman

Russet Lederman: **The Watson Library has a rich assortment of artists' books. How was the collection formed?**

Jared Ash: The Watson Library is as comprehensive as the Metropolitan Museum of Art, maybe even more so, because it's a lot easier to acquire a book than it is a work of art—and storage is a lot less expensive! For a long time, individual departments, like Drawings and Prints, selectively collected artists' books, but twentieth-century and contemporary examples weren't well represented. About eight years ago, a defined collection of artists' books was formalized to fill this gap.

RL: **You often share books on your Instagram feed, @MetLibrary. Can you discuss some of the treasures you have highlighted?**

JA: Instagram is an exceptional calling card for us. Our account features unusual materials, especially photobooks and artists' books that don't fall squarely within a specific curatorial department's range, such as object-like books that have inventive formats or include atypical elements made from textiles or glass. *By the Piece* (2016), by the artist, typographer, and researcher Tabea Nixdorff, is a good example. Printed in a limited edition of twenty copies, it evolved from her research at the Chicago Historical Society and is centered on Agnes Nestor, an early twentieth-century glove-maker and suffragette, who was also a labor rights activist.

RL: **How does a book like Nixdorff's come into the collection?**

JA: We acquire works through different means: about a third are gifts and two-thirds are purchases. Nixdorff and her fellow students were in the city for Printed Matter's New York Art Book Fair, and we invited them to visit the Watson Library. We shared some books from our collection, and they showed us some of the works they were exhibiting at the fair. When objects stand out, like Nixdorff's book, we see an opportunity.

RL: **What are some other acquisitions that cross boundaries?**

JA: Sandra C. Davis's *Queen Anne's Lace* (2006) is a small-scale book composed of cyanotypes on handmade Japanese paper, overlaid with hand stitching. A play on words, it tells the history of the wildflower, embellished with lace thread and a real bloom. Clarissa Sligh's *What's Happening with Momma?* (1988), published by the

Women's Studio Workshop, is cut in the shape of a house and illustrated with screenprinted photographic images from a family album. Sligh is an exceptional artist whose biography includes work at NASA and Goldman Sachs alongside her social-justice-focused art practice. In this volume, she explores notions of domesticity and class, elucidating childhood memories through texts printed on folded sheets of paper that drop down like sets of stairs.

RL: **More recently you acquired the Beijing-based photographer Thomas Sauvin's *Until Death Do Us Part* (2015), which is distinctive for its slipcase that looks like a cigarette pack.**

JA: Yes, I believe you could buy this book either individually or by the carton! Inside is a board book of found photographs, sourced from the Beijing Silvermine archive of salvaged negatives from a Chinese recycling plant, celebrating a Chinese wedding

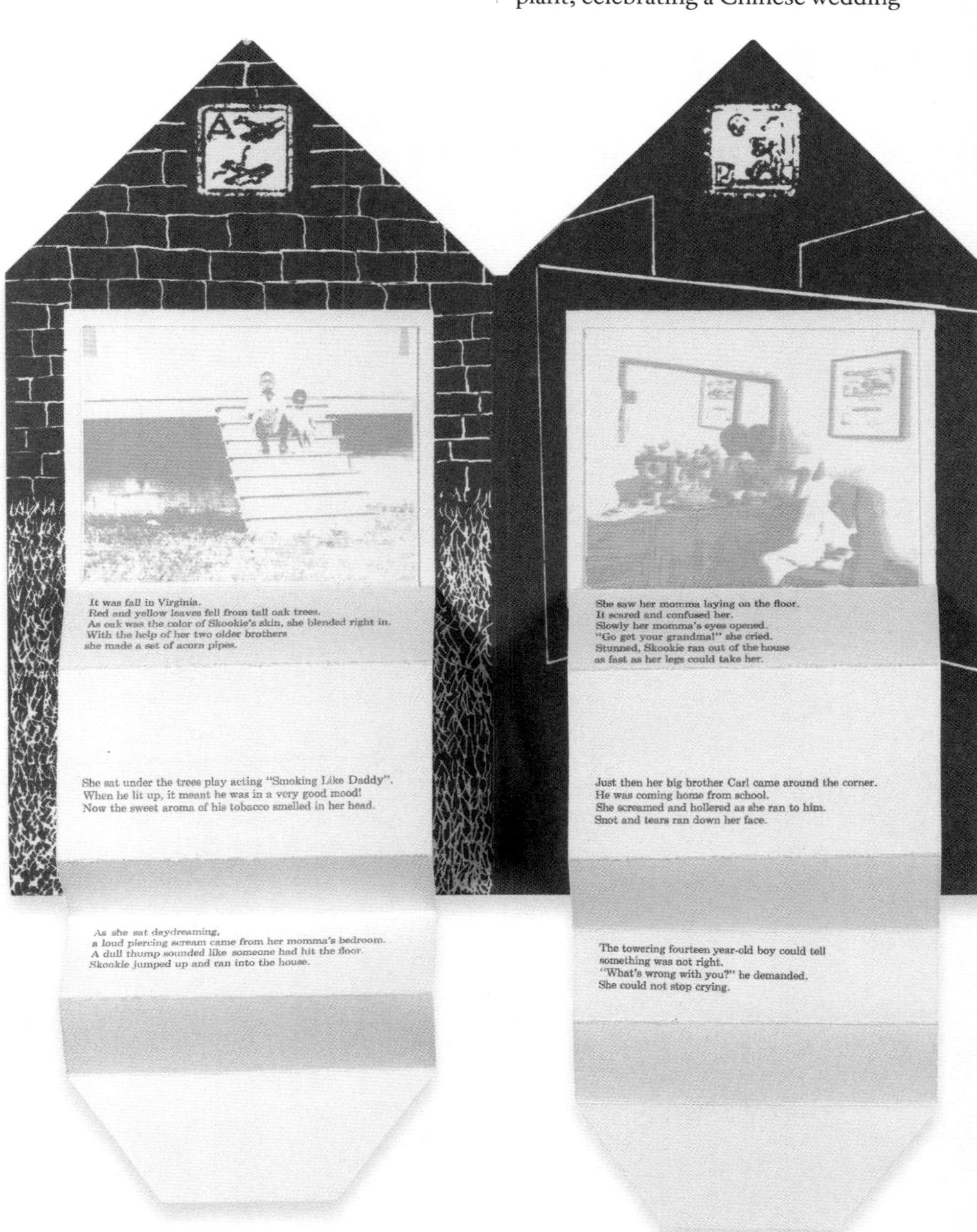

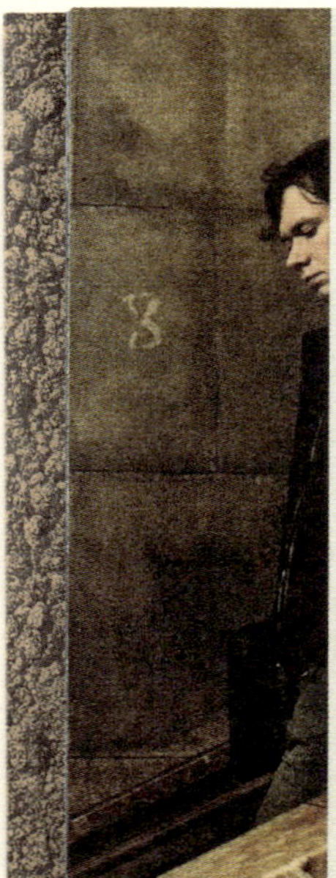
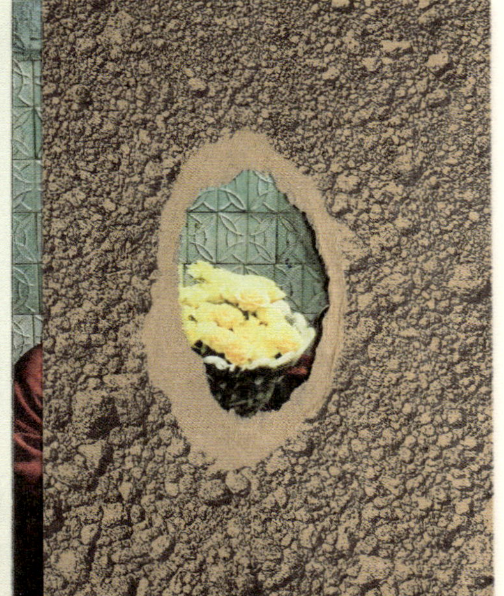

Top:
Irina Popova, *If You Have
a Secret* (Dostoevsky
Publishing, 2017); bottom:
Slipcase for Thomas
Sauvin, *Until Death Do
Us Part* (Jiazazhi, 2015)

We value books that challenge people's perceptions of what a book is.

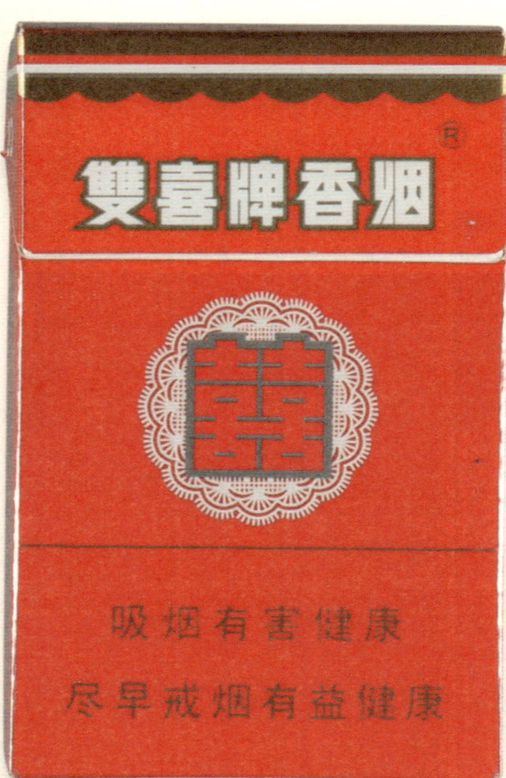
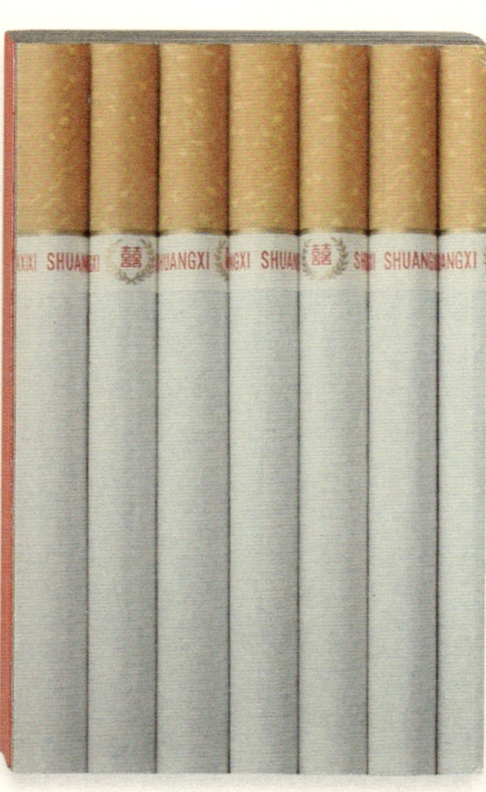

tradition where the bride lights a cigarette for each male guest and the couple plays smoking games that include stuffing as many cigarettes in one's mouth as possible and then lighting them all at once. We value books that challenge people's perceptions of what a book is.

RL: Some of the books in your collection did not start as fine-art objects, such as a trade catalog of cast-glass samples that is nearly one hundred years old.

JA: As part of the twenty-one departmental libraries that are centralized through the Watson Library, we have a substantial collection of trade catalogs. They show how art movements like Art Deco, Art Nouveau, and Constructivism found their way into everyday life, whether on wallpaper patterns or baby carriage designs. This notion of art into life and life into art is important for us.

The *Album des principaux modeles de verres: produits spéciaux en verre coulé* (1913), a.k.a. "The Glass Book," is a trade catalog from a French firm, Manufactures des glaces & produits chimiques de Saint-Gobain, Chauny & Cirey, that has made glass for centuries, including for the Hall of Mirrors in Versailles. From the outside, the book doesn't look like much, but inside are pages filled with more than a hundred samples of multicolored decorative glass panes, including the glass that Hector Guimard used for the Paris Métro. It's a good example of how ordinary materials can be beautiful and inspire wonder. I also really like the backstory of how this book came to us. It was delivered to the library on New Year's Eve by a book dealer who transported it on his bicycle!

RL: More contemporary yet equally inspiring is Irina Popova's *If You Have a Secret* (2017). What is its design and concept?

JA: This book's inventive design requires activation to discover its message. In this second printing of *If You Have a Secret*, Popova, a Russian photographer now living in the Netherlands, interweaves personal and public images taken in her former homeland with poems and vignettes printed on semitranslucent, half-cut sheets to reflect on her past life. Most of the text appears on the front of each page, but in several instances, words or lines of type are printed on the reverse side of the sheet— forcing the viewer to hold the book up to the light to read the full text and understand its deeper meaning.

RL: Radically different, but just as inventive, is *Ezoshi Urotsuki Yata* (Yata, the

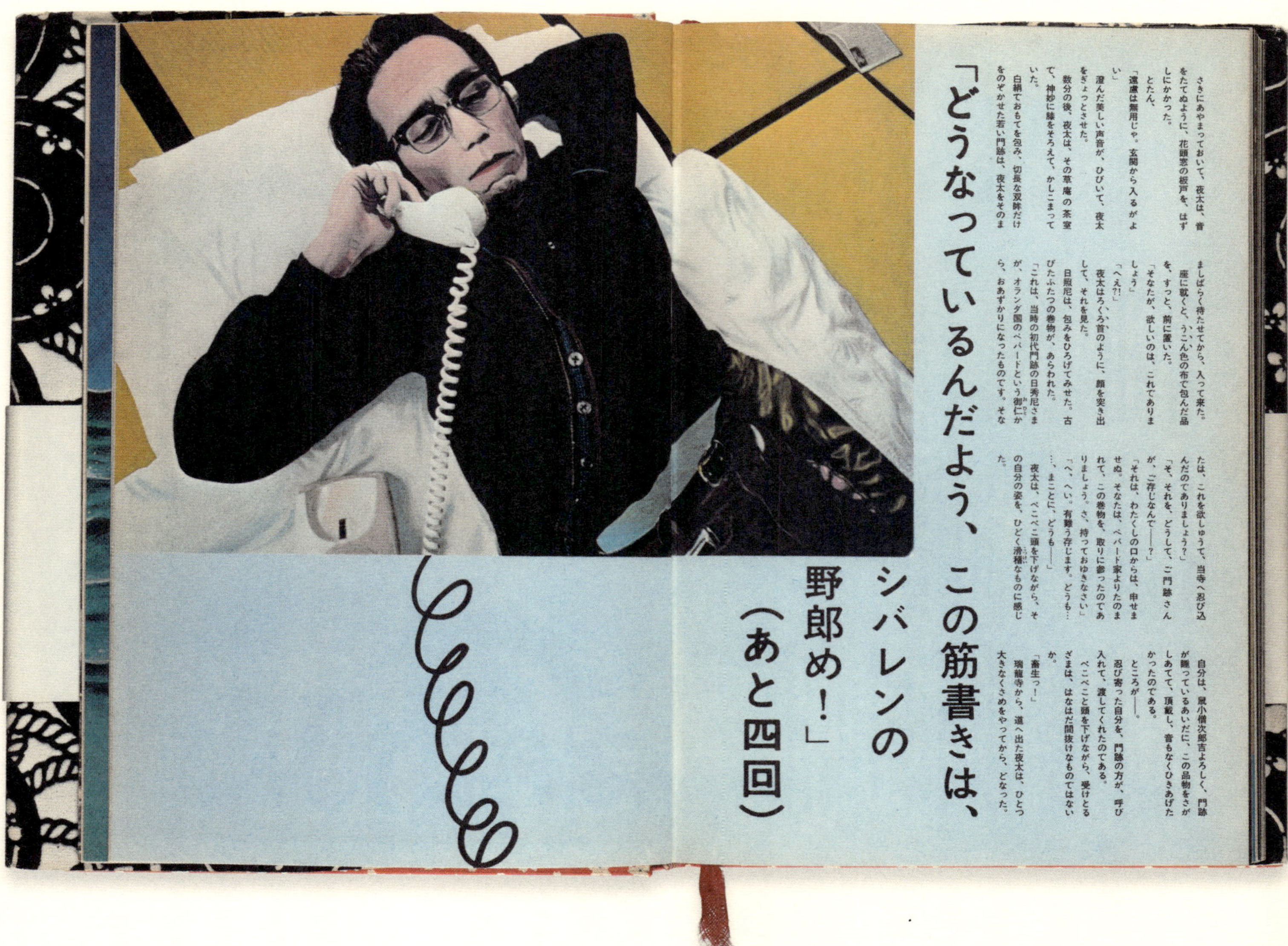

Spread from Tadanori Yokoo and Renzaburo Shibata, *Ezoshi Urotsuki Yata* (Yata, the Vagabond; Shueisha, 1975)

All photographs by Elizabeth Legere. Courtesy the Metropolitan Museum of Art, New York

Vagabond; 1975), a collaboration between the designer Tadanori Yokoo and the novelist Renzaburo Shibata.

JA: I think our Yokoo holdings are a good example of how the Watson Library is a study collection. In this case, we've collected an artist in-depth, providing a comprehensive collection for research. During the New York Art Book Fair, a dealer from Japan had nearly an entire booth filled with books by Yokoo, which made us realize our lack. We wound up buying about fifteen books from the dealer, *Ezoshi Urotsuki Yata* among them. Even without knowing its fablelike narrative, the work can be appreciated for its experimental visual elements and dynamism alone. It never fails to wow people.

RL: With so many to choose from, I imagine it is hard to have a favorite book, but if you had to pick one, which would it be?

JA: The collection that I feel closest to is a series of zines that evolved from *Teens Take The Met!*, a free, museum-wide public program that we co-organize every year with community partners. For several of these events, the Watson Library partnered with Endless Editions, who brought a Risograph machine that the teens used to make zines. We had a group of Russian teens from Brighton Beach, Brooklyn, this past May, right before Mother's Day, and one of them made a zine about piroshki that is a tribute to his babushka. Every year, program participants include kids from all over the city, many speaking different languages. These are our future visitors, and this event lets them know that this space exists for everyone.

Russet Lederman is a researcher and writer based in New York, and a cofounder of 10×10 Photobooks and the Gould Collection.

The Lives of Documents

A recent exhibition considers how publications can inform and inflect the creative process.
Sara Knelman

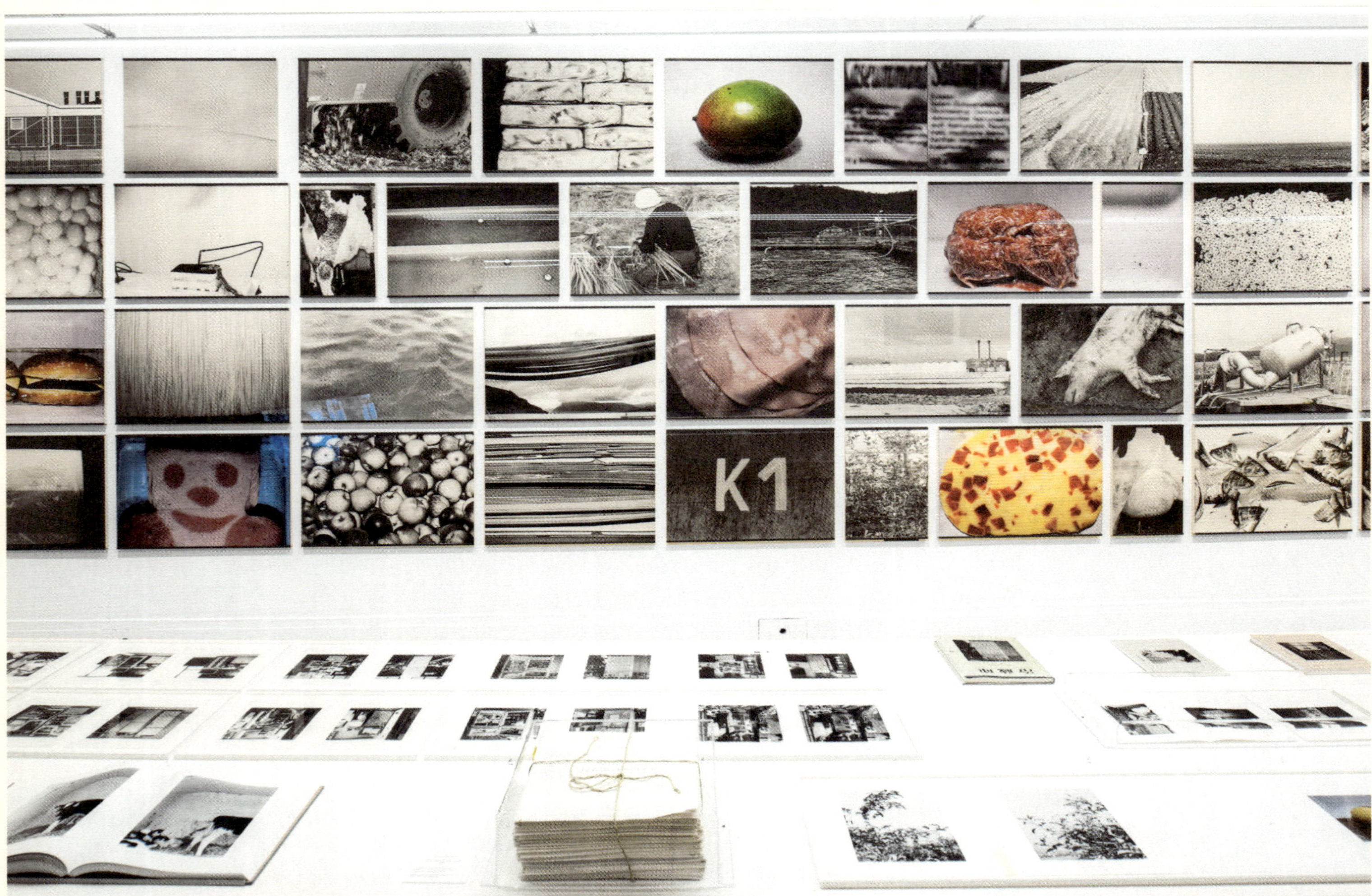

The artist Gordon Matta-Clark's whimsical personal library includes volumes on architectural history, urban planning, art, philosophy, and poetry, as well as a lovely 1962 edition of John Milton's *Paradise Lost*. Many contain personal markings—not only notations and underlines but, in some instances, telephone numbers and even recipes. His collection is a reminder of how books can inform and inflect the creative process, and weave their way into our lives. Seventy volumes from his library are part of the collection of the Canadian Centre for Architecture (CCA), in Montreal, which

recently opened *The Lives of Documents— Photography as Project*. The nearly yearlong exhibition is the first in a planned trilogy of shows over the next decade that will take stock of the organization's vast and impressive photography collection. With work by Lewis Baltz, Bernd and Hilla Becher, Lynne Cohen, Luigi Ghirri, Takashi Homma, Matta-Clark, Richard Misrach, Michael Schmidt, Jeff Wall, and Marianne Wex, among many others, this first iteration is a deluge of some of the most formidable photographic projects of the last fifty years.

The depth of the CCA collection was first showcased in *Photography and Architecture: 1839–1939*, a touring exhibition that traveled to the Centre Pompidou, Paris, and the Art Institute of Chicago, among other venues, between 1982 and 1984. The current show picks up decades later, with works from the 1970s to today, and broadly seeks to explore the way artists document the built environment. Selections from the CCA collection, related ephemera, and in-depth interviews emphasize the process and research of photographers. Each project is treated with reverence. With books at its center, the show functions in part like a curated library, with copies of many relevant photobooks available and accessible. The spaces of exhibition extend to include the CCA library itself, the center of research for the institution, which includes the selection from Matta-Clark's library.

In the main galleries, we also find many volumes, often chosen to reflect the "life" of a photographic project. Lara Almarcegui's *Guide to the Wastelands*, for instance, comprises small artist books made between 2006 and 2023 in response to sites in the urban landscape deemed failed or abandoned, most recently the Francon quarry in Montreal. Lewis Baltz's *The New Industrial Parks Near Irvine, California*, originally published by Leo Castelli in 1974 and rereleased by Steidl in 2023, has achieved iconic status. Many examples connect clearly and directly to architecture, such as Bernd and Hilla Becher's *Framework Houses of the Siegen Industrial Region* (Schirmer/Mosel Verlag, 1977), a discrete typology of building structure, or Lynne Cohen's *Occupied Territory* (Aperture, 1987), a searing look at the fabrication of corporate aesthetics. In some cases, other forms of printed matter— magazines, letters—stand in as a record. Dan Graham's image *Toronto Two-Way Mirror Tower* (1974), from the series *Private Public Spaces: The Corporate Atrium Garden* (1987), was originally published in *Artforum*.

Perhaps most intriguing, however, are books and projects that don't immediately relate to ideas of architecture or urban planning but instead consider the way we inhabit public and domestic space, the way our lives unfold within the world we build around us. For Takashi Homma's *New Waves, 2000–2013* (Longhouse Projects, 2013), the artist returned to the same beach in Hawaii for more than a decade, photographing the sea and presenting the waves as a mode of self-reflection; Roni Horn's *You Are the Weather* (Scalo, 1997) considers the human face as changing landscape; Richard Misrach's *Destroy This Memory* (Aperture, 2010) shares images of messages of love and despair, left—often as graffiti—following Hurricane Katrina; Tokuko Ushioda's *Ice Box* (BeeBooks, 1996) unfolds as a lyrical exploration of Japanese domestic interiors through diptychs of refrigerators, first open, then closed; Marianne Wex's *Let's Take Back Our Space: "Female" and "Male" Body Language as a Result of Patriarchal Structures* (Frauenliteratur Verlag Hermine Fees, 1979) is a constructed exposition of posture and gender through train commuters in Germany.

Though books form a significant element of the show, the curators, Bas Princen and Stefano Graziani, sought to elaborate the projects on view. In addition

to series of prints sprawled across walls and ephemera atop long metal tables alongside the books, nearly every room includes a large monitor, low to the ground, humming with the voices of the curators interviewing artists in studios across the globe. Though the conversations are often insightful and the videos meticulously produced, their presence can feel intrusive, like curatorial excess. There is much to admire in the curiosity and transparency of the discussions, but the curatorial presence, in transposed introductory texts and the video interviews, shifts our focus away from the works themselves.

Yet the show remains compelling and energetic, in part because it is grounded in the exhilarating struggle of learning itself.

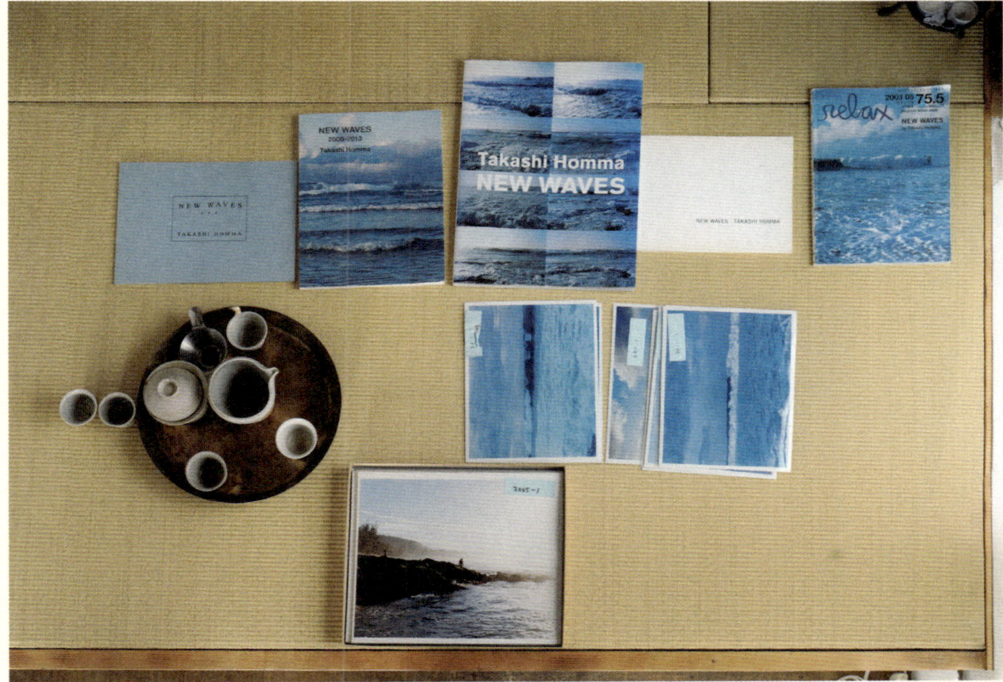

This page: Photographs and books from Takashi Homma's series *Waves* (2000–ongoing) at his studio in Tokyo, 2023. Photograph by Bas Princen. Opposite: Installation view of *The Lives of Documents—Photography as Project*, with works by Michael Schmidt and Tokuko Ushioda, Canadian Centre for Architecture, Montreal, 2023. Photograph by Matthieu Brouillard
Courtesy the Canadian Centre for Architecture, Montreal

It's a reminder that great photographic collections—and indeed, libraries—often live in service to other disciplines and can be more expansively understood in relation to their usefulness in myriad contexts unrelated to art or the history of image making: urban sprawl and cartography, for instance, or, more grandly, the cycles of decay, destruction, revision, and rebuilding that propel us forward. The blankness of "documents" is not bureaucratic or objective but, like a book, an invitation to use a way of seeing or thinking as a frame for meaning.

Sara Knelman is a writer and curator based in Toronto, and the executive director and publisher of C Magazine.

Reviews

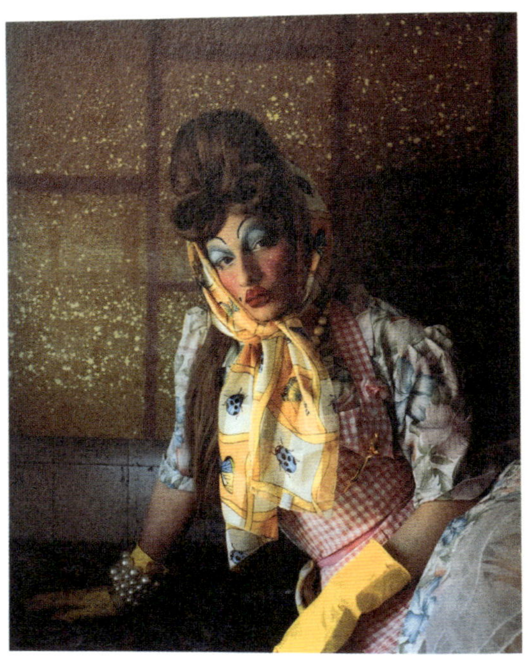

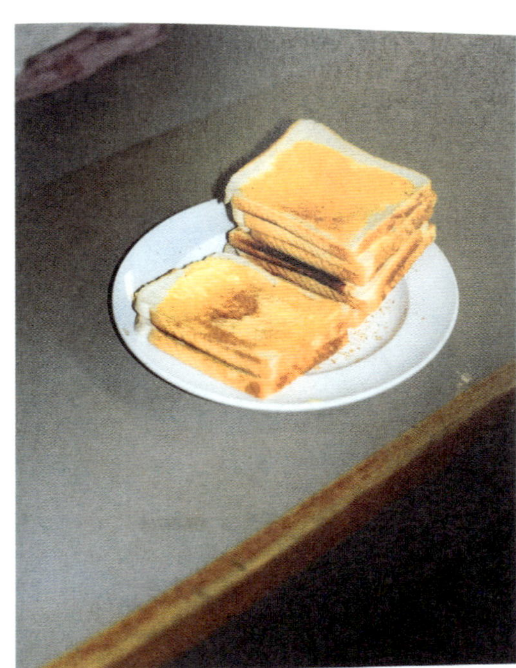

Oliver Frank Chanarin

The opening pages of Oliver Frank Chanarin's ***A Perfect Sentence*** (**Loose Joints, 2023; 240 pages, $60**) relay a set of rules to the reader. "Don't reduce me to tears as a form of control." "Don't capture my image without consent." "Don't walk with your hands in your pockets." The true meaning of these statements is oblique, yet their anxious tenor inflect our reading with a particular unease. When we encounter the first image in the book—a photograph of a middle-aged man, wide-eyed, face injured and violently fractioned by the uneven exposure lines of the photographer's test print—the combination of the subject's and Chanarin's anxieties begins to foment our own.

As one moves through the book, this sense of apprehension reveals itself to be the true focus of the artist's photographic inquiry. Chanarin explores a variety of subjects: bondage group members, drag performers, shelter residents, young men in military uniform. The connections are vague, but common threads of performance, eccentricity, and the particularities of British culture fill the photographer's wide net. Yet what really binds the images together is the way they interrogate the uncertainties of the photographic process itself and the fallibility of the documentary language; the images are reproduced with Chanarin's darkroom notes, tests, and mishaps, but more potently, his subjects seem acutely aware that they are being photographed. This awareness amplifies their performance, or in other cases, their trepidation.

An essay by Chanarin in the back of the book distills his thoughts, doubts, and musings on the project, which was incepted in 2022 from a commission by Forma and several other institutions. Here, the pleasures of image making and misgivings around (mis)representation are clarified through the artist's narrative. He admits, "I've tried to make these encounters positive and inspiring experiences, but every human interaction is fraught, especially when the camera is involved."
—**Noa Lin**

Lynne Cohen and Marina Gadonneix

Published to accompany an exhibition at the Centre Pompidou, Paris, this double-volume set of catalogs presents two individual bodies of work: the unexpected and inspiring pairing of ***Lynne Cohen: Observatories*** and ***Marina Gadonneix: Laboratories* (Atelier EXB, 2023; 104 pages, each $46)**. *Observatories* features (mostly) black-and-white images by the late Canadian photographer, an artist whose work falls squarely within the Venn diagram overlap between Social Landscape and the New Topographics. *Laboratories* presents pictures by the contemporary French artist, a photographer whose work resonates with and expands upon Cohen's sharp-eyed descriptions of social and functional spaces. Cohen photographed empty banquet halls, classrooms, showrooms, laboratories, living rooms, and lobbies; Gadonneix focuses on depicting the mise-en-scène of science labs and sites where simulations of natural phenomena are modeled, measured, and analyzed. This artistic pas de deux is prompted by Gadonneix's close study of Cohen's work, which she discovered after stumbling upon her first book, *Occupied Territory* (Aperture, 1987), as a student at the École nationale supérieure de la photographie in Arles. In a text that appears at the close of *Observatories*, Gadonneix describes this encounter as one that "came to upend [her] way of looking." Cohen's oeuvre treads a fine line between cool observation and earnest curiosity—a photographic inquiry at equal turns sardonic and sympathetic. Gadonneix shares her interest in constructed space rendered in flattened, sculptural terms and emptied of human presence, but turns up the heat in her images through carefully selected scenes drenched in electrified industrial color and abstracted through the elision of detail within the frame. Her work also incorporates found images of scientific phenomena—appropriated illustrations of color charts, nebulae, and star showers, as well as works by contemporary artists, such as Christopher Williams and Tacita Dean, that deal with the phenomenology of vision and representation of the natural world. Twinned via parallel designs in complementary black-and-white graphic treatments, *Observatories* and *Laboratories* offer a wonderfully generous, intergenerational dialogue that fires the imagination.

—Lesley A. Martin

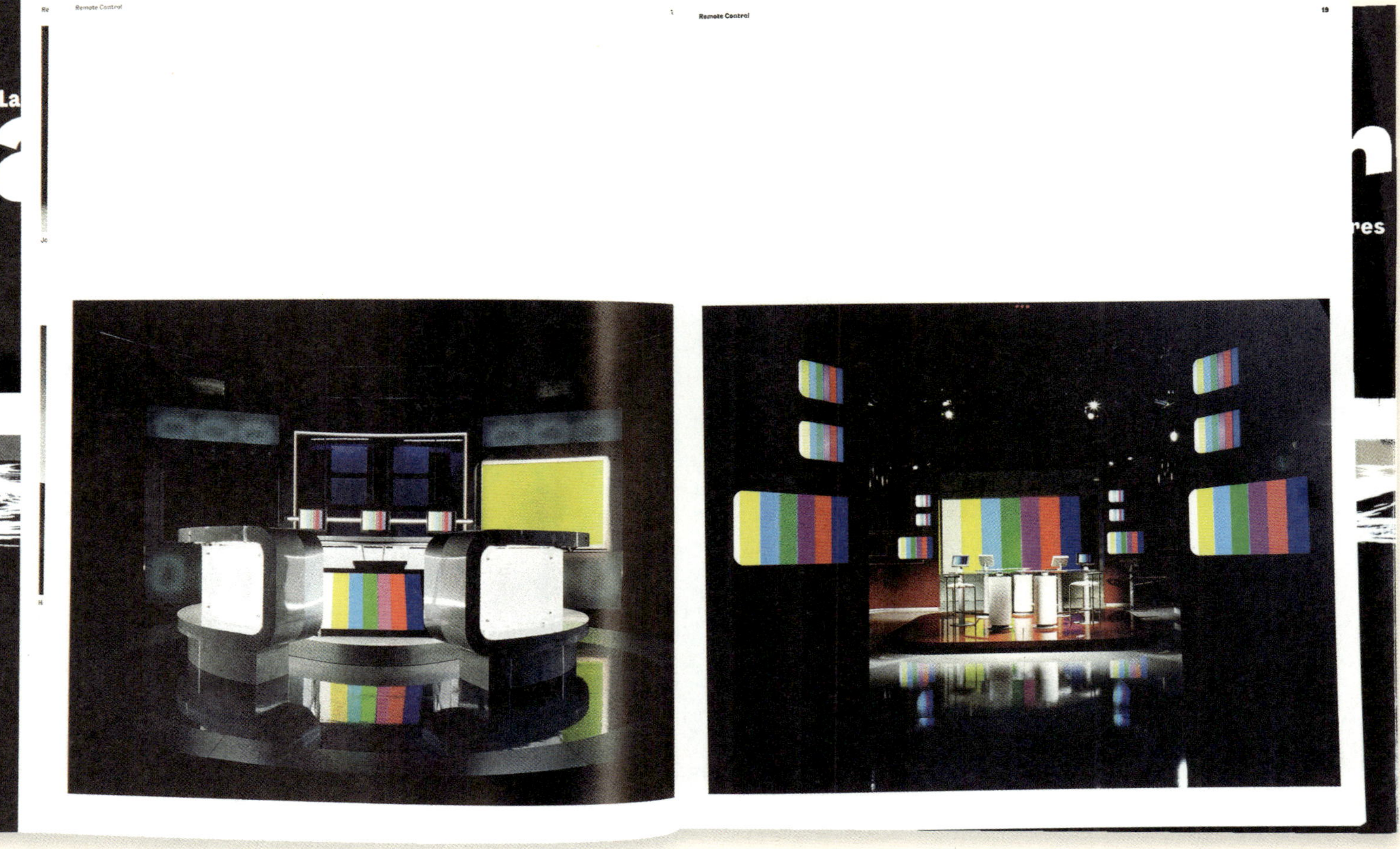

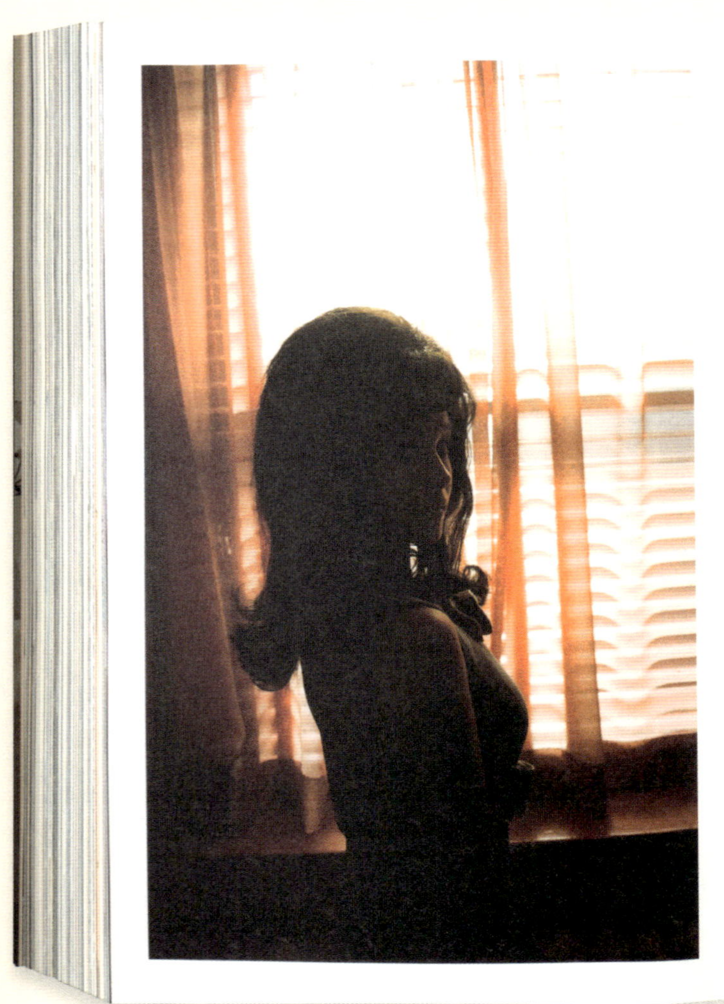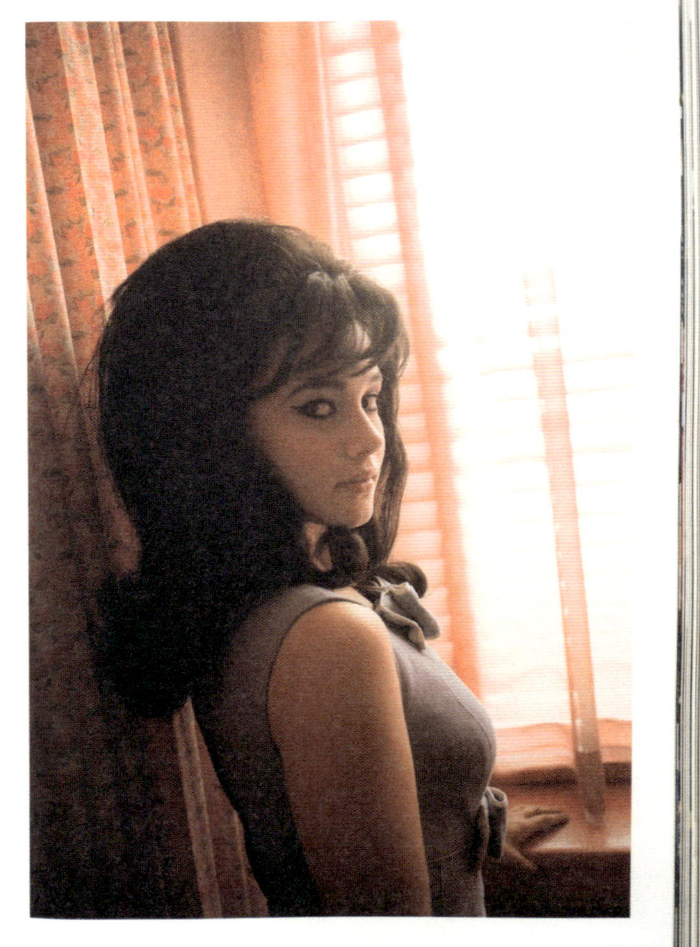

Sofia Coppola

As a filmmaker, Sofia Coppola creates highly stylized, lush visual worlds. Those with a knowledge of photographic history can delight in decoding the image references from which her stories are built. The signature image for *Lost in Translation*, for instance, features a resigned Bill Murray seated on the edge of a hotel bed, a re-creation of a central image from Larry Sultan's 1992 opus *Pictures from Home*. (A project that has now, surprisingly, also inspired a Broadway play.)

Coppola's new book, **Sofia Coppola: Archive** (**MACK, 2023; 488 pages, $65**), is structured as a scrapbook of reference images, magazine tear sheets, and pen-marked script pages, as well as on-set, behind-the-scenes images by various photographers, including some alluring moments caught by Corinne Day during the production of *The Virgin Suicides*, Coppola's 1999 directorial debut.

Many of the images in the book, however, were made by Coppola, who studied photography with Paul Jasmin at California Institute of the Arts. She amply credits him here for believing that she had a valuable artistic point of view, and even cast him as an extra in her candy-pop retelling of Marie Antoinette's decadent reign. This publication showcases an obsessive attention to every detail of filmmaking—lighting, costume, mood, location—and reveals how images by Guy Bourdin inspired the opening scenes of that historical drama. It reveals other direct references to well-known photographers throughout her oeuvre: Bill Owens and Tina Barney for *The Virgin Suicides*; William Eggleston for *Priscilla*; Jo Ann Callis for *The Beguiled*. Some critics have griped that Coppola's films at times indulge visual pleasure at the expense of story or character, but this book opens up the director's creative process, showing how she diligently pairs an aesthetic with a script. Her absorbing cultural chronology, from the late 1990s through the aughts to the present, makes clear (through the many images of people napping on set) that filmmakers create their seductive worlds through complex, often grueling work.
—**Michael Famighetti**

A Field Guide to Photography and Media

In their introduction to **The Art Institute of Chicago Field Guide to Photography and Media** (**Yale University Press, 2023; 424 pages, $65**), the book's coeditors, Antawan I. Byrd and Elizabeth Siegel, assert that "any collection is a product of its own social and historical context." As such, any catalog of a museum's collection is a product of the present. Spanning seventy-five essays and illustrated by nearly four hundred works, the *Field Guide* considers the evolution of photography through the fixed perspective of a single institution and its collection. It's been more than a century since the Art Institute's first photography exhibition and nearly seventy-five years since its first acquisition. How, then, might a book address this historical arc and meaningfully distill its lessons?

One answer is in finding many pathways. Despite the implications of order and classification suggested by its name, the *Field Guide* presents an open and evolving vocabulary, "less as a declaration of ownership than as a map of new directions." Recalling, at least in spirit and shape, Raymond Williams's sweeping *Keywords* project from the 1970s, each essay links to a single term—from the specific ("Book," "Negative," "Street") to the more abstract ("Intimacy," "Public," "Morality"). In "Collaboration," Nadya Bair questions the figure of the lone photographer and asserts the importance of reconceiving creativity through partnerships and communities; Thy Phu, in "Home," relates the nineteenth-century parlor ("the

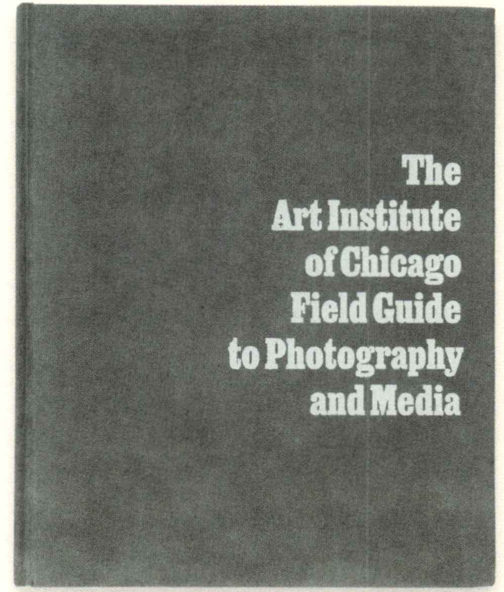

Top:
Cover of Antawan I. Byrd and Elizabeth Siegel, *The Art Institute of Chicago Field Guide to Photography and Media* (Yale University Press, 2023)

Bottom and page 137:
Cover and spread from Julie Ault, Jason Fulford, and Jordan Weitzman, *Ordinary Things Will Be Signs for Us: Photographs by Corita* (J&L Books and Magic Hour Press, 2023)

most exterior of interior domestic rooms") to the studio, highlighting photography's traversal of public and private spaces; Patricia Hayes, in "Travel," imagines a commons for photography that can be transformative through its ability to facilitate and visualize human exchange. The real pleasure of spending time with the *Field Guide* is discovering what these connections might reveal, and the many smaller books that sit hidden within the larger project. —**Varun Nayar**

Corita Kent

Sister Corita Kent was still a nun when she visited Andy Warhol's infamous exhibition of soup can paintings at the Ferus Gallery in Los Angeles in the summer of 1962, just a few months before John XXIII convened Vatican II. Corita taught art and made Pop art–style silk-screens and posters. By the end of the 1960s, Corita—like Cher or Pelé, she had no need for a surname—had dispensed with her vows. Her order, the Immaculate Heart of Mary, was released from the Vatican and became a nonprofit community center. "I'm sure if I had been a nice proper housewife, I would not have bumped into these ideas," she once said. "And of course once they get into you, you start noticing and expanding."

What she noticed is the subject of **Ordinary Things Will Be Signs for Us: Photographs by Corita** (**J&L Books and Magic Hour Press, 2023; 144 pages, $45**), a rollicking journey through selections from Corita's fifteen thousand 35mm color slides held by the Corita Art Center and recently preserved and digitized. Corita had a voracious appetite for the signs and symbols of daily life—"ordinary things" like cookies, flowers, confetti, toothpaste, festivals, hats, balloons, nuns, Brillo boxes, the Marshmallow Love Seat, and kites. They were kept in idiosyncratic categories such as "mad hat party" and "ideas for problems."

Ordinary Things is the rare photobook that appeals to children and adults alike, bursting as it is with joy and curiosity. The width of two paperback novels, the book opens to panoramic spreads, across which are grids of laundry detergent packaging or a close-up of a geodesic dome, all printed in a bright, Kodachrome palette. "We did a lot of looking exercises," reads the epigraph, one of many quotes from Corita interspersed throughout, a line that likely also refers to the daunting task faced by the editors, Julie Ault, Jason Fulford, and Jordan Weitzman. Corita never made prints from her slides. Instead, she considered herself a collector or archaeologist, and her eyes were always wide open. "Everything," she said, "is a source."
—**Brendan Embser**

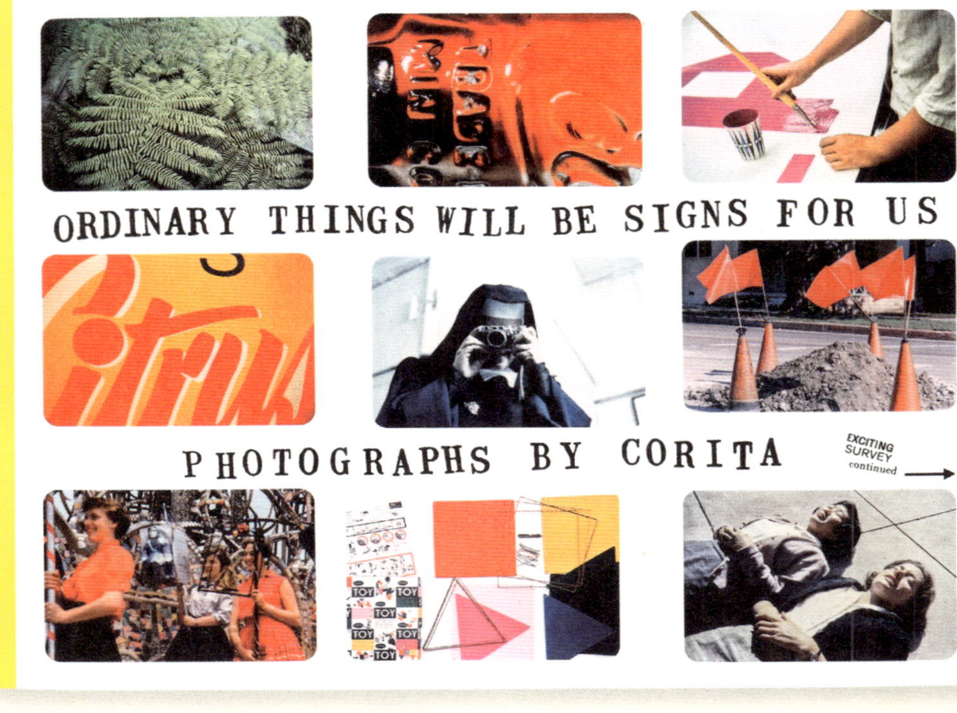

Endnote
Heji Shin

The German photographer Heji Shin is drawn to complicated, at times fraught subjects. She has intrigued, and provoked, audiences with her images presented in galleries and at the Whitney Biennial, and through her work as a sought-after fashion photographer. Her most recent series, *The Big Nudes* (2023), comprising large-scale portraits of pigs, borrows its title from Helmut Newton.

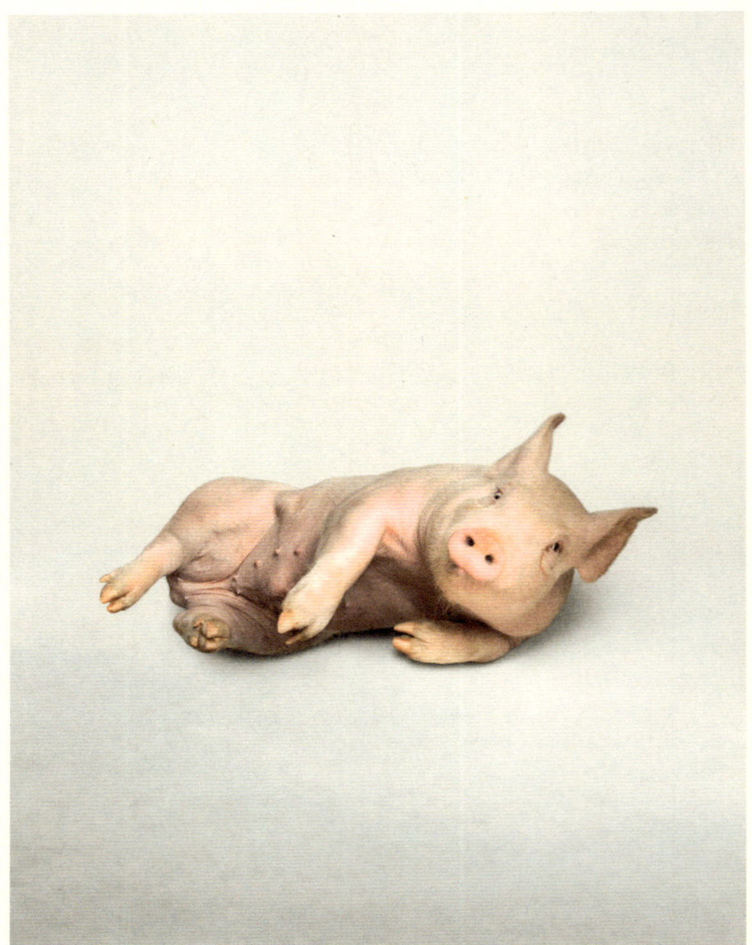

Heji Shin, *Reclining Nude*, 2023
© the artist and courtesy 52 Walker, New York

Why is Helmut Newton important to you?
Every fashion photographer loves—or at least knows—him. I've loved him for as long as I can remember. The *Big Nudes* are his huge, sculptural photographs of women. They are not very light or feminine. There's a bar in Berlin, Newton Bar, near the German parliament, where you can smoke cigars, that has reproductions or maybe even original *Big Nudes* on the walls.

Is this a critique of Newton? His work has been criticized for its objectification of women.
It's not a critique. It's up to the viewer to see what they want to see in the pigs, or what the pigs are.

You have a longstanding interest in making large-scale pictures of animals, as in your earlier series of roosters, titled *Big Cocks* (2020).
I like the psychological aspect of portraits. And here, because it's an animal, people project onto them. I also just like animals. There's an unpredictability; it's very similar to working with a child. You can't direct them. There's a lot of chaotic energy. They are very giving subjects.

Unlike in your fashion work, you get to work with a subject with zero self-consciousness.
I actually think that animals have a self-consciousness; it's just different from ours.

There is a strong sense of a desire to look in your work—in a direct, at times uncomfortable way.
The voyeuristic aspect of photo and pleasure is connected, especially in fashion. To aestheticize, to be an extreme visual person—there is a genetically immoral aspect to that. You can't control that. The process itself is objectification and there is something very male about it still—the masculine gaze. Even if romantic young women photographers deny they make sexualized photographs—they do. But their projection into the model can be different. It's complicated.

In a recent interview, you referred to art as the sublimation of one's shadow. What did you mean by that?
Things that are dark or perverted or evil, you can recognize them and turn them into art, which is the process of sublimation. Some people aren't even aware of certain dark shadows of their own, or they reject that they have this shadow in them, and so it sometimes comes out in an unrefined, unsublimated way, a lashing out. These are old psychological concepts. The principle of shadow is from Carl Jung. I think he is having a comeback.

You've photographed a number of well-known people, including pop stars such as Robyn, Kanye West, and others. How does celebrity change the terms, or not?
With a celebrity, I work with what people already perceive about someone. You see sexy, or funny. I'm only interested in photographing a famous person when I think people already project a very certain thing onto them. Then there's a tension between my perspective, the general perspective, and the person.

Is there someone you'd like to photograph?
There's Trump, there's Elon Musk.

Powerful, complicated—toxic—men?
Yes—and they are such personas.

Musk and Mark Zuckerberg have been threatening to have a cage fight. Maybe you could photograph that?
I was just thinking the same. Musk said he has a move called "the Walrus." He can just lay on top of the opponent and do nothing. I hope it's happening.